The Performing Century

Nineteenth-Century Theatre's History

Edited by

Tracy C. Davis

and

Peter Holland

Redefining British Theatre History Series
General Editor: Peter Holland
In Association with the Huntington Library

palgrave
macmillan

First published in hardback 2007
First published in paperback 2010 by
PALGRAVE MACMILLAN

Palgrave Macmillan in the UK is an imprint of Macmillan Publishers
Limited, registered in England, company number 785998, of Houndmills,
Basingstoke, Hampshire RG21 6XS.

Palgrave Macmillan in the US is a division of St Martin's Press LLC,
175 Fifth Avenue, New York, NY 10010.

Palgrave Macmillan is the global academic imprint of the above companies
and has companies and representatives throughout the world.

Palgrave® and Macmillan® are registered trademarks in the United States,
the United Kingdom, Europe and other countries.

ISBN 978–0–230–57256–0 hardback
ISBN 978–0–230–25040–6 paperback

This book is printed on paper suitable for recycling and made from fully
managed and sustained forest sources. Logging, pulping and manufacturing
processes are expected to conform to the environmental regulations of the
country of origin.

A catalogue record for this book is available from the British Library.

A catalog record for this book is available from the Library of Congress.

10   9   8   7   6   5   4   3   2   1
19   18   17   16   15   14   13   12   11   10

Printed and bound in Great Britain by
CPI Antony Rowe, Chippenham and Eastbourne

The Performing Century

Redefining British Theatre History

General Editor: Professor Peter Holland

Redefining British Theatre History is a five-volume series under the general editorship of Professor Peter Holland. The series brings together major practitioners in theatre history in order to establish ways in which previous assumptions need fundamental questioning and to initiate new directions for the field. The series aims to establish a new future for theatre history, not least by making theatre historians aware of their own history, current practice and future.

Titles include:

Michael Cordner and Peter Holland (*editors*)
PLAYERS, PLAYWRIGHTS, PLAYHOUSES
Investigating Performance, 1660–1800

Tracy C. Davis and Peter Holland
THE PERFORMING CENTURY
Nineteenth-Century Theatre's History

Peter Holland and Stephen Orgel (*editors*)
FROM SCRIPT TO STAGE IN EARLY MODERN ENGLAND
From Performance to Print in Shakespeare's England

Peter Holland and Stephen Orgel (*editors*)
FROM PERFORMANCE TO PRINT IN SHAKESPEARE'S ENGLAND

W. B. Worthen and Peter Holland (*editors*)
THEORIZING PRACTICE
Redefining Theatre History

Redefining British Theatre History
Series Standing Order ISBN 978–0–333–98219–8 (Hardback)
978–0–333–98220–4 (Paperback)
(*outside North America only*)

You can receive future titles in this series as they are published by placing a standing order. Please contact your bookseller or, in case of difficulty, write to us at the address below with your name and address, the title of the series and the ISBN quoted above.

Customer Services Department, Macmillan Distribution Ltd, Houndmills, Basingstoke, Hampshire RG21 6XS, England

Contents

List of Illustrations

Notes on the Contributors

Emily Allen is Associate Professor of English at Purdue University, where she teaches in the literature programme and in the programme for Theory and Cultural Studies. She is the author of *Theater Figures: the Production of the Nineteenth-Century British Novel* and is currently at work on a book about the royal weddings of the Victorian period, one of which she discusses in her essay for the present volume.

Jacky Bratton is Professor of Theatre and Cultural History at Royal Holloway, University of London. Her most recent books are *New Readings in Theatre History* and *The Victorian Clown*. She is currently involved in two large-scale projects. One is beginning to re-catalogue the Lord Chamberlain's collection of nineteenth-century plays. The other, in collaboration with Dr Ann Featherstone, aims to produce a series of books and articles rewriting mid-Victorian entertainment history on a more inclusive plan.

Catherine Burroughs is Professor of English at Wells College and Visiting Lecturer in English at Cornell University. In addition to her many articles on British Romantic theatre and drama, her publications include: *Reading the Social Body*, co-editor (1993), *Closet Stages: Joanna Baillie and the Theater Theory of British Romantic Women Writers* (1997) and *Women in British Romantic Theatre: Drama, Performance, and Society, 1790–1840*, editor (2000).

Gilli Bush-Bailey is Senior Lecturer in Drama and Theatre, Royal Holloway, University of London. Following a first career as a professional actress, she combines her interest in women's theatre history with practice-based research. Her work on early nineteenth-century actress/writer Jane Scott includes a special edition of *Nineteenth-Century Theatre & Film* (2002) and a contributing chapter to *Women in British Romantic Theatre* (2000), both co-authored with Jacky Bratton. Her monograph *Treading the Bawds: Actresses & Playwrights on the Late-Stuart Stage* (2006) looks at the work of seventeenth-century actresses and female playwrights and she has also contributed a chapter on the early actress to the *Cambridge Companion to the Actress* (2007).

Jeffrey N. Cox is Professor of English and of Comparative Literature and Humanities at the University of Colorado at Boulder where he is also Associate Vice Chancellor for Faculty Affairs. His work on the drama includes *In the Shadows of Romance: Romantic Tragic Drama in England, Germany, and France, Seven Gothic Dramas, 1789–1825* and the *Broadview Anthology of Romantic Drama*, co-edited with Michael Gamer. He is also the author of *Poetry and Politics in the Cockney School: Keats, Shelley, Hunt and their Circle*.

Jim Davis is Professor and Chair in the School of Theatre, Performance and Cultural Policy Studies at the University of Warwick. He is co-author with Victor Emeljanow of *Reflecting the Audience: London Theatregoing 1840–1880* (University of Iowa Press, 2001) and has published widely on nineteenth-century theatre. He is currently working on the iconography of comic performance, 1780–1830.

Tracy C. Davis is Barber Professor of Performing Arts at Northwestern University and President of the American Society for Theatre Research. In addition to nineteenth-century British theatre, she specializes in the economics and business history of theatre; performance theory; gender and theatre; research methodology; museum studies; and Cold War studies. She is editor of the forthcoming *Cambridge Companion to Performance Studies*.

Heidi J. Holder is Professor of English at Central Michigan University. Her articles on British, Irish and Canadian drama have appeared in such journals as *Essays in Theatre* and the *Journal of Modern Literature*. She is currently engaged in a full-length study of the working-class theatre of Victorian London and on an anthology of plays from those theatres.

Peter Holland is McMeel Family Professor in Shakespeare Studies and Department Chair in the Department of Film, Television, and Theatre at the University of Notre Dame. From 1997 to 2002 he was Director of the Shakespeare Institute, Stratford-upon-Avon. He is General Editor of *Shakespeare Survey, Oxford Shakespeare Topics* (with Stanley Wells), and *Great Shakespeareans* (with Adrian Poole), as well as of *Redefining British Theatre History*. Among his books are *The Ornament of Action* (1979) and *English Shakespeares* (1997). He is currently President of the Shakespeare Association of America.

Jane Moody is Professor in the Department of English and Related Literature at the University of York. She is the author of *Illegitimate Theatre in London, 1770–1840* (2000) and co-editor of *Theatre and Celebrity in Britain, 1660–2000* (2005) and *The Cambridge Companion to British Theatre, 1730–1830* (forthcoming, 2007). Her essays on nineteenth-century theatre have appeared in a number of volumes including *Women and Playwriting in Nineteenth-Century Britain* (1999), *Women in British Romantic Theatre: Drama, Performance, and Society, 1790–1840* (2000) and *The Cambridge Companion to Shakespeare on Stage* (2002).

Mark Phelan is a lecturer in Drama at Queens University, Belfast. His research focuses on Irish Theatre, specializing in theatre and performance in the North of Ireland and nineteenth-century theatre history and historiography. He has written a number of articles on Irish theatre and recently received his doctorate (from Trinity College Dublin) on the Northern Revival and the Ulster Literary Theatre for publication.

Thomas Postlewait, University of Washington Seattle, Ohio State University, was President of the American Society for Theatre Research (1994–7) and is the author of *Prophet of the New Drama: William Archer and the Ibsen Campaign* (1986) and *The Cambridge History of Theatre Historiography* (forthcoming). He edited *William Archer on Ibsen* (1984), co-edited *Interpreting the Theatrical Past* (1989) and is editor of the book series 'Studies in Theatre History and Culture' for University of Iowa Press. He is working on a study of George Edwardes and the transformation of the London entertainment industry (1886–1914).

Richard Schoch is Professor of the History of Culture at Queen Mary, University of London, where he is also Director of the Graduate School in Humanities and Social Sciences. His most recent book is *The Secrets of Happiness: Three Thousand Years of Searching for the Good Life* (Scribner, 2006). He is currently writing a book on leisure.

Edward Ziter is Associate Professor of Theatre History in the Department of Drama at NYU. He is the author of *The Orient on the Victorian Stage* and has published articles in *The Wordsworth Circle, Theatre Survey* and *Theatre Journal* as well as edited volumes. He has edited the book reviews section for *Theatre Survey* and co-edited the performance reviews section for *Theatre Journal*. He is currently working on a monograph examining contemporary Syrian Theatre.

Series Introduction: Redefining British Theatre History

Peter Holland

On the surface, it doesn't look like much of a problem: conjoining the two words 'theatre' and 'history' to define a particular practice of scholarship has a long and illustrious history. Nor does it appear to over-complicate matters to add the word 'British', for all that the word is so furiously questioned at different moments of history (and especially at the moment). Yet what kind of history theatre history is and what kind of theatre theatre history investigates, let alone what the Britishness is of its theatre history, is endlessly problematic. For all the availability of shelves full of the outcomes of its practices, theatre history is in need of a substantial reassessment. This series is an attempt to place some markers in that vital project.

It is hardly as if theatre history is a new area of scholarly enquiry and academic publication. Within a general, varyingly academic mode of publication, one could point, in the UK, to the longevity of *Theatre Notebook*, a journal founded in 1945 by the Society for Theatre Research; its subtitle *A Journal of the History and Technique of the British Theatre* neatly sets out its scope and the assumed scope of theatre history. A number of US journals have had similar concerns, including *Theatre Survey* (from the American Society for Theatre Research) and more narrowly defined examples like *Restoration and Eighteenth-Century Theatre Research* or *Nineteenth-Century Theatre Research*. Lying behind such work is the complex institutional history of the formation of university drama and theatre departments on both sides of the Atlantic and their vexed and often still unformulated connection both to theatre training (the university as feed to a profession) and to departments of English Literature.

For the early modern period theatre historians might chart the subject's early twentieth-century history as being encapsulated by the work of E. K. Chambers (especially *The Elizabethan Stage*, 4 vols [Oxford: Clarendon Press, 1923]) or G. E. Bentley in his continuation (*The Jacobean and Caroline Stage*, 7 vols [Oxford: Clarendon Press, 1941–68]), phenomenal individual achievements of documenting theatrical events, theatre performers and theatrical contexts. Their work might be matched for a later period by, say, E. L. Avery et al., eds, *The London Stage 1660–1800*, 11 vols (Carbondale, Ill: Southern Illinois University Press, 1960–8) or Philip Highfill, Kalman Burnim and Edward Langhans, eds, *A Biographical Dictionary of Actors, Actresses, Musicians, Dancers, Managers and Other Stage Personnel in London, 1660–1800*, 16 vols (Carbondale, Ill: Southern Illinois University Press, 1973–93). Further back still comes the fundamental work of such people as Boaden (*Memoirs of Mrs Siddons*, 2 vols [London, 1827]) and Genest (*Some Account of the English Stage from the Restoration in 1660 to 1830*, 10 vols [Bath, 1832]), who saw themselves neither as scholars nor as academics and yet whose work implicitly defined the accumulative function of data collection as a primary purpose of theatre history. Behind them comes the achievement of the greatest of eighteenth-century editors of Shakespeare, Edmond Malone.

Yet, seeing that there is a practice of theatre history is not the same as understanding or theorizing such a project. While many academics are engaged in the practice of something they would unhesitatingly term 'Theatre History' and while they would differentiate it carefully from a variety of other contiguous fields (e.g. performance theory or history of drama), there has been remarkably little investigation of the methodological bases on which the shelves of accumulated scholarship have been based or the theoretical bases on which Theatre History has been or might be constructed. Even within organizations as aware of the need for theoretical sophistication as IFTR/FIRT (Fédération Internationale pour la recherche théâtrale) the emphasis has been placed more squarely on performance theory than on the historiographical problems of theatre. In part that can undoubtedly be traced to the disciplines or institutional structures out of which the work has evolved: one would need to examine its early and still troubled connection to literary studies, to the analysis of drama and, most visibly, to the study of the history of Shakespeare in performance or, on another tack, to consider the ways in which theatre departments have structured their courses in the US and UK.

By comparison with the traditionally positivist accumulation of data that marks, say, *Theatre Notebook*, one could, however, see signs of the emergence of a new concern with the processes of historiography as it affects the specific study of a massive cultural institution like theatre in, to take just one significant example, the collection of essays edited by Thomas Postlewait and Bruce McConachie, *Interpreting the Theatrical Past: Essays in the Historiography of Performance* (Iowa City: University of Iowa Press, 1989). But, while individual theatre historians are demonstrating an expanding awareness of the specific areas of historiography relevant to their work (e.g. economic history) and while theorizing of performance including its historical traces has grown immensely over the past fifteen years, there is little enough to set out on a large scale the parameters of something that might hope by now to see itself as a discipline. The shelves of libraries and bookshops and the reading lists of courses do not show major resources for understanding what theatre history is, while an unending stream of books offering to help students understand the history of theatre pours from presses. In part this may be connected to the absence of departments of theatre history and the further substantial absence, within theatre departments, of courses concerned to do more than teach theatre history as an assumed and shared methodology based on an acceptance of what constitutes evidence and of how that evidence generates the potential for meaning.

Redefining British Theatre History sets out, extremely ambitiously, to make a major statement by bringing together, in the course of its series of five volumes, some fifty major practitioners in theatre history in order to establish ways in which previous assumptions need fundamental questioning and in which a future for the field can be enunciated in modes as yet undervalued. It aims to be a significant review of where we are and what we think we are doing.

The project began from an unusual collaboration between research library and publisher. My gratitude goes first and foremost to Dr Roy Ritchie of the Huntington Library and Josie Dixon of Palgrave Macmillan for contacting me to see whether I would develop a proposal that would create a series of conferences and subsequent volumes based on a single theme. Their support, not least financial, has been crucial in bringing the project to a reality both in the pleasures of the conference and the creation of this book. If we succeed, *Redefining British Theatre History* should chart the beginnings of a new future for theatre history, not least by making theatre historians newly and self-consciously aware of their own history, their practice and their future.

Introduction: the Performing Society

Tracy C. Davis and Peter Holland

The taxonomies of writing about theatre morph with time. What originated as memory was committed to the page in reviews, diaries or letters; anecdotes were codified in memoirs;[1] the theatre was increasingly remembered through biographies of its stars and histories of its buildings; and only later did the recording of performance become a scholarly activity of theatre history. Recounting that history – the history of theatre history itself – thus inherently poses a problem of methodology as well as creating a falsely precise stratification of generations of scholarship and criticism the history produces.

From one perspective, the history necessitates a chronological exposition. The academic study of nineteenth-century British theatre might be marked by a clear point of origin: Allardyce Nicoll's *A History of English Drama, 1660–1900* reached the early nineteenth century in 1930 and the second half in 1946, cataloguing thousands of plays and summarizing playhouse conditions and major trends in dramatic writing. Decades later, in his study of melodrama, Michael Booth took a more sympathetic outlook towards what Nicoll had termed 'this type of despised and neglected entertainment',[2] and opened up the field to the first wave of revisionist investigations. In *English Melodrama* (published in 1965) and his prefaces to *English Plays of the Nineteenth Century* (1969–76), Booth showed how genre-based studies of repertoire can be grounded in performance traditions. Further work was dependent upon and enabled by the availability of dramatic materials, initially in the ambitious microform collection *English and American Plays of the Nineteenth Century* (which issued over 25,000 plays from acting editions, manuscripts and the Lord Chamberlain's licensing copies between 1965 and 1984), continuing when the series switched from using migraine-inducing microcards to the more user-friendly and up-to-date medium of microfiche. J. P. Wearing's series *A London Stage*, whose multi-volume calendars begin with 1890, added a wealth of basic information about plays from the end of the century and the Edwardian years, including cast and crew lists, length of runs and locations of reviews. Diana Howard's *London Theatres and Music Halls 1850–1950* made the confusing history of over 900 London venues traceable, a boon to everyone trying to untangle a succession of names for sites, architectural histories and the cavalcade of managements.[3]

1

These tools eased the work of a generation of scholars including George Rowell (whose long career of writing on the period's actors, plays and criticism began in the 1950s), David Mayer (on melodramatic music, Regency pantomime, later popular entertainments and silent film), Joseph Donohue (on Romantic-era theatre), Jane Stedman (on W. S. Gilbert and his corpus), Terence Rees (on theatre lighting) and Kurt Gänzl (on musical theatre). They insisted on the vitality of theatre in the nineteenth century, especially during the formerly derided Victorian years and the belletristic late-Georgian and Regency period, establishing a solid foundation based in theatre practice, eschewing judgements about literary quality and instead establishing the characteristics of a succession of managers, performers and other artists who presented the repertoire. Together, they established that a populist repertoire was sustained by a wide swathe of the British public, by which they almost always meant Londoners. Refinements to this outlook, offered by scholars such as Clive Barker and Penny Summerfeld, showed persuasively that populism did not erase politics (especially radicalism), while Peter Bailey and Jacky Bratton's collections opened up studies of the parallel entertainment of music hall to social, aesthetic and economic implications. Martin Meisel's *Realizations* demonstrated abiding connections between visual practices of the theatre and exhibitions of fine and popular art, nuancing Michael Booth's important work on spectacularism and, by tracing connections between theatre and the novel, reconnecting literary and theatrical studies in a new mode.[4]

After 1990, nineteenth-century theatre scholars looked even more earnestly beyond the boundaries of conventional dramatic genres, with Dagmar Kift's study of music hall programming and spectatorship, Alexandra Carter's detailing of English ballet, John McCormick's work on marionette theatre, Jane Goodall's excavation of evolutionist pseudo-science, Brenda Assael's study of circus and Jacky Bratton and Ann Featherstone's investigation of the Victorian clown. Post-structuralists showed how stage performance seeped into – or steeped – ideas and practices beyond the playhouse, in forms as varied as Elaine Hadley's *Melodramatic Tactics*, Daniel O'Quinn's *Staging Governance*, Joseph Donohue's *Fantasies of Empire* and Joel Kaplan and Sheila Stowell's *Theatre and Fashion*, as well as within theatre as exemplified by Marc Baer's study of the Old Price Riots at Covent Garden. Feminism occasioned a major revision of nineteenth-century historiography, capped by Jacky Bratton's *New Readings in Theatre History* and supported by Tracy C. Davis's *Actresses as Working Women*, collections by Catherine Burroughs on Romantic theatre, and Tracy C. Davis and Ellen Donkin on women playwrights and Katherine Newey's *Women's Theatre Writing in Victorian Britain*, a counterpart to John Russell Stephens's *The Profession of the Playwright* which fleetingly mentioned but a few women dramatists. Explicit manifestations of politics found advocates with varied outlooks: Jane Moody's *Illegitimate Theatre in London, 1770–1840* and Tracy C. Davis's *The Economics of the British Stage, 1800–1914* set the performance industry in relation to competition and capitalist theory, while the pervasiveness of racialized outlooks was explicated in Jennifer DeVere Brody's *Impossible Purities*, Edward Ziter's *The Orient on the Victorian Stage* and Brian Singleton's *Oscar Asche, Orientalism, and British Musical Comedy*. Books by Richard

Schoch and Richard Foulkes exemplified how current perspectives on Shakespeare production, always a staple of Victorian theatre studies, took into account British imperialism, while the composition of localized audiences preoccupied Jim Davis and Victor Emeljanow's *Reflecting the Audience: London Theatregoing, 1840–1880*.[5] A recent overview (in Joseph Donohue's volume in *The Cambridge History of British Theatre*) shows how the field has now been redefined from at least some of these perspectives.[6]

This chronicle, too abbreviated, too dense with names and titles and inevitably over-simplified in its divisions,[7] effectively moves beyond its own apparent chronological account by sketching two major shifts in the historiography. In the first wave, there is an emphasis on establishing scholarly credibility for nineteenth-century theatre studies, relying most often on empiricist approaches – only in a few cases embracing materialist histories – and frequently preoccupied with establishing taxonomies (for plays, acting and production styles, venues and paratheatrical entertainments). After 1990, there is a robust engagement with critical theory, ranging from new historicism to feminism, post-colonial studies, critical race studies and Marxist-inflected microhistory. This reflects not only a more secure footing for nineteenth-century theatre studies – no longer in a defensive mode vis-à-vis literary studies – but also the confidence to take on the debates arising from various disciplines and fields and contribute simultaneously to multiple ongoing controversies in theatre studies and elsewhere. It is not surprising, therefore, that theatre and performance are currently embraced by Romantic and Victorian scholars alike as pervasive practices of the historical past as well as indispensable discourses for the study of what, until recently, had not been terrain claimed even by the most enterprising of theatre scholars. The interaction between Romantic (or Georgian) and Victorian scholarship is still minimal, an unnatural divide awkwardly bifurcating the period before the first Reform Act (1832), Victoria's accession (1837) or the Theatre Act (1843) from what followed (or, arguably, what continued, relatively seamlessly). Yet nineteenth-century theatre – a designation now followed almost invariably by 'and performance' with variants such as 'spectacle', 'exhibition' and 'spectatorship' – is at last a hot button and, to mix the metaphor, no longer some kind of impoverished, embarrassingly dull or pedestrian descendant of glorious early-modern forebears.

One of the most significant developments has been the broadening of focus from repertoire, production values and architecture to an inclusive view of performance beyond theatre buildings. This is reflected in the present volume by Emily Allen's approach to public celebrations of royal ceremonials and, at the other end of the imperial spectrum, Mark Phelan's chapter on the presence of popular rites and populist ebullience in Belfast theatres and other civic celebrations. Both authors significantly review, revise and overturn narratives of high/low cultural premises and the locus of aesthetic meaning-making. Allen shows how British royalty and the public made theatre, engaged in theatricality and commemorated royal milestones in versions of a peaceful and consensual polity, in contrast to contemporaneous French recourse to rebellion, revolution and war. The link between folk practices of a recently urbanized Belfast working class and the management of public affairs in a divided society undermines the prevailing noisy attributions of modernism linked indivisibly both to the Irish Revival and Dublin, which Phelan overturns as minor practices in comparison to the industrial and cosmopolitan Irishness of the more northerly city.

Phelan's case study reflects meta-textual concerns that bind cities, regions and nations together. Similar ideas are also taken up in chapters by Tracy C. Davis, Jane Moody and Heidi Holder. Fairies, characterized by twentieth-century critics who dwell on the nostalgic depictions of Neverland in *Peter Pan*, have been relegated by historiography to children's theatre, childish sensibilities and juvenilia. Davis argues instead that *Peter Pan* is an aberrant text, both for the Victorian and Edwardian traditions. Adult players' abiding interest in theatre fairies is equatable to the fascination with the Other, an Other which, in this case, has sovereign power distinct from the British nation and coexists peacefully with mortals but may choose to express dissatisfactions about human encroachments and breaches of land, ethics and law, making Britons subservient to fairies' will. Thus, the theatre is not a corruption of tales collected by folklorists but an outlet for aestheticizing data gathered by dispassionate ethnographers who observed and/or chronicled fairydom.

Heidi Holder explores a different manifestation of the Other in East End plays with Jewish themes, setting them against the West End theatres' and West End audiences' well-known fascination with a drama of location, an exploration from the West End perspective of what London signifies as a social entity and cultural phenomenon. What has been assumed to be representative of London (both geographically and culturally) can, however, be contrasted powerfully by the ways in which a different London is figured by the East End theatres – or spaces of performance that the West End patronizingly refused to acknowledge as theatres – where Jewish managers, playwrights and audiences were important enough and self-identified sufficiently to create their own images of their place in the culture. In this Holder tracks the diversity within British culture and the multiplicity of the ethnos within the East End.

For Jane Moody, another assumption of theatre history needs to be queried and revised. Where the history of the theatrical representation of capitalism has assumed it to be narrowly limited in the nineteenth century to the problems of working-class labour as a subject for melodrama, Moody argues that capital offered a far wider range of drama, drama of the middle and upper classes, a commercial and psychological need for new kinds of theatrical characters and stage plots. Hence, far from being dourly depressing, as capital has appeared to be when seen through the lens of Shaw, it can be seen as exhilarating and bewildering when its location is a suburban villa rather than a worker's cottage. Instead of privileging the anti-capitalist vision created by melodrama, Moody proposes a theatre history in which capital is moralized in contradictory and far more ambivalent ways.

For early chroniclers of Victorian and Edwardian theatre, such as W. Macqueen-Pope, Raymond Mander and Joe Mitchenson, recognizing the ebullience of performers went hand in hand with expressions of their own connoisseurship of excellent acting, playwriting and productions. Three contributors to this volume show the obsolescence of such an approach by acknowledging the importance of consumption and spectatorship, not as connoisseurship but as instances of mass culture. Gilli Bush-Bailey reverses the polarity of attention in the 1813–14 season by turning rapidly from the often considered ways in which Edmund Kean impressed audiences at Drury Lane through his arresting approach to tragic acting (leaving behind his provincial career and multi-genre repertoire), to the ways the Sans Pareil, a minor theatre around the corner from Drury Lane, utilized performers in a wide range of roles and plays. Where specialization was not an option, players garnered admiration precisely for their ability to embody disparate creations in a single evening. Bush-Bailey finds in the Sans Pareil a way to question what constitutes depth and skill, and how audiences recognized and acknowledged versatility in a theatre known for its homegrown plays, responsive topicality and stable acting corps. Jim Davis's focus on the performances of pantomimes on Boxing Day, a phenomenon of great significance for a broad spectrum of spectators across classes, tracks the evolution of this popular Christmastime entertainment through traditions of its spectatorship, a significant reversal of the usual presumption that writing and production shape consumer demand rather than spectators reforming customs collectively. In his preliminary study of the impresario, producer and theatre-owner George Edwardes, Thomas Postlewait shows the centrality of Edwardes for late nineteenth- and early twentieth-century London theatre, as a successful producer of long-running and financially profitable shows. Where Irving, Wilde and Shaw are usually taken as the key figures of the period (to judge by the number of biographies they are accorded), Postlewait argues that Edwardes and, especially, his brand of musical theatre are of far greater cultural significance, not only because they were popular and profitable but also as part of the process of urbanization and its cultural and social transformations. George Edwardes appears in this guise as the perfect definer of London, its theatre and culture, its society and its Edwardian forms.

These thematic concerns link spectatorship to consumer choice and ultimately to the success and durability of three formulae important to nineteenth-century theatre – the mixed bill, pantomime and musical comedy – that cut across practices of art, theatre governance and popular culture. Catherine Burroughs complicates the picture by posing a paradox: if the legitimacy of drama is not based upon production at all, how can theatre historians understand unperformed 'closet drama' of the early part of the century as necessarily and centrally a mode of reception? Where should reception be located, especially when gender is a factor to be kept constantly in the scholar's focus? What is the distinction between a censored or rejected play (resulting in what Burroughs terms 'disappointed authorship') and drama that was deliberately written to be read? When visuality is removed from the product and relegated to a reader's imagination, scholarship has delineated a false division between literary and stage history, and between intellectuality and popularity, instead of acknowledging valid and not incommensurate choices regarding authorial agency and consumer volition.

Attention to performance issues has significantly changed from earlier studies about the mechanics of stagecraft, idiosyncrasies of actors and the staff rotas in a pre-director theatre. For example, Bush-Bailey asks tangentially how performance itself can be a research strategy to try to (re)discover an historicized aesthetic.[8] Edward Ziter marshals visual artefacts of a consummately somatic art to argue that portraiture is equally apt as eye-witness accounts and critical theory in piecing together an actor's approach to character. Indeed, in the case of Charles Mathews's solo performance, together the evidentiary categories make sense of low comedy as an aesthetic praised by Romantic critics. Jeffrey Cox demonstrates how genre continues to be a useful category, not to separate Romantic drama from a truly new form, melodrama, but to see how sensationalism is 'the artistic machine to mould the quiet spectator'. Melodrama was effective, and persistent, Cox argues, because its virtuality remade and redefined the real. Exhibited at top speed, it is understood by Cox as an experience, not as a set of writerly or performative conventions.

Two contributors pose questions about how theatres defined their turf and innovated, either when aspiring to 'higher' forms or in freely combining popular tropes. Richard Schoch's perspective on the 1866 Parliamentary Select Committee, which probed anxieties about the viability of dramatic theatres in the midst of a burgeoning entertainment industry, questions the orthodox view about protectionism around Shakespearean repertoire.[9] The differences in licensing authorities and conditions for theatres (with dramatic repertoire) and music halls (featuring a succession of brief turns, including singers and specialty acts) created conflict about what was fair or unfair restriction of trade. The Committee recommended that the halls be allowed to produce Shakespeare, as a potentially uplifting stimulus for the audiences and a coalescing effect on the British public. But this was not what music hall managers wanted, and ultimately was not what the British public got. Jacky Bratton explores the hybridity and distinction of a different competitor, the circus, which invariably featured equine acts and sometimes deployed a stage as well as the sawdust-dappled equestrian ring. In presenting stories that reiterate national tropes and cement national identity, the circus epitomizes nineteenth-century audiences' lack of concern for genre divides and indifference to stylistic intermixing. Bratton demonstrates how, in the transmission of a compelling story, the concerns of audiences are at odds with the traditional concerns of scholars.

Readers who are brand new to this field might be surprised by some absences. These absences reflect current preoccupations and priorities as well as belie traces of what scholars of nineteenth-century theatre have endeavoured to overcome as prevalent narratives. There is scant discussion of the Irish playwright whose witty criticism of art, music then theatre paved the way for his extraordinary output of comic drama, beginning in 1892 and lasting until the middle of the twentieth century, and none of the other writers and artists who were featured at the Royal Court, independent or non-commercial theatres of the late-Victorian and Edwardian years is mentioned. There is no overview of playwriting styles or dramatic theory at all; only one manager is featured, and though a prominent businessman he was far from a society figure; and the only starring actor who is analysed produced sui generis one-person shows which he devised and performed. The great nineteenth-century enterprises of journalism and novel-writing, though important parallel pursuits to theatre, are sidelined both as historical inquiries and scholarly subjects. Modernism – which various theatre historians have cast as the saviour, bane, usurper or inevitable successor to nineteenth-century styles, practices and priorities – is invoked either as a minor (and over-blown) counter-narrative to an ebullient populist tradition or a zeitgeist in tension with traditionalism. But invocations of *modernity* are peppered throughout the volume: in the advent of melodrama, the hybridity of genres, consumer-driven aesthetic change, and the scale of enterprises. Nineteenth-century theatre and performance, in other words, are neither preceded nor succeeded by a more valid (literary and recondite) aesthetic.[10]

Bratton sketches what is the abiding problem with nineteenth-century British theatre historiography: it is a tale *re*told, and thus altered. In the recombination forged in various conditions of mass entertainment, social and political anxieties, the relationship of repertoire to audiences, or the definitional parameters of performance, we simply cannot recuperate eye-witness experience as testimony of play-going any more than we can find the most robust ideas in a calendar of productions, a chronicle of locales or an aristocracy of styles. And thus, nineteenth-century theatre is inevitably misunderstood (again). We may attribute innovation or consistency, custom or tradition, and excellence or mediocrity in changing our reasons for *what* mattered, but we also belie our interest in *why* theatre mattered. Embedded in this book's title is the concept that nineteenth-century society itself performs. Theatre is culture's palimpsest, written upon again, as traces of the old show through with more or less insistence despite inscriptions of the new seeming to have easiest legibility. Theatre history itself mimics the palimpsestic layering and scraping back, performing (or demonstrating) subsequent centuries' preoccupations, claims for legitimacy, and echoic multiplicity. Never 'authentic', theatre history is now more valenced, reflecting how nineteenth-century performance was neither contained by neat taxonomies (despite what the first generation of its historians strove to demonstrate in order to bring an inchoate field into view) nor strictly populist (as the second generation of historians suggested in bringing a host of non-dramatic forms and non-literary features to the fore). To the extent that a third generation of historians, including several contributors to this volume, subsequently showed theatre to be intricately connected to abiding social and imaginative formations, *The Performing Century: Nineteenth-Century Theatre's History* again revises the story, as different evidence is accorded credibility, some analytical polarities are reversed, new ideas draw focus, different interests accord importance to neglected phenomena and a unique version of comprehensiveness finds expression.

Notes

1. See, for example, W. J. Macqueen-Pope, *Carriages at Eleven* (London: Hutchinson, 1947); *Haymarket: Theatre of Perfection* (London: Allen, 1948); or *The Footlights Flickered* (London: H. Jenkins, 1959). See also Jim Davis and Victor Emeljanow, 'Wistful Remembrancer: the Historiographical of Macqueen-Popery', *New Theatre Quarterly*, 17.4 (2001): 299–309; and Jacky Bratton, *New Readings in Theatre History* (Cambridge: Cambridge University Press, 2003), 95–132. The editors thank Jacky Bratton, Jeff Cox, Jim Davis,

Tom Postlewait and Richard Schoch for comments and correctives to our recounting of this history.

2. Allardyce Nicoll, *A History of English Drama, 1660–1900*, 6 vols (Cambridge: Cambridge University Press, 1952–9), 4: 100. The very first academic survey may be Ernest B. Watson's *Sheridan to Robertson; a Study of the Nineteenth-Century London Stage* (Cambridge, MA: Harvard University Press, 1926), building on his Harvard dissertation of 1913.

3. Michael Booth, *English Melodrama* (London: H. Jenkins, 1965); and Michael Booth, *English Plays of the Nineteenth Century* (Oxford: Clarendon, 1969–76). *English and American Plays of the Nineteenth Century* (New Canaan, CT: Readex, 1965–84); this continued under the title *Nineteenth Century English and American Drama* (New Canaan, CT: Readex, 1985–), and is partially indexed in James Ellis, comp. and ed., assisted by Joseph Donohue, with Louise Allen Zak, *English Drama of the Nineteenth Century: an Index and Finding Guide* (New Canaan, CT: Readex Books, 1985). J. P. Wearing's series begins with *A London Stage, A Calendar of Plays and Players 1890–99* (Metuchen: Scarecrow, 1976). Diana Howard, *London Theatres and Music Halls 1850–1950* (London: Library Association, 1970).

4. George Rowell, *The Victorian Theatre: a Survey* (London: Oxford University Press, 1956); George Rowell, *Victorian Dramatic Criticism* (London: Methuen, 1971); David Mayer, *Harlequin in His Element; the English Pantomime, 1806–1836* (Cambridge, MA: Harvard University Press, 1969); David Mayer, *Four Bars of 'Agit': Incidental Music for Victorian and Edwardian Melodrama* (London: Samuel French, 1983); David Mayer, *Henry Irving and 'The Bells'* (Manchester: Manchester University Press, 1980); Joseph Donohue, *Theatre in the Age of Kean* (Oxford: Basil Blackwell, 1975); Joseph Donohue, *Dramatic Character in the English Romantic Age* (Princeton: Princeton University Press, 1970); Jane Stedman, *Gilbert Before Sullivan; Six Comic Plays* (Chicago: University of Chicago Press, 1967); Jane Stedman, *W. S. Gilbert: a Classic Victorian and His Theatre* (Oxford: Oxford University Press, 1996); Terence Rees, *Theatre Lighting in the Age of Gas* (London: Society for Theatre Research, 1978); Kurt Gänzl, *The British Musical Theatre, Volume I: 1865–1914* (Basingstoke: Macmillan, 1986); Clive Barker, 'A Theatre for the People', in K. Richards and P. Thomson, eds, *Essays on Nineteenth Century British Theatre* (Manchester: Manchester University Press, 1971), 1–17; Penny Summerfeld, 'The Effingham Arms and the Empire: Deliberate Selection in the Evolution of Music Hall in London', in Eileen Yeo and Stephen Yeo, eds, *Popular Culture and Class Conflict 1590–1914: Explorations in the History of Labour and Leisure* (Brighton: Harvester, 1981), 209–40; Peter Bailey, *Music Hall: the Business of Pleasure* (Milton Keynes: Open University Press, 1986); J. S. Bratton, *Music Hall: Performance and Style* (Milton Keynes: Open University Press, 1986); Martin Meisel, *Realizations: Narrative, Pictorial, and Theatrical Arts in Nineteenth-century England* (Princeton: Princeton University Press, 1983); and Michael Booth, *Victorian Spectacular Theatre, 1850–1910* (London: Routledge & Kegan Paul, 1981).

5. Dagmar Kift, *The Victorian Music Hall: Culture, Class, and Conflict* (Cambridge: Cambridge University Press, 1996); Alexandra Carter, *Dance and Dancers in the Victorian and Edwardian Music Hall Ballet* (Aldershot: Ashgate, 2005); John McCormick, *The Victorian Marionette Theatre* (Iowa City: University of Iowa Press, 2004); Jane Goodall, *Performance and Evolution in the Age of Darwin: Out of the Natural Order* (London: Routledge, 2002); Brenda Assael, *The Circus and Victorian Society* (Charlottesville: University of Virginia Press, 2005); Jacky Bratton and Ann Featherstone, *The Victorian Clown* (Cambridge: Cambridge University Press, 2006); Elaine Hadley, *Melodramatic Tactics: Theatricalized Dissent in the English Marketplace, 1800–1885* (Stanford: Stanford University Press, 1995); Daniel O'Quinn, *Staging Governance: Theatrical Imperialism in London 1770–1800* (Baltimore: Johns Hopkins University Press, 2005); Joseph Donohue, *Fantasies of Empire: the Empire Theatre of Varieties and the Licensing Controversy of 1894* (Iowa City: University of Iowa Press, 2006); Joel Kaplan and Sheila Stowell, *Theatre and Fashion: Oscar Wilde to the Suffragettes* (Cambridge: Cambridge University Press, 1994); Marc Baer, *Theatre and Disorder in Late Georgian London* (Oxford: Clarendon, 1992); Jacky Bratton, *New Readings in Theatre History* (Cambridge: Cambridge University Press, 2003); Tracy C. Davis,

Actresses as Working Women: Their Social Identity in Victorian Culture (London: Routledge, 1991); Catherine Burroughs, ed., *Women in British Romantic Theatre: Drama, Performance, and Society, 1790–1840* (Cambridge: Cambridge University Press, 2000); Tracy C. Davis and Ellen Donkin, eds, *Women and Playwriting in Nineteenth-century Britain* (Cambridge: Cambridge University Press, 1999); Katherine Newey, *Women's Theatre Writing in Victorian Britain* (Cambridge, Cambridge University Press 2005); John Russell Stephens, *The Profession of the Playwright* (Cambridge: Cambridge University Press, 1992); Jane Moody, *Illegitimate Theatre in London, 1770–1840* (Cambridge: Cambridge University Press, 2000); Tracy C. Davis, *The Economics of the British Stage, 1800–1914* (Cambridge: Cambridge University Press, 2000); Jennifer DeVere Brody, *Impossible Purities: Blackness, Femininity, and Victorian Culture* (Durham: Duke University Press, 1998); Edward Ziter, *The Orient on the Victorian Stage* (Cambridge: Cambridge University Press, 2003); Brian Singleton, *Oscar Asche, Orientalism, and British Musical Comedy* (Westport, CT: Praeger, 2004); Richard Schoch, *Shakespeare's Victorian Stage: Performing History in the Theatre of Charles Kean* (Cambridge: Cambridge University Press, 1998); Richard Foulkes, *Performing Shakespeare in the Age of Empire* (Cambridge: Cambridge University Press, 2002); and Jim Davis and Victor Emeljanow, *Reflecting the Audience: London Theatregoing, 1840–1880* (Iowa City: University of Iowa Press, 2001).

6. Joseph Donohue, ed., *The Cambridge History of British Theatre, Volume 2: 1660–1895* (Cambridge: Cambridge University Press, 2004).

7. Some of the continuities of previous practices can be shown in the publications in journals, with *Theatre Notebook* (1945–) continuing to publish positivist accounts of details of theatre materials while, say, *Nineteenth Century Theatre Research* (from 1973), continued as *Nineteenth Century Theatre* (from 1987) and as *Nineteenth Century Theatre and Film* (from 2003) publishes more analytic work.

8. This is taken up in other published work: see Gilli Bush-Bailey, 'Putting it into Practice: the Possibilities and Problems of Practical Research for the Theatre Historian', *Contemporary Theatre Review*, 12.2 (2002): 77–96.

9. This problem recurred more generically in the 1892 Select Committee as the 'sketch issue', which also concerned the conflict between protectionism and laissez faire. See *Select Committee on Theatrical Licences and Regulations With Proceedings Minutes of Evidence Appendix and Index*, British Parliamentary Papers Report (1866; rpt. Shannon: Irish University Press, 1970); and *Select Committee on Theatres and Places of Entertainment With Proceedings Minutes of Evidence Appendix and Index*, British Parliamentary Papers Report (1892; rpt. Shannon: Irish University Press, 1970).

10. This bears comparison with David Mayer's essay 'Some Recent Writings on Victorian Theatre', a review essay in *Victorian Studies* 20.3 (Spring 1977): 311–17.

Part I
Performance Occasions

1
Boxing Day

Jim Davis

Each successive Boxing Day finds us in the same state of high excitement and expectation. On that eventful day, when new pantomimes are played for the first time at the two great theatres, and at twenty or thirty of the little ones, we still gloat as formerly upon the bills which set forth tempting descriptions of the scenery in staring red and black letters, and still fall down upon our knees, with other men and boys, upon the pavement by shop doors, to read them down to the very last line.[1]

Throughout the nineteenth century the Boxing Day performances of the annual pantomime at theatres throughout Britain were a highlight of the theatrical calendar. Traditionally, the Christmas festivities spilled over into Boxing Day on 26 December, the day on which tradesmen and servants received their Christmas boxes, a seasonal gift of money from employers or customers, and so had an unaccustomed amount to spend. This was also the day which saw the first performance of hundreds of Christmas pantomimes, combining spectacle, comedy, music and, for most of the century, the Harlequinade in a performance that appealed to both adults and children through a strange blend of fairy tale and topical allusion. The solvency of many theatres depended on the success of these pantomimes, which could run for several months and would hopefully recoup the substantial financial investment involved. Most studies of British pantomime give some attention to the extraordinary size and behaviour of theatre audiences on these occasions, to the uproar drowning out the words of the plays (traditionally *The London Merchant* and *Jane Shore*) which preceded the pantomimes and to the inevitable technical problems encountered as transformation effects went wrong through lack of adequate preparation or rehearsal. The spectators' expectations were high, no doubt accentuated by the sort of advertising Dickens describes above and by the 'puffs' that appeared in the newspapers just prior to Christmas. Such advertising had a strong impact on Victorian stage spectacle and pantomime:

[t]he primary result was to instigate a continual escalation of representation. This escalation had its own logic of one-upmanship: everything had to outdo what had come before it, and in turn everything had to be outdone by what

came after it. The spectacles of the early Victorian stage conditioned their audiences to expect more – and more and more.[2]

If this was the case, then the anticipation of pantomime audiences increased year by year, accentuating the 'state of high excitement and expectation' to which Dickens refers. Indeed, 'an exceedingly large proportion of the community would as soon think of giving up their plum pudding on Christmas Day as abandoning their pantomimes the night after', claimed the *Daily Telegraph* (27 December 1865), 'On no other dramatic venture of the year is such a vast amount of thought and capital expended . . . ' But this was only part of the picture.

For Boxing Day and Boxing Night were occasions when audiences re-enacted their own spectacle, reviving through rowdiness, fights and the throwing of orange peel exactly those conditions to which foreign visitors to England referred with such disdain in the late-eighteenth and early-nineteenth century. However self-regulating the Boxing Day audiences were, especially once the pantomime had commenced, they also demonstrated their power through the creation of a saturnalian event, in which disorder, chaos and anarchy never seemed far away. The issue of class also crept into these events, since the disorderliness was invariably associated with the working classes or with working-class elements within the audience. In so far as the gallery audience reigned supreme on Boxing Day, the lower classes asserted their temporal and spatial control over the events that occurred both on stage and within the auditorium. They refuted such perceptions as those of Henry Morley, whose description of *Twelfth Night* at Sadler's Wells Theatre includes the statement that, 'There sit our working class audiences in a happy crowd, as orderly and reverent as if they were at church.'[3] Indeed, pantomime audiences were engaged in what Marc Baer calls 'social theatre', in which audiences themselves become actors or active participants. The Boxing Day performance of pantomime in fact provided almost the last glimmer of the 'activist audience' defined by Baer. But it was generally an audience that justified Baer's notion that we should reconceptualize the disorderly 'crowd', allowing for its definition along a continuum from riot to protest to celebratory events.[4] Among factors celebrated by Boxing Night audiences throughout the century were notions of liberty and community, and – judging from their enthusiastic singing of the National Anthem, 'Rule Britannia' and, on occasions, 'God Bless the Prince of Wales' – a sense of patriotism and national identity. The temporary hedonism of Boxing Day enabled a saturnalian ritual of disorder, hallowed by tradition, which was actually quite orderly and predictable in its customary re-enactments. The object of this disorder was unfocused: rioting and protest of a political, social or economic nature were practically non-existent.

The *Daily Telegraph* (27 December 1865) confirmed the saturnalian inversion of pantomime audiences, describing how 'on and after Boxing-night the stalls – the usual ruling powers – are dethroned by the pit and gallery. The regular *habitués* surrender their exclusive sway, and a boisterous, but by no means revolutionary, mob, reigns . . . ' In itself, with its disorder and cruelty, crime and insubordination, pantomime too embodied saturnalian transgression. Recent revisionist accounts of pantomime have suggested that both the genre and its audiences were populist rather than radical:

> There is, of course, always an element of the Lord of Misrule in popular culture, and pantomime certainly incorporated it. It is significant, however, that the humbling of the mighty and the elevation of the clown is in pantomime, as in carnival and other traditional festivals, a temporary affair that emphasises rather than questions the normal order of things.[5]

This is far too easy and simplistic an assertion. While there is a clearly discernible pattern in both the behaviour and the journalistic representation of pantomime audiences, particularly those who attended Boxing Day performances, there is a dynamic that press reports frequently seek to contain and through this an assumption that agency lies somewhere other than among those spectators who both created and controlled the continuum from order to disorder that typified this unique occasion.

The challenge presented by an investigation of Boxing Day audiences in the nineteenth century is two-fold. A discussion of a generic audience over a range of theatres and across a considerable timespan seemingly counters the argument that historical studies of theatre audiences needed to be focused and discrete in order to avoid the sort of generalization that has too often bedevilled this topic.[6] Yet the phenomenon of the Boxing Day audience stretches across many decades of the nineteenth century and manifests itself in a variety of venues. It is a unique aspect of theatre-going in this period and merits further investigation in isolation from the rest of the theatrical year. Secondly, the formulaic descriptions of such audiences – invariably focused on the occupants of the cheaper seats in the gallery – remain fairly constant throughout the century, whether the theatre was located in London's West End or in east and south London or in the provinces. The Boxing Day audience, particularly as mediated by the press, is partly the construction of journalists, but we need to look beyond the formula and uncover what lies beneath the condescension and voyeurism embedded in description after description of working-class spectators by middle-class observers. Paradoxically, the major source for our evidence of Boxing Day audiences must also be the object of our inquiry.

The problem of sources is one familiar to historians of the crowd. Mark Harrison draws attention to it in a study of pre-Victorian English crowds, but believes that, for all their faults, newspapers were 'the carriers of much apparently incidental information which can be profitably re-interpreted'.[7] Harrison considers the language of crowd description and how precisely the 'crowd' is defined as the antithesis of the 'mob' or the 'riot', meaning 'quite specifically a *non-riotous* (or at least non-threatening) grouping'.[8] The city crowds, the result of urban expansion from the late eighteenth century onwards, created feelings of both awe and anxiety in those who observed them. But, says Harrison, 'the complexity and motive and action which informed attendance at crowd events of very different kinds was nevertheless beyond the explanatory interests or abilities of most contemporary observers.'[9] Although Harrison is not discussing theatrical events and his focus is pre-Victorian, these are useful strictures to keep in mind. Those who reported crowd behaviour effectively 'wrote' the crowd, enabled by language to determine the nature of its mediation. Nevertheless, '[t]his labelling, and the management of this problem object – the crowd loathed and adored – had...to operate in constant conflict with the object's essentially independent, and formidably coherent, self-definition.'[10] In the discussion which follows, Harrison's provisos provide a useful counterbalance to undiscriminating acceptance of the evidence provided by the press.

Throughout much of the nineteenth century, especially the Victorian period, the Drury Lane pantomime became particularly notorious, its gallery audience frequently selected as the focus for generic accounts of Boxing Night spectators. As late as 1881 the *Era* (1 January 1881) described a typical Drury Lane gallery audience on Boxing Night:

> How they pelted the pittites far down below with orange-peel and nut-shells and any missiles that happened to be at hand! How they chaffed the better dressed people who had paid higher prices, and whom they delighted to designate as swells! How, too, they chaffed one another, and roared greetings of recognition from side to side!... But the chaff, and the orange-peel throwing, and the horse-play were curiously enough to find their master... The conductor [Mr Waller-stein] faced round to the dwellers up on high, and enlisted them as friends and assistants. No sooner had the overture commenced than those rough, but good-humoured, fellows up above seemed, as it were, to lay in wait for the familiar air which they were certain would come, and directly it made its appearance they sprang eagerly upon it, and made it their own. How they enjoyed the vocal exercise is evidenced by the fact that they wanted it all over again, and got it. The style in which they joined in the National Anthem and 'Rule Britannia' left not the shadow of a doubt as to their loyalty and patriotism.[11]

The *Daily Telegraph* (28 December 1880) confirms this account, suggesting that as well as the spectacle, the music, the dancing and the humour the audience themselves were a major feature of attraction, especially the 'gods' and their 'bedlamite bellowing': 'They shrieked, they yelled, they holloaed, they bawled, they barked, they whistled, in every key of maniacal cacophony.'

'The screeching of a thousand peacocks and the gobbling of five hundred turkey-cocks... a forest of steam-whistles, a *plaza de Toros* filled exclusively with roaring bulls of Basshan, a Niagra of cat-calls, and a wilderness of howling monkeys' were just some of the ways in which this critic chose to describe the clamour

> which last night impelled the ladies in the stalls and boxes to stop their ears from time to time, but which caused them, nevertheless, to smile, knowing, as they did, that all the appalling din was due simply to the jovial good humour of the 'gods', who were enjoying themselves in true Boxing Night fashion, and who were indeed training themselves for behaving with admirable propriety during the performance by roaring themselves hoarse before it commenced.

The idea that Drury Lane, England's 'national theatre' in the eyes of many, could accommodate such a spectacle was not received with equanimity in all quarters. In 1845 George Cruikshank's illustrations for *The Comic Almanack* included one entitled 'BOXING-NIGHT – A picture in the National Gallery'. Cruikshank's punning picture shows a swirling mass of chaos and disorder in which almost the entire gallery appears to be caught up in a fist fight. Along the front of the gallery railing a black demonic figure – perhaps a chimney sweep, perhaps something more sinister – makes its way. The overall scene could perhaps represent any and every Boxing Night audience of the period, but the reference to 'the National Gallery' implies that Drury Lane is the venue. Cruikshank's illustration is comical, satirical, quite possibly exaggerated and, I suspect, rather disapproving. In 1832 Cruikshank had published an attack on Bartholomew Fair entitled 'The Fiends [sic] Frying Pan or Annual Festival of Tom Foolery and Vice, under the Sanction of the Lord Mayor and the Worshipful Court of Aldermen! – In The Age of Intellect'. As in 'BOXING-NIGHT' the spectators are immersed in a drunken brawl. Thirteen years on Cruikshank is still signalling the same unease about popular amusements and the behaviour they provoked.

BOXING-NIGHT – A picture in the National Gallery.

Illustration 1 George Cruikshank, 'BOXING-NIGHT – A picture in the National Gallery', from *The Comic Almanack*, 1845. Courtesy of Bristol Theatre Collection.

From before Cruikshank's 1845 illustration to after the 1880–1 pantomime at Drury Lane disorder reigned supreme. Pelting, singing and noise emerge as predominant activities in the *Telegraph* and *Era* reviews, although the *Era* is at pains to stress the spectators' patriotism and the *Telegraph* emphasizes the 'propriety'

THE FIENDS FRYING PAN or Annual Festival of Tom Foolery & Vice.
Under the Sanction of the LORD MAYOR and the Worshipful Court of ALDERMEN! _ In THE AGE OF INTELLECT

Illustration 2   George Cruikshank, 'The Fiends Frying Pan or Annual Festival of Tom Foolery and Vice, under the Sanction of the Lord Mayor and the Worshipful Court of Aldermen! – In the Age of Intellect', 1832. Courtesy of Bristol Theatre Collection.

of their behaviour once the pantomime commenced. There is indulgence and complacency in these accounts, a sort of containment by proxy, wherein a sense of national identity and the order imposed by the performance itself render the spectators docile and their prior behaviour acceptable. Their behaviour in itself is part of the spectacle and just as vital to a full critical account of the Boxing Day pantomime as the outline of the complicated and convoluted plots that usually appeared in the reviews.

To understand critical responses to Boxing Day pantomimes we need to place them in a broader context. Boxing Day was for many a holiday and through much of the nineteenth century was notorious for the drunkenness and fights that occurred not only in the theatres during the first performances of the pantomime, but also among those who did not get in. It was also a holiday during which, as the century progressed, Londoners for instance might visit the Tower, the Monument, the Zoological Gardens at Regent's Park or the South Kensington Museum, take railway excursions to the seaside or Windsor Castle, visit the Crystal Palace or Alexandra Palace, frequent those parks within which large expanses of water were frozen over for the purpose of skating, or just visit family and friends. Weather inevitably determined the success of Boxing Day entertainments, bright frosty weather always ensuring that the theatres were crowded with holiday-makers. J. Ewing Ritchie vividly describes the streets on Boxing Night c.1857:

But the thousands outside who did not get in [to the theatres] – what are they about? Look at that respectable mechanic; you saw him in the morning as happy as a prince, and almost as fine; he stands leaning against the lamp-post, apparently an idiot. His hat is broken – his coat is torn – his face is bloody – his pockets are empty; not a friend is near, and he is far away from home. It is clear too what he has been about. Come on a few steps further – three policemen are carrying a woman to Bow-street. A hooting crowd follow; she heeds them not, nor cares she that she has lost her bonnet – that her hair streams loosely in the wind – that her gown (it is her Sunday one) is all torn to tatters – or that her person is rudely exposed. The further we go, and the later it grows, the more of these sad pictures shall we see. Of course we do not look for such in Regent-street, or Belgravia, or Oxford-street, or the Strand. Probably in them we shall meet respectable people staggering along under the influence of drink – but they are not noisy or obstreperous – they do not curse and swear – they do not require the aid of the police. We must go into the low neighbourhoods – into St Giles', or Drury-lane, or Ratcliffe-highway, or the New-cut, or Whitechapel – if we would see the miseries of London on Boxing night. We must take our stand by some gin-palace. We must stay there till the crowds it has absorbed and poisoned are turned loose and maddened into the streets. Then what horrible scenes are realized . . . In the metropolis in 1853, the number of public-houses was 5729 – the number of beer-shops 3613 . . . If on this night we suppose on an average one fight in the course of the evening takes place in each of these drinking shops, we can get some idea of what goes on in London on a Boxing night. In passing at midnight down Drury-lane, I see three fights in a five minutes' walk. Enlightened native of Timbuctoo, will you not pity our London heathens and send a few missionaries here![12]

Ritchie had grounds for his description in that drunkenness was a recurrent urban problem,[13] the consumption of drink peaking in the mid-1870s. Nineteenth-century press reports also highlighted the problem of drunkenness. On Boxing Day 1840 the *Era* (27 December 1840) reported that

the different police-offices were occupied for the greater part of yesterday in hearing charges against individuals for drunkenness. The delinquents were of all sorts, young and old, male and female, and belonged to almost every class of society from the highest to the lowest. The excuses they made were for the most part the same, viz., – an undue indulgence in the festivities of the season. In the great majority of the cases the magistrates inflicted very trifling punishments on the offenders.

In 1865 a reporter at the Sadler's Wells pantomime claimed that 'the proximity of a young gentleman who has imbibed so large a quantity of rum that it has disagreed with him, is not an agreeable mental preparative for the reception of a fairy tale.'[14] In 1876 the *South London Press* (1 January 1876) reported nineteen cases of drunkenness or assault as well as four further cases of assaults on the police brought before the Southwark police court on Boxing Day. The ejection of a commercial traveller from the Surrey Theatre for being drunk and disorderly was also reported in the same edition. While it would be inaccurate to imply that life on Boxing Day and Boxing Night degenerated into a Bacchanalian orgy within the theatres as well as without, this was certainly a holiday in which excess was exhibited and tolerated beyond the norm.[15]

The presence of inebriated spectators at the Boxing Day performances of the pantomime must have created a degree of unpredictability, even danger, at these events, but this aspect receives little attention from the press, perhaps because it undermines the concept of a boisterous yet ultimately good-humoured and compliant working class perpetuated in so many reviews. Yet generic accounts did not only originate in journals and newspapers. In 1837 James Grant contributed this portrait of the Boxing Night audience in his account of *The Great Metropolis*:

> The pantomimes are a great source of attraction to young people; and as they are always brought out on 'Box-night', when there is something in the pockets of the lower classes, the galleries of the various theatres are...crowded to suffocation...A very large proportion of the 'deities'...consists of chimney-sweep apprentices, who are by far, considering their limited means, the most liberal patronizers of the drama...There is also a fair sprinkling of bakers' apprentices on box-night...The unlimited play which the 'divinities' give their lungs on these nights often, in fact, has the effect of drowning the voice of the actors on the stage. The truth is, that they claim a prescriptive right to be as noisy as they please on box-night, and all efforts to preserve order would be perfectly useless.[16]

Grant inevitably pinpoints the gallery, drawing attention to the youth of its occupants and to the noise, implying that the imposition of any sort of order is out of the question. Twenty years later J. Ewing Ritchie described the Victoria's audience:

> And now the dull, dark day, by the magic power of gas, has been transformed into gay and brilliant night. The thousands who have spent the day sight-seeing are not satiated, and are flocking round the entrances of the various theatres. Let us stand on the stage of the Victoria, and see them to the number of fifteen hundred mounted upon the gallery benches. Through the small door near the ceiling they come down like a Niagara, and you expect to see them hurled by hundreds into the pit. What a Babel of sounds! It is in vain one cries 'Horder!' 'Ats off!' 'Down in front!' 'Silence!' Boys in the gallery are throwing orange peel all over the pit; Smith halloos to Brown, and Brown to Smith; a sailor in a private box recognises some comrades beneath, and immediately a conversation ensues; rivals meet and quarrel; women treat each other to the contents of their baskets – full of undigestible articles, you may be sure, with a bottle of gin in the corner...This night in every theatre of London is a similar scene witnessed. The British public is supposed to be unusually weak at Christmas, and tricks that were childish and stale when George the Third

was king, and jokes venerable even in Joe Miller's time, are still supposed to afford the most uproarious amusement to a people boasting its Christianity, its civilisation, and enlightenment.[17]

Despite the exuberance of his account, Ritchie seems uncomfortable with the infantilism to which pantomime arguably reduced its audiences, perhaps a continuation of the 'precise and largely unquestioned correlation . . . between the lowly cultural status of pantomime and its alleged patronage by unsophisticated infantile audiences'[18] that was prevalent earlier in the century.

Generic accounts of Boxing Day audiences take a number of forms, but invariably the tone is both rhetorical and voyeuristic so that we too become voyeurs, on the outside looking in, enfolded in descriptions made comfortable (and therefore containing) through their predictability. Certain theatres, which established a reputation both for the quality of their pantomimes and the vitality of their audiences, repeatedly draw such reports. In London, Drury Lane, the Surrey, the Britannia and the Grecian were particularly renowned for their offerings. The *Era* (1 January 1871) describes a typical Surrey Boxing Night, which captures the performative nature of the Surrey pantomime audience in just this sort of way:

A transpontine audience is not at any time the most orderly; but a transpontine audience on Boxing Night almost defies description. For what purpose did the crowds in the gallery visit the Surrey on Monday? Professedly they paid their money to see the Christmas Pantomime and to see and to listen to the dialogue, to witness the absurdities and to laugh at the jokes . . . But is this all? Decidedly not. If the Fairies sing, why should not they? If the Fiends roar, why should the 'gods' not howl and scream and whistle? If Harlequin dances a clog hornpipe, why should they not stamp? And if Clown plays practical jokes on 'butchers and bakers and candlestick-makers,' why should they not pelt the occupants of the pit and boxes with orange-peel? Why not? We ask. It was Boxing Night, and these proceedings in the gallery formed as much a part of the evening's performance as the doings upon the stage.[19]

The Britannia Theatre's audiences, from one of the poorest areas of London, also delighted in singing, which the following report suggests at least kept them away from more violent or disruptive pursuits:

At the very commencement the audience were propitiated by a number of those popular airs which, because England is an unmusical nation, everybody is able to sing in time *and* tune, and the sound of four thousand people, in a jovial holiday mood, chanting these lively strains in chorus, was infinitely to be preferred to the 'Marseillaise' roared by a band of dirty, blood-thirsty Communists.[20]

The uniqueness and performative nature of the Britannia's pantomime audience was described by the *Daily Telegraph* (27 December 1881):

> What other audience would have consented to squeeze up into all sorts of corners to make room for strangers, or to let half-a-score of persons enter each of its private boxes when they were already full? Hoxton was bent upon enjoying Christmas, and on helping everyone else that wished to enjoy it, too; and the cordiality which was thus exhibited was really part of the pantomime performance, the players in which had the duty of amusing and the spectators that of being amused.

When in 1867 the Britannia pantomime attracted a relatively youthful audience for its morning Boxing Day performance of *Abon Hassan*, the *Era* (28 December 1867) was impressed by its discipline and good behaviour:

> We have never before seen so large, so respectable, and so orderly an assemblage of young people on one occasion, and their conduct speaks in favour of the management of the establishment. The place was literally crammed with principally boys [sic]; not above one-tenth of the entire audience were above the age of boyhood.

No fear of Communist revolution here! Yet the perpetual emphasis on good behaviour also implies the possibility of its opposite. The audience performs itself yet also behaves itself. It prefers to sing popular songs badly rather than engage in more revolutionary airs. In 1867, the year of the second Reform Bill, the potential for political agitation seems remote among the 'orderly' and 'respectable' youths of Hoxton. The reductio ad absurdum of all these accounts would be that the annual license of the pantomime creates a carnivalesque liberation, in the Bakhtinian sense, which is short-lived and easily controllable. However, the power and agency of the gallery audience, its own control of the situation, is either overlooked or ignored.

The audiences at the minor theatres did not always attract critical commendation. An audience at the Queen's Theatre in 1861 elicited very different comments:

> Long before the time of opening the entrances to this Theatre were besieged by an immense crowd, the principal portion of which seemed to comprise 'roughs' of the lowest grade and boys of young age, and the scene of uproar that took place was disgraceful, and at one time assumed a somewhat threatening aspect. All respectable persons who wished to enter the Theatre could not for a time get near the doors, and, to add to this, fights were of most frequent occurrence, the whole forming a scene of uproar and confusion seldom equalled ... The Box-keeper seemed to be in the utmost difficulty to carry out his duties, and was frequently threatened and abused as he would not show females to the Dress Circle ... without removing their bonnets.[21]

Unease of a different nature surfaces elsewhere. A critic for the *Bristol Times* (1 January 1859) was relieved to note, as he entered the boxes for the local pantomime, that 'policemen, with baton in hand, have taken up their position as a barrier to all further advance' to the gallery.[22]

The class bias in the representation of Boxing Day audiences emerges not only in relationship to behaviour, but also to dress sense. In an editorial in the *Theatrical Journal* (21 January 1857) on Boxing Night at the Theatre reference is made to the way in which the boxes have lost their fashionable look and 'white kid gloves have been superseded by hands covered with less elegant materials or, perhaps shining in their natural and unadorned state of redness'. The transformation of the boxes in this way was a social transgression unacceptable to some critics. Thus one year *The Times* complained of the Surrey that

> The house was crowded in every part, not excepting the private boxes in which we were very sorry to perceive that what used to be 'gallery company' were admitted and behaved worse than they did in the gallery. We were told that this was done from a wish to accommodate those who could not find room in the pit or gallery and were anxious to gain admittance. We have no doubt that it was done from a wish to oblige, but surely if there are such scenes as we witnessed from some of the drunken occupants of the private boxes on Saturday night, respectable parties will not be in a hurry to take seats with them.[23]

Removal of clothing was also frowned upon:

> To a foreigner studying the manners and customs of the English people no stranger sight could be presented ... Full dress he would report to be an abandonment of coats, an unlimited *exposé* of dirty shirt-sleeves, and a violent display of red and other coloured pocket-handkerchiefs.[24]

The questionable etiquette of watching the pantomime in one's shirt sleeves alarmed critics far more than the unbearable heat and poor ventilation which had occasioned the removal of jackets in the first place.

Overcrowding during the pantomime season was fraught with dangers, especially when one performance followed another and queues for the second performance were blocking exits in the event of an emergency. On Boxing Day 1858 a matinee at the Victoria Theatre was coming to its conclusion when a young man in a box apparently struck a match and set alight some furnishings. Some other members of the audience screamed out 'Fire' and a panic ensued. The gallery audience fled straight into the waiting crowds and in the crush eighteen spectators were killed. The *Illustrated Times* (1 January 1859) described how

> The whole mass of people on the upper portion of the stairs ... precipitated themselves on the crowd below, while those on the stairs of the first landing unconscious of what had occurred kept ascending. The result was that more than one hundred people became compactly wedged between the two masses.

The shrieks, cries and smothered groans that arose as the crowd swayed about or got dashed against the balustrades or were thrown down and trodden upon were awful.

Some of those on the top flight of stairs fairly threw themselves down onto the heads of people below and unable to recover their legs fell through and were smothered in the crowd; some threw themselves over the balustrades while others, wedged in and unable to move, held put against suffocation and broken ribs as they best could.

A similar catastrophe occurred at the New Theatre Royal in Park Row, Bristol, on Boxing Night, 1869. Queues on the down gradient leading to the pit and boxes were so immense that, when the doors were opened, those at the front of the queue were pushed over and trampled as a result of the crowd behind them surging forwards. Not only were many hurt, but up to eighteen people died in the crush. In 1881, on the night after Boxing Day, there was a panic at the Grecian Theatre in East London after a quarrel broke out in the gallery. Such occurrences, according to the *Daily Telegraph* (28 December 1881), were not unusual in theatres like the Grecian, 'situated in the midst of a densely-peopled working-class neighbourhood'. The quarrel led to blows and a woman whose husband was being beaten up shrieked for assistance. It seemed to observers 'like a sort of Irish affray, in which every spectator felt himself called upon to take part, and blows were being distributed right and left in the most indiscriminate manner'. The *Telegraph* criticized the police for not intervening more promptly (there were five policemen on duty in the theatre), especially as a cry of 'Fire!' from the back of the pit led to the transformation of the audience into 'a seething mass struggling to escape' from the theatre. Nevertheless, the 5000-strong audience evacuated the theatre without major mishap:

A number of those who occupied side-boxes leapt upon the stage and fled across it in an affrighted way . . . The pit, where there were probably 1,000 persons densely packed, rose *en masse*. A number of the more reckless rushed headlong over the seats to the rear, trampling on whoever was in their way. One man was seen lying on a seat, his head thrown back, while a continuous rush of persons passed over his prostrate form . . . One poor, affrighted woman, carrying a child in her arms, actually threw it to a waitress at the bar situated behind this partition, exclaiming, 'Oh take my child, I don't care for myself.'

Panics such as these, an inevitable danger when large and potentially disorderly crowds had congregated, were always a possibility, but they did not generally deter the large Boxing Day audiences from attending the theatre. Indeed, they were relatively rare, which suggests that self-discipline rather than indiscipline prevailed among spectators, even at holiday times.

Despite the possibility of such disasters and despite the unruliness and inebriation of some Boxing Day audiences, there were many who took a benign view of the proceedings. If Cruikshank's illustration was a reprimand, two sets of illustrations by Phiz (Hablot K. Browne) from the *Illustrated London News* of 1848[25] and the *Illustrated Times* of 1855 emphasized pleasure and communality. In the 1848 illustration (Illus. 3) the gallery audience are certainly eating and imbibing and there is one fight in progress, but this audience seem to be largely focused on the entertainment on offer and one gets the impression that they are enjoying themselves. This is generally true of the audiences in the pit and boxes, which clearly include a number of families with children. And, despite variations, the 1855 illustration makes much the same point (Illus. 4, 5 and 6). The theatre brings together not just the different classes of society, but more specifically families and children to celebrate the festive season.[26]

Illustration 3 Phiz (Hablot K. Browne), 'Pantomime Night: The Gallery', *Illustrated London News*, 8 January 1848. Courtesy of Bristol Theatre Collection.

Illustration 4 Phiz (Hablot K. Browne), 'Pantomime Night: The Boxes', *Illustrated London News*, 8 January 1848. Courtesy of Bristol Theatre Collection.

Illustration 5 Phiz (Hablot K. Browne), 'Pantomime Night: The Pit', *Illustrated London News*, 8 January 1848. Courtesy of Bristol Theatre Collection.

The 1855 illustration was accompanied by a commentary written in the usual formulaic mode by Edmund Yates. A striking feature of this description is the distinctions it makes between the different groups arriving for the pantomime. Some are queuing on 'a sharp, bitter evening, [with] the sleet driving in heavy clouds, and . . . sharp gusts of wind rushing over Waterloo Bridge', until the doors open and '[c]oat-tails part company with their skirts, ownerless sticks and hats fall from the head of the stairs on to the heads of the crowd below; women shriek, and cry, and laugh convulsively; and at last, after an immense amount of pushing, yelling, laughing and hustling, the goal is attained.'[27] The entry of the more affluent part of the audience is somewhat easier, for '[a]ll this time cabs and private carriages have been driving up to the box-entrance, and depositing their cargoes of girls in scarlet opera-cloaks, with bandolined tresses, and the nicest fitting Jouvin gloves, happy and shiny-faced children, glorious old gentlemen, all bald heads and bland smiles, and portentous-looking swells in white chokers and embroidered shirts.'[28] The boxes house grandfathers and grandchildren, papas and mammas, 'delighted at the delight of their darlings'. In the pit, '[t]he place above all others from which to see the pantomime', we find Jack Meggott, 'who keeps the coal and potato shop in Holborn', his wife and children. His children take 'a special delight in the repeated downfalls of the policemen, beadles, and other authorities, who are hated by them with a truly British-middle-class hatred'. Their mother takes exception to the ladies of the *corps de ballet*, who she styles 'bold creeturs', and who she firmly believes are constantly to be found in that airy condition of tarlatan and muslin in which they appear on stage. As for the Boxing Night gallery, it defies description, for it is 'a chaos, a confused mass of shirt-sleeves, fustians, and belcher handkerchiefs, of whistles and cat-calls, screams, yells and fights, shouts of "Ar-ree!" "Bill Jo-ones," "Music," "Tippety-witchet," and "Hot Codlins," of diabolical *jödels* [yodels], and fierce invectives, of suspended bonnets and lost hats, of warm porter and sodden oranges, of escaped gas and exuded perspiration, of policemens' staves and single combats and stolen handkerchiefs, of black eyes and hoarse voices, and maudlin discontent, and childish laughter!'[29] This sort of personalizing of the Boxing Day audience in Yates's narrative reflects a tendency in a number of similar accounts.[30] They are invariably very jovial, but the tone is condescending, containing and even voyeuristic.

The pantomime itself had the power both to subdue and to transform its audience, at least as far as the press was concerned. The *Era* noted how, in the period between the opening of the doors at the Victoria Theatre and the start of the pantomime, one might 'observe a marked difference in the behaviour of the people. From rollicking fun, which drowns the bawling and the hammering of the stage carpenters, he will see a transition to the sedateness which sits on a man in church, and the only apparent indications of the waiters and viewers being the same persons after the piece has commenced are the warm greetings with which every successful change of scene or graceful dance is met.'[31] The Surrey audiences were praised by the *Telegraph* (28 December 1860) for their good behaviour:

They have been tutored into an admirable state of quiescence by the mild yet firm discipline of the management. They express their delight without unseemly uproar; and, which is more gratifying, instead of having to bestow their plaudits upon senseless vulgarity or unmeaning glitter, they are enabled to bestow their applause upon very capital actors and very beautiful scenic effects.

Five years later, the same newspaper (27 December 1865) claimed that, whether it was a sign of the times or not, it was a certain fact that 'Boxing-night audiences, even in their roughest and noisiest mood, are many degrees more civilized than a few years before... and, in the matter of chaff they are abstinent almost to the verge of dullness.'

Throughout the Victorian era many asserted that public behaviour on Boxing Day was improving both within and without the theatre. In 1872 the *South London Press* (28 December 1872) commented that 'One fact notable as indicating the improved and improving habits of the poorer classes came under our observation. Peculiar circumstances compelled us to walk from Mile End road to Temple Bar between ten and eleven o'clock on Boxing Night, and even in Whitechapel we did not see a single person intoxicated. Perhaps it was too early; but seeing that the day had been devoted to festivity and the spending of Christmas boxes, even that was a creditable fact.' In 1865 the *Telegraph* (26 December 1865) had also celebrated Boxing Day, stating that it was 'no longer what it was – a day of senseless drinking and ugly debauchery'. People now made 'a rational use of this bye-day, as of their other holidays'. These changes, claimed the *Telegraph*, have come from the people themselves; 'nobody can teach them self-respect and human dignity; they must be their own masters... But that they know as much, the streets, even on Boxing Day, will abundantly prove.' Even pantomime, when 'the magic realms of fairyland open to the world' and 'Harlequin waves a wand that could almost turn a Tory into a reasonable creature' was included by the author of these sentiments as reflecting 'the improving disposition of the people'.

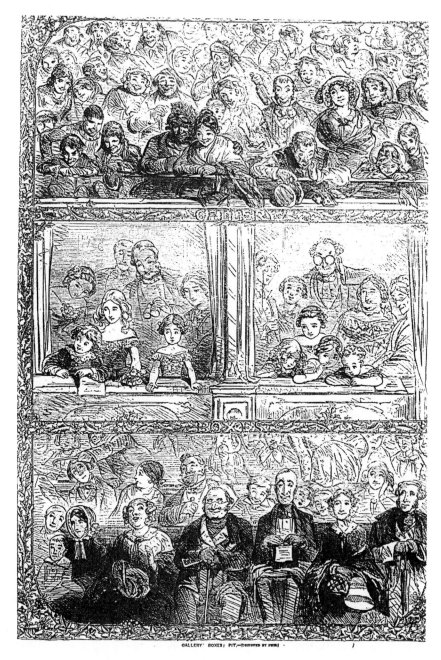

Illustration 6 Phiz (Hablot K. Browne), 'The Pantomime', *Illustrated Times*, 1855. This illustration subsequently reappeared in the *Illustrated Sporting and Theatrical News*, 16 January 1869. Collection of Jim Davis.

The *Era* (1 January 1871) felt that the Boxing Day pantomimes not only gave pleasure to audiences but also secured seasonal employment for a great many performers, something that should convince the puritanically minded that the good accomplished far outweighed 'the most exaggerated calculation to be made of any evil that can possibly arise from the habit of frequenting places of amusement'. In Hoxton enjoyment of the pantomime was treated with the same seriousness as 'a sturdy day's work' (*Era*, 31 December 1871). Earlier, in 1837, the *Theatrical Journal* (21 January 1837) noticed how during the pantomime 'all regret for the past, anxiety for the future, all of our less-kindly nature seems to be forgotten. Due honour we say to that pursuit that can impart such a kindly feeling to thousands and thousands of human creatures. Talk of the immorality of the thing – pshaw! Is there one man, woman, or child in the place who, if called upon to act, would not do so wholesomely and better than if still tied to their everyday drudgery of trade or pursuit?'

These are sentiments worthy of Dickens. Indeed, just as Phiz's illustrations imply the benevolent impact of pantomime on the community, so the majority of descriptions of pantomime audiences either predict or echo Dickens's own advocacy of the value of popular entertainments, especially as seen in the power of pantomime to turn an unruly mob into an absorbed and submissive audience. But we need to be wary of certain factors. One is the tone of these accounts, which is often patronizing, condescending, implicitly containing and highly class-conscious. The second is their specificity to one day of the year and to exceptional rather than normal conventions of audience behaviour. As the nineteenth century drew to its conclusion, the pantomime audience became more disciplined, as Jimmy Glover, conductor of the Drury Lane pantomime orchestra, attests. In 1869 he tells us there were fewer rows of stalls, 'a huge eightpenny pit, and a seething mass of sixpenny and fourpenny galleryites, who cat-called the "Opening" on Boxing Night till not a word was heard', and who shouted the latest music hall songs. However,

> The better educated audience of today is not the chorus-singing urchin or patron of the seventies. The top gallery disappeared under the London County Council during the end of the Harris management, and the stalls on Boxing Night have developed into a kid-gloved army of *dilettante* patrons, across whose well-dressed and gloriously-gloved personalities it is a far run to get to the pit for a good honest round of applause.[32]

Yet no doubt the new configurations in the auditorium brought greater profit to managements, whatever the nostalgia for the boisterous audiences of the past. And throughout the latter part of the century many theatres drew the ire of traditionalists because they opened their pantomimes prior to the Christmas period rather than on Boxing Day. Saturnalia gave way to consumerism and to the commercial interests of those very managements which, when it suited them economically, had allowed full rein to the excesses of Boxing Day audiences. But these excesses themselves had always been controlled by tradition, convention and the self-fashioning of a mob which, when the conductor raised his baton and encouraged them to sing, evolved into the vital yet compliant crowd celebrated (and to some extent constructed) in thousands and thousands of newspaper reports of Boxing Day pantomimes throughout the 1800s. Nevertheless, I would like to suggest that Boxing Day audiences were not intimidated or coerced into acquiescence; their self-regulation was in itself an indication that they owned the occasion and that they chose as and when they responded to the performance and how they wielded the power that they undoubtedly possessed. Such power, it has been argued, was merely temporary and ultimately an illusion. It has also been argued that newspaper descriptions of pantomime audiences indicate how thoroughly middle-class observers 'would identify the Christmas pantomimes as rituals of social order and control, which "humanised" those who saw them'.[33] But that is to assume that these audiences lacked agency and that the condescension of the press descriptions accurately encapsulates and defines them. I beg to differ. Far from merely enabling a saturnalian inversion of everyday life, the Boxing Day performances of the nineteenth-century British pantomime were repeatedly the site for a celebration of disorder, self-regulation and power by a crowd which, however out of control it might seem, was far more in control than the press accounts imply.

Notes

1. Richard Findlater, ed., *Memoirs of Joseph Grimaldi* by Charles Dickens (London, 1838; revised edition London: MacGibbon & Kee Ltd, 1968), 11.
2. Thomas Richards, *The Commodity Culture of Victorian England: Advertising and Spectacle 1851–1914* (Stanford, CA: Stanford University Press, 1990), 56. For a fuller discussion of Richards's ideas in relation to pantomime see Jill Sullivan, 'The Business of Pantomime: Regional Productions 1865 to 1892', unpublished PhD thesis, University of Nottingham, 2005.
3. *The Journal of a London Playgoer* (London, 1869; reprinted Leicester: Leicester University Press, 1974), 138.
4. Marc Baer, *Theatre and Disorder in Late Georgian London* (Oxford: Clarendon Press, 1992), 182–5.
5. A. M. Golby and A. W. Purdue, *The Civilisation of the Crowd: Popular Culture in England 1750–1900* (Stroud: Sutton Publishing, 1999), 71.
6. See Jim Davis and Victor Emeljanow, *Reflecting the Audience: London Theatre Audiences 1840–1880* (Illinois: University of Illinois Press, 2001).
7. Mark Harrison, *Crowds and History: Mass Phenomena in English Towns, 1790–1835* (Cambridge: Cambridge University Press, 1988), 45–6.
8. Ibid., 170.
9. Ibid., 190.
10. Ibid., 191.
11. The *Illustrated Times*, 2 January 1858, writes of Drury Lane that 'From the topmost row of the gallery to the very back of the pit seethed a sea of human faces; and though at most of the other houses quiet was observed, here the cat-calls, shrieks, whistles, cries of "Ar-ree!" and objectionable epithets, raged in all their pristine vigour.' The following year the *Illustrated Times*, 1 January 1859, refers repeatedly and rhetorically to the Drury Lane pantomime audience as 'Mob'.
12. J. Ewing Ritchie, *The Night Side of London* (London: 1857), 170–2.
13. Golby and Purdue, *Civilization of the Crowd*, 116. 'In London alone arrests for this offence never fell before 17,000 per year in the 1860s and arrests throughout the country for

drunkenness or being drunk and disorderly were far larger than for any other category of offences.'

14. *Daily Telegraph*, 27 December 1865.
15. A tacit recognition of this may be seen in the drop curtain painted for the pantomime at the Theatre Royal Bristol in 1853, which depicted a monstrous Bacchus and huge assembly drinking punch, *Bristol Times*, 31 December 1853. And four years earlier, at the Princess's Theatre in London, a personification of Alcohol participated in the magical transformation of characters from the Opening into the figures of the Harlequinade in *King Jamie; or, Harlequin and the Magic Fiddle*.
16. James Grant, *The Great Metropolis* (London: Saunders & Otley, 1837) quoted in Russell Jackson, ed., *Victorian Theatre* (London: A & C Black Ltd., 1989), 16–17.
17. Ritchie, *The Night Side of London*, 168–70.
18. Jane Moody, *Illegitimate Theatre in London, 1770–1840* (Cambridge: Cambridge University Press, 2000), 224–5.
19. The *South London Press*, 28 December 1872, says the occupants of the gallery seemed to be supporting the roof with their heads. The audience's behaviour was fine except for certain occupants of a box who 'dressed as gentlemen, behaved as ruffians. These cads sat on the front of the box and pelted the orange-peel until they were suddenly pounced upon by an official, and, after a scuffle, thrown out into the street amid universal cheers. Let us hope for the credit of South London that they came from over the water.'
20. *Era*, 31 December 1871.
21. *Era*, 29 December 1861.
22. Protests that were not specific to Christmas sometimes affected Christmas entertainment. Thus the Gaiety's 1881 Christmas Eve performance of the burlesque *Aladdin; or, The Sacred Lamp* was the occasion for an expression of indignation at the curtailment of places in the pit. Some occupants of the pit 'vented their indignation on occupants of the back row of the stalls and sang a chorus of "Never again, never again; We won't come back no more" ', something that alarmed the *Daily Telegraph* (26 December 1881) more on account of bad grammar than anything else.
23. Undated, quoted in A. E. Wilson, *Christmas Pantomime: the Story of an English Institution* (London: George Allen & Unwin, 1934), 138–9.
24. Undated, quoted in ibid., 137–8.
25. This was used again in the *Illustrated Sporting and Dramatic News* in 1869.
26. A particular feature of Phiz's illustrations is the number of children and families depicted in the audience. The Boxing Day pantomime was for many associated with childhood and the family, although boxes were not always full on Boxing Night, a fact partly attributable to the weather and partly to 'a general disinclination that many families feel to encounter the noise and excitement of the first week of the holiday period'. But for those who did attend it evoked nostalgic memories such as those of F. C. Burnand, who recalled in detail his own childhood reminiscences of pantomime at Drury Lane, including the 'stout women with big baskets . . . struggling between the seats in pit and gallery, hawking their "ginger beer, lemonade, and bill o' the play" ' and then 'Oh glorious moment in the Christmas life of a town-bred child – the overture to the pantomime commences! What overture can ever equal the overture to a pantomime on the first night of performance!'
27. *Illustrated Times*, 1855.
28. Ibid.
29. Ibid.
30. In 1860 *The Players* (2 January 1860, 7) described the gallery of a minor theatre on Boxing Night, focusing particularly on a Mrs Gullins and her four blooming daughters.
31. *The Era*, 1 January 1871.
32. J. M. Glover, *Jimmy Glover: His Book* (London, 1911), p. 159.
33. See Janice Carlisle, 'Spectacle and Government: Dickens and the Working-class Audience', in Sue-Ellen Case and Janelle Reinelt, eds, *The Performance of Power: Theatre Discourse and Politics* (Iowa City: University of Iowa Press, 1991), 173.

2
What are Fairies For?

Tracy C. Davis

In recent research, attention has been paid to the prominence of fairies in nineteenth-century folklore, literature and fine arts. Two other areas of fairies' proliferation have been neglected: ethnography and the theatre. Variously regarded as the products of invention or documentation, fairies figured consistently in the nineteenth-century imaginary as well as the more empirical realms of scholarship and stage embodiment, suggesting that they may have served more, or deeper, purposes than mere lighthearted distraction and aestheticized diversion. In particular, examination of a relationship between ethnography and theatre challenges the historiography on fairies and suggests this chapter's abiding question: 'what are fairies for?'[1]

Ethnographic writing on fairies and related beings is a pan-European phenomenon that stems from the Romantic period and lasted, with steady output and particular emphasis on English and Celtic populations of supernaturals, until the end of Victoria's reign.[2] Fairy ethnographies are the products of fieldwork, interviews and collecting of accounts from people who sought out or accidentally came upon fairies and could then describe to researchers their physiology, social organization, customs and celebrations, beliefs and law.[3] Whereas ethnographic studies collate accounts of meeting fairy-folk and document these encounters dispassionately; folklore favours customary tales and makes no pretext of their accuracy except as tradition; literature typically explores the subjective experience of encounter and utilizes narrative to express perceptions of fairies' otherness; illustration renders the data from ethnographies, folklore and literature in a visual interpretation of the fairy world; and music provides a corresponding aural interpretation of subjective perception.[4] Theatre combines all five traditions, discursive media and expressive forms in order to present a compound of received data and fanciful expressions and, though it does this with extraordinary fecundity, until now commentary has been limited to just a handful of plays and productions.[5] In addition to the Shakespearean canon (which dominates the commentary) and W. S. Gilbert (the only Victorian dramatist of fairy fare that endures in popular memory), fairies appear in productions from every decade and in every genre, including opera, ballet, tragedy, drama, comedy, farce, melodrama, extravaganza, pantomime and burlesque, in countless permutations of the serious, frivolous, parodic, allegorical, sentimental, nationalistic and sensational. In some genres, fairies are cornerstones of the repertoire; in others, they are less often deployed.

To some people, fairies were commensurate with theatre and theatrical practice, indelible to the idea of theatre as a metonym of faith in magicality.[6] This idea, probably adopted from pantomime and extravaganza, was generalized to the entire medium of theatre. J. M. Barrie's *Peter Pan* (1904) famously poses this as a crisis of belief: belief in fairies implicates the effaceability of frames containing disbelief, which signals the instability and fragility of theatre's entrancement of the imagination. As I have written elsewhere, 'Barrie proposes an alternative to the ritualized responses to Victorian pantomime while also taunting his audience to develop their own position on the extrinsic purpose of mimesis, spectatorship and the theatrical contract.'[7] As a stage play, *Peter Pan* has a unique hold on twentieth-century ideas about fairies; however, Tinkerbell – who bestows flight on young monarchists faithful to King Edward VII – should not be regarded *post hoc* as representative of Victorian stage fairies.[8] Barrie's play effects a momentous breach with Victorian stage traditions of the fairy as a corporeal, vocal and often terpsichoral and musical being. Tinkerbell was instead played by a bobbing light reflected in a mirror, her 'voice' portrayed by a bicycle bell.[9] Tinkerbell represented Barrie's concerns about children's loss of innocence: he asked them to attest belief in fairies – even this rather vicious one – as an affirmation of their immaturity. Many adults joined the clamour, but this was decidedly not what was at stake in the tradition of stage fairies, before or immediately after *Peter Pan*, for their undeniable comeliness in genres like burlesque, extravaganza and pantomime and sexualized femininity in the plot lines of tragedy, comedy and farce asseverates their adult, if not R-rated, connotation. Both in terms of social anxieties and personal desires, the Victorian stage fairy tracks a problem about the unseen – or the unseen made manifest – linking ideological problems to material and narrative renditions. Barrie's Edwardian preoccupation of wishing impish spirits upon children belies supreme confidence in British culture's ability to prevail over traditional fairy primitivism. Genuine danger from Puck's meddling had become enchanting mischief in Richard Doyle's *In Fairyland* (1870), and Barrie concurs that at the end of this period the odds of survival in inter-species encounter had shifted in favour of humanity.[10] But along with humanity's apotheosis – and ability to decide the fairy's fate – came a formulary of Britishness. Through their manifest difference, fairies demonstrated what ideologically united audiences.

The study of fairies always necessitated adoption of the precept that absence of verifiable evidence is not per se evidence of non-existence. Ethnography changed the paradigm to posit fairy encounter as a phenomenon of human experience. Ethnographers observed that fairy folk were fast deserting the British Isles as a consequence of urban expansion, industrial encroachment on the countryside, loss of traditional rural folkways and ecological degradation.[11] Fairies largely moved on beyond the purview of ethnographic data collectors by the end of the nineteenth century. Thus in Britain, if not elsewhere, the experience of fairy encounter was demarcated historically. The Cottingley hoax, hatched in 1918, serves to emphasize that the era of fairy spotting had definitively closed, however much nostalgia was generated for those bygone days when ethnographers and folklorists roamed the countryside collecting data.[12] In the theatre, the question of intercultural encounter between humans and fairies endured, as fairies continually attracted a broad-based audience. Their persistence begs the question of whether theatrical fairies remained suspended in the timeless netherworld of literature and folklore, if they were artefacts of antiquarians' research into the fairy-filled past, or if they somehow modernized to adapt to changing times despite the dwindling ethnographic record.[13] Presumably, this would be evident in the plots of plays; however, I have found that variants in generic, kinetic and sonic conventions are also indicators of the fairy's status and, consequently, of the sense of their contemporaneity.

In the Georgian period, fairies were studied by learned worthies devoted to 'popular antiquities'; the field made way for folklorists in the Victorian period, but throughout the nineteenth century there is a discernible lineage of ethnographic collecting, a practice which combines fieldwork with qualitative description.[14] Translated into performance, according to Dwight Conquergood, ethnography 'brings self and other together even while it holds them apart. It is more like a hyphen than a period.'[15] The performance of fairies is comparable: performer and role, or self and persona, are the hyphen holding together logic and pretence as well as humanity and fairydom. Cognizant of these concurrent iterations, my argument is at odds with what is generally presumed about the historical arc of fairies and fairydom evident in the theatre or any aspect of Victorian culture. Perceptions of a gradual dilution of the cultural potency of fairies, paralleling their 'farewell' from Britain and Ireland and culminating in their relegation to the newly minted Edwardian genre of 'theatre *for* the child' (not only *Peter Pan* but also plays like *Bluebell in Fairyland*, Vaudeville 1901–2; and *The Water Babies*, Garrick 1902–3) thoroughly sentimentalizes what had been a folklore of the gruesome and macabre, newly palatable only to the young.[16] Instead, I have tracked an ongoing relevance of fairies to adults and adamant assertion of this fact.

This, in part, is what fairies are for. Ethnography and theatre both set aside questions of belief, or doubt, in fairies to challenge how the unseeable can be sought, known and rendered. They provoke fundamental questions about memory as knowledge, the durability of a mortal life span and cultural tradition. As such, the theatrical presentation of fairies expressed socio-political concerns at the very heart of the British ethnos: (1) does the irrational have a place in national identity; (2) what, or who, suffers in the wake of progress; and (3) is it too late to turn back?

Pinkie and the Fairies

Although my database of approximately ninety fairy plays is light in its sampling of pantomimes in favour of other genres, it is comprehensive of genres and the fare consistently produced in London and licensed by the Lord Chamberlain between 1828 and 1914. His Majesty's Theatre's production of *Pinkie and the Fairies* is the test case at one end of this array. Written by W. Graham Robertson, with music by Frederic Norton, it ran for sixty-nine performances in 1908–9 and was revived for a similar run the following Christmas season. Herbert Beerbohm Tree directed rehearsals but did not act in the piece. Instead, the marquee performer in the original run was Ellen Terry, who offered to come out of retirement to play a 'dull but genial spinster aunt', her costume suggesting that her ideas (like her ringlets) were settled in the early 1870s.[17] The premise of this Surrey idyll is that a girl named Pinkie, her brother Tommy and their older cousin Molly take a nighttime ramble in the wood and encounter fairies' Mayday revels. Robertson describes this as Pinkie's vision, influenced by illustrators:

> The elves who dwell in the haunted wood of Pinkie's vision were, of course, Fairies as they exist in a child's imagination; figures evolved partly from picture books, partly from dreams of personified flowers, birds or insects. They were, I hope, removed from the acrobatic sprites and ballet ladies of pantomime, but were no more, though no less, real than the rest of the children's dream world.[18]

This equation of youthful dreaming with fairyland alludes to the contemporaneous debate about continuity of consciousness during fairy sightings. Supernatural lapses of time were accounted for as trance states and thus Evans Wentz concludes 'Fairyland, stripped of all its literacy and imaginative glamour and of its social psychology, in the eyes of science resolves itself into a reality, because it is one of the states of consciousness co-ordinate with ordinary consciousness.'[19] The question remained open, however, as to who or what was encountered in such a state. Wentz explains that the rarity of fairy visions in psychical research is overwhelmed by other evidence of 'phantasms supposed to be of the dead, the dying and the absent.'[20] This is one way of accounting for fairies' farewell, and thus elusiveness, by the Edwardian period: they were no longer fairies sighted by the naïf but ghosts seen by the psychically endowed.[21] Ghosts, unlike fairies, were internal: not mystical but psychological, not folkloric but scientific, not a lost pygmy race (human or otherwise) but a new explanatory paradigm heralded by cognitive research. What they were *for*, figures such as physicist and spiritualist Sir Oliver Lodge imply, remained consistent: continuity with conditions of existence and contact with other minds.[22]

For Robertson, however, encounter with fairies was still intrinsic to humans and held a positive relation to Nature. Pinkie and the other children enter a wood where 'but for the constant ripple of the stream running over the ledges of rock in the tiny waterfall...the scene is one of absolute stillness and quiet' amidst flitting fireflies. The children encounter green-clad fairies and singing flowers, frogs, rabbits, dragonflies, a ladybird and a moth intoning the virtues of flowers and the beauty of the moon.[23] The Queen of the Fairies is played by a diminutive eleven-year-old child (Elsie Craven, making her debut), elevated on a lily pad and costumed in an 'early Victorian ballet-dancer's garb, her dress of bright gold tissue set out by innumerable stiff muslin skirts.'[24] She performed the 'steps and airs and graces of a conventional *prima ballerina assoluta*' *en pointe* and thrilled the audience when she archly instructed an adult player to stop pulling focus by standing centre stage and hogging the limelight.[25]

Illustration 7   The Fairy Queen (Elsie Craven) enthroned on a water lily. From *Pinkie and the Fairies*, Act II. Courtesy of Bristol Theatre Collection.

While this meta-theatricality destabilizes the idea of theatre-as-magic, a self-referential trick common to pantomime, the Fairy Queen's narratological function is to explain that the intrinsic connection between babyhood and fairyland, a co-constitutive paradise, fades as a child grows into its humanity. The Queen leads fairies, frogs and children in a farandole chain-dance, then they partake of a banquet. When the children's stodgy uncle (played with suppressed comedy by Frederick Volpé) wanders into their midst, smoking a cigar on his evening constitutional, he stares right at the Queen yet sees nothing. In fairy logic, this confirms the 'reality' of the children and fairies in contravention to the adult world. Elaborating on this idea, *the Daily Telegraph* compares Robertson's approach with what is, inferentially, recognizable as ethnography:

You can write about fairies from the point of view of grown-ups, or you can write about grown-ups from the point of view of fairies. In the first case you

PINKIE AND THE FAIRIES

MISS MARIE LOHR
AS "CINDERELLA".

MISS STELLA PATRICK CAMPBEL
AS "MOLLY".

MISS ELISE CRAVEN
AS "QUEEN OF THE FAIRIES"

MISS IRIS HAWKINS
AS "PINKIE".

Illustration 8 Cinderella arriving in her coach (extreme left); fairies flank the Fairy Queen and Frog King (centre back); Pinkie sits in the foreground (right). From *Pinkie and the Fairies*, Act II. Courtesy of Bristol Theatre Collection.

get . . . a good deal of accurate science; in the second case you get no science, but sheer fantasy . . . Mr. Robertson's play is, accordingly, written from the second standpoint. The dreams of children are the real thing and therefore the fairyland which belongs to children is also real. Middle-aged men and women are not realities, but unworthy phantoms, of whom really there is nothing valuable to be said.[26]

Mixing the mysticism of an atmospheric fairyland with the vernaculars of panto-mime, a thoroughly up-to-date resplendent Cinderella drops by, pausing in her gruelling social schedule, as do Jack of the Beanstalk, Jack the Giant Killer, Sleeping Beauty (whose singing lulls Pinkie to the verge of sleep) and Beauty and the Beast. After various ironic interactions, Cinderella (reduced to rags at the stroke of midnight) climbs into her withered half-pumpkin (formerly a green-lit crystal carriage) drawn by four piebald mice and departs in the wake of the other fairy tale notables.

The fairy Pickle urges the children to return home too. Alluding to accounts of abductions of mortals by fairies and other dalliances in fairyland,[27] Pinkie expresses fear that twenty years may have passed in what seemed like one night. But, according to fairy Twinkle, 'that sort of thing never happens to Invited Guests.'[28] The Queen also denies that they will remember this merely as a dream, saying, 'Of course not. That's a Grown-up's ending.'[29] As Sleeping Beauty's 'dust cloak' rises, the children are engulfed by a grey mist. 'Shadows begin to gather over the stage, gradually blotting out all but the crowd of Fairies clustered round the enthroned

Queen.'[30] They sing as the light fades on them: initially, a chorus of first and second sopranos are heard and seen, then just a semi-chorus, sextet, and trio until finally the Queen alone, a light shining on her face 'like a star in the darkness', sings this melody to a chromatic accompaniment (Illus. 9):[31]

> Never wholly children of the day, dears,
> In your ears the ring of elfin rhyme:
> Once to Fairyland you found your way, dears;
> Once upon a time.

The arpeggios played on the subdued harmonium accompaniment fade away.[32] And then, 'as darkness is complete the curtain falls.'[33]

In an interview, Robertson stressed the importance of imagination, cultivated in childhood and retained in adulthood. Through fairies, he claimed, we reach into a trans-cultural consciousness, for fairies are known in every part of the world. In this, Robertson is in concert with the Society of Folklore, but he becomes much more explicit than folklorists about his motives for promoting fairies to Edwardians. Fairies create wonder and cause joy and thus serve the common good: 'so far as the nation is concerned, the fairy-minded childhood is whole gold and whole gain.' Fairies are essential for both sexes. Though the British matron may seem antithetical to 'the fairy-mind', belief produces compassion and mothers need to be compassionate. Men, who have a different responsibility to the commonweal, must not only be stoic and severe. 'Grown-ups, unless they are as little children, are so drearily dense. And we cannot run an empire on density, therefore my plea for the fairy-mind is the child of to-day. It means the understanding man and the sympathetic woman to-morrow. It means a new-born nation.'[34]

He may have had a point. The play did appeal to children but, according to Robertson's memoir, *Pinkie and the Fairies* had another surprising fan base:

'Pinkie,' intended to capture the Nursery, captured – the Military. Night after night the stalls at His Majesty's looked like a parade at Aldershot. I was much puzzled by this phenomenon and finally asked a little soldier of my acquaintance to enquire into it . . . He returned to me with a most unexpected explanation – 'They say it makes them cry.' Apparently, what they found most devastating was the close of the second Act, when the children's dream ends and the vision of Fairyland slowly fades, the lights twinkling out, the music dying away, until all is darkness and silence save for the murmur of the stream among the shadows. And in the darkness Aldershot sat weeping for its lost Fairyland and the lights went up upon rows of bedewed shirt-fronts.[35]

This striking emotional testament did not come about by overtly challenging the audience to take a stand on fairies but rather because it moved the epitome of masculine empire-builders, administrators and defenders – regimental officers in the British Army – to tears at the sheer beauty of its fairy sensescape and the effect of it as a dream remembered in the wakeful lights of a re-illuminated auditorium.[36] Whether this was spurred by catharsis, nostalgia, grief or something else, the theatre's claim on a presentational arena for fairies and their efficacy in stimulating fascination suggests that what fairies were for was to remind adults of the human arc from childhood to maturation and the retention of the best part of the former

Illustration 9   Finale score for *Pinkie and the Fairies*, Act II. This is scored for Sleeping Beauty to sing, but according to the script she has already exited. This is sung by the Fairy Queen, accompanied by a harmonium and gradually fading chorus.

Illustration 9   (Continued)

in the latter state. As the *Sunday Times* reviewer opined, 'I really envy Pinkie and Tommy! They can see fairies all the time! They see them in broad daylight – in the grass and amongst the bluebells; they see them weaving the colours of the sunset, whilst we, poor, foolish grown-ups, talk with Aunt Imogen about Turner's atmospheric effects and quote Ruskin!'[37] Adults, in other words, have supplanted the folktale with the newspaper, and nature with aesthetic theory.[38] Children, for their part, *see* fairies, like the informants to ethnographers, whereas adults have come to understand their trace merely as constructs. Continuity with others, in this case, is infra-species continuity even though it was dramatized as inter-species contact.

Pinkie and the Fairies is a late instance of a long line of plays devoted to such seeing, perceiving and comprehending. Unlike *Peter Pan*, where 'they talk a lot about fairies, but . . . you never see fairies. A bicycle-bell and a number of little lamps: that is all you get of them',[39] proper fairy plays depict the witnessing of 'Every elf and fairy sprite/Hop as light as bird from brier.'[40] Corporeality and co-presence are essential to the satisfaction. This is the core element enabling dramatic characters – and thus their audience – to bear testament to encounter, like Conquergood's hyphen of dialogical performance, struggling 'to bring together different voices, world views, value systems and beliefs so that they can have a conversation with one another.'[41] On stage, the encounter is between two worlds. Between stage and auditorium, by metonymic implication, the encounter is between two conscious human states.

Fairy mimesis

Ethnographies provide taxonomies of fairy folk, distinguishing the elf, gnome, pixie, *Sidhe* and so on, from each other. Some general, but no absolute, physical characteristics are described. They are the size of giants, humans, children, birds or insects (Illus. 10).[42] W. B. Yeats claimed fairies were capricious about their size, changing from one to another.[43] The theatre, not surprisingly, tended use performers whose stature was in the mid-range of what ethnography allowed.

Corporealizing fairies for the theatre rested most critically not on their proportions but on their visibility, but here too the theatre utilized conventions of manifesting out of thin air, dancing and flight.[44] J. R. Planché spoofed this in the extravaganza *The Golden Branch*, where Pastorella, 'a Fairy of the New School', enters through a keyhole and proclaims:

> No use! You're no great conjurors I doubt,
> To think a door can keep a fairy out.
> At Christmas too, of all times in the year,
> When we have special licence to appear.
> But to be short, as fairies short you see,
> And to be quick, as fairies ought to be . . . [45]

The fairy-actor's body was not typically costumed in the green or brown of antiquarians' documentation to code authenticity for ethnographic display but in the white muslin petticoats of the ballerina or fantastical allegories recognizable from extravaganzas (Illus. 11 and 12).[46] This specifically theatrical code visually signalled difference from mortals and kinetically showed separateness from humans' abilities.

It is not my intention to conflate the fictional depictions and thematics on stage with what may (or may not) have been a real phenomenon as chronicled by ethnography and captured by illustrators. What this points to, instead, is theatre's capacity to question (and ignore) 'the real' while either evoking belief or reinscribing awareness through mimetic conventions relating to a remote spectrum of belief.[47] Fairies functioned aesthetically, to be sure, but also served to keep alive experiences, deeds and ideas from the past, connecting the past and present to cement personal and collective identities. This cultural tradition, like any branch of history, expressed shared ideas, values and experiences about national, ethnic and racial tradition as a 'symbolic universe' legitimating claims to power, morality and collectivity rooted in the past. Fairy ethnography was interpreted to line up evidence – including archaeological remains, pre-historical and historical waves of ethnic immigration, natural history and vestiges of one religious system not quite supplanted by another – in accord with other patterns in order to show continuity as well as breaks with the past.[48] The theatre presented a comforting version of how ideas lingering from the past modelled, contrasted and challenged rapid modernization.[49] The fairy, corporealized on stage, externalized intuitive knowledge: 'the *locus* of truth', despite disbelief, which Emmanuel Levinas argues is the 'wisdom of perception, the wisdom of everyday life and the wisdom of nations'.[50] A rational connection between fairy encounter and normal life was not required – that was exactly its appeal – though a form of rationality allowed passage from representation to the concept underlying it.[51] Or, in Edmund Husserl's contemporaneous view: 'Shifts and displacements of being (*Sinnverschiebungen*), enchanting or enchanted games, are played out at the heart of objectifying consciousness – good, clear and distinct consciousness – without, however, in the least jarring its spontaneous, naive and rational gait . . . The full intelligence of the undistorted,

Illustration 10 Cruickshank's illustration for Thomas Keightley's *The Fairy Mythology* (1828), indicating a mortal asleep before a fairy mound. Note the fairies' diminutive size. Courtesy of Northwestern University Library.

Illustration 11 Fairy Bluebell, pantomime costume design by Wilhelm (1882). Courtesy of Bristol Theatre Collection.

Illustration 12   'Feeding the Fairies Christmas Cheer', a backstage view of child fairies in a pantomime. *Illustrated London News*, 27 December 1903. Courtesy of Northwestern University Library.

objective gaze remains defenceless against meaning's displacements.'[52] Knowledge of the world, in other words, comes about not just through what is seen, certain and demonstrable.[53] Reducible neither to intermittent consciousness nor transcendental memory, theatre drew implicitly upon racial and national characteristics accepted into the idea of the British – explicitly not just English – as a group, a nation-state and ethnos experienced in part through these depictions.

Fairy repertoire

This idea is realized over and over as the pretext of staged versions of fairy encounters. Adaptations of Dickens's *The Cricket on the Hearth* provide an exceptional tracking of this through the fourteen versions produced in England from 1845 through 1914 for which scripts can be identified. The earliest versions – there were up to seventeen within days of the novella's appearance as a Christmas confection in 1845 – faithfully adhere to the story of the happily married Peerybingles whose joy and fidelity are symbolized by the cricket who chirps as cheerfully as the kettle steams for their tea, establishing the locus of warmth with the shrill sound of the insect, both at the hearth, the feminized core of familial contentment.[54] A cricket-hating toy-seller bent on besmirching the idea of marital bliss leads John Peerybingle where he can witness his wife, Dot, in intimate conversation with another, much younger man. John despairs of his illusory happiness and spends a mournful night seated at his fireside, gun at the ready to ensure this man does not approach his wife again. (The man is actually an old friend who has assumed a disguise but shared his secret only with Dot so she can help reunite him with his true love.) Albert Smith's version for the Keeleys, premiering at the Lyceum the same day the book was published, opens up the hearth to reveal the Fairy Cricket. She recites John's own loving words back to him and admonishes him to conflate his sweet wife with the quiet sanctuary of his hearth. Above, the chimney parts to reveal miniature facsimile scenes reprising earlier tableaux of Dot and the baby by the fireside. As these are shown, a 'troop of small Fairies appear from every available position; some forming a sort of border to the tableaux [sic], others run to John, pull him by the skirts, to call attention to the picture'. The tableau changes again to show a miniature John arriving from work, as in the first scene, and Dot running to greet him.

The Music becomes louder and hurried. A film descends in front of the tableau. The scene becomes darker and a shadow appears to obscure it. The Fairies express consternation and strive to rub it out, or put it on one side. When it goes away, it discovers DOT, sitting by the side of the cradle, with her hands clasped on her forehead and her hair hanging down. The Fairies get round her, kiss her and try to fondle her.
Cricket: It this the wife who has betrayed your confidence? Do you think that these household spirits, to whom falsehood is annihilated, would thus comfort her, if they did not believe her to be true? Reflect on this; for in all truth and kindness has it been presented to you.

The tableau closes and John starts out of his sleep.[55]

In Thomas Archer's version for the Princess's and Victoria, the cricket rises up from the fender, steps into the room and stands 'in fairy shape' before John. The rest, according to the author, is 'Vide book.' At this moment, the novella stipulates:

And while the Carrier, with his head upon his hands, continued to sit meditating in his chair, the Presence stood beside him, suggesting his reflections by its power and presenting them before him, as in a glass or picture. It was not a solitary Presence. From the hearthstone, from the chimney, from the clock, the pipe, the kettle and the cradle; from the floor, the walls, the ceiling and the stairs; from the cart without and the cupboard within and the household implements; from every thing and every place with which she had ever been familiar and with which she had ever entwined one recollection of herself in her unhappy husband's mind; Fairies came trooping forth. Not to stand beside him as the Cricket did, but to busy and bestir themselves. To do all honour to her image. To pull him by the skirts and point to it when it appeared.[56]

Archer's Fairy asserts the truth of the hearth and home that speak for Dot's innocence. Six other fairy crickets, accompanied by music, appear from various parts of the room and form a tableau around the spirit. The mantelpiece separates to show visions of Dot, her baby, then John slumped over the table.[57] This closely adheres to the novella and is standard stuff for the versions produced at the Royal Albert Saloon, City of London, Marylebone, Haymarket and Apollo Saloon.[58] Only E. L. Blanchard's burlesque varies the formula, as King Cricket emerges from a chorus of merry crickets and shares a smoke with John.[59] In the 1845–6 stage versions, the cricket-as-fairy – accompanied by chirping or soft music – is considered indispensable at this point and the play's sensationalism rests on the combined device. The chorus of fairies is dispensed with, however, in Joseph Halford's 1855 version for the Strand,[60] and reworked in Dion Boucicault's 1859 adaptation, *Dot* (produced at the Adelphi in 1862 and frequently revived). *Dot* commences in fairyland, as Oberon, Titania, Ariel and Puck, marginalized by the loss of forest land to agriculture, are depicted as down-at-heel scavengers. An updated fairyland pantheon is presided over by Home (aided by personified Kettle, Cradle and Cricket), who provide visions of the long-lost friend and the Peerybingles at ease, by way of exposition. The fairies reappear through the chimney at the end of Act I, singing Dot's praises and that of the cricket who watches over her. John's customary vision is foregone and instead the revelations of identity and reunifications are enhanced. The play ends with the fairies in the chimney overseeing the country dance that customarily concludes the story.[61] H. C. Hazlewood's 1867 version for the Alexandra Theatre restores the usual structure and characters, but also forgoes John's sleeping visions.[62]

The idea that fairies infuse everyday life – if only we could see them – and personify Victorian values of domesticity and femininity exists in all versions. Sound modulates the overtness of this motif. We do not need to see fairies if we know what to listen for.[63] The idea of fairies' ubiquity in the Peerybingles' home is metatextual in Dickens's story and explicit in the illustrations by Daniel Maclise, Richard Doyle and John Leech for the first edition, but curiously it is precisely at the point that the cricket-fairy becomes incarnate in the story – John's reverie – that there is *no* fairy in Leech's accompanying drawing.

Illustration 13   D. Maclise, frontispiece to Charles Dickens, *The Cricket on the Hearth* (1846). Courtesy of Northwestern University Library.

CHIRP THE FIRST.   17

bringing himself to sudden
stops ; now eliciting
a shriek from Tilly
Slowboy, in the
low nursing-chair
near the fire, by
the unexpected
application of his

Illustration 14   J. Leech, Bertha Peerybingle and Tilly Slowboys awaiting John's arrival, in Chirp the First, Charles Dickens, *The Cricket on the Hearth* (1846). Courtesy of Northwestern University Library.

One thing that prose can merely describe and an illustration can merely show is the production of sound. The theatre makes it audible. Given fairies' well-known devotion to music – especially on woodwinds, trumpets and strings – and fairy music's ability to arrest humans' attention, it is a frequent harbinger of the

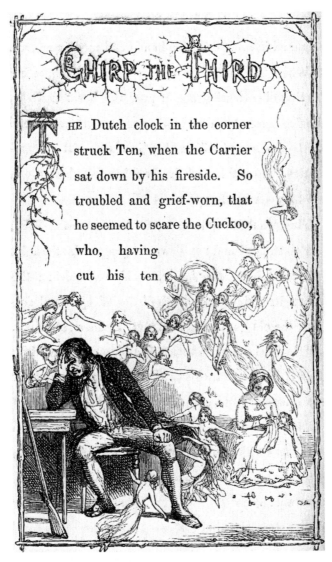

Illustration 15 R. Doyle, Chirp the Third, from Charles Dickens, *The Cricket on the Hearth* (1846). Courtesy of Northwestern University Library.

theatrical fairy's entrance. As Percy Fitzgerald typifies the revelation of fairyland in pantomime,

> First the 'gauzes' lift slowly one behind the other... giving glimpses of 'the Realms of Bliss,' seen beyond in a tantalising fashion. Then is revealed a kind of half-glorified country, clouds and banks, evidently concealing much. Always a sort of pathetic and at the same time exultant strain rises and is repeated

Illustration 16   J. Leech, John's Reverie, from Charles Dickens, *The Cricket on the Hearth* (1846). Courtesy of Northwestern University Library.

as the changes go on. Now we hear the faint tinkle – signal to those aloft on 'bridges' to open more glories. Now some of the banks begin to part slowly, showing realms of light, with a few divine beings – fairies – rising slowly here and there... While, finally, perhaps, at the back of it all, the most glorious paradise of all will open, revealing the pure empyrean itself and some fair spirit aloft in a cloud among the stars, the apex of all. Then all motion ceases; the work is complete; the fumes of crimson, green and blue fire begin to rise at the wings; the music bursts into a crash of exultation.[64]

Ethnographers also describe the peculiar voice and language of fairies,[65] and though this is less directly realized on stage, it finds musical expression through onomatopoetic stylization in instrumentation, kinetic simulation in syncopated rhythmic lines and generic synechdochal substitution through adaptation of orientalist musical styles utilizing harmonic colour, enharmonic modulation, chromaticism, tonal ambiguity, augmented intervals, chains of parallel thirds and ornamental devices.[66] In Douglas Hyde's *The Tinker and the Fairy* (1902), music calls the transformed fairy back to her own kind.[67] In *The Cricket on the Hearth*, the cricket's chirp either signals the fairy's imminent manifestation or reminds theatregoers of its presence as an untransformed insect. Fairy music, replete with convention, is an unmistakable anaphone of fairy speech.

The cricket's association with homeliness was borrowed from folklore, its chirping a lucky omen especially at Christmastime.[68] Despite vague resemblance between crickets and brownies or *uruisg*s as household spirits signifying hospitality,[69] Dickens invents – and seemingly cements – the connection of chirping cricket to feminized fairy life.[70] Within a decade, however, the fairy chorus (but not the chirping fairy) is stripped away from Halford's *The Cricket on the Hearth* dramatizations; more radically, Boucicault replaces the chorus with panto-mimic personifications of household objects and burlesqued Shakespeareans, though the spirit of the Cricket is still synonymous with music and the play ends with a tacit fairy benediction on the household as it breaks into joyous dancing. An anonymous version of *The Cricket on the Hearth* for the Brixton Theatre in 1900 counts on a multi-generational audience to be thoroughly familiar with Dickens's story, as well as later fairy literature; it interpolates new ideas, such as the song sung behind the scenes at the start of Act I, describing the elves and fairies that wait for night to guard and bless mortal dwellings. When John has his vision, the Cricket leaps out of a bush and intones soothing thoughts. A choir of crickets and elves then dance by moonlight. The next day, when the whole plot is revealed, the Cricket jumps forth and says a blessing directly to John and Dot. Then, a trick veil envelops the stage, obscuring the characters. The Cricket comes to the footlights and addresses the audience, Puck-like. When the veil rises, the Cricket holds a frame of wild flowers around the characters in tableau. A soprano, at a distance, sings the refrain 'A simple tale of human joys/Of love and trust unchanging.'[71] An operatic version from 1914 also opens with a fairy song, though set in the Peery-bingles' parlour. The Fairy-Cricket appears at the hearth and, when it determines that all is well with Dot, it vanishes and the usual business commences. In the final Act, the Fairy-Cricket lingers by the hearth for John to come home, sings him to sleep and conjures visions of Dot at various ages. When John awakes, he is peaceful.[72]

Not all stage fairies are sentimental. Some delight in the corruption of literature by the mundane. In J. B. Buckstone's burletta *The Sylph* (1834), the kitchenmaid Betty takes a tipple on her wedding morning to calm her nerves and is magically surrounded by sylphs liberated from their barrel prisons in the cellar. (They're *spirits*: get it?) Betty's bridegroom-to-be, John, does a dance around her parodying Richard III's 'Now is the winter of my discontent' and *La Sylphide* (1832). The Sylph causes antic mischief between Betty and her beau, pelting him with his sunflower bouquet, snatching the ring and absconding up the chimney with the marriage contract. Suspecting sorcery, John shoots a gun up the fireplace. The Sylph rolls down all sooty and vanishes through a trap. Moments later, it reappears perfectly clean.[73] Burlesque fairies are particularly fond of causing discord between humans, whether in the debased form of these 'spirits' or as monarchs. In *A Fairy's Frolic* (1863), the pantomime fairy Queen and King, bored with the opera, music halls, dinners and balloon rides, entertain themselves by causing mischief between human lovers.[74]

In *Dot*, Boucicault draws upon the tradition of adapting Shakespeare, Spenser and folklore. Like *Oberon* (1846), *Robin Goodfellow or the Frolics of Puck* (1848) and *Oberon; or the Charmed Horn* (1852),[75] he utilizes the Oberon–Titania story of marital discord and reconciliation, never shying away from didactic direct address to draw the homily between sets of fairy and mortal characters. More soberly, in the domestic sketch *A Household Fairy* (1859), a good-natured young woman embodies 'fairyness' because she jollies a despondent aristocrat, disappointed in an inheritance, into participating in normal household tasks and taking pleasure in tea and plain bread and butter. She restores his taste for simple things and zest for life, as well as carrying news of his fortune.[76] *Queen Mab* (1874), a three-act comedy, is a more convoluted variant, as the eponymous fairy – adopted daughter of an actor residing in artists' bohemian lodgings – is 'the good fairy that turns this place into a paradise'.[77] *Fairy Madge; or, the Slavery of Drink* (1891), a musical comedietta, also abstracts the fairy to a good daughter; in this case, she is an actress recently hired to play a fairy. Madge's drunkard father contrives to pawn her fairy costume, but before he can do this sees a green-eyed devil in the fireplace (actually, it is one of Madge's masks contorted by his delirium). When Madge interrupts him breaking into their savings, he strikes her on the head and she falls, seemingly lifeless. The moon breaks through the clouds and limelight shines brightly on Madge's insensate body. Mistaking her for his late wife, the father repents, Madge rouses and he is delivered from the slavery of drink.[78]

As different as these plays are in genre, they all demonstrate that despite the range of attributes accorded the fairy, whether poetically mischievous immortals or prosaic dutiful humans, together they signify the importance of appreciating mundane blessings, daily comforts and the goodness of others. A rhetorical convention equated to a fortuitous coincidence of action suffices to establish the connection to 'fairies'.[79] In plays for adults, banshees, lurelies and fairy queens may cause mayhem or it is discovered that someone taken for a fairy is actually human (a variant on the pantomimic fairy's propensity to unite lovers).[80] In plays for children, maudlin pandering may predominate or plots resolve in the Golden Rule.[81] A 1902 musical version of *The Water Babies* portrays this as well as any other example: Tom the chimney-sweep does a good deed for a lobster who enables him to become a water baby. The Fairy Queen's sister, Mrs Bedonebyasyoudid, aids him on an epic journey to the Other End of Nowhere and he is ultimately rewarded for his consistent acts of kindness.[82] She has an adult-oriented precursor in Planché's *The Island of Jewels*, where the Fairy Benevolentia brushes off the dispiriting effects of her malevolent counterpart, the Fairy Magotine, from the Princess Laidronetta, with the words

> Remember, love should love be won by,
> And the best rule is, 'do as you'd be done by.'[83]

Remarking on the illustrators Helen Allingham and Kate Greenaway, John Ruskin observed 'we are, in the most natural and rational health, able to foster the fancy', which he differentiates from knowing, 'up to the point of influencing our feelings and character in the strongest way'.[84] Social scientists were not so discerning. Herbert Spencer observed that as a society becomes more refined, the world of supernatural beings becomes less tangible, visible or audible. Yet ghosted figures inhabit the gap between observable phenomena, from whence they sometimes transmit uncanny communications to the living. This foundational idea in Victorian sociology explained a fundamental condition of human experience and law.[85] My emphasis is not on communication with the dead (the domain of spiritualism) but rather with a culture living amongst the human, yet separate and sovereign (the domain of supernaturals). Ethnographies describe and plays animate this realm: neither is scientifically verifiable (though ethnography aspires to it) and that is perhaps part of their appeal. While supernaturals may subscribe to a different ethic than Victorians, fairies are allied with commonly held notions of the Good: childlike innocence, the *quid pro quo* of deeds, household felicity and the mating of true loves. Mischief may be rampant, but order reigns in the end. Fairies, as 'lost' or 'muted' races, are the vehicles to express ideals fundamental to Britain's internal harmony.

While it is tempting to think of fairydom as a domain subject to rule by British ideology, its sovereignty is inviolate. As much as fairy queens (or kings) may exemplify benevolence through femininity, they are creatures with power and authority and withdrawal of their sympathy is catastrophic for humans. They represent both the highest aspirations of British character and the potential for resistant action, either as a corrective to misrule or sheer unmotivated malevolence. If anything, Britain is subject to the interference, meddling or visitation of fairies and incapable of stopping their incursions. In our era of post-colonial criticism, it is a delicious irony to recognize this vulnerability to fairies' prerogative turned to serve core cultural values of those who were 'other' to the fairies.

H. M. Walbrook protested in 1908 against 'the violent anti-Fairy attitude of the average theatrical manager, pantomime writer and pantomime actor and actress', who 'distort and mangle' stories of the fairies until they are unrecognizable.[86] I read the evidence very differently: the distortions are merely cosmetic adaptations of casting, costuming and topicality. Fairyland, as realized on Victorian and Edwardian stages, was not merely a vision of the world they had given up for modernity but a reflection on modernity bowed by nostalgia, tradition and mild rebellion. One could proceed, as Angela Bown suggests, 'as if one believed in it without actually doing so', but belief was no longer the point.[87] Fairies represented a minority discourse – whether they were a minority people is beside the point – in a nation adamant about homogeneity within the confines of its native shores. Like the perpetually 'medieval', rural and feudal world of European musical comedy, fairies provided a comforting fiction about backwardness in the midst of progress.[88] Yet they also reminded Victorians and Edwardians about the biopolitics of struggle with the non-human: a struggle for land and resources on the species level; for ethics on a moral level; and for justice and good government on a political and domestic level.[89] Uniting the remnants of a peasant culture, or culture of innocence, with the concept of event-based or political history, fairies accorded well to Victorian ideas of cultural tradition and social evolution. Ruthless or benevolent, fairies represented a code of consummate firmness and certainty in their ancient and stable society, itself a mirror of intercultural strife and imposition. What seemed impetuous, random or fabulous was the result of highly codified and venerable practices: there were absolute guidelines for convention and etiquette that kept the fairy world in order and sometimes Britons' too, when fairies deigned to interfere.

Notes

1. I am indebted to my research assistant, Adrian Curtin, for his genial and indefatigable labours on this project and particularly on the musical analysis.
2. These characteristics of culture or civilization are taken from E. B. Tylor's foundational work of British ethnography, *Primitive Culture: Researches into the Development of Mythology, Philosophy, Religion, Language, Art and Custom*, 2 vols (1871; rpt. London: Murray 1920). See also Christopher Herbert, *Culture and Anomie: Ethnographic Imagination in the Nineteenth Century* (Chicago: University of Chicago Press, 1991), 4; and Archibald MacLaren, *The Fairy Family: a Series of Ballads and Metrical Tales Illustrating the Fairy Mythology of Europe* (London: Macmillan, 1874).
3. While there is also an extensive folkloric literature on African, Middle Eastern and Asian fairies, with many plays focused on the *peri*, my focus is explicitly on non-Orientalist versions. I do not exclude plays set in German-speaking and Scandinavian lands, but the vast majority of my sampling from the Lord Chamberlain's Plays at the British Library favours British and Celtic settings (including, in one case, Brittany).
4. Robert A. Gilbert, ed., *Victorian Sources of Fairy Tales: (1) A Collection of Researches*, 5 vols (Bristol: Thoemmes, 2002); Robert A. Gilbert, ed., *Victorian Sources of Fairy Tales: (2) A Collection of Stories*, 5 vols (Bristol: Thoemmes, 2003); Alison Stella Beddoe Packer and Lianne Jarrett, *Fairies in Legend and the Arts* (Brighton: Cameron and Tayleur, 1980); Jane Martineau, ed., *Victorian Fairy Painting* (London: Merrell Holberton, 1997); Michael Maier, ' "Mine ear is much enamoured of thy note": Musikalische Grundbegriffe in Shakespeare's *A Midsummer Night's Dream*', *Archiv für Musikwissenschaft*, 59.1 (2002): 33–50; and Linda Austern and Inna Naroditskaya, eds, *Music of the Sirens* (Bloomington: Indiana University Press, 2007).
5. Gary Jay Williams, *Our Moonlight Revels: 'A Midsummer Night's Dream' in the Theatre* (Iowa City: University of Iowa Press, 1997); and Jane W. Stedman, *W. S. Gilbert: a Classic Victorian and His Theatre* (Oxford: Oxford University Press, 1996). A much slighter literature exists for James Robinson Planché, e.g. Paul Buczkowski, 'J. R. Planché, Frederick Robson and the Fairy Extravaganza', *Marvels & Tales: Journal of Fairy-Tale Studies*, 15.1 (2001): 42–65. For the French tradition, see Paul Ginisty, *La Féerie* (Paris: Louis-Michaud: 1910); Arthur Pougin, *Dictionnaire Historique et Pittoresque du Théâtre et des Arts qui s'y Rattachent* (Paris: Firmin-Didot, 1885), 360–4; and Frank Kessler, 'On Fairies and Technologies', *Moving Images: From Edison to the Webcam*, ed. John Fullerton and Astrid Söderberg Widding (London: John Libbey, 2000), 39–46.
6. This view frequently appears in pantomime reviews, e.g. 'Harlequin Fairy Morgana!' *All the Year Round*, 12.278 (1864): 40–8.
7. Tracy C. Davis, 'Do You Believe in Fairies?: the Hissing of Dramatic License', *Theatre Journal*, 57 (March 2005): 57–81.
8. I strenuously disagree with the conclusions about *Peter Pan* expressed by Juliette Wood, Diane Purkiss and Nicola Bown (on the BBC 4 programme *In Our Time*, aired 11 May 2006) with regard to Tinkerbell's function in the dramatic version of *Peter Pan* and the *post hoc* applicability to the Victorian period. They are correct, however, in attributing influence to *Peter Pan* on twentieth-century ideas about fairies.
9. R. L. Green, *Fifty Years of Peter Pan* (London: Peter Davies, 1954), 79.
10. Robert A. Gilbert makes a related point in the introduction to his reprint of Victorian fairy tales. The shift from oral to printed conveyance sometimes resulted in liberties with conventions, however as Dickens and William Roscoe argued the essential aspects

of the tales must be preserved as if factual, which made them fundamentally unsuited to children (Vol. 1, p. xi).

11. Anxiety over the fairies' farewell dates from Chaucer's Wife of Bath, and became a keynote in the Renaissance, as a poem by Richard Corbet (Bishop of Norwich) jests: the fairies fled after Mary's reign out of disgust over Puritanism. For nineteenth-century updates, see Thomas Crofton Croker, *Fairy Legends and Traditions of the South of Ireland*, vol. 3 (London: John Murray: 1826), 70–1; William Dowe, 'A Talk About the Fairies', *Sharpe's London Magazine of Entertainment and Instruction for General Reading*, 17.2 (1853): 10–16; Katharine M. Briggs, *The Vanishing People: a Study of Traditional Fairy Beliefs* (London: B. T. Batsford: 1978); Diane Purkiss, *At the Bottom of the Garden: a Dark History of Fairies, Hobgoblins and Other Troublesome Things* (New York: New York University Press, 2000), 215.

12. Arthur Conan Doyle, *The Coming of the Fairies* (1922; rpt. London: Pavilion, 1997); Geoffrey Hodson, *Fairies at Work and at Play* (1922; rpt. Wheaton, IL: Theosophical Publishing House, 1982); Alex Owen, ' "Borderland Forms": Arthur Conan Doyle, Albion's Daughters and the Politics of the Cottingley Fairies', *History Workshop Journal*, 38 (1994): 48–85; and Nicola Bown, 'There Are Fairies at the Bottom of Our Garden: the Cottingley Photographs – Fairies, Fantasy and Photography', *Textual Practice*, 10.1 (Spring 1996): 57–82.

13. George Chauncey documents that in New York 'fairy' was homosexual slang by the 1890s; however, I have identified no such early usage in Britain. Some American 'fairies' adopted femininity and cross-dressing, suggesting that to be fairy was to be discernible, double-coded, distinct in appearance amid a differently coded reality, and aberrant. See *Gay New York: Gender, Urban Culture, and the Makings of the Gay Male World, 1890–1940* (New York: Basic Books, 1994), 47, 60–1, 106, 112.

14. These designations are conventions, not absolutes. Both methodology and contents blur across types and my classifications do not always concur with standard choices; see Neil C. Hultin, 'Anglo-Irish Folklore from Clonmel: T. C. Croker and the British Library Add. 20099', *Fabula*, 27.3–4 (1986): 288–307; and Jennifer Schacker, *National Dreams: the Remaking of Fairy Tales in Nineteenth-Century England* (Philadelphia: University of Pennsylvania Press, 2003). However, for indicative examples of antiquarianism, see James Orchard Halliwell, ed., *Illustrations of the Fairy Mythology of 'A Midsummer Night's Dream'* (London: Shakespeare Society, 1845); Henry Fothergill Chorley, ed., *Personal Reminiscences by Chorley, Planché and Young* (New York: Scribner Armstrong: 1874); Thomas Crofton Croker, *Recollections of Old Christmas: a Masque* (privately printed, 1850); and D., M. A., *A Few Fragments of Fairyology, Shewing its Connection with Natural History* (Durham: Will Duncan and Son: 1859). For folkloric studies, see Thomas Keightley, *The Fairy Mythology* (London: William Harrison Ainsworth, 1828); Edwin Sidney Hartland, *The Science of Fairy Tales* (London: Walter Scott, 1890); George Laurence Gomme, *Ethnology in Folklore* (New York: D. Appleton, 1892); and Juliette Wood, 'Folklore Studies at the Celtic Dawn: the Rôle of Alfred Nutt as Publisher and Scholar', *Folklore*, 110 (1999): 3–12. For ethnographic studies, see Anna E. Bray, *A Description of the Part of Devonshire Bordering on the Tamar and the Tavy; its Natural History, Manners, Customs, Superstitions, Scenery, Antiquities, Biography of Eminent Persons, &c. &c. in a Series of Letters to Robert Southey, Esq.* (London: John Murray, 1836); Croker (1826); Charlotte Sophia Burne, *The Handbook of Folklore* (London: Folk-Lore Society, 1914); and David MacRitchie, *The Testimony of Tradition* (London: Kegan Paul, Trench, Trübner & Co., 1890).

15. Dwight Conquergood, 'Performing as a Moral Act: Ethical Dimensions of the Ethnography of Performance', *Turning Points in Qualitative Research: Tying Knots in a Handkerchief*, ed. Yvonna S. Lincoln and Norman K. Denzin (Walnut Creek, CA: Altamira Press, 2003), 408.

16. Jacqueline Rose, *The Case of Peter Pan or the Impossibility of Children's Fiction* (London: Macmillan, 1984), 94.

17. Bristol Theatre Collection HBT/TB/000039, *Pinkie and the Fairies*, press cuttings [part I], 1908, 'His Majesty's. Miss Ellen Terry in a Fairy Play', *People*, 20 December 1908; and 'His Majesty's Theatre. Pinkie and the Fairies', *Morning Post*, 21 December 1908.

18. W. Graham Robertson, *Time Was* (London: Quartet Books, 1931), 315.
19. W. Y. Evans Wentz, *The Fairy-Faith in Celtic Countries* (London: Oxford University Press, 1911), 468.
20. Wentz, 476.
21. A change in how ghostly characters might be posited by comparing the Wilis of *Giselle* (1841) to late-Victorian versions of plot manipulation through behavioural control, such as *Trilby* (1895). Planché spoofs the rage for *Giselle* in *The New Planet; or, Harlequin Out of Place* (1846) in *The Extravaganzas of J. R. Planché*, vol. 3, ed. T. F. Dillon Croker and Stephen Tucker (London: Samuel French, 1879), 172.
22. Sir Oliver Lodge, 'Psychical Research', *Harper's Magazine* (August 1908), cited in Wentz, 478–9.
23. A complete character list is included in the promptbook Bristol HBT/0002161/2, Graham Robertson (music by Frederic Norton), *Pinkie and the Fairies*, 1902.
24. Bristol Theatre Collection HBT/TB/000039, *Pinkie and the Fairies*, press cuttings [part I], 1908, 'Picturesque Costumes at His Majesty's', *Sunday Times*, 20 December 1908.
25. Bristol Theatre Collection HBT/TB, *Pinkie and the Fairies*, press cuttings [part II] 1908, 'Dramatic Notes'. *The Planet*, 26 December 1908; and 'The Theatre', *World*, 22 December 1908: 1195.
26. Bristol Theatre Collection HBT/TB/000039, *Pinkie and the Fairies*, press cuttings [part I], 1908, 'Pinkie and the Fairies. A Christmas Play at His Majesty's Theatre'. *Daily Telegraph*, 21 December 1908.
27. Edwin Sidney Hartland, *The Science of Fairy Tales* (London: Walter Scott, 1890); Lewis Spence, *The Fairy Tradition in Britain* (London: Rider and Company, 1948), 298–9, 305.
28. W. Graham Robertson, *Pinkie and the Fairies* (London: William Heinemann, 1909), 98.
29. Robertson (1909), 99. See also Spence, 305.
30. Robertson (1909), 99.
31. Bristol HBT/0002161/2.
32. Bristol Theatre Collection HBT/TB, *Pinkie and the Fairies*, press cuttings [part II] 1908, Arthur Poyser, 'A Fairy Play – with Music'. *The Musical Standard*, 26 December 1908.
33. Robertson (1909), 100.
34. Bristol Theatre Collection HBT/TB/000039, *Pinkie and the Fairies*, press cuttings [part I], 1908, Raymond Blathwayt, 'The Child in Fairyland', *Black and White*, 5 December 1908.
35. Robertson (1931), 320–1.
36. Non-commissioned officers and soldiers in uniform were not admitted to all parts of theatres, a caution against the rank and file's reputation for drunkenness and brawling, so the military in the stalls were almost certainly officers. David French, *Military Identities: the Regimental System, the British Army, and the British People, c. 1870–2000* (Oxford: Oxford University Press, 2005), 232–3. At this time, officers were still public school educated and represented the interests of landed gentry. Following military service at home or abroad, second careers frequently involved parliamentary service, usually as Tories, or stints in local administration as magistrates or Chief Constables. Gwyn Harries-Jenkins, *The Army in Victorian Society* (London: Routledge & Kegan Paul, 1977), 216–73.
37. Bristol Theatre Collection HBT/TB/000039, *Pinkie and the Fairies*, press cuttings [part I], 1908, A. G., 'Last Night's Premiere', *The Sunday Times*, 20 December 1908.
38. 'Fairy Poetry'. *Times*, 1 April 1914: 5.
39. Bristol Theatre Collection HBT/TB, *Pinkie and the Fairies*, press cuttings [part II], 1908, Owen Stair, '*Pinkie and the Fairies* at His Majesty's'. *Outlook*, 26 December 1908.
40. *Midsummer Night's Dream*, 5.1.393–4.
41. Conquergood, 408.
42. Briggs, 18, 28; John Graham Dalyell, *The Darker Superstitions of Scotland, Illustrated from History and Practice* (Edinburgh: Waugh and Innes, 1834), 535; Rev. John O'Hanlon, rpt. from *The Gentleman's Magazine* (1865) in *The Gentleman's Magazine Library: English Traditional Lore*, ed. George Laurence Gomme (London: Elliot Stock, 1885), 32–41; John

Arnott MacCulloh, 'Fairy', *Encyclopedia of Religion and Ethics*, vol. 5 (Edinburgh: T. & T. Clark, 1912), 671.

43. Cited in Wentz, 242.

44. Gustav Kobbe, 'Staging a Fairy Play', *The Cosmopolitan*, 1 (1902): 3–13.

45. J. R. Planché, *The Golden Branch* (London: S. G. Fairbrother and W. Strange, 1848), 7. This extravaganza was based on 'Le Rameau d'Or', by the Countess D'Anois.

46. Anna E. Bray, *A Description of the Part of Devonshire Bordering on the Tamar and the Tavy; its Natural History, Manners, Customs, Superstitions, Scenery, Antiquities, Biography of Eminent Persons, &c. &c. in a Series of Letters to Robert Southey, Esq.* (London: John Murray, 1836), 173; Dalyell, 535; Lang, 131; Spence, 132–46; and George Waldron, *The History and Description of the Isle of Man* (London: W. Bickerton, 1744), 64–5. Alexandra Carter details the repertoire of supernatural ballets and typical costuming in *Dance and Dancers in the Victorian and Edwardian Music Hall Ballet* (Aldershot: Ashgate, 2005), esp. 57–9 and 82–5.

47. Compare Gay McAuley, *Space in Performance: Making Meaning in the Theatre* (Ann Arbor: University of Michigan Press, 1999), 25. Michael R. Booth speculates on the possible influence of fairyologists such as Thomas Keightley, T. Crofton Croker and the Grimms on staged interpretations of *A Midsummer Night's Dream*, but only via illustrations by painters such as Daniel Maclise. *Victorian Spectacular Theatre* (London: Routledge & Kegan Paul, 1981), 36–7.

48. For explanatory frames for fairies, see D., M. A., *A Few Fragments*; David MacRitchie, *Fians, Fairies and Picts* (London: Kegan Paul, Trench, Trübner, 1893); John Rhys, 'Welsh Fairies', *Nineteenth Century*, 30 (1891): 564–74; Grant Allen, 'Who Were the Fairies?' *Cornhill Magazine* (March 1881): 335–48; and David MacRitchie, *The Testimony of Tradition* (London: Kegan Paul, Trench, Trübner, 1890). Secondary studies include Richard M. Dorson, *The British Folklorists: a History* (London: Routledge & Kegan Paul, 1968); Philippa Levine, *The Amateur and the Professional* (Cambridge: Cambridge University Press, 1986); Carole Silver, 'On the Origin of Fairies: Victorians, Romantics and Folk Belief', *Browning Institute Studies*, 14 (1986): 141–56; and Stephen R. L. Clark, 'How to Believe in Fairies', *Inquiry*, 30.4 (1987): 337–55.

49. See Gerda Lerner, *Why History Matters: Life and Thought* (Oxford: Oxford University Press, 1997), 116–17.

50. Emmanuel Levinas, *Entre Nous: On Thinking of the Other* (New York: Columbia University Press: 1998), 77.

51. Levinas, 79.

52. Levinas, 82.

53. Levinas, 83. This is comparable to Jacques Derrida's 'understanding of "absence" as an *activity* of the presence *in* representation'. Catherine M. Soussloff, 'Like a Performance: Performativity and the Historicized Body, from Bellori to Mapplethrope', *Acting on the Past*, ed. Mark Franko and Annette Richards (Hanover, NH: Wesleyan University Press, 2000), 74.

54. Malcolm Morley, ' "The Cricket" on the Stage', *The Dickensian*, 48.1 (1951/2): 17–24; and Elaine Ostry, *Social Dreaming: Dickens and the Fairy Tale* (New York: Routledge, 2002), 79–104.

55. Albert R. Smith, *Cricket on the Hearth* (London: John Dicks, 1845), 11–12.

56. Charles Dickens, *The Cricket on the Hearth* (London: Bradbury and Evans, 1846), Chirp the Third.

57. BL Add MSS 42990, Thomas Archer, *Cricket on the Hearth*, 1845.

58. BL Add MSS 42998, C. T. Barnett, *Cricket on the Hearth, or the Carrier and His Wife, a Fairy Tale of Home*, 1845 [Royal Albert]; BL Add MSS 42990, W. J. Townsend, *Cricket on the Hearth*, 1845 [City of London]; BL Add MSS 42990, W. J. Lucas, *Cricket on the Hearth*, 1845 [Marylebone]; BL Add MSS 42990, B. N. Webster, *Cricket on the Hearth*, 1845 [Haymarket]; and BL Add MSS 42991 ff. 113–28, B. F. Rayner, *The Cricket on the Hearth, or a Fairy Tale of Home*, 1846 [Apollo]. See also *The Dramatic and Musical Review*, 24 January 1846: 37–8.

59. BL Add MSS 42991, E. L. Blanchard, *Cricket on Our Own Hearth; a Fairy Burlesque*, 1846.
60. BL Add MSS 52953 M, Joseph Halford, *Cricket on the Hearth*, 1855.
61. Dion Boucicault, *Forbidden Fruit and Other Plays* (Princeton: Princeton University Press, 1940), 109–49. *Dot* became best known through J. L. Toole's performance; in 1869 Henry Irving joined him as John Peerybingle; Toole reprised the play at the Gaiety in 1870 as *A Christmas Story* and retained it in his repertoire thereafter. It was revived in 1903 at the Garrick, retitled *The Cricket on the Hearth* (Morley, 20–1). Ostry (101) points out that the novella does not end with the dance, but with a coda stipulating that the dancers have vanished, 'A Cricket sings upon the Hearth; a broken child's-toy lies upon the ground; and nothing else remains'. The narrator is all alone in a narrative conceit that parallels Caleb Plummer's deception of his daughter regarding Tackleton's benevolence. None of the plays hints at this, preferring the *pas d'ensemble* ending.
62. BL Add MSS 53063 H, H. C. Hazlewood, Jr., *The Cricket on the Hearth*, 1867. D. W. Griffith makes the same choice to eliminate the vision scene in his 1909 Biograph film; Tom Gunning regards the glowing hearth as both 'a realistic detail and psychological sign' developed through 'character psychology' that dispenses with 'subjective imagery and its *feerique* trappings'. Tom Gunning, *D. W. Griffith and the Origins of American Narrative Film: the Early Years at Biograph* (Urbana: University of Illinois Press, 1991), 177. See *Cricket on the Hearth*, Grapevine Video, *D. W. Griffith Director*, vol. 2 (1909).
63. This may be a tradition picked up by Tinkerbell, who though not corporeal is audible.
64. Percy Fitzgerald, *The World Behind the Scenes* (1881; rpt. New York: Benjamin Blom, 1972), 89.
65. O'Hanlon, 1–3, 12; Bray, 173; Dalyell, 535, 538; Clark, 342; Hinton, 41; Lang, 131; and MacCulloch, 679.
66. See Philip Tagg, 'Toward a Sign Typology of Music', in *Secondo Convegno Europeo di Analisi Musicale*, ed. R. Dalmonte and M. Baroni (Trento: Università degli studi di Trento, 1992), 369–78.
67. Douglas Hyde, trans. Belinda Butler, 'The Tinker and the Fairy', *New Ireland Review* (June 1902): 183–92. Incidental music was written by Michele Esposito.
68. Jacqueline Simpson and Steve Rand, *A Dictionary of English Folklore* (Oxford: Oxford University Press, 2000), 83; W. Carew Hazlitt, *Faiths and Folklore of the British Isles*, vol. 1 (1905; New York: B. Blom, 1965), 155; David Pickering, *A Dictionary of Folklore* (New York: Facts on File, 1999), 64; and Alison Jones, *Larousse Dictionary of World Folklore* (Edinburgh: Larousse, 1995), 126. The rapid cementing of the association is demonstrated by Planché's *Golden Branch*, an extravaganza produced at the Royal Lyceum in December 1848. In the final scene, the Fairy Tree of Entertaining Knowledge contains a cricket and a grasshopper in the hollow of its trunk immediately before their transformation into the Prince and Princess. The Prince sings, to a tune from *Don Pasquale*, 'The "Golden Branch"/By friends so staunch,/In this parterre now planted,/A Christmas tree/Of mirth shall be/By all good spirits haunted.' Planché (1848), 39.
69. The resemblance to household spirits is evident in both Scottish and English traditions. John Arnott MacCulloh, 'Fairy', *Encyclopedia of Religion and Ethics*, vol. 5 (Edinburgh: T. & T. Clark, 1912), 683; Archibald MacLaren, *The Fairy Family: a Series of Ballads and Metrical Tales Illustrating the Fairy Mythology of Europe* (London: Macmillan, 1874), xxi; and Spence, 22, 34–41.
70. George Bernard Shaw seems to parody this in *John Bull's Other Island*. At the start of Act II, Keegan, a defrocked priest, engages a shrilly responding grasshopper on the subject of Ireland's resemblance to heaven or hell. I am indebted to Heidi Holder for pointing out this passage.
71. LC Plays 1900/23, *Cricket on the Hearth*, 1900.
72. BL LC Plays 1914/20, *Cricket on the Hearth*, 1914. Presumably, this is Julian Sturgess's libretto for music by Alexander McKenzie produced by the Royal Academy of Music. See Morley, 24.
73. BL Add MSS 42928, J. B. Buckstone, *The Sylph (The Kitchen Sylph)*, 1834.

74. BL Add MSS 53028 U, *The Fairy's Frolic*, 1863–4. In some burlesques, extravaganzas and pantomimes, the good fairy is poised to resist an embodied evil fairy. *The Black Crook* as licensed for the Alhambra in 1872 is a typical example. BL Add MSS 53115 D; see also Raymond Knapp's discussion of the play's indebtedness to *Der Freischütz*, in *The American Musical and the Formation of National Identity* (Princeton: Princeton University Press, 2005), 20–9.

75. BL Add MSS 42996 ff. 92–117, G. Dance, *Oberon*, 1846; BL Add MSS 43015, *Robin Goodfellow of the Frolics of Puck*, 1848; and BL Add MSS 52935(S), Thomas W. Beckett, *Oberon; or the Charmed Horn*, 1852. Source texts include Ben Jonson's masque *Oberon* (1616), Carl Maria von Weber's opera *Oberon or the Elf King's Oath* (1826).

76. BL Add MSS 52988 V, Francis Talfourd, *A Household Fairy*, 1859.

77. BL Add MSS 53135 I, George William Godfrey, *Queen Mab*, 1874.

78. BL Add MSS 53486 F, Claude Trevelyan, *Fairy Madge; or, the Slavery of Drink*, 1891.

79. See, for example, BL LC Plays 1902/15, *Fairy Prince*, 1902.

80. BL Add MS 52930 I, Edward Fitzball, *The Last of the Fairies*, 1852; BL Add MSS 53000, J. Baxter Langley, *The Fairy*, 1861; BL Add MSS 53271, John Joseph and William Watson (adapted from the French of Halery and Busnach, music by Offenbach), *The Banshee's Spell; or, the Magic of Woman's Wit* (also known as *The Blush Rose; or, the Fairy Tempter*), 1882.

81. Compare BL Add MSS 53162 L, John C. Levey, *The Banshee; or, the Spirit of the Boreen*, 1876; BL Add MSS 53338 E, John Simpson Palgrave (music by Arthur Hervey), *The Fairy's Post Box*, 1885; BL Add MSS 53364 J, Oswald Brand (music by Immanuel Liebich), *The Fairy Ring*, 1886; BL LC Plays 1903/35, Philip Carr, *Snowdrop and the Seven Little Men*, 1903; BL LC Plays 1913/17, *Fairy Story*, 1913.

82. LC Plays 1902/35, Rutland Barrington, *Water Babies*, 1902.

83. J. R. Planché, *The Island of Jewels* (London: S. G. Fairbrother, 1849), 28.

84. John Ruskin, *The Art of England: Lectures Given in Oxford* (Sunnyside, Kent: George Allen, 1884), 122–3.

85. Herbert Spencer, *The Principles of Sociology* (1897–1906; rpt. Westport, CT: Greenwood, 1975), vol. 3: 162–3; vol 2: 514. See also Herbert, 15.

86. H. M. Walbrook, 'A Plea for the Fairies and their Cruel Treatment in Pantomimes', *Pall Mall Magazine*, n.s. 8 (December 1908): 715.

87. Compare Nicola Bown's perspective in *Fairies in Nineteenth-Century Art and Literature* (Cambridge: Cambridge University Press, 2001), 1–2.

88. Len Platt, *Musical Comedy on the West End Stage, 1890–1939* (Basingstoke: Palgrave Macmillan, 2004), 65.

89. Compare Giorgio Agamben, *The Open: Man and Animal*, trans. Kevin Affell (Stanford: Stanford University Press, 2004).

3
Communal Performances: Royal Ritual, Revolution and National Acts

Emily Allen

For a woman who was famously unamused, Queen Victoria took her pleasures both liberally and seriously, and she bid her subjects do the same, both in her advocacy of rational pleasure and in the nation-wide parties she threw to celebrate the weddings of her children. These celebrations were part choreographed pageant of state and part 'spontaneous' overflow of national feeling, spilling out as they did into the streets and communal spaces of the country, not to mention the nation's illustrated press, souvenir shops and curio cabinets. Newspaper coverage of Victorian royal weddings focused closely on the nation's crowds, on their order-liness, their joviality and their public expression of national pride and goodwill. By addressing both verbal and visual representations of English crowds at play during the royal wedding festivities, I want to think about the serious work performed by such national enjoyment. I want also to think about the category of performance itself, which I use here in both its broadest sense of action and enactment and its more theatricalized sense of public presentation and display. Ultimately, I am interested in what it meant, in 1871, to 'act' like a nation or in the interest of a nation, and why the scene of national action keeps returning to the theatre – or, at least, to the well-worn tropes of theatre and spectacle. What is at stake in terms of national identity formation when English crowds turn out for what is essentially a command performance of group affect? What happens when pleasure becomes a national duty, who takes part in this performance, and where and how does it take place?

I have argued elsewhere that in such commanding pleasures the disciplinary subject of the nineteenth century achieves its fullest articulation.[1] I will argue here that this articulation is achieved over and against the image of national affect gone rampant and awry – which is to say, over the Channel and against the French. I will argue, too, that the scene of national enjoyment that took place when Princess Louise Caroline Alberta married John George Edward Henry Douglas Sutherland Campbell, the Marquess of Lorne, on 21 March 1871, made itself available for consumption in many and sometimes material ways, extending the possibilities for participation, collectivity and performance, in numerous senses. While the Victorians may have been a 'performing society' in their love of theatre, spectacle and state pageantry, they also can be said to *be* 'performing society', or at least forming one idea of the social, in their collective attendance at or attention to state spectacle. This essay focuses on the public and private acts of spectating, reading, playing, buying, collecting and fantasizing by single and massed individuals that came to constitute the nation.

Vive la Commune!

In the last two weeks of March 1871, two events dominated the headlines of English newspapers and the imagination of the English public: the English royal wedding and the French civil war. The former was remarkable for its pomp and circumstance, for its carefully staged union between royal and 'commoner' (the groom was merely an aristocrat, not a royal), and for the tidiness of its sizeable crowds. The latter was marked – at least in the mainstream London press – by its bloody chaos, as crowds of working-class Frenchmen took Paris from the 'aristos' and the National Assembly looked on from the safety of a theatre in Versailles.[2] These two events were linked not only by their close proximity on the newspaper page, a proximity that produced for the events an uncanny simultaneity, but also by a logic of inversion in which the nightmare of France plays out as the frightening obverse of England's dream of order, restraint and benign collectivity. As Victorian England celebrated its first 'democratic' and truly domestic royal union, welcoming Lorne, whose family hailed from Scotland, as the first British noble to marry into Victoria's family and as proof positive that Britain's previously warring factions had learned to play nicely together, France's republic was being ripped apart by domestic antagonism, the long-simmering class warfare that England congratulated itself on having dealt with peacefully.[3] English newspapers dwelt upon this contrast as a longed-for performative: representing it will make it so. The lawless, blood-thirsty, hysterical Mob props up a most joyfully imagined community, the English crowd-as-nation, coherent, rational, and made up of private individuals capable of disciplining themselves and each other.[4]

This contrast was seen most clearly on the wedding day itself, when English readers of middle-class newspapers were offered competing images of English and French collectivity.[5] Not surprisingly, the English ones reproduce the familiar idea of the nation as happy family.[6] *The Times* begins its wedding coverage like this: 'To-day a ray of sunshine will gladden every habitation on this island, and force its way even where uninvited. A daughter of the people, in the truest sense of the word, is to be married to one of ourselves. The mother is ours and the daughter is ours. We honour and obey the QUEEN.'[7] In its tangle of interrelation, the piece proclaims both national and familial ownership of the royals and its own obsequiousness towards a monarch whose joy the country shares, apparently without exception. As it continues, the Queen is portrayed as a strange hybrid of all-powerful deity and family member, absolute monarch and servant of the people, a representation explained when the other shoe drops:

> Good reason, indeed, have we to be thankful that, at a time when the oldest and strongest principles of society are most severely tried, Royalty exists here

in the meekest, the wisest, and the most unpretending forms. It offers a symbol of union, a type of family life, and an example of resignation to Divine decrees and submission to human laws. Royalty with us has no ambition. What it most affects is that privacy which is the charm of English life. The QUEEN is one of us, and her family is an English family.[8]

Less than six months after the ouster of Emperor Napoleon III following his capitulation in the Franco-Prussian war, three days after the outbreak of civil war in France, and the day after the opening of the French republic's National Assembly in exile at Versailles, London's *Times* portrays royal power as both incontestable and ultimately harmless, a model for lawful Englishness and familial unity, and, above all, private in ways that only a massive public spectacle can demonstrate.

What English crowds (and readers) saw in the very public enactment of their own 'private' Englishness was a form of national feeling that could be both collective and individual at once. The doubleness of royal marriage – private affair of the heart/public affair of state – modelled the tension of the national individual, distinct and yet grouped. This part-for-whole logic, which is by necessity reversible (whole-for-part), can be glimpsed in the way that the wedding crowd comes to stand in for the whole nation: 'if the part taken by sight-seers who thronged the little but loyal town of Windsor can be accepted as an example of national feeling – and we believe it may – the popularity of this marriage [. . .] must be thoroughly national.'[9] The discipline of each individual spectator is such that the crowd made up of these spectators is cordial and malleable, although feeling shivers through them communally. Newspaper accounts of the crowd focus on both the exuberance of its emotion and the extreme ease with which the crowd is controlled: only a small constabular force, we are told repeatedly, is necessary to guide the movements of a crowd in which there is an 'agreeable absence of the "rough" element'.[10] As with coverage of previous royal weddings, an issue is made of the crowd's inability to hear and see the royals, but this lack of access only manages to underscore the 'privacy' of the occasion, during which the crowd appears content to cheer and wave at royals they cannot recognize but must only (and this is the point) imagine. The royals are on some level redundant, as what the crowd cheers is finally itself, or an idea of itself in all of its size and singularity.

The *Illustrated London News* plays up this focus on the crowd with a series of national wedding tableaux that show the royal pair framed by massive but orderly crowds, docile bodies massed in harmless jubilation. We see Louise and Lorne leaving St George's chapel as figures in the foreground and the background doff their hats and a bobby and plenty of guardsmen look on; we see them driving down the long walk in Windsor Park, as blocks of spectators look on from either side and converge behind their carriage as it passes; and we see the royal couple arriving at Esher for their wedding night to a large and cheering crowd.[11] These images perform the work of representing the people en masse and as the true object of the national gaze, and they follow a familiar visual grammar that John

MARRIAGE OF PRINCESS LOUISE: THE CASTLE HILL, WINDSOR

Illustration 17 'Marriage of Princess Louise: The Castle Hill, Windsor', *Illustrated London News*, 1 April 1871, p. 324.

Plunkett describes as iconographic of Victorian populism: the royals are small and unostentatious, and necessarily so, since what such images display is popular support for the Crown, rather than the Crown itself.[12] Most interesting is an image of the royal cortege disappearing through the crowd at Castle Hill, where Eton boys line the wall and a working-class man sells souvenir images of the royal pair in the foreground (Illus. 17). We cannot see the royals, but we don't need to see them: they are the focus around which the collective gathers, but they are not the spectacle itself. Instead, we have the crowd, made up of soldiers, schoolboys, gentlemen and ladies, police, and an African clutching a mandolin, all apparently united in celebration. Kilted musicians in the foreground remind us of Lorne's Scottishness, which mixes in here, as it does in wedding coverage generally, as a pleasing, homegrown exoticism, a mark of British cultural diversity and political unity.

In the midst of this hubbub, at the left margin, a woman returns the viewer's gaze as though she knows herself, alone in the crowd, to be the real object of public scrutiny – as well she might be, as she appears to be standing on a pair of stilts. Here is a kind of visual surplus, one merrymaker aware of the day's script and produced as if by the sheer counterforce of ideological iteration. If the other members of this crowd are absorbed in the spectacle itself, witnessing the scene with a certain unthinking complicity, this woman stares out from the margins with self-awareness, a possible model for and invitation to critical distance, the 'theatricality' that Tracy Davis identifies as a spectatorial stance.[13] Here is a rare moment in which the viewer, most often described and inscribed as docile, is invited to 'act back', something anti-revolutionary wedding coverage generally discouraged in its promotion of uncritical unification.

À Paris: coup de théâtre

This idea of a unified, disciplined nation that is (almost seamlessly) embodied by the Windsor crowd finds its undoing in the French mob that haunts its construction. Indeed, the most amazing thing about the 'Paris Mob' as English newspapers describe it is that it ever managed to take over the city at all. The mob is mindless, irrational, leaderless and absolutely chaotic. What appears to frighten English journalists most is the almost complete illegibility of the mob: 'no one can say what, from fright or desperation or sheer inability to stand still, they may do.'[14]

Unlike the *pars pro toto* logic of the Windsor wedding crowd, this minority is completely unrepresentative of the nation and unable to act meaningfully or nationally. The mob is formless, huge, yet insignificant in all the ways that might count politically or socially because made up of so many nobodies. Indeed, this is what seems to gall English journalists the most: that 'no one' multiplied in any amount could equal someone (or something) in power. As *The Times* has it, with all the incredulity and outrage of a paper that on the facing page celebrates a wedding of England's ruling minority, 'They are a minority, *and yet they rule.*'[15] The *Illustrated London News* is similarly flummoxed: 'Such a spectacle as the past week presented has certainly never before been recorded in history – the utter abandonment by a Government of its capital . . . because a *small fraction* of the population, unsupported by so much as a *single representative* of its wealth, intelligence, and respectability, have risen in arms.'[16] The point here is that the mob by definition excludes both the singular *and* the representative subject, for it swallows up the unwashed and the uncivilized into its vast red maw, where they become a vicious hoard, massive yet oddly miniaturized, incapable of individual thought or feeling, and surely incapable of *national* thought or feeling. The mob's mastery of Paris causes *The Times* to question France's nationhood altogether: 'France does still claim to be, not an aggregate of Municipalities, but a nation, and yet what are we to say of France when such things as these are done at Paris ... no one knows how or why?'[17]

England's illustrated newspapers show the mob engaged in various acts of bloodshed and brutality. The mob turns on the bourgeoisie in the Place Vendome, as massed but indistinct bodies clash and scramble; it turns on General Chanzy, who looks out helplessly at the viewer from a great crowd of jostling bodies; and in Place Pigalle, it apparently battles itself, as the two sides of armed National Guardsmen are indistinguishable from one another.[18] When the actions of the mob are particularized, they are focused on its victims, singular and strangely familiar images of suffering taken from the stock poses of sensation fiction, theatre and journalism and designed to move the melodramatic Victorian imagination: a woman puts one hand to her brow and the other to the chest of a wounded man as she leans over his insensible body; a mother clutches her baby to her breast and extends one arm in panic; a young bourgeois clutches himself in fear as he is impressed by working-class roughs, his face registering the terror of the bourgeois individual swallowed by the mob.[19] While the image of the single individual, alone in the crowd and aware of her isolation, has been described as the quintessential representation of bourgeois sensibility, the press-gang image of the individual threatened with compulsory belonging should be considered its necessary corollary, the violent flipside to the fantasy of discriminating exclusion.[20]

While English representations of the French mob include all the things that one might expect – the shadow of the Terror, the fear of contagion, the rhetoric of instability, etc. – what seems all the more loathsome to English onlookers is the suggestion that the mob might be enjoying itself. Newspaper accounts return, again and again, to what is offered up as the bizarre spectacle of wartime crowds watching street-side theatrical performances or watching each other promenade through the streets with an air of carnival.[21] The mob comes to embody the confusions of the carnivalesque: 'Here are the rowdy Quarters in full possession of the whole city, mounting guard over its most fashionable resorts, pointing cannon into the houses of wealthy fathers of families ... *waving flags, beating drums, blowing bugles in an ostentatious manner*, and demeaning themselves generally in a fashion which must combine the pleasing sensation of gratified vanity with all the charm of novelty.'[22] What Lenin would later famously refer to as 'the festival of the oppressed' appears differently to *The Times* special correspondent: 'Paris resembles a vast madhouse.'[23] With 'a caravanserai of roving and hostile bands' in control of Paris, while the National Assembly met in Versailles's converted Theatre of the Château, France appears to the English eye as nothing short of insanely theatrical, in that term's most ostentatious, stagey and pejorative sense.[24]

By way of contrast, and in the triangulating spirit with which news reports consider the Anglo/Franco/Prussian connection, it is instructive to glance at the wedding-day coverage of Germany, which was celebrating the triumphant return of its warring monarch (and the husband of Victoria and Albert's oldest daughter, Victoria). *The Times* assures us that 'Nothing could be more decorous than the streets, and the enjoyment of the crowd was thoroughly Teutonic. It swayed calmly along on quadruple currents.'[25] Unlike the faceless, illegible and irrational French mob, the German crowd is 'cheerful rather than jovial' and 'Most of their faces showed calm reasoning satisfaction.'[26] Restraint is the order of the day, and *The Times* reports approvingly that 'Sovereign and subjects at Berlin were equally determined that their feelings should not run away with them . . . The enthusiasm is there, and it is genuine; but there is nothing noisy, nothing extravagant, above all things, nothing theatrical.'[27]

Ritual space

Nothing theatrical, extravagant, ostentatious: it sounds English. And, indeed, the English crowd at play is imagined as perfectly natural, filled with sincere feeling and 'natural' duty to the nation and royal family. The comparatist gambit that propped up this naturalness and sincerity at the expense of the theatrical, hysterical, abnormal and dangerous French continued in the weeks and months following the royal wedding, as the Paris Commune took over the governance of the city for seventy-two days and was then removed from power in a bloody massacre that left over 60,000 working-class Parisians dead.

One signature way that the English press, especially the illustrated press, continues to construct this comparison is by sustained focus on public gatherings, public ritual and the public buildings that in their magnitude, grandeur and civic purpose embody the 'people' and the nation. Here, for example, is the self-congratulation that greets Victoria's opening of the Royal Albert Hall in the week following Louise's wedding: 'Eight thousand well-dressed Englishmen and Englishwomen brought together, and no skirt damaged, no nerves shaken, no eager rush by six people to pass through an entrance meant only for one!'[28] The pinnacle of middle-class rational amusement, the Royal Albert Hall was designed 'for invention and discovery, for the achievements of genius, for all that addresses itself to the cultivated eye and ear' and dedicated to the late Prince consort's belief in 'order, unity, goodness, and happiness'.[29] Comparing the building to its French analogue, *The Times* declares that 'We may be comforted to reflect that if we have not such a building as the Palace of Industry in Paris, we have been spared the pain of lodging in it ten thousand triumphant invaders.'[30] If England's 'people, including all classes' have taken on a more 'public and common character', their communality is the sort that shakes no national nerve but rather steadies the national character.[31] The civilizing rituals of public life govern the behaviour of and unify England's citizens. The dowdiness of England's public buildings, long a source of anxiety and inferiority, is here embraced as the antidote to French flash and pretension. Here we have nothing extravagant, above all things, nothing theatrical.

Illustrations of the Royal Albert Hall are juxtaposed to the sumptuous public buildings of Paris occupied by armed 'invaders' (French, not German). Scenes of the English at public play are published side by side with images of Paris under siege and aflame. While English crowds enjoy the Second International Exhibition,

Derby Day, and various other amusements, the Tuilleries burn and the Biblio-thèque Nationale is destroyed. Nowhere perhaps is the juxtaposition clearer than in a pair of *Illustrated London News* crowd scenes from London and Paris museums: in one, the rational English crowd amuses itself at the South Kensington Museum; in the second, a woman is shot outside the Louvre for spreading petroleum. I take these images to be the culmination of a visual argument about the national use of public space. The ideologically charged space of the public museum, on which rested national hopes for the civilizing education of the masses, becomes here both a decorous playground for the English lower and middle classes, who talk and flirt and look within this secular temple, and a literal backdrop for French violence.[32] The South Kensington Museum, which later became the Victoria and Albert Museum, was key to the English programme for mass education, class paci-fication and crowd control, and its collection of 'fine arts applied to industry' made it a particularly English enterprise. The Louvre, on the other hand, was an icon of French national identity, tied as it was to revolutionary history and to the French assumption of aesthetic and cultural superiority.[33] Turning the Louvre back into a symbol for lawless revolution (rather than, say, the democratization of art in France after the fall of the *ancien régime*), the *Illustrated London News* associates it with *les pétroleuses*, the female arsonists who became the Commune's most potent symbols of revolutionary fervour and civilization gone bad.[34] While London's public spaces host the rituals of nation building and the enactment of public collectivity, Paris witnesses the spectacle of its own disintegration and demise.

These spaces are not only stages for class ritual and national action, but they are also performative in a more deeply interpellative sense. Public buildings such as these intend and mould action. They call forth the subjects who inhabit them. Even unoccupied, they embody a dream of collective behaviour. These theatres of activity, in other words, are both hosts to and agents of performance, and not any less so in their ideologically charged newspaper representations, which themselves create (national) realities.

With its usual bluntness, *Punch* captures the binary logic by which England is the rational obverse of France and through which the English press sought to create, far more than to represent, national unity. In a diptych called 'Two Fire Engines', the mechanics of national fantasy are laid bare. In one image, French soldiers fire into Paris in a scene that looks like many other realistic depictions of the civil war; in its allegorical companion piece, Britannia commands a hose brigade made up of representatives of every class (and including Benjamin Disraeli), who together douse a crowd carrying banners that read 'Republic League London' and 'Vive la Commune'.[35] Such images teach English readers a 'French Lesson', as a *Punch* cartoon has it, and allow them to misrecognize their own connection to France and to French crowds.

Festival of the repressed

The public relations campaign that took place during the spring of 1871, juxta-posing England's royal wedding and other public rituals with the events in Paris,

Illustration 18 'Whit Monday at the South Kensington Museum', *Illustrated London News*, 10 June 1871, p. 553.

yielded an image of the English unified in the national performance of pleasure. While Queen Victoria is often portrayed as a kind of Victorian superego – the strict mother of the nation and the royal lid on the rampant id of 'other' Victorians – she appears in the spring of 1871 not only as the mother of the bride (walking Louise down the aisle herself) but also as the mother of enjoyment, urging her subjects towards serious pleasure and rational play. But what is the political and national psychology behind this imperative to enjoy, which, like any imperative, includes a certain incipient violence?

REGISTERED AT THE GENERAL POST-OFFICE FOR TRANSMISSION ABROAD.

4.—VOL. LVIII.   SATURDAY, JUNE 10, 1871.   PRICE FIVEPENCE
BY POST, 5½D.

Illustration 19 'The Late Events in Paris: A Woman Shot at the Louvre for Spreading Petroleum', *Illustrated London News*, 10 June 1871, p. 557.

PUNCH, OR THE LONDON CHARIVARI.—April 8, 1871.

A FRENCH LESSON.

Britannia. "IS *THAT* THE SORT OF THING YOU WANT, YOU LITTLE IDIOT?"

Illustration 20 'A French Lesson', *Punch*, 8 April 1871, p. 141.

The violent overthrow of authority in France was not, ultimately, discon-
nected from the docile performance of national approval that occurred simultaneously in England. Rather than the lawless opposite of the lawful English
crowd, the Parisian 'mob' is ultimately the obverse (not the contradiction) of those
acting out England's own festive imperative. The carnival crowds on Paris streets
should therefore be seen not as the illegible opposite of England's disciplined

Illustration 21   'Street Scene in Bordeaux', *Illustrated London News*, 25 March 1871, p. 301.

subjects, but as a kind of apotheosis of national enjoyment, a French mirror from which England could gaze back upon itself. Small wonder, then, that the English public relations machine worked overtime to advertise and occlude this reflective identity.

We see a trace of this festive imperative at work in an *Illustrated London News* image of a crowd gathered on the street in Bordeaux, where National Guardsmen, provincial *Gardes Mobiles*, and regular Army troops prepare to march on Paris. In the centre, a stationery peddler sells paper and ink for soldiers to write home to their families. In the front right, a mother attends to her young son. In the background, a female performer stands upon a man's shoulders and juggles gilt balls in the air. This is a scene of conscription, and not just the military kind. Around the tools for its own inscription – the sentimental letters home penned by those in service of the state – the French crowd gathers as an object lesson in carnivalized nationhood, the bizarrely theatrical nature of the scene underscoring – and hopefully erasing by outdoing – the ritual theatre of life on the other side of the channel, where the English crowd is compulsively (and compulsorily) bid to perform.

Here, in this lurking circus performer, is another kind of performative surplus. Like the Windsor stilt-walker, hers is an odd body out that reminds us how theatrical, how staged are the performances of public life. But unlike that previous woman, who met our gaze almost confrontationally, daring us to a critical awareness of the scene and our place in it, this juggler as performing object does little, to my mind, to challenge the English reader's self-conception. She may be theatrical, in other words, but she does not produce theatricality in the viewer, who is invited to see French life – not his own – as underwritten at various social levels by the instabilities of carnival. (Something along the lines of 'France, what a circus!') It is for the English reader to feel, once again and with all the force of ideological necessity, that it is the French who have been caught in the act.

Collecting the nation

French and English crowds operated as potent symbols for the national collective. Their representation performed the work of national fantasy, allowing the Victorians to recognize and misrecognize their own complicated relation to the nation-state, as it allowed them to work through the related issues of communal affect and disciplinary individualism. Wedding crowds and the revolutionary mob, while played off each other, function similarly as representative crowds, removed from daily life by extraordinary circumstance but nonetheless indicative of national character and desire. With only the rare exception, London's papers either drew readers into the crowd, as was the case with the royal wedding, or asked them to discriminate themselves from the mob, as with the Commune. Such representations provided a tutorial in aggregate identity, a tutorial that continued in other guises as these national events were merchandized to a public hungry both for collective experience and the experience of collecting.[36] The ephemeral performance of the crowd took shape in the material afterlife of commodity culture.

Royal collectibles performed the symbolic work of nation making, and the royal weddings of the Victorian period presented England with grand and festive opportunities to collect itself, in most senses of that phrase. Not only did these occasions prompt an almost hysterical display of national togetherness – the people collected around and for the wedding of one of their 'own' children – but they also allowed the nation to gaze at its own, collectible, reflection. We have already seen that reflection in the wedding crowds themselves, touted over and over in the public press as representing the national collective. We see it also in the official collection of wedding presents that was offered both on public display and in the pages of the illustrated news for voyeuristic consumption; and we see it in the commemorative items that were sold to the public in honour of the occasion.

These overlapping forms of collection express national fantasies of and about Victorian England, from the image of the unified 'family' coming together in communal good will and celebration to the idea that collecting commodities allows one to participate in the larger and communal life of culture. To collect commodities is in this instance to collect as a nation, to cohere as a people. But it is also to adhere around an experience of exclusion, as the traditional display of royal wedding gifts makes abundantly clear: these expensive luxury items are on limited view to a public that can never hope to own them. What is at stake in the museum-like display of these gifts, given as they are both to 'the nation' and to the 'private' couple whose wedding is both state ceremony and (as the newspapers insist) romantic event? How does a nation of shop-goers participate in this ceremony by collecting their own bit of it? Such collections massage, even while they magnify, the separation between the 'individual' citizen and the royals, as well as the distance between the 'people' and the nation-state that the royal family uneasily represents. The collectible souvenir – the commemorative tea cup, or spoon, or print – allows the purchaser to remember, even as they forget, their own place in the exalted pageant of state. It is in this space between memory and forgetting that the nation collects itself.

If the nation is not just a place, an imagined community, but a set of collective practices, or ritualized performances, then viewing the royals in celebration was an important and identifying practice. Viewing their *things* was equally important. Plunkett stresses the everydayness of royal media exposure, and I agree that quotidian practice is crucial, but so is the *specialness* of the royal wedding day. The role of the royals in nation making is not just a populist one whereby royal transparence and inclusiveness help construct collective identity. The royals also exist above and apart, and royal pageantry works to supercharge the everyday, to imbue the life of the nation with glamour, and to lift it into the realm of the sacred, with its own set of holy relics.

The interplay between national access and necessary distance is on display in the numbingly detailed coverage of the wedding presents received by Victorian royalty. In page after page of exhaustive description and visual image, illustrated newspapers like the *Graphic* and *Illustrated London News* publicly catalogued the gifts, from the silver and the plate to the jewels and the paintings and the gewgaws. Readers of the illustrated press enacted their participation and its limits by viewing the wedding presents on display in the newspaper, and particularly in such 'collectible' editions as the *Illustrated London News* special wedding number, or in the South Kensington Museum gift display and catalogue that literalized the archival quality of wedding news coverage.

It seems natural that royal gift display should take us back to the South Kensington, itself a space of what Carol Duncan calls 'civilizing ritual' and a monument to English crowd control. When English crowds in the spring of 1871 attended the South Kensington for a gander at the royal booty, they participated in such a ritual, collecting themselves around a collection of quasi-national artefacts. Somewhere between the Louvre's nationalizing of royal property and the Crown's gathering of a private hoard, the South Kensington show demonstrated both the public nature and the limits of English royal display. And, again, the important part of the collection was the crowd itself.

Can we connect these two forms of national collecting – as crowds and of materials – with the Victorian rage for royal wedding souvenirs? The most obvious connection is between these souvenirs and the royal wedding gifts. Here is the gift you give yourself. And, indeed, it is worth noting that souvenirs fall into the same basic categories as the wedding gifts: household objects, personal objects and adornment. It is less easy to see what these souvenirs, sold for individual purchase, have to do with the massed, national wedding crowds who filled London's streets, the nation's newspapers, and the national imagination. The default way of thinking of collectors, after the work of Baudrillard and Debord, is as isolated individuals, driven by serial acquisition and in thrall to the commodity spectacle that promises the unification it will never deliver.[37] But when it comes to the nation, isn't promise what it's all about? Where do we draw the line between national fantasy and political reality? If fantasy is its own political performance, then the collection of royal souvenirs is a fantastic investment in the idea of the nation as space and practice. Like massing in the streets, purchasing mass-produced royal commemoratives is a performance of collectivity, of belonging. You own a bit of the royals but also declare your citizenship within the nation every time you gaze upon your collectible portraits of the wedding couple, perhaps purchased in Windsor from the street vendor in Illus. 17, or mark your triple-decker novel with a silk Louise and Lorne wedding bookmark. This last commemorative suggests how royal spectacle might be tied to the nation's favourite and most binding ritual: serialized reading. Just as the bookmark's owner participates vicariously in national celebration, Louise and Lorne participate in the very private act of reading that collected the nation as a reading public and bound one individual reader to the next.

Of course, very few political institutions have been toppled by mobs brandishing silk bookmarks, and if individual purchase takes the potential mob out of the masses, so much the better for a nation petrified of revolution. While the English were buying up souvenirs of the royal wedding, they were also collecting the *other* must-have item for spring 1871: images of the Paris ruins, which were avidly sought by English buyers who made of them souvenirs of disaster.[38] Here was another way in which the grand buildings of Paris could provide a civilizing

No. 1656.—VOL. LVIII.   SATURDAY, JUNE 24, 1871.   PRICE FIVEPENCE
BY POST, 5½D.

RUINS OF PARIS.

Illustration 22   'The Ruins of Paris', *Illustrated London News*, 24 June 1871, p. 605.

ritual. Through the ritual of purchase, the site of recent violence was made into an aesthetic commodity, an instant antiquity rather than a present anxiety. The visual and material capture of Paris's ruins itself became a purchasable image when the *Illustrated London News* ran a cover illustration of French rubble in the process of being photographed.

Like the wedding merchandise with which I would like to link them, these *cartes des désastres* were offered for sale to the public as souvenirs, rather than as part of a collection, per se. The difference seems both crucial and obviated: crucial, in so far as the souvenir is an object of personal memory, something that takes its value from the affect of the owner and that points to the past, whereas the collection points only to itself, giving objects a new context in the present tense of their formal association; obviated, in so far as these souvenirs are part of a national collection that links individual owners through the practice of mass consumerism.[39] Here are objects that recall an event never witnessed, a place never visited, except in the imagination. They 'remember' events enjoyed vicariously. They mark an affective engagement that is personal only in so far as it is first national. They are, in other words, souvenirs that have personal power only if they belong to others also, which runs counter to the accepted logic of the 'rare' collectible. These artefacts assume a collective context both outside of and including the individual buyer, fostering the sense of shared experience and aggregate memory.

The Victorian desire to collect (both as a people and as individual collectors) around an image of national unity created its own form of exclusive populism, one that discriminated itself from the disastrous populism of France. The middle-class monarchs of Victoria's family were icons of both popular accessibility and royal glamour. I tend not to think of the collectors who invested in these icons, either emotionally or materially, as dupes, lulled into political passivity by the power of the commodity spectacle. I think of them instead as willing fantasists who made of royal commemoration a national and even quotidian practice. In such ritual performances as these, powerful in their very ordinariness, the Victorian nation collected and recollected itself.

By including in the term 'performance' a wide range of activities, my hope has been not to dull the term's specific use but to track its movements from the openly spectacular, political and communal into the everyday, material life of culture. I want, in other words, to follow the crowd home. If the main act I have been interested in is 'to collect', I have tried to put pressure on the many ways that might be done and to follow it onto the many stages where it takes place, from the city street to the museum hall, newspaper page and shop counter. The final regress of that move is more intimate, even, than the drawing rooms and curio cabinets of the domestic interior, for it lies within the subject who becomes, through acts of fantasy, consumption and belief, part of something larger than herself, something national, something ephemeral but nevertheless extremely powerful.

If we return in closing to the earlier image Louise and Lorne disappearing through the wedding crowd at Windsor, we will recall the man in the lower right corner hawking souvenir prints of the wedding pair (Illus. 17). Here is the collectible written into the fabric of the crowd experience, and here too is an English solution to French revolution. This worker, so similar to *Punch*'s allegorical figure of 'republicanism' (Illus. 20), has certainly learned his 'French lesson': he attends the pageant of state as the agent of its successful reproduction, catering to the spectators who together perform an act of union and communion. With his mouth wide open ('Louise and Lorne! Get your pictures here!'), he is a figure for public enunciation, saying, in the braying tones of commerce, what the nation would have him and all others say, that sweet and longed-for performative: 'I do.'

Notes

1. Emily Allen, 'Culinary Exhibition: Victorian Wedding Cakes and Royal Spectacle', *Victorian Studies* 45.3 (2003): 458–84.
2. The causes of the French civil war are too complicated to rehearse in any detail here, but the roughest outline of the conflict is as follows: following France's defeat by Germany in the Franco-Prussian war, the government led by Adolphe Thiers allowed German troops into Paris. Paris workers reacted in anger and the best part of the National Guard defected to form the Central Committee and take control of Paris. Thiers attempted unsuccessfully to disarm Paris and moved the National Assembly to Versailles. Civil war began on 18 March 1871. On 26 March, Paris elected a worker's government, the Paris Commune, which held the city until 21 May, when the French Army entered Paris and began the massacre of as many as 60,000 French citizens.
3. I use the terms England and English (as opposed to Britain or British) throughout because the London journals I discuss do so. Clearly, the addition of Lorne to Victoria's family makes visible the England/Britain split, which the representations I address ignore in favour of English/French competition. Lorne's Scottishness is everywhere in evidence as cultural diversity and touristic opportunity, but nowhere apparent as potential political strife.
4. On imagined communities, see Benedict Anderson's *Imagined Communities: Reflections on the Origin and Spread of Nationalism* (London and New York: Verso, 1983). On the formation of Victorian England's 'signifying' national crowds, see John Plotz, *The Crowd: British Literature and Public Politics* (Berkeley: University of California Press, 2000).
5. My focus here will be on the most visible and mainstream press organs: London's *Times*, *Illustrated London News* and *Graphic*. The radical and provincial press gave a different view of the events of 1871, which is outside of the scope of this essay.
6. The idea of the nation as a family with Victoria as both monarch and mother has been discussed in the many recent books that treat the Queen's image as public (and private) figure. See especially the essays in Margaret Homans's and Adrienne Munich's edited collection *Remaking Queen Victoria* (Cambridge: Cambridge University Press, 1997) and Margaret Homans's *Royal Representations: Queen Victoria and British Culture, 1837–1876* (Chicago: University of Chicago Press, 1998).
7. *Times*, 21 March 1871, 8.
8. Ibid.
9. *Times*, 22 March 1871, 9.
10. Ibid.
11. These images appeared in the *Illustrated London News* on the following dates: 'Marriage of Princess Louise: Leaving St. George's Chapel, Windsor', 1 April 1871 (316); 'The Long Walk: Windsor Park', 1 April 1871 (325); and 'The Newly Married Pair Receiving an Address of Welcome at Esher', 1 April 1871 (325).
12. John Plunkett, *Queen Victoria: Media Monarch* (Oxford: Oxford University Press, 2003).
13. In 'Theatricality and Civil Society' (*Theatricality*, ed. Tracy C. Davis and Thomas Postlewait [Cambridge: Cambridge University Press, 2003], 127–55) Davis takes this meaning of 'theatricality' from Thomas Carlyle's first uses of the neologism, coined, perfectly

enough for the purposes of this essay, in his *French Revolution* (1837). Davis defines theatricality as 'a spectator's dédoublement resulting from a sympathetic breach (active dissociation, alienation, self-reflexivity) effecting a critical stance toward an episode in the public sphere, included but not limited to theatre' (145), and writes that 'in public life . . . the onus for instigating this theatrical moment is on the spectator, who by failing to sympathize and instead commencing to think becomes the actor' (154). I take this *Illustrated London News* moment as one such, in which the viewer is invited to become a critical spectator of the royal pageant and her consuming role in it.

14. *Times*, 22 March 1871, 5.
15. Ibid., 9. My italics.
16. *Illustrated London News*, 1 April 1871, 306. My italics.
17. *Times*, 27 March 1871, 9.
18. See the *Illustrated London News*: 'The Conflict in Paris: Massacre at the Place Vendome', 1 April 1871 (328); 'Assault on General Chanzy', 1 April 1871 (329); and 'Encounter at the Place Pigalle', 1 April 1871 (329).
19. See the *Illustrated London News*: 'Return of the Wounded', 29 April 1871 (425); 'Shell at Suresnes', 29 April 1871 (413); and 'Impressment in the Streets of Paris for the Army of the Commune', 29 April 1871 (428).
20. As Peter Stallybrass and Allon White put it, 'There is no more easily recognizable scene of bourgeois pathos that the lonely crowd in which individual identity is achieved over against all the others, through the sad realization of not belonging. That moment . . . is as the very root of bourgeois identity' (*The Politics and Poetics of Transgression*, Ithaca: Cornell University Press, 1986), 187.
21. The carnivalesque has a long history both with political crowds and with people who write about them. While the topsy-turvy spirit of carnival may be taken for (or feared as) liberating, however, it is easily turned into a disciplinary spectacle, as the newspaper reports I quote make clear.
22. *Times*, 22 March 1871, 5. My italics.
23. *Times*, 23 March 1871, 9.
24. Ibid.
25. *Times*, 21 March 1871, 10.
26. Ibid.
27. *Times*, 22 March 1871, 8.
28. *Times*, 30 March 1971, 9.
29. *Times*, 29 March 1871, 9.
30. Ibid.
31. Ibid.
32. On the public museum as a space of civilizing ritual, see especially Carol Duncan's *Civilizing Rituals: Inside Public Art Museums* (London and New York: Routledge, 1995). On Victorian museums particularly and the South Kensington in specific, see Barbara Black's *On Exhibit: Victorians and Their Museums* (Charlottesville: University Press of Virginia, 2000).
33. The Louvre is, of course, the former palace of French royalty, which was in 1793 opened as a public art institution by the revolutionary government. Its holdings were once the King's private art collection. See Duncan, 22–33, for the history of the Louvre and its status as paradigmatic public institution.
34. On les pétroleuses, see particularly Gail Gullickson's *Unruly Women of Paris: Images of the Commune* (Ithaca: Cornell University Press, 1996).
35. 'Two Fire-Engines' can be found in *Punch*, 60 (10 June 1871): 236–7.
36. It should be noted that Queen Victoria herself was an avid collector and a model for the nation's collecting passion. See Gail Turley Houston's *Royalties: the Queen and Victorian Writers* (Charlottesville: University of Virginia Press, 1999).
37. Jean Baudrillard, *The System of Objects* (London: Verso, 1996 [1968]) and Guy Debord *The Society of Spectacle* (London: Verso, 1990). My ideas about collections and souvenirs

have been most influenced by Susan Stewart's *On Longing: Narratives of the Miniature, the Gigantic, the Souvenir, the Collection* (Durham, NC: Duke University Press, 1993). On commodity culture more generally, I am indebted to Thomas Richard's *The Commodity Culture of Victorian England: Advertising and Spectacle, 1851–1914* (Stanford: Stanford University Press, 1990).

38. On photographing and merchandizing the Commune, see Alisa Luxenberg, 'Creating "Désastres": Andrieu's Photographs of Urban Ruins in the Paris of 1871' (*Art Bulletin*, 80.1, (March 1998): 113–38) and Jeannene M. Przyblyski, 'Moving Pictures: Photography, Narrative, and the Paris Commune of 1871' (*Cinema and the Invention of Modern Life*, ed. Leo Charney and Vanessa R. Schwartz [Berkeley: University of California Press, 1995], 253–78).

39. For this distinction between the souvenir and the collection, see Stewart, 132–67.

4

George Edwardes and Musical Comedy: the Transformation of London Theatre and Society, 1878–1914

Thomas Postlewait

I

On the evening of 26 November 1911 most of the leading members of the London theatre establishment gathered at the Savoy Hotel for a banquet – a 'Jubilee' to honour George Edwardes, the lessee/manager of three West End theatres: the Gaiety, Daly's and, most recently, the Adelphi. Musical comedies, which had charmed the Edwardian age, reigned supreme at all three theatres. Close to two hundred people, 'representing the highest and best traditions of the stage', packed the dining room: 'managers, actor-managers, actors, dramatists, critics, and famous theatre patrons'.[1] The chairman for the event was Sir Herbert Beerbohm Tree of His Majesty's Theatre. Sir George Alexander of St James's Theatre served as the vice-chairman.

Tree commended Edwardes for his 'happy record of twenty-five years' management' in the West End theatres (99), and he praised Edwardes's ability to run three theatres and to manage the many world tours of his productions. Reflecting upon his own responsibilities at His Majesty's Theatre, Tree said: 'I know what it is to manage one theatre; what must it be to manage three?' (100). In an apparent spirit of mischief, Tree made a few jokes about Edwardes and the famous Gaiety girls of the musical comedies. Then, after praising the 'beauty' of Edwardes's theatrical productions (and making a bad joke about Edwardes laying his hands on beauty), Tree commented upon Edwardes's prosperity, his modesty, and his success in horse racing, for his horse Santoi had won the Ascot Gold Cup in 1901. He then bestowed on Edwardes another gold cup, which he identified as a 'loving-cup of friendship' (100).

In response, Edwardes downplayed his accomplishments, which he characterized as merely 'making a living in the theatre. An honest living, I hope' (101). He did not name his many successes in musical comedy, including *The Shop Girl*, *The Geisha*, *San Toy*, *The Toreador*, *Veronique*, *The Merry Widow*, *Our Miss Gibbs* and *The Quaker Girl*. Instead, in a self-deprecating manner, he noted that his 'class of entertainment' lacked the importance of Tree's Shakespearean productions. He made fun of his occasional attempts to write and produce social comedies and serious plays. Unlike Alexander, who had established his reputation with the works of Oscar Wilde and Arthur Wing Pinero, Edwardes had achieved his success in the 'play with music', which, he felt compelled to explain, did not appeal to people who wanted the theatre to 'improve our minds' (101). After this demonstration of modesty (and perhaps forced deference to Tree and Alexander), he defended his accomplishments, for he believed that the 'musical play' had actually done much 'for the art of the theatre':

> If the energies and activities I have given to the theatre have not been misspent, if I have cultivated my own little patch in the world of the theatre to some use and advantage, then I am satisfied. I have attempted nothing more, nothing less. I hope I may say for this Cinderella of the drama that it is a little better cared for, better housed, most considerably treated, better dressed than it used to be in the old days.
>
> (101)

Concluding his speech, Edwardes thanked Tree and Alexander for the Jubilee: 'To you, Sir Herbert Tree, I am indeed grateful for the signal compliment you have paid me in presiding at this dinner . . . and to you, gentlemen, one and all, who have paid me the honour to come here I feel myself greatly indebted for an evening you have made memorable for me. It has been worth waiting twenty-five years for!'[2]

The Jubilee ceremony, which displayed certain contradictory aspects of George Edwardes's theatrical reputation and social standing in the West End community, provides a convenient touchstone for an investigation of not only Edwardes's career but also the place of musical comedy in our histories of British theatre. In recent years musical comedy has received attention from a few musicologists, most notably Kurt Gänzl.[3] It has also been investigated for its social and cultural significance by Peter Bailey and Len Platt.[4] But with rare exceptions theatre historians have shown little interest in this popular form of entertainment. It has remained marginal to our histories of modern British theatre. And Edwardes, who was celebrated in the 1950s by W. Macqueen-Pope in his series of nostalgaic books about the late Victorian and Edwardian theatre, is now represented in negative terms by most theatre scholars. The historical challenge, then, is to understand not only why Edwardes was being honoured in 1911 but also why his reputation has experienced a major reversal, from high praise at mid-century to dismissal and even indictment today.

II

Who, then, was George Edwardes? What did he actually contribute to the British theatre? In his time, Edwardes was widely known as the 'Gov'nor', the man who created the amazingly popular musical shows at the Gaiety and Daly's, from the early 1890s to 1914. No other entrepreneur, impresario, actor-manager or playwright came even close to this popular success. Besides crafting the shows in rehearsal, he (1) oversaw a creative team of writers, lyricists and musical composers, (2) employed and managed several hundred employees, (3) controlled hundreds of musicians and performers through contracts, (4) launched and helped to maintain the careers of some of the most popular stars of the era, (5) renovated several West End theatres, (6) built several new theatres, (7) formed business partnerships that integrated the various elements of the entertainment package, and (8) organized tours of shows that travelled the world. Because of the provincial and world tours, the musicals spread to cities large and small, generating the profits that sustained Edwardes's production system. Some of the productions travelled for years, not only through the British Isles but in Europe, the United States, Australia, New Zealand and South Africa.[5]

Unlike some theatre producers who specialized in financial management (e.g. Oswald Stoll who built the Coliseum), Edwardes not only oversaw all business matters (e.g. owning, leasing and building theatres, hiring staff, commissioning productions and arranging tours) but also guided the production teams, making many of the decisions on casting, design, costume, script revision and final rehearsals. This comprehensive involvement in all phases of theatre distinguished him, on the one hand, from the actor-managers (e.g. Tree and Alexander) who oversaw production at one theatre, and, on the other hand, from the theatre entrepreneurs (e.g. the Gatti family) who often controlled more than one theatre but had little or nothing to do with the details of production. Consequently, though Edwardes attained great success as a theatre entrepreneur, he did not develop the kind of capital partnership and limited liability company that Oswald Stoll and others created before the war and expanded after the war. Instead, by joining the artistic director to the entrepreneur, Edwardes tried to serve two distinct principles of West End theatre. This balancing act is also part of the story of Edwardes and the kind of theatre enterprise that he developed and maintained.

He began his career as an assistant manager with Richard D'Oyly Carte in the late 1870s, staging the Gilbert and Sullivan operettas. Then in 1885 he established a joint-partnership of the Gaiety Theatre with John Hollingshead. A year later he became the owner of the Gaiety, where he presented farcical burlesques for a few years. Between 1885 and 1892 he managed and produced close to a dozen productions of the 'new burlesque', featuring not only Nellie Farren and Fred Leslie, the dominant stars of Gaiety theatre burlesques, but also two new stars, Seymour Hicks and Ellaline Terriss. Then in a two-year period, 1892–1893, he created the first of his new musicals, *In Town* and *A Gaiety Girl*, which had long runs at the Prince of Wales's, thereby launching a popular revolution in the theatre. For the next twenty years, beginning with *The Shop Girl* in 1894, he staged a series of light-hearted musical comedies at both the old and new Gaiety Theatre. Also, in 1895 he took over Daly's Theatre, where he created sophisticated musical comedies, beginning with *An Artist's Model* (1895), *The Geisha* (1896), *A Greek Slave* (1898) and *San Toy* (1899). In 1910, while still running productions at the Gaiety and Daly's, he acquired the Adelphi Theatre, which served as a special venue for featuring Gertie Millar in several musicals, with music by Lionel Monckton.

The Gaiety and Daly's were the home for many productions, but Edwardes also took over other theatres in order to accommodate long runs. For example, in the period between 1902 and 1904 he also had productions running at the Apollo, the Prince of Wales's, the Comedy and the Lyric. During a twenty-year period he managed, leased or owned not only these six theatres but also Shaftesbury, Terry's, Opéra Comique, Hicks and the Vaudeville for specific productions. He thus produced entertainment in over 25 per cent of the West End theatres. Also, between 1887 and 1908 Edwardes co-owned and managed the Empire Theatre of Varieties in Leicester Square. He was the very model of the modern theatre entrepreneur, the empire builder of musical entertainment. In sum, for thirty years (1885–1915) he was the most successful producer of theatre in London, with over sixty musical productions (see Table 1). Thirty-one productions had at least 300 performances. Amazingly, only three ran for less than 100 performances.

The length of each run, as listed in Table 1, includes the occasional transfer to other theatre buildings during the extended run in London, but the perform-ance numbers do not count the many revivals and tours in Great Britain, France, Germany, USA, Canada, Australia, India, etc. Some productions toured for a decade or longer. Touring was a major component of Edwardes's entertainment empire; many of his productions toured in England, Wales and Scotland. And some production companies toured to the empire (e.g. Australia, South Africa). Edwardes also worked in tandem with various producers, such as Charles Frohman in New York City. The NYC productions, for example, often had long runs. Sometimes key London performers would transfer with the production, but the New York productions were usually adapted in libretto and songs to accommodate the star appeal of American performers and the perceived tastes of New York audiences.[6]

The pattern of long-running productions offers an impressive record of busi-ness success. But they are important not simply as commercial ventures but also as aesthetic achievements, for Edwardes created new kinds of popular entertain-ment. Between 1885 and 1892 he had a hand in creating the 'new burlesque' that brought the middle class into the old Gaiety Theatre. And then, with his talented production teams – featuring the composers and song writers Sidney Jones, F. Osmond Carr, Ivan Caryll, Lionel Monckton and Paul Rubens, and the librettists and lyricists 'Owen Hall' [James Davis], James T. Tanner, Harry Nicholls, Adrian Ross, George Grossmith, Jr., Basil Hood, Harry Greenbank and Percy Green-bank – Edwardes put a new type of musical comedy on the London stage.

The Edwardes musical comedy was derivative in some of its elements yet quite new in its overall style. It took elements from operetta, burlesque, French vaudeville, opéra-comique, music hall routines, and popular song, then trans-formed them into a new musical entity. As John Hollingshead proclaimed in 1903: 'The invention or discovery of Musical Comedy was a happy inspiration of Mr. George Edwardes's.'[7] As early as 1895, William Archer, the theatre critic and translator of Ibsen's drama, took notice of a new development:

I have a very sincere liking for the class of entertainment to which *An Artist's Model* belongs. As it began with *In Town*, I presume we may assign to Mr.

Table 1   George Edwardes: musical productions from 1885 to 1915

Work	Theatre	Number of performances	Opening date	Type[8]
Little Jack Sheppard	Gaiety	55	26 Dec. 1885	Burlesque
Dorothy	Gaiety	931	25 Sept. 1886	Musical comedy
Monte Cristo Jr.	Gaiety	166	23 Dec. 1886	Burlesque
Miss Esmeralda, or The Monkey and the Monk	Gaiety	87	8 Oct. 1887	Burlesque
Frankenstein, or The Vampire's Victim	Gaiety	110	24 Dec. 1887	Burlesque
Faust Up-To-Date	Gaiety	188	30 Oct. 1888	Burlesque
Ruy Blas and the Blasé Roué	Gaiety	282	21 Sept. 1889	Burlesque
Carmen Up-To-Data	Gaiety	248	4 Oct. 1890	Burlesque
Joan of Arc	Opéra Comique	181	17 Jan. 1891	Burlesque
A Pantomime Rehearsal	Terry's	438	6 June 1891	Burlesque
Joan of Arc, 2nd edition	Gaiety/Shaftesbury	106	30 Sept. 1891	Burlesque
Cinder-Ellen Up Too Late	Gaiety	314	24 Dec. 1891	Burlesque
In Town	Prince of Wales	292	5 Oct. 1892	Musical farce
A Gaiety Girl	Prince of Wales	413	14 Oct. 1893	Musical comedy
Don Juan	Gaiety	221	28 Oct. 1893	Burlesque
His Excellency	Lyric	161	27 Oct. 1894	Light opera
The Shop Girl	Gaiety	546	24 Nov.1894	Musical comedy
Hansel and Gretel	Daly's	161	26 Dec. 1894	Fairy tale opera
An Artist's Model	Daly's	392	2 Feb. 1895	Musical comedy
The Geisha	Daly's	760	25 Apr.1896	Musical comedy
My Girl	Gaiety	183	13 July 1896	Musical comedy
The Circus Girl	Gaiety	497	5 Dec. 1896	Musical comedy
A Runaway Girl	Gaiety	593	21 May 1898	Musical comedy
A Greek Slave	Daly's	349	8 June 1898	Musical comedy
San Toy, or The Emperor's Own	Daly's	778	21 Oct. 1899	Musical comedy
The Messenger Boy	Gaiety	429	3 Feb. 1900	Musical comedy
The Toreador	Gaiety	675	17 June 1901	Musical comedy

Title	Venue	Date	Performances	Genre
Kitty Grey	Apollo	7 Sept. 1901	220	Musical comedy
A Country Girl	Daly's	18 Jan. 1902	729	Musical comedy
Three Little Maids	Apollo/Prince of Wales	20 May 1902	348	Musical comedy
The Girl from Kay's	Apollo/Comedy	15 Nov. 1902	432	Musical comedy
The School Girl	Prince of Wales	9 May 1903	333	Musical comedy
The Duchess of Dantzig	Lyric	17 Oct. 1903	236	'Light opera'
The Orchid	Gaiety	28 Oct. 1903	559	Musical comedy
The Cingalee (or Sunny Ceylon)	Daly's	5 Mar. 1904	365	Musical comedy
Veronique	Apollo	18 May 1904	495	Opéra-comique
Lady Madcap	Prince of Wales	17 Dec. 1904	354	Musical comedy
The Little Michus (Les P'tites Michu)	Daly's	29 Apr. 1905	401	Opéra-comique
The Spring Chicken	Gaiety	30 May 1905	401	'Comic opera'
The Little Cherub	Prince of Wales	13 Jan. 1906	114	Musical comedy
The Girl on the Stage	Prince of Wales	5 May 1906	29	Musical comedy
See See	Prince of Wales	20 June 1906	152	'Comic opera'
The New Aladdin	Gaiety	29 Sept.1906	203	Burlesque
The Lady Dandies (Les Merveilleuses)	Daly's	27 Oct. 1906	196	Opéra-comique
Two Naughty Boys	Gaiety	8–27 Jan. 1907	matinees only	Fairy tale musical
The Girls of Gottenburg	Gaiety	25 May 1907	303	Musical comedy
The Merry Widow (Die Lustige Witwe)	Daly's	8 June 1907	778	Comic operetta
A Waltz Dream (Ein Walzertraum)	Hicks	7 Mar. 1908	146	Comic operetta
Havana	Gaiety	25 Apr. 1908	221	'Comic opera'
The Dollar Princess (Die Dollar-prinzessin)	Daly's	24 Dec.1908	428	Comic operetta
Our Miss Gibbs	Gaiety	23 Jan. 1909	636	Musical comedy
The Girl in the Train (Die Geschiedene Frau)	Vaudeville	4 June 1910	340	Comic operetta

Table 1 (Continued)

Work	Theatre	Opening date	Number of performances	Type
The Quaker Girl	Adelphi	5 Nov. 1910	536	Musical comedy
Peggy	Gaiety	4 Mar. 1911	270	Musical comedy
The Count of Luxembourg (Der Graf von Luxemburg)	Daly's	20 May 1911	340	Comic operetta
The Sunshine Girl	Gaiety	24 Feb. 1912	336	Musical comedy
Autumn Manoeuvres (Ein Herbstmanöver)	Adelphi	25 May 1912	75	Comic operetta
Gipsy Love (Ziegeunerliebe)	Daly's	1 June 1912	299	Comic operetta
The Dancing Mistress	Adelphi	19 Oct. 1912	242	Musical comedy
The Girl on the Film (Filmzauber)	Gaiety	5 Apr. 1913	232	Musical comedy
The Marriage Market (Leányvásár)	Daly's	17 May 1913	423	Comic operetta
The Girl from Utah	Adelphi	18 Oct. 1913	195	Musical comedy
After the Girl	Gaiety	7 Feb. 1914	105	Musical comedy
Betty	Daly's	24 Apr. 1915	391	Musical comedy
The Maid of the Mountains[9]	Daly's	10 Feb. 1917	1,352	Comic operetta

Adrian Ross [the librettist] the credit of its invention. These musical farces are certainly an immense improvement on the old-fashioned burlesques and third-rate operettas which they have so largely supplanted. I believe there is a future before this admirably supple and adaptable art-form.[10]

Hollingshead and Archer alike, from two distinct perspectives on the London theatre, recognized that something special had occurred in the 1890s.

There seems to be scholarly accord on this point, for a century later in *150 Years of Popular Musical Theatre*, Andrew Lamb assures us that 'the credit for establishing modern-dress musical comedy as a specific genre belongs to London theatre manager George Edwardes.'[11] And from the perspective of Kurt Gänzl, the leading authority on British musical theatre, Edwardes was the supreme master of the form: 'One of the most important producers of musical plays in the history of the genre, Edwardes, by his activities at the end of the 19th and in the early 20th century, set styles and standards in the musical theatre throughout the world.'[12] This perspective is shared by Gerald Bordman, the major chronicler of the American musical. He points out that Edwardes provided the catalyst for the creation of the modern American musical: 'The influence of the Gaiety musicals, coupled with the vogue of American farce-comedy, led directly to modern musical comedy.'[13] For over two decades this new musical comedy at the Gaiety dominated the London theatre, with many imitators. In addition, Edwardes developed a more sophisticated and less farcical model of musical comedy at Daly's Theatre, from 1895 to 1904. Then as it began to trail off in popularity, he reinvigorated it by adapting opéra-comique from France (e.g., *Veronique*) and operetta from Austria and Hungary (e.g., *The Merry Widow, Leányvásár*). In the process of adapting the new tunes and plots, his team always created an English version that still delivered some of the familiar traits of the successful Daly's musical.

Far more than Henry Irving, Oscar Wilde or Bernard Shaw, Edwardes defines an entertainment era in London theatre. Yet while there are approximately thirty biographical studies of Irving, forty-five of Wilde and forty of Bernard Shaw, there is only one of George Edwardes, written by Ursula Bloom in 1954. It is a nostalgic, sentimental story of musicals and their stars (presented without documentation). Edwardes does appear regularly in histories of famous West End theatres. He is, necessarily, a key figure in W. Forbes-Winslow's *Daly's: the Biography of a Theatre* (1944) and W. Macqueen-Pope's *Gaiety, Theatre of Enchantment* (1949). And his name pops up in various anecdotal autobiographies and reminiscences, especially those of performers who worked at the Gaiety or Daly's, such as Seymour Hicks and Rutland Barrington. But in great measure he has disappeared from our histories of late Victorian and Edwardian theatre. If he is known today, it is usually because of his suspect reputation for two things: running the infamous Empire Theatre of Varieties, which had a balcony promenade that attracted prostitutes, and packaging the fetching 'Gaiety Girls' in elaborate costumes in the musicals. These two sexual matters are significant factors in his career, and they must be addressed; but they are hardly the definitive features of his contributions to British theatre and London society.

III

In order to recover the historical importance of George Edwardes and musical comedy in the late Victorian and Edwardian eras of London theatre, we need to consider both the positive and the negative versions of the man and the age. I start with the celebratory, often nostalgic versions that appeared before the 1960s. Then, in the spirit of equal representation, I will present the unsentimental, critical studies of recent decades. Only after both perspectives are presented will I attempt to put in place the basic groundwork for a third, alternative history of Edwardes, musical comedy, and the Edwardian theatre. This overview thus offers the initial terms for the kind of theatre history that we need to produce if we wish to do full justice to not only Edwardes and musical comedy but also London theatre in the modern era.

The positive representations of Edwardes show up not only in the theatre histories written before 1960 (e.g. Walter Macqueen-Pope, Ernest Short and A. E. Wilson) but also in anecdotal reports on London nightlife by people who lived in the late Victorian and Edwardian eras (e.g. the reminiscences of H. G. Hibbert and J. B. Booth). In addition, Edwardes appears in a number of the auto-biographies and biographies of the performers of the era, such as Seymour Hicks, Ellaline Terriss and Ada Reeve. These histories, memoirs and biographies tend to recall a lost age in the theatre. A steady refrain runs through them: once upon a time, a golden age of theatre and social order existed.

In *Twenty Shillings in a Pound*, W. Macqueen-Pope recalled those glorious days: 'George Edwardes had invented musical comedy. He gave shows which for quality, polish and workmanship cannot be matched today. Their memories and their music live on – the tunes of Ivan Caryll, Lionel Monckton, Sidney Jones, Paul Rubens and the rest of them, who filled the Golden Age with melodies which, if not classic, at least rank as true and chimed as melodiously as the golden sovereign itself.'[14] A. E. Wilson concurs; Edwardes and the age go hand in hand: 'He certainly made his stamp upon his time. Even now his name stands for a very definite species of entertainment – joyous, florid, tuneful, irresponsible, yet not without a measure of taste.'[15] In 1900, for example, all of London society gathered nightly for the pleasure of musical comedies at Daly's and the Gaiety Theatre. *San Toy* occupied Daly's from late 1899 to early 1902 for 778 performances. And at the Gaiety, *The Messenger*, which ran for 429 performances, had replaced *A Runaway Girl*, whose run was for 593 performances. No other London producer could match these popular successes, one after another.

Both Macqueen-Pope and Wilson point out that Edwardes carefully created two distinct types of musical comedies at the Gaiety and Daly's. In Wilson's words: 'The Daly's productions were nearer to genuine operetta, showing less robust humour, a more refined type of music, a closer attention to plot; whereas in the Gaiety productions the plot was always more sketchy and on more conventional lines, with a greater opportunity for the principals, more particularly the comedians, to display themselves in numbers irrelevant to whatever plot could be discerned' (213–14). Or as Macqueen-Pope succinctly defined the difference: 'The Gaiety sold laughter, Daly's sold Romance.'[16]

Both Macqueen-Pope and Wilson praise the display of beautiful women in musical comedy, especially 'those lovely ladies, the Gaiety girls'. Wilson has no reservations about those girls: 'It was a golden age for stage beauty, and the astute Edwardes, who had an unerring taste that way and a talent for spotting them, gathered the cream of them under his banner' (215). Costumed in the latest styles, they were the height of fashion. The chorus girls were carefully coached in their diction, their choice of clothes, their social etiquette, and their public behaviour. Under Edwardes's guidance, as Macqueen-Pope proclaimed, a refined sexuality was achieved.

The actresses who played the leading roles in musical comedy – Katie Seymour, Ellaline Terriss, Marie Tempest, Marie Studholme, Letty Lind, Rosie Boote, Topsy Sinden, Evie Greene, Gabrielle Ray, Phyllis and Zena Dare, Eva Stanford, Ethel Oliver, Florence Collingbourne, Lily Elsie and Gertie Millar – were blessed with not only great beauty but also charm and talent. Their fetching ability to deliver a song charmed the spectators and created a series of popular hits. The sales of sheet music skyrocketed. Consequently, an aura of stardom attended the beauty and talent of these actresses, who performed in spectacles of fairy-tale glamour. In this world of beauty and happiness, romance occurred on and off the stage. Several of the actresses and Gaiety Girls, in the spirit of impossible dreams, married into the nobility.

We must keep in mind, though, that the girls were beloved by all observers, male and female alike, not just by the young rakes or a few aged nobles. During the era, hundreds of thousands of postcards were sold of the actresses. 'Everyone seemed to collect them, the prime favourites being those of Marie Studholme, the Dare sisters, and Gabrielle Ray . . . Was there ever a lovelier example of fair English womanhood than gracious Marie Studholme? Or such piquant dainty prettiness as that of petite Gabrielle Ray?' (Wilson, 215). The magazines and newspapers regularly printed photographs of the actresses, dressed in the flowing dresses and hats of the era. And shop windows featured them, even though the actresses had little or nothing to do with the products being sold.

As the successful producer of the glamorous spectacles of beauty and music, Edwardes had the admiration of the spectators. He was also admired by most of the performers. In the words of Seymour Hicks, whose career began with Edwardes at the old Gaiety (before he and his wife Ellaline Terriss created their own series of musicals), Edwardes was the one who put all of the creative pieces together:

> There is no man living who can deal with any sort of theatrical problem in such a masterly manner as he can, no matter from which quarter of the compass the wind blows . . . His taste theatrically is unequalled, and while, like many of us, he may not always know what to do, he is a past master at knowing what not to do, which is, in our business, a most valuable asset . . . His judgment of artists is unerring.[17]

For Hicks and many others who worked for him, Edwardes was the creative genius of popular entertainment.

This is the judgement of Walter Macqueen-Pope (1888–1961), who worked in the London theatre during this period. No one has written about this golden era with more love and dedication.[18] 'Popie', as he was called, was a historian of the British stage, especially the London stage of stars and actor managers. In a series of books – including *Carriages at Eleven* (1947), *Twenty Shillings in the Pound* (1948), *Gaiety, Theatre of Enchantment* (1949), *Ghosts and Greasepaint: an Evocation of Yesterday and the Day Before* (1951), *Shirtfronts and Sables: a Story of the Days When Money Could Be Spent* (1953), *Pillars of Drury Lane* (1955), *Nights of Gladness* (1956), and *St. James's: Theatre of Distinction* (1958) – he recreated the lost world of late Victorian and Edwardian theatre and society. In these books as well as his television show, which older people watched with gratitude, Popie served as the collective voice of the lost heritage of the popular theatre.[19]

Looking back longingly at the lost era, Macqueen-Pope wrote: 'Those who live in our land today who did not know it before the year 1914, that fateful year of all years in history, have never known England...But before 1914, England...(or Great Britain as it is now called) was the greatest country in the world and when it was indeed worth while being a son or daughter of that fortunate land.'[20] In those days of proud sons and daughters, the experience of going out to the theatres offered not merely a night of entertainment. The fullness of the event delivered a way of life, a way of perceiving the wonders of London theatre and the glories of the city, country and empire, as Macqueen-Pope insisted:

> London in the days of King Edward VII was a city of smiles, the habitation of wealth, of peace, of security, and of power. London was an English city, speaking its own language, conscious that it was the centre of the whole world, that it called the tune and held the balance as the capital of the greatest Empire ever known. And that word Empire then meant what it said...The Empire was our god and Kipling was its prophet.[21]

A patriotic rhetoric runs through Maqueen-Pope's books: God bless the Empire, Edward VII and, not least of all, George Edwardes.

IV

Of course, for most of us today the imperial tone of this statement grates and grinds against our sensibilities. The sentiment comes across as an unappealing mixture of hyperbole, chauvinism and jingoism. Consequently, we may reject not only Macqueen-Pope's rhetoric but also his idea of the greatness of those golden days. That world is anything but golden to many historians today. From our perspective, there is much to criticize. We lament the failure of the West End establishment to take up and support the new drama of Ibsen, Shaw, Granville Barker, and the emerging women playwrights. We reject its class values and prejudices, with the actor-managers chasing after respectability and knighthoods. And we indict the actor-managers, mostly male, for their sexist treatment of women in the theatre. From our modernist perspective, the West End theatres failed almost completely to do justice to modernist culture and values. Beyond the theatres, there are additional reasons to reject the idea of a golden age.

One of the sharpest attacks on the West End theatre was presented by John Pick in *West End: Mismanagement and Snobbery* (1983). Pick criticizes the economic organization of West End theatres since the late Victorian age because of their 'luxurious and extravagant style of management' that has served an agenda of social snobbery and class prejudice.[22] In the process of making his indictment of the West End theatres and their actor-managers, Pick offers his own version of a lost golden age. Returning to mid-nineteenth-century theatre, he praises the 1843 Theatres Act because it allowed the theatres to re-establish a populist spirit in the London theatres. As in Shakespeare's age, he proclaims, common people attended and enjoyed the London theatres. But this opportunity for a truly populist entertainment was lost as commercialism took over. 'After 1865,' Pick explains, 'the ordinary folk who had, for a short time, enjoyed the new populist theatre, did not choose to take their pleasures elsewhere; they were, by a series of deliberate managerial decisions, excluded from the new respectable theatre of the later Victorian age' (11). The theatres of the West End, if not those of the surrounding neighbourhoods, turned away the ordinary folk. The leaders of this new West End theatre establishment 'took a delight in the enclosed world they inhabited, and kept financial records secret, their contractual arrangements private and their aims obscure' (12). These theatres, appealing to the tastes and values of the middle and upper classes, became the homes of snobbery and the abodes of philistines. Joining Henry Irving in his chase after a knighthood, the West End managements were driven by the ambition for respectability. Fashion, social status and commercialism became the organizing principles that guided these theatres. 'Between 1890 and 1914 the term "West End" became a synonym for high sophistication and expense, a term which could be used by advertisers to sell fashionable clothes, luxury, make-up, perfumes, and entertainment equally' (99). Spectators were taught to want the new refinements that theatre delivered. Not surprisingly, for Pick the spokesman for this corrupt world was Macqueen-Pope, 'whose theatre histories may be said not so much to analyze West End attitudes as to embody them' (100).[23]

Because of 'a club-like confidentiality' (12) in these commercial theatres, the working-class spectators disappeared from the West End. Where did they go? That story is yet another one of our historical narratives about the era, for if Pick and others have nothing positive to say about the West End theatres, they are quite prepared to celebrate the music halls, their performers and their audiences. But an overly neat opposition gets presented, with West End theatres attacked as representatives of elite culture and music halls celebrated as emblems of popular culture. West End commerce is evil, East End community is good. Though Jacky Bratton has warned against a sentimental celebration of popular culture and the folk in our studies of the music halls, the temptation has been hard to resist. Supposedly, the pure identity of the working class was expressed and realized in the halls. Bratton and Peter Bailey have cautioned us that the cultural politics of pleasure and leisure in the halls did not operate outside of commercial motives and procedures.[24] Necessarily, the halls were commercial enterprises for all involved – performers, employees, managers and property owners. And the halls had several identities, not just one. This fact was most obvious in the distinction between small-scale pub halls in the neighbourhoods and the big-business halls built in the city centre. As Bratton notes: 'At first the growth of halls provided a leisure service to growing urban populations, and enabled talented individuals to develop star careers and fortunes. [But] cultural change and aspiration, the broadening of the audience to include more segments of society, and concomitant moves to increase discipline and market control shifted power into the hands of business managers and investors.'[25]

One of those investors was George Edwardes. He helped to turn the entertainment world of the music hall into a capital venture for his own profit. So characterized, Edwardes is emblematic of everything wrong with the theatre of the era. Then and now, for many people Edwardes is identified as the notorious manager of the Empire Theatre of Varieties in Leicester Square. In 1894 a major controversy developed when the social reformer Laura Ormiston Chant campaigned against the relicensing of the Empire because of its reputation for the slight costumes of the ballet dancers and the parading prostitutes who would pick up customers on the infamous promenade at the back of the balcony. This battle between Chant and Edwardes became a tremendous public controversy, played out not only at the London County Council, which controlled theatre licences but also in the newspapers and magazines. For a few weeks, Chant succeeded in her campaign. The Empire was closed down and the promenade was boarded up. But Edwardes cunningly appealed to public sentiment, especially the men who wanted to protect their right to visit the theatre. Chant was identified as a sexual 'prude', and Edwardes successfully dramatized his battle for keeping the Empire open as a defence of liberty and individual rights. After a few months Edwardes had regained control of the Empire.[26]

In the eyes of most historians, Edwardes emerges from the Empire controversy as a theatre manager who exploited women – his dancers and the prostitutes – for profit. Driven by commercial considerations, he placed the sexual display of women at the centre of his enterprises. This image was reinforced by his practice of parading young, beautiful women in dozens of burlesques and musical comedies. Likewise, the librettos of the musical comedies featured young heroines who, because of their beauty, charm and youth, are rewarded with wonderful marriages. Flirting and frolicking, they excelled at the social skills of sexual conquest, just as Edwardes excelled at packaging sex. He was, in the words of social historian Peter Bailey, the entrepreneur who filled the stage with shows that 'celebrated the modern chorus girl'.[27]

Because Edwardes was 'the man most responsible for the exaltation of the woman as girl' (177), Bailey describes him as a chauvinistic businessman: 'Variously Svengali, martinet, snooper, and sugar daddy, George Edwardes is a more complex and darker figure than standard accounts allow' (178). Regimenting the chorus girls, who performed in well-designed production numbers year after year, he brought the order and efficiency of factory production to the world of entertainment. The Gaiety Girl, naughty but nice, was packaged, duplicated and 'routinised' as a sexual product and object. From Bailey's perspective, the orderly routines of musical comedy produced a cultural industry of mechanical girls, 'performing repetitious, standardized operations in a . . . closely supervised workplace' (178).

Thus, while Macqueen-Pope celebrated Edwardes and musical comedy in a sentimental manner, Bailey removed all sentiment from this popular entertainment which packaged sexual appeal as the chief product of the leisure industry: 'In musical comedy the bidding and dealing in sexual favours echo the speculative transactions of the market and the risks and rewards of the business deal. Thus sex itself is a resource or commodity like the nitrates, the oil, soap or pork that generated the spectacular new wealth of the era' (188). In a world increasingly under the sway of advertising and consumerism, Edwardes created a product that could be sold by clever publicity and gossip.

Joel Kaplan, in the new *Cambridge History of British Theatre*, fully agrees with Bailey's social critique. He makes the case for seeing Edwardes's production of *The Shop Girl*, which opened in 1894 and ran through 1895, as the quintessential theatrical embodiment of the modern consumer society. The shop-girl heroine, working in a modern department store, represented 'the period's commodity culture'. Sex and shopping went hand in hand: 'Such trajectories were central to the form, as the sumptuous replication of consumer goods became in the end an endorsement of the economic status quo.'[28] The Edwardes musical, by exploiting the figure of the liberated women while yet presenting her as a 'girl', achieved the 'commodification' of sexual identity. Attending the theatre, the London spectators participated in a commercial experience delivered by the sexual appeal of the girls.

V

Although I agree that popular entertainment should be placed in the contexts of social institutions, commercial culture, capitalism, popular values, leisure culture and political conditions in Victorian and Edwardian England, I find this critique of musical comedy too reductive.[29] Such critiques, though often insightful about certain kinds of social attitudes and institutional practices that operate in popular culture (e.g. social codes for gender representation in the fashion world and the commercial theatre), do not explain sufficiently how and why these entertainments supposedly contributed to the maintenance of the traditional orders. Nor do such critiques of capitalist practices address the fact that social change and transformation, not just maintenance of the old order and its values, operated in the popular culture and entertainment. Moreover, the artistic qualities of musical comedy and the particular talents of the performers disappear in this kind of social analysis. And the aesthetic pleasures and judgements of the creators and spectators alike are not just ignored but systematically denied.

If we have any hope of understanding who George Edwardes was and what he accomplished, we need to acknowledge, first of all, that he produced popular entertainment that pleased a generation of spectators from all classes. Our descriptive terminology, our analytical categories and our historical understanding must begin with some basic aesthetic facts. Musical comedy, phenomenally successful and appealing, was a major artistic development, a new genre which has continued to grow and appeal throughout the twentieth century. The librettists and composers were very good at their artistic jobs. The productions achieved high artistic standards in design and performance. The charming and clever performers were the best of their types – and that is saying something for London was blessed with many accomplished singers and comedians during this era. So, despite the analysis of Edwardes as the purveyor of 'brokered sex', as Peter Bailey succinctly defines his business practices, musical comedy was not merely the delivery system of a commercial enterprise of sexual representation and exploitation. Bailey is not wrong about the sexual motifs, for the productions at the Gaiety Theatre always had a sexual component and appeal. But the Edwardes productions were much more than just a parade of beautiful women.

In our social critiques, we have often failed to capture the innovative, liberating energy of this entertainment which helped to realign the processes of urbanization and democratization. We have failed to investigate the organizational and business practices of Edwardes's theatres, the Gaiety and Daly's. And we have failed to describe the place of Edwardes, who was not an actor-manager, in the commercial developments and transformations in the West End. Yes, those department stores on stage in the musicals may have served certain capitalist ventures, but for the spectators who flocked to both the theatres and the department stores, the experience contributed to an accelerated, exciting and liberating process of change and empowerment in a new modern environment of metropolitan life. We are blind to the nature of urban activity, in a city like London, if we reduce the experiences and opportunities of millions of people, with all kinds of energy and drives, to a formula about the ideological hegemony and control of capitalism. The practices and consequences of musical entertainment are far more interesting and complex than the making of regulated products of sexual identity. By focusing rather exclusively on the gender issues, to the exclusion of other key factors in the making of not only theatre and culture but also new attitudes and values, we have failed to understand George Edwardes, musical comedy, the West End theatre district, and the social, economic and political contexts for the era.[30]

VI

Interestingly, Peter Bailey himself, in a recent essay, provides a way to move beyond the either/or polarities that have predominated in our descriptions and analysis of Edwardes and musical comedy. He grants that scholarship on Edwardian popular entertainment has, with few exceptions, been either a celebration of 'the legends of some prelapsarian golden age (bourgeois or populist)' or an assault on 'the vapid products of a capitalist mass culture'.[31] Bailey also recognizes that for most theatre historians today the era is only important because of its 'New Drama', which is seen as the modernist alternative to the conservative West End theatre. But Bailey urges us to rethink our idea of modernity, for he wants to argue that the popular entertainment, such as Edwardes's musical comedy, generated its own dialectical responses to the modern world.

Bailey suggests that musical comedy achieved 'a popular modernism that was the dynamic complement to that of the avant-garde' (6). His essay, which attempts to spell out the theoretical basis for this claim, is based upon the familiar proposition that modernism in the arts is a response to the processes of modernization in Western society. Modernity is the short-hand name for various developments of mass society in the industrial world: new technologies, new modes of communication, urbanization, corporate business practices, consumerism, bourgeois society, growing bureaucracies, democratic movements, the transformations of the national state, and imperialist governmental policies. Romanticism offered one response (e.g. the return to nature as expressed by Wordsworth, Chateaubriand and Thoreau); modernism offered another response (e.g. a direct assault on these developments as expressed by the drama of Ibsen, Strindberg, Shaw and Wedekind). This basic understanding, though informative, is still tied, all too often, to the oppositional narrative of the culture of commerce versus the culture of rebellion.

So how, where and why does musical comedy, as a model of popular entertainment, find a place in modernity? Ironically, some of the very traits that Bailey had criticized previously, such as the representation of gender and sexuality in the display of the Gaiety Girl, serve to qualify musical comedy as an important voice in the development of modernity. Musical comedy, he is prepared to argue, contributed to the emergence of the new woman, including the changing economic conditions for some women. This possibility had already emerged in his previous study of musical comedy. After reducing the Gaiety Girl to a sexual commodity, packaged and standardized by Edwardes, Bailey wrote a concluding statement in his 1998 essay that began to oppose his basic argument. He declared that musical comedy may have stimulated 'new imaginative gains for women in a more overtly sexualized identity that was no longer merely hostage to the designs of men'.[32] I would suggest that these gains, however imaginative they may have been on stage, were acted out in the lives of thousands upon thousands of women spectators. When we let go of our regimented versions of modernity, we may begin to see a far more complex development – for women and everyone else. And these musicals, which featured a range of working-class, middle-class and upper-class women, from plot to plot, offered some intriguing – and problematic – versions of social mobility, opportunity and uncertainty that the women in the audience, from shop girls to well-heeled society women, responded to and applied to their own lives. The challenge is to take the measure of this complex dynamic of representation, recognition and response. Instead of dismissing the shop girl, as presented on stage, we need to acknowledge and even respect those many different kinds of shop girls among the spectators.

Bailey admits as much. He now calls for new scholarship on musical comedy that will engage with the contradictory conditions of modernity, especially the energy released by urbanization, new job opportunities and 'new institutions trading in various forms of leisure, entertainment and consumption' (7). Although still committed to an analysis of capitalist control, he notes that musical comedy, more than the avant garde drama, captured the qualities of modern city life in its representations of everyday experiences, especially for women. Musical comedy 'legitimized the new social fact of women abroad in public spaces' (14). I agree, but I would add that a new conception of social roles and personal identity was being developed and played out both on stage and in the auditorium at the Gaiety and Daly's. This is not simply the factor of new fashions being paraded on stage and taken up by spectators in a voyeuristic exchange. The popular theatre, on and off stage, was becoming a new kind of social process for articulating the texture and conditions of urban life. It served as a timely representative of urban values, both silly and sophisticated. In part, this laboratory generated new roles defined by fashions and colloquialisms. Just as today young people learn much about the accoutrements and slang for their social roles from television shows and movies, so too at the beginning of the twentieth century did popular entertainment in the urban setting provide a new resource for articulating social behaviour. But beyond the trends, the process generated new models and goals for daily life; new social rules were created and old ones were laughed at and disdained. Popular modernity was a spectacle in which people could participate, in part because the lyricists and librettists were using the new genre to express the new sensibilities of modern life.

Drawing upon some astute comments of William Archer, Bailey tracks how a new kind of 'knowingness' was generated in the public spaces of music hall and popular theatre. The sources for this process of being in tune with the times were various. 'In the new theatres of entertainment, its "authors" were to be found in a diverse army of showpeople, journalists and admen, variously writing, staging, performing, puffing and dissecting a hybrid and multiple text' (17). That text provided, in a playful manner, the full culture of modern urban society. The social text and the roles were multiple, and no one – not the captains of industry nor the leaders of government – controlled it. And George Edwardes, like everyone else, gambled on what the text might express each week, month and year. We now know that Edwardes threw the dice successfully for an amazing twenty-five years, with only a few miscalculations about the texture of contemporary values and attitudes. But at the time, he was guessing just like everyone else. Unless we recover the historical sense of contingency and chance that operated for him in that era, we will fail to understand and appreciate what was so special about his accomplishments and the qualities of musical comedy. We then retreat into formulas of a golden age or a commodified culture.

Taking up Bailey's suggestion about the significance of modernity in musical comedy, Len Platt has written a preliminary survey of the development of the popular entertainment. In *Musical Comedy on the West End Stage, 1890–1939* (2004) Platt, who is a social historian not a theatre historian or musicologist, sees musical comedy as an 'important prototype of "mass" culture' and 'one of the earliest "star" vehicles'.[33] Of course, he ignores that fact that actors since the sixteenth century (e.g. William Kemp, Edward Alleyn and Richard Tarlton) had 'vehicles' in which they starred. Platt insists that musical comedy after the 1890s 'utilized the most modern forms of technology, distribution and marketing available, and was intensely consumerist in its design, execution, and general orientation' (4). In accord with Bailey, he places popular entertainment in the history of modernity.[34] Platt notes that the audiences drew upon women especially, and that the stars had become 'household names'. He offers some promising insights on how new theatre magazines responded to the emerging fan culture: *The Play Pictorial* (began publication in 1896), *The London Stage Annual* (1903), *The Stage Souvenir* (1904) and *The Actor Illustrated* (1905). By focusing on the appeal of such magazines to the middle class, Platt opens up a promising way to recapture certain aspects of the appeal of musical comedy. But he soon abandons these individual insights as he prepares his general analysis:

> Musical comedy was part of the much wider process by which the idea of modernity, of urban, industrial and commercial life, became newly imagined, not as an alien contamination of British culture, dismantling tradition and custom in its inexorable march, but as the 'natural' state of everyday existence. (58)

This development, which Platt credits to 'the profound transformation in the culture of the popular classes which occurs between the 1880s and 1920s' (58), signals the arrival and acceptance of popular entertainment by the urban middle class. Accordingly, as burlesque transforms into musical comedy, the modern world arrives, imposing itself upon the traditional British way of life:

> No longer an anti-culture, in mainstream urban culture the innovative became the new, unassailable reality, the universal dynamic that somehow now could be constructed as 'belonging' to everybody. Musical comedy with its astonishing facility to 'charm' and 'amaze' was very much part of that deeply ideological orientation. It helped secure modernity for posterity by rendering it the pleasure dome and the condition of the civilized. (58)

Thus understood, musical comedy – the Cinderella of a play as Edwardes defined it – performs a kind of dream work, like a fairy tale. But unlike traditional folk tales, its representative mode of spectacle served most of all to articulate the modern transformations of the social realms of being.

The Edwardes musicals, with their modern settings, revealed to British society its modern identity. But Platt (who depends upon the ideas of Stuart Hall as well as those of Peter Bailey) misleads us if his argument implies that these developments were specific to Great Britain. The definitive attributes of modernity emerged in several countries during this period of transformation, followed by the catastrophic war. The key factors that Platt names were also operating in France, Germany, the United States and, to a less accelerated extent, in other European countries, from Sweden to Italy. And, I would contend, one of the reasons that Edwardes's musical comedies – and then those by other people – were so successful on tour throughout the world is that bits and pieces of the transformative messages of modernity emerged within the seemingly familiar and traditional stories of the musical comedies. These suggestive, if sometimes contradictory motifs, were recognized and responded to by various spectators, from London to Sydney, from New York City to Cape Town.

The problem with Platt's study, besides the overly generalized nature of this social discourse for describing musical comedy, is the lack of attention on the specific traits of the genre and the productions. Modernity explains everything. His organizing topics are 'musical comedy as cultural intervention' (19) and 'musical comedy as modern commodity' (33). Though he wants to move beyond the analysis of productions as 'sites of consumption' for fashion-starved women, he still sees stage spectacle as a means for celebrating 'modernity's astonishing capacity for reproduction and assimiliation' (36). Even when he taps the vital scholarship of Kurt Gänzl, which provides many details about each production, Platt tends towards thematic analysis that illustrates his argument about modernity. He shows little interest in the specific individuals (though he is pleased – and perhaps surprised – to note that many of the librettists and composers were well educated).

Most notably, from my perspective, this method of social history fails to address the mystery of who George Edwardes was. How did he achieve such success? What was the nature of the specific musical comedies? He remains an enigma in Platt's survey. There is no real attempt to look beyond the business category of successful producer. Platt acknowledges that Edwardes developed musical comedy, but how and why he did so is not addressed. Apparently, when modernity is running the show, the contributions of individuals are beside the point.

VII

In order to do full justice to George Edwardes and musical comedy, we need to proceed in both a specific and a general way. Consider, for example, some specific facts and general conditions for London theatre at the turn of the century, the heart of the Edwardes era of musical comedy and the beginning of the Edwardian age. By 1900, London had expanded to six million people. The metropolis had become an imperial centre for a world empire and a commercial nexus for trade and finance. In the process, it also had become a cosmopolitan centre for entertainment and leisure. Forty West End theatres, located in central London, presented everything from Gilbert and Sullivan operettas and Wagnerian operas (sung in Italian) to comedies, farces, musicals, melodramatic spectacles and Christmas pantomimes (that often ran until Easter). Another forty neighbourhood theatres operated beyond the central area (eleven to the north, fourteen to the south, seven to the east, and eight to the west). And fifty to sixty music halls, distributed throughout the city, entertained working-class audiences nightly with a popular array of songs, dances, variety acts and a steady flow of comic performers.

In the West End alone, twenty-four new or renovated theatre buildings and upscale music halls opened between 1880 and 1914. Basically, the number of venues, productions, employees and spectators doubled during this era. The government's Examiner of Plays (who had censorship power over productions) read 297 plays in 1890, 466 plays in 1900, and 604 plays in 1910. And the number of productions that ran for 300 or more performances expanded from twenty-five in the 1890s to seventy in the 1910s.[35] This successful growth of the theatre district was made possible in part because of a transportation network that included the underground sections of the Metropolitan Railroad and the new underground or 'Tube' system, linking a ring of railway stations around central London (e.g. Paddington, Euston, King's Cross, Waterloo and Victoria). Travel to and from the theatres was becoming an easy, affordable venture for London residents as well as for people beyond the city. Dozens of new hotels and restaurants opened to serve the approximately 100,000 people who poured into the area most evenings for entertainment. And another 100,000 people attended the neighbourhood theatres and music halls each evening for various kinds of drama and variety entertainment. So, every month or two, approximately six million spectators – the equivalent of London's population – saw some kind of theatrical event. The entertainment industry had arrived – before film, before radio, before television. By 1900 this entertainment juggernaut generated jobs, either directly or indirectly, for approximately 15–20 per cent of the city's employees.

Accordingly, in order to appreciate and do justice to Edwardes and musical comedy, we need to place both the man and the productions within the urban context of London and the series of cultural and social transformations, beginning in 1878 when Edwardes took his first London job with D'Oyly Carte and carrying forward to 1915, when he died and the First World War changed everything. At the very least, then, we need to investigate the following topics: (1) the hybrid theatrical form of the modern musical comedy that emerged under Edwardes's guidance; (2) the teams of accomplished writers, composers and lyricists that Edwardes put together; (3) the series of stars who emerged in the musicals; (4) the increasing mobility of performers to move across the boundaries (aesthetic and social) that separated types of entertainment: music hall, burlesque, musicals and society plays; (5) the theatre audiences, men and women, middle and upper classes, central and suburban, in Edwardes's London theatres, especially their changing social and gender traits from the 1880s to the 1910s; (6) the representation of women – not only the famous 'Gaiety Girls' but also various other kinds of women that the musicals featured; (7) the gossip and implications of the series of marriages of Gaiety Girls to young (and not so young) men of the peerage; (8) the recurring social and political motifs in the musicals, for the shows represented everything from current events to the colonial policy of the empire; (9) the emergence of modern business practices in the entertainment industry; (10) the expansive touring syndicate that Edwardes helped to develop; (11) the relationship between the London stage and the class system of British society; and (12) the kinds of business partnerships that Edwardes developed with various people in the financial markets and banking.

Step by careful step, this investigation will then begin to reveal what was once obvious in 1911 at the time of the Jubilee for George Edwardes. The entrepreneur and musical comedy provided the defining features of London theatre and society in the Edwardian era.[36]

Notes

1. W. Forbes-Winslow, *Daly's: the Biography of a Theatre* (London: W. H. Allen, 1944), 99.
2. Alan Hyman, *The Gaiety Years* (London: Casell, 1975), 187–8.
3. Kurt Gänzl, *The British Musical Theatre*, 2 vols (New York: Oxford University Press, 1986). Kurt Gänzl, *The Encyclopedia of the Musical Theatre*, 2 vols (New York: Schirmer Books, 1994), 1: 398.
4. Peter Bailey, *Popular Culture and Performance in the Victorian City* (Cambridge: Cambridge University Press, 1998). Len Platt, *Musical Comedy on the West End Stage, 1890–1939* (Basingstoke: Palgrave Macmillan, 2004).
5. Some of the touring figures are tabulated by Kurt Gänzl in *The British Musical Theatre* (e.g. length of runs in New York City, productions in Paris, Vienna, Sydney). But no one has done a serious study of the touring of musical comedy. Even without such a study, it is quite apparent that the Gaiety and Daly's musicals reached into almost every corner of the world.
6. In great measure, the information in this catalogue of productions is derived from the scholarship of Kurt Gänzl: *The British Musical Theatre* and *The Encyclopedia of the Musical Theatre*.
7. John Hollingshead, *Good Old Gaiety: a Historiette and Remembrance* (London: Gaiety Theatre, 1903), 72.
8. The types or genres of the various musical shows that Edwardes staged are not easy to categorize. There was no consistent terminology developed by Edwardes and his teams of librettists and composers. Nor did reviewers at the time agree on the types. One reviewer would call a Gaiety musical a farce, another would proclaim it was a comedy, and yet another would call it an opéra-comique. About the only term that seems reliable is 'burlesque', which names the early productions at the Gaiety in the 1880s and early 1890s. After that, confusion reigns. But there is general agreement that the productions at Daly's, which required a larger orchestra, were more sophisticated and expensive than those of the Gaiety. The Daly's productions required more accomplished singers; the plots were more fully developed. In turn, when Edwardes began to adapt French, Hungarian and Austrian musicals, the productions at Daly's usually had traits of the opéra-comique and operetta.
9. This comic operetta or opéra-comique, produced after Edwardes's death, was a sensational success, running for years, longer than any of his other productions. It was produced by the Edwardes estate and, overseen by his daughter Bobbie Evett, serving as manager, rescued Daly's Theatre from financial disaster. After its long London run, twelve companies toured the show around Britain. Subsequently, the Edwardes estate sold Daly's at a nice profit.
10. William Archer, *The Theatrical World of 1895* (London: Walter Scott, 1896), 43. Two years later, Archer had this to say: 'Whatever its value, a new literary movement set in with the production of *The Second Mrs. Tanqueray* in May 1893; and it was about the same time, or a little earlier, that the all-conquering "musical farce" began its triumphal progres.' 'Epilogue Statistical', *The Theatrical World of 1897* (London: Walter Scott, 1898), 354.
11. Andrew Lamb, *150 Years of Popular Musical Theatre* (New Haven: Yale University Press, 2000), 116.
12. Gänzl, *The Encyclopedia of the Musical Theatre*, vol. 1, 398.
13. Gerald Bordman, *The American Musical Theatre* (New York: Oxford University Press, 1978), 118.
14. W. Macqueen-Pope, *Twenty Shillings in a Pound* (London: Hutchinson, 1948), 271.
15. A. E. Wilson, *Edwardian Theatre* (London: Arthur Barker, 1951), 212.
16. W. Macqueen-Pope, *Shirtfronts and Sables: a Story of the Days When Money Could Be Spent* (London: Robert Hale, 1953), 131.
17. Seymour Hicks, *Twenty-Four Years of an Actor's Life* (New York: John Lane, 1911), 185.
18. In a recent essay on Macqueen-Pope, Jim Davis and Victor Emeljanow make the case that those books offer us an avenue into popular memory – not in spite of his sentiments and

prejudices but because of them. His chronicles, they argue, 'retain a value as documents' because of their mixture of memory and nostalgia. See Jim Davis and Victor Emeljanow, ' "Wistful Remembrancer": the Historiographical Problem of Macqueen-Popery', *New Theatre Quarterly*, 17.4 (Nov. 2001): 304. This essay is a vital starting place for any historian who is prepared to take the measure of Macqueen-Pope's value as a historical source.

19. In the 1950s, during the early days of television, Macqueen-Pope had a television show called *Popie*. It featured his nostalgic commentary on the theatre of the past and his conversations with people of the theatre. Although 'Popie' may not have appreciated the situation, it is rather ironic that he used the new medium of television to pay homage to the lost traditions of the theatre, which had been partially displaced by the media of film, radio and television.

20. Macqueen-Pope, *Twenty Shillings in the Pound*, 9.

21. W. Macqueen-Pope, *Carriages at Eleven: an Account of the Theatre from 1897–1914* (London: Hutchinson & Co., 1947), 7–8.

22. John Pick, *West End: Mismanagement and Snobbery* (East Sussex: John Offord, 1983), 17.

23. Pick is hardly alone in this judgement, which dismisses Macqueen-Pope's books as failed apologies for the West End system of actor-managers. Attacks on *Carriages at Eleven*, the one book that theatre historians may still read, have become the norm.

24. J. S. Bratton, ed., *Music Hall: Performance and Style* (Milton Keynes: Open University Press, 1986); Peter Bailey, ed., *Music Hall: the Business of Pleasure* (Milton Keynes: Open University Press, 1986). Also see Dagmar Kift, *The Victorian Music Hall: Culture, Class, and Conflict* (Cambridge: Cambridge University Press, 1996).

25. J. S. Bratton, 'Music Hall', in *The Oxford Encyclopedia of Theatre and Performance*, ed. Dennis Kennedy (Oxford: Oxford University Press, 2003), vol. 2, 903.

26. For a lively, well-written microhistory of this whole battle between Edwardes and Chant, see Joseph Donohue, *Fantasies of Empire: the Empire Theatre of Varieties and the Licensing Controversy of 1894* (Iowa City: University of Iowa Press, 2005). On ballet at the Empire, see Ivor Guest's *Ballet in Leicester Square: the Alhambra and Empire, 1860–1915* (London: Dance Books, 1992).

27. Bailey, *Popular Culture and Performance in the Victorian City*, 176.

28. Joel Kaplan, '1895: a Critical Year in Perspective', in *The Cambridge History of British Theatre*, ed. Joseph Donohue (Cambridge: Cambridge University Press, 2004), vol. 2, 425.

29. See, for example, Bailey, *Popular Culture and Performance in the Victorian City*; Peter Bailey, *Leisure and Class in Victorian England; Rational Recreation and the Contest for Control, 1830–1885* (London: Routledge & Kegan Paul, 1978); John M. MacKenzie, *Propaganda and Empire: the Manipulation of British Public Opinion, 1880–1960* (Manchester: Manchester University Press, 1984); Thomas Richards, *The Commodity Culture of Victorian England: Advertising and Spectacle* (Stanford: Stanford University Press, 1990); Paul Richard Thompson, *The Edwardians: the Remaking of British Society* (New York: Routledge, 1992); F. M. L. Thompson, *The Rise of Respectable Society: a Social History of Victorian Britain, 1830–1900* (Cambridge, MA.: Harvard University Press, 1988).

30. Of course, gender-based scholarship has proved to be very important in our new and more comprehensive understanding of Victorian and Edwardian theatre, culture, society, economics and politics. But Bailey and Kaplan do not draw upon this new understanding sufficiently in their representation of the Gaiety Girl, who becomes a faceless type in their presentation.

31. Peter Bailey, 'Theatres of Entertainment/Spaces of Modernity: Rethinking the British Popular Stage 1890–1914', *Nineteenth Century Theatre*, 26.1 (Summer 1998): 5.

32. Bailey, *Popular Culture and Performance in the Victorian City*, 193.

33. Platt, *Musical Comedy on the West End Stage, 1890–1939*, 4.

34. Platt is impressed by the middle-class appeal of musical comedy (though he ignores the valuable statements by Macqueen-Pope on Edwardian theatre and middle-class values).

35. For data on London theatre in this era, see scholarship by John Pick, Tracy C. Davis, J. C. Trewin, J. P. Wearing and Kurt Gänzl.

36. For a vital perspective on the business practices and commerce in the Edwardian theatre, see Tracy C. Davis, 'Edwardian Management and the Structures of Industrial Capitalism', in *The Edwardian Theatre: Essays on Drama and the Stage*, ed. Michael R. Booth and Joel H. Kaplan (Cambridge: Cambridge University Press, 1996), 111–29. Her essay has its full demonstration in her book, *The Economics of the British Stage: 1800–1914* (Cambridge: Cambridge University Press, 2000).

Part II
Performance Anxieties

5
Nation and Neighbourhood, Jews and Englishmen: Location and Theatrical Ideology in Victorian London

Heidi J. Holder

Fascination with the representation of place, of location, is an obvious feature of nineteenth-century theatre, and one that requires contextualizing. Audiences of this era delighted not merely in spectacle but in a highly particular realization of their world on stage; their theatre displays a visceral sense of the domestic and the local. The beginnings of this trend are evident if we look to the enormous success of the dramatic adaptations of Pierce Egan's *Life in London*, better known as *Tom and Jerry*, following its serial publication in 1820–1. Egan builds on works such as John Gay's *Trivia, or The Art of Walking the Streets of London* (1716) and the anonymous *Midnight Spy . . . or London from 10 in the Evening until 5 in the Morning, Exhibiting a Great Variety of Scenes of High Life and Low Life* (1766), which provided surveys that organized city life. *Life in London* would inspire and inform the later urban dramas of the nineteenth century, plays that relied heavily on the *mise-en-scène* to define character and shape plot. Egan's work had an enormous impact on the stage, setting off a vogue for a comprehensive urban realism that would endure through the century. By the end of 1821, several dramatic adaptations had appeared, the most notable being William Moncrieff's at the Adelphi Theatre. Other versions were staged in London at Sadler's Wells, Astley's Amphitheatre, Covent Garden, the Olympic, the Royalty, and the Coburg. The characters' travels take them to the Burlington Arcade, Tattersall's, Almack's Assembly Rooms, the Temple Bar by Moonlight, a Watch House, a 'fashionable Hell' (a gambling room in the West End), the 'Back Slums of the Holy Land' (lodgings in St Giles), a gin house in the East End, Fleet Prison, and a grand masquerade in Leicester Square.

London is here subject to an extensive process of demystification: the Oxonian Bob Logic is a 'walking map' of the city, and the progress of our three gentlemen creates a kind of order out of the multitude of urban types, locales and experiences. Egan's introduction to the book, published in 1821, insists that this kind of mastery of space is necessary to 'an accurate knowledge of the manners, habits, and feelings of a brave and free people'.[1] A comprehensive knowledge of the national character is the payoff. It is important to note, however, that this display-and-consumption of knowledge is not equally accessible at all London theatres: the vogue for urban realism emerges at a time when theatres are jostling for power and the Lord Chamberlain's office is expanding its control over the London houses. Jane Moody has usefully examined the earlier emergence of the concept of the 'legitimate' as evidence of 'a feverish desire to distinguish between authentic and spurious dramas and between loyal and seditious performances'.[2] In this contest between high and low, and between theatrical insiders and outsiders, the 'illegitimate' taste for spectacle emerges victorious. *Tom and Jerry* was a hit for the upstart minor theatre the Adelphi (and other minor theatres that rushed to stage their own adaptations); among the patent theatres Covent Garden eventually gave in to the craze. And the play's success signalled the inevitability of the intrusion of its sort of domestic realism into the 'legitimate' theatres. By late in the century impatience with the persistence of such tastes is evident. A reviewer for the *Illustrated London News* rather sadly concedes the success of such dramas at Augustus Harris's Drury Lane: audiences, he admits, '[long] to see on the stage what they behold everyday in real life. So without more ado Mr. Harris takes them to Trafalgar Square, and shows them the gala day of a London crowd. The arrival of the guards at Charing Cross is as fine and striking a picture of its kind as has ever been . . . if we cannot get Julius Caesar at DL . . . we must be content with crowds at Charing Cross.'[3] The enduring desire for intensely localized plays suggests that the audience's enjoyment was not only in seeing the recreations of urban spaces, but more precisely in the embedding of melodrama in such a fully realized world, a visual realm that authenticates the action on stage.

But could just any theatre conjure up such powerful recreations of London life and London types? Plays such as those based on Egan's novel showed a range of settings in both East and West London, and a slew of character types from high and low life. On the lower end of the scale were sailors and sweeps, blacks and Jews, all staged for the amusement and edification of largely West End audiences. The key dramatizations of Egan – at the Adelphi, Sadler's Wells and the Olympic – gave to the West End theatres a compelling model for depictions of city life. More to the point, these plays, at venues such as the Princess's and Drury Lane, were a prime source of images of London's working-class neighbourhoods. Could East End theatres, in turn, stage the world of London? (Remember, Egan pointedly made Londoners stand-ins for the national character.) William Moncrieff could summon up East End scenes for audiences at the Adelphi; could East End playwrights authoritatively stage their own peoples and neighbourhoods, let alone those to the west?[4]

This question points to a greater significance for the role of location, which matters not just on stage but also in the larger politics of the theatrical world. The site of theatres themselves is a matter of constant commentary across decades that saw the debate over the end of the theatrical monopoly and the transition of key minor theatres from so-called 'saloons' to theatres proper. I have been struck by the unwillingness of many commentators to admit that some institutions might even *be* theatres. This effect is of course due in part to the very real question of legal status: *Knight's Cyclopaedia of London*, one of the innumerable guides written for visitors to the 1851 Great Exhibition, gives a taste of this kind of dismissal, when, after surveying the town's amusements, it asserts, 'There are in addition a number of taverns at which dramatic performances of a humbler kind are exhibited, such as the Eagle Tavern, City Road, the Britannia, Hoxton, and many other places. They are not theatres, however, and so we leave them.'[5] But the resistance to conceiving of such places as theatres goes well beyond the parameters of legality.

Reviewers and commentators on the East End and transpontine theatres spend an inordinate amount of time directing attention not to the stage but at the audience in and the neighbourhood surrounding the theatre, suggesting that the only kind of drama such venues can provide is found off the boards. *The Thespian and Dramatic Record* provides some good examples of this effect in its series 'The Travels of Thespis'. Take its 1857 account of 'The Bower Saloon on Boxing Night':

Suppose t'were Boxing Night, and I Asmodeus, willing to conduct you high over the roofs and steeples of this vast metropolis, and show you a few of the foibles of humanity. Grant all this is true – I am Asmodeus, and you are clinging to the skirts of my cloak; up, up higher and higher we ascend, and now the huge city lies far beneath us; look down upon those buildings, round the doors of which people have already begun to assemble – they are our theatres. I see your eye is fixed upon that one the other side of the mighty Thames, the Bower Saloon. Come, we will descend; and, so, having perched ourselves on the iron railing in front of the gallery, we wait impatiently for the tide of life which in a few moments will flow into the vacant space before us . . . Look upon yon squalid-looking man in the further corner; that is his wife seated next to him. He is a poor artisan, whose weekly earnings do not amount to the cost of a single meal for his employer; the world reproaches him with improvidence, but the world sees not the heart, or it would know the mind needs amusement as the body needs sleep.[6]

While more sympathetic – certainly less disgusted – than many visitors to such theatres, the author quite literally makes a show of venturing out to such a place. The kind of panoramic view of the city that might well be expected in the melodrama onstage is here provided by the journey. Another image of the ways in which the environs can literally get between an audience member and the performance is provided by Cornelius Webbe, on his visit to the Coburg to see *The Gamblers* in 1823: 'the smoke and fume from the frying of sausages, and preparation of trotters and stewed eel on the New Cut, seemed to permeate the Coburg, and even to obscure spectators' views of the stage.'[7]

There are many such examples. But some journalists go even further, re-imagining the theatre or venue itself, under the influence of audience and location, as undergoing an identity shift. In *Figaro in London* in 1838, the Standard is dealt with thus: 'This place will never do any good as a theatre, and the sooner it is converted into something else the better. From the number of murders committed there, it would make an excellent slaughterhouse.'[8] Some plays went so far as to mock this intrusion of location into the theatrical space. J. B. Johnstone's *London Highways and Byeways* (Grecian 1864) makes the target a Penny Theatre, a venue even lower down the hierarchy: at one point in the proceedings a character cries, 'Behold, here comes the specter.'[9] A policeman enters instead, closing the theatre and arresting everyone.

Figaro in London provides a notable example of such an inversion of theatrical and urban space. In 1838 the Victoria, after sitting closed following Davidge's departure, fell into the hands of one Lawrence Levy (later the lessee of the Garrick Theatre in Whitechapel). These were the so-called 'dark days' of the Vic, about which its 'biographers' cannot bring themselves to speak in any detail. Cicely Hamilton and Lilian Bayliss pass briefly over the 'vulgarized' theatre of this period. George Rowell at least mentions Levy, only noting that he was 'apparently not a theatre man, and the first of several lessees who may have seen the sale of liquor as more profitable than the provision of entertainment'.[10] Rowell's comments suggest that he read pieces such as those in *Figaro*, which deny not only Levy's status as a 'theatre man' but also the Victoria's standing as a theatre while under his influence. Castigating Levy as the keeper of a lock-up house for debtors (and I have found no evidence that he in fact was), *Figaro* imagines the inevitable transformation that will result:

> the tribe of Levy have at last got possession of the Victoria, and *Jacob* and his brethren are to be installed in the various departments immediately . . . We do not think parties will be very fond of visiting the private boxes. One might as well be looking through Levy's grated windows in Fetter Lane. We have heard, but cannot vouch for the truth of it, that the whole of the boxes are to be partitioned off, and iron bars placed in front of all of them. The gallery will be made into a kind of House of Call for the Court of Requests, and sums under forty shillings. The opening pieces are, we have heard it rumored – a drama, called '*Uncertificated; or, Bullybrawl the Bankrupt*'; with an interlude called '*Nabb'd at Last*,' in which Mr. Levy, who has a grasping talent, will take all the characters; to conclude with a melo-drama, entitled the '*Withered Cognovit*'; the last of which will introduce the place of *Entering up Judgement*, and the *Immolation of a Debtor*. – If the theatre does not *take*, the lessee will, we believe, continue to *take* as usual.[11]

This sort of thing goes on for months, with plays on words such as 'take' and 'bill' in economic and theatrical contexts. In November the imagined transformation seems complete:

> The treasurer is the discharged turnkey of Coldbath Fields Prison, and all of the money and check-takers are gentlemen who have been highly successful in their performances on the tread-mill. That such a set can be thought attractive is perfectly out of the question. The police generally forms the majority of the audience, amongst whom it is generally expected they may find somebody they have been wanting.[12]

Such transposition of worlds, the conflation of theatrical space and business with that of other professions, is a tactic familiar from the satirical prints of Cruikshank and Gillray. But the persistence with which this strategy is applied to the 'low' theatres of the Victorian period invites scrutiny.

A connection may usefully be made between two cultural compulsions: the apparently bottomless desire to see local scenery onstage, and heightened aware- ness of the site of the theatre itself. Some of the reluctance to grant houses such as the Britannia, the Pavilion, the Surrey and the Victoria full status as theatres has to do with the presumed power of the theatre to present an authentic image of the people. Although it is immediately accepted that theatres ranging from the Adelphi and Olympic to Covent Garden and Drury Lane can accurately stage all localities, the theatres identified with the working classes and with 'alien' types such as Jews meet resistance on this point. Reviewers commonly and pityingly reveal the ways in which such theatres get things wrong, especially in the attempts to stage the worlds beyond their own neighbourhoods.[13] That said, I would like to suggest that working-class theatres could engage the politics of location, and do so in ways that addressed issues not only local but national. And one avenue of approach may be found precisely in the accounts of Lawrence Levy's control of the Vic, which clearly point to a central problem of his administration: he was a foreign element, a Jew. Playhouses controlled by Jews or located in neigh- bourhoods with large Jewish populations were persistently depicted as foreign, as orientalized, as 'Houses of Israel' – a matter recently analysed by Jim Davis and Victor Emeljanow.[14] Yet in the years following the emancipation of England's Jews in 1858, the East End theatres would show a real determination to recast the Jewish type as English, to domesticate the figure, and, engaging in a kind of mimicry, they used the prevailing fascination with locality to do so.

The East End theatres, in their revision of the stage Jew, were building on a tradition of representation, one in which locality proved extremely important. Consideration of the placement of Jews in Victorian drama is necessary here in order to chart the path by which such figures were made 'Londoners' in produc- tions at theatres which were themselves marked as unrepresentative, as less than fully English. Concluding her essay 'The History of the Jews of England' (1847), the Anglo-Jewish writer Grace Aguilar observes that the 'exiles of Judea' have been granted in Britain 'a home of peace and freedom'; they are, however, still 'regarded as aliens and strangers'.[15] Over the course of the nineteenth century, many writers, Jewish and otherwise, produced work that illuminated the debate over the status of Jewish men and women as 'English'. Strikingly, much of this literature places the Jewish community at a certain distance, temporally or geographically: Spain during the Inquisition was a favourite, as in Aguilar's *Vale of Cedars* or Bulwer- Lytton's *Leila*. In the theatre, many of the plays featuring Jews – especially Jewish families – exhibited a similar displacement: from the hugely popular adaptations of the French opera *La Juive* during and after the 1835 season to the numerous, and likewise successful, mid-century stagings of Salomon Mosenthal's tale of the vengeful Jewess in *Deborah*, Jews, even – indeed especially – when treated sympath- etically, were located in the past and in foreign realms. So, in our examination of the stage Jew of the period, we must spend a good deal of time on the continent and work our way back to the local scene, following the trajectory of the dramas.

This displacement might seem to coincide with views of the Jewish people as essentially anti-modern and alien. I would argue, however, that in the works of some Victorian playwrights of Jewish descent, such as C. Z. Barnett (Charles Zachary) and E. Manuel (Johnny/Emmanuel Gideon), and in those written partly with a Jewish audience in mind (those of C. H. Hazlewood at the East End Britannia Theatre and J. Stirling Coyne at the Surrey-side Victoria), the avoidance of a contemporary British setting allows the Jewish characters to emerge in opposition to the foreign/historical setting: they become the proxies for the audience in their struggles against dark and backward foreign powers. Paradoxically these characters appear *less* alien when they appear in a non-domestic scene.

Certainly the prevalent images of the Jew on the Victorian stage were negative. Dominated by such alien and menacing figures as Fagin, in the many adaptations of *Oliver Twist* that appeared on the British stage from 1838 onwards, and Svengali, in Paul Potter's dramatization of George Du Maurier's *Trilby* (initially produced at the Haymarket in 1895), the role of the stage Jew has largely been that of antagonist, corrupter and source of vice. The Jew was very frequently an emphatically un-English character. The counterbalancing tradition of the virtuous Jew was somewhat weaker, but provided a persistent source of opposing imagery. The virtuous Jew tended to be an old man or a young maiden. The former is exemplified by Sheva, in Richard Cumberland's *The Jew* (Drury Lane 1794), a work that provided the model for this character type. Sheva, a Londoner, retains notably stereotypical characteristics – he is constantly concerned about money – but his goodness always gets the best of his greed. When sneered at as a miser, Sheva laments the caricature:

> I live sparingly and labour hard, therefore I am called a miser – cannot help it – an uncharitable dog, I must endure it – a blood-sucker, an extortioner, a Shylock – hard names . . . but what can a poor Jew say in return, if a Christian chooses to abuse him? . . . We have no abiding place on earth, no country, no home; everybody rails at us, everybody flouts us, everybody points us out for their May-game and their mockery. If your playwrights want a butt or a buffoon, or a knave to be made sport of, out comes a Jew to be baited and buffeted through five long acts for the amusement of all good Christians – Cruel sport, merciless amusement![16]

Sheva will make an elaborate display of kindness in the course of Cumberland's play. It is the manner in which his goodness affects the other characters that proves to be the most significant element of his portrayal, even more than his frequent lamentations, for Sheva is a rescuer and a reuniter of fractured English families. At the end, the man who called himself 'a solitary being, a waif on the world's wide common', is praised as 'the widow's friend, the orphan's father, the poor man's protector, the universal philanthropist'.[17] In case the lesson of fellowship and tolerance has not been made clearly enough to a London audience, it emerges in the course of the play that the family Sheva aids had once rescued him, years earlier, from an anti-Semitic mob in Cadiz.

Sheva's role provides a kind of template for the 'good Jews' to follow. Such characters manifest their virtue by coming to the aid of gentile families, even as they themselves are denied any visible home life or future. This peculiar feature of the nineteenth-century stage Jew is observed also in the female variants – the most popular being, perhaps, the endless parade of Rebeccas in the many adaptations of Walter Scott's *Ivanhoe*. In J. Stirling Coyne's *The Miser's Daughter* (Victoria 1860) a young Jewish maiden sacrifices her very life for an Englishman who loves another woman. Her reward is ironic: the couple name their first child for her (a detail also found in another story of spurned Jewish maidenhood, Mosenthal's *Deborah*). In such plays Jewish virtue proves very useful to gentile families – but the Jewish characters are safely alone, or dead, at the conclusion.

It is possible to find Victorian plays in which Jews are given a central role, even a home life, though the stereotype remained the lone, menacing male Jew. But it seemed easier to deal with powerful Jewish figures in historical and period dramas, and particularly in plays set safely in other European nations. When a Jewish character appears in a contemporary English setting, an overwhelming desire is evident to assimilate him out of existence, as if his very presence in that particular location is unendurable. Tom Taylor's play *Payable on Demand* (Olympic, July 1859), obviously inspired by such banking families as the Rothschilds, centres on one Reuben Goldsched. We first meet him in the Juden-Gasse in Frankfort in 1792, as French troops are about to enter the city. Reuben, jubilant at the arrival of the soldiers of the revolution, nonetheless helps a French nobleman, St. Cast, sell goods to save money. Reuben's status as a Jew is already threatened by a marriage outside the faith: 'I married a Christian, and cut myself off from fellowship with my brethren.'[18] Reuben is a character divided: he is shown to have a 'Jewish' love of money, but his love for a Christian draws him towards the right thing (his wife is always setting him on the virtuous path).

It is in London, twenty-two years later, that Reuben finally and definitively does the right thing. St. Cast was killed by the French troops, and Reuben grew rich on his money, not knowing how to find the dead man's family. This being a Victorian melodrama, such lack of knowledge is no problem: St. Cast's son turns out to be Reuben's daughter's penniless music teacher, with whom she has fallen in love. The son's identity is uncovered, and Reuben must decide whether or not to give back the money. If he does, he is ruined (men from the city – and even farther east – are constantly visiting to arrange complicated financial schemes). His daughter encourages him to make the sacrifice. In the end, he offers the money to St. Cast's son, who allows him to continue his speculation (to considerable success). Everyone is rich, and Reuben goes from being married to a Christian to being the father – and father-in-law – of one. In the Frankfort scenes, references to Jewish identity were constant. In England, Jewish identity apparently fades away – a point made visually by having the same actress play Reuben's Christian wife *and* daughter – and that's obviously part of the happy ending, and a marker of Reuben's ultimate 'success', of a kind of conversion to an 'English' identity. It is clear that there remained real stumbling blocks to the notion of Jews as 'domestic' in both senses: they have no viable family life, and they are not really 'English'.

The vexed matter of Jewish family life can perhaps best be dealt with by looking at the plays written in response to the Mortara kidnapping case of 1858. This incident galvanized the international Jewish community and pointed to a particular source of anxiety for European Jews: that their children might be lured away, or even kidnapped, by gentiles bent on converting them. In England, the London Society for Promoting Christianity Among the Jews, an organization whose tactics angered and frightened London's Jewish community, specifically targeted perceived 'weak links': the poor and children. The fears of the Jewish community were realized in the case of Edgardo Mortara, a six-year-old Jewish boy in the city of Bologna. On 23 June 1858, officers of the Papal police detail removed the boy from his home and turned him over to the custody of Pope Pius IX. The boy, it emerged, had been secretly baptized by a Catholic servant and was now considered, in the eyes of the church, a Catholic living among Jews – an unacceptable arrangement. Edgardo, never returned to his family despite lengthy court battles and political manoeuvring, became a Catholic priest and died in a Belgian monastery in 1940, shortly before citizens of Jewish birth were rounded up during the German occupation.[19] The Mortara affair was a *cause célèbre*, and not just among Jews. The matter played into the hands of the Pope's enemies, particularly Napoleon III and the forces of Italian unification. But the case was a flashpoint in the Jewish community, and was heavily covered in Jewish newspapers such as London's *Jewish Chronicle*. For years afterward the case provided a point of reference in tales of conversion.[20]

This sense of an endangered Jewish family was embodied on the stage in the dramatizations (often quite loose) of the Mortara episode, and it is in the reading of these plays, in their continental and British variations, that we can see London's East End theatres pushing the stage representation of Jews in a new direction. The key dramatization of the Mortara case was French: Victor Séjour's *La Tireuse des Cartes* (*The Fortune Teller*). A heavily romanticized version of the story, the play retains the baptism but makes the child a girl, placing her in a loving Catholic home, where she is ignorant of her origins. The star role of the piece is that of the ever-seeking mother, who adopts the disguise of a fortune-teller. In this version, the daughter is a pathetic figure, torn between two mothers. The father has died, and the reunion with the Jewish mother is a sad affair.

The links and contrasts between the versions of this play staged at the West End and East End theatres are instructive. The most popular was undoubtedly Joseph Stirling Coyne's *The Woman in Red* (staged at the St James's Theatre in the West End in 1868), which featured the popular actress Madame Celeste in the highly dramatic role of the disguised mother. Interestingly, most reviews do not even mention the Jewish element, focusing rather on the theme of maternal suffering and revenge. Indeed, in Coyne's version, the Jewish mother Miriam becomes a figure of overwhelming power when she takes on the persona of Rudiga, a fortune-teller. She says to her daughter, 'I have drunk the cup of bitter misery to the dregs. Look at these wasted limbs, these hollow cheeks, this hair, once dark as the raven's wing now grey and scant. Misery has done this. Misery has been my sole companion through life.'[21] While a sympathetic figure, Miriam/Rudiga is clearly linked to traditional Jewish stereotypes: she is vengeful, and she maintains vast, hidden stores of wealth (she even buys a palace for her recovered child). While Rudiga finds her daughter, there is no clear restoration of the Jewish family. The girl – Naomi to her Jewish mother and Francesca to her Catholic mother – will keep her ties to both women. Rudiga extends her hand to Constanza, the adoptive mother, insisting, 'we shall love her better united'.[22] Most significantly, Naomi/Francesca will marry Claudio, her gentile lover. As in *Payable on Demand*, we anticipate the daughter's assimilation into a gentile world.

In the East End theatres the Mortara case and Séjour's dramatization of it provided the path to a very different sort of ending. Most striking is the production at the City of London Theatre (in Norton Folgate) of *The Fortune Teller; or The Abduction of the Jew's Daughter* (September 1860). This version places squarely in the foreground the specifically Jewish context of the play, featuring scenes with the Grand Inquisitor and the threat to the fortune-teller – the mother here is named Gemea – of death by burning. The basic outline of Séjour's play is retained, but the ending is radically different. The Gemea who discovers her grown daughter in a Catholic home is here described as 'wild wolf': 'squalid and tattered, hair gray ... a repulsive old hag'.[23] While the wandering mother of Séjour and Coyne is authentically on the brink of madness, here Gemea merely feigns. And, more importantly, she is not alone. Her husband, Gideon, dead in the other versions of the tale, here survives. In the City of London production, he is the one who gains financial control over the family that has stolen his daughter (a much less sympathetic crew here). The members of this lost family gradually move towards recognition and reunion. This family, in its victory over what is represented as a specifically continental Catholic and degenerate elite, becomes a source of identification not only for Jewish but Protestant English theatregoers.

In Séjour's *The Fortune Teller* and most of the plays descended from it the mother remains a mournful figure, and though the daughter is found, the Jewish family is hardly restored. The City of London version adds a remarkable twist to this ending. Gemea, her daughter found, throws off her disguise, crying, 'witness the springing forth of a new life':

> She in an instant throws off the squalid rags, in which she is enveloped, tears off the faded cowl from her head to which the long gray hair is attached, and appears clad in a crimson robe, a plain gold zone around the waist, a plain gold tiara with one jewel in the center of her head. She stands in a proud and dignified attitude, little older in appearance than in the first act.[24]

Gideon engages in a similar act of transformation when he reveals himself to his rediscovered wife and daughter: 'Behold me as I am,' he says to Gemea, 'your husband': 'He throws off wig and beard and appears neatly as in Act I.'[25] More is being thrown off here than wigs and costumes. A tradition of Jewish representation is being cast aside, one in which a happy ending points to a vanishing of Jewish characters into a gentile world, and in which the happy family is, inevitably, a Christian one. The magic of 'transformation' scenes, so much a part of Victorian spectacular theatre, from melodrama to pantomime, is here used to effect a reversal of the expected trajectory of the play. At the City of London Theatre, the audience enjoys not the pathos of the suffering mother, but the reconstitution of the happy family of Gideon, Gemea and Naomi, first encountered at the opening of the drama. The conclusion provides that most miraculous of effects, at least on the British stage: a Jewish family that survives the ending. (They also pointedly drop their exotic disguises.) Other East End plays on Jewish themes feature similar reversals: young gentiles uncover hidden Jewish identities, and even convert and become Jews.

Such plays, however creative in their attempts to use contemporary theatrical models to provide alternative endings to stories of Jewish life, all rely on foreign settings. It is a commonplace in theatre history that the domestic life of Victorian East London's steadily growing Jewish community was not a focus of British drama until the end of the century, after the huge wave of immigration from Russia had dramatically increased the number of Jews in the nation, particularly in London. Israel Zangwill's theatrical adaptation of his own *Children of the Ghetto* (1899) is often pointed to as the first play of Jewish life in London. There is, however, a playwright of the 1870s who anticipated Zangwill, in dramas staged at the Britannia Theatre in Hoxton. The playwright 'E. Manuel' (note the pun) rose to a position of some influence at the Britannia early in the management of Sarah Lane. (This is likely the pen name of Emmanuel Gideon, although input by his father Johnny, a friend of Lane's, is possible.)[26] In his work, another kind of adaptive strategy is present. Rather than attempting to create a drama of the 'other', of a strange, exotic, alien group that had to be rendered comprehensible to a mixed audience, E. Manuel simply ignored the 'problem' of representation, deliberately inserting Jewish characters into the conventional and familiar subgenres – and local settings – of British theatre.

Two domestic melodramas are relevant here. *Rachel's Penance; or, A Daughter of Israel*, staged at the Britannia in April 1878, is easily recognizable as a variation on the melodrama of temptation. A young country girl considers throwing over the eminently respectable suitor selected by her father for the charms of a handsome but unscrupulous adventurer. She gives in to temptation, absconds with her seducer, and commences a slow downward spiral into degradation and murder. Ultimately, she poisons the man and finds herself being chased by an angry mob. Elements of this play can be found in such reliable hits as Watts Phillip's *Lost in London*, the various adaptations of Mrs Henry Wood's *East Lynne*, and Wilkie Collins's *The New Magdalen*. Even the adventurer's name, 'Rupert Rockley', is typical. The ending provides a clear echo of earlier plays. Just as Rachel is set upon by an angry mob, she awakens from what has only been a dream; chastened by her vision of suffering, she obeys her father and agrees to marry her father's choice, assuring him, 'I shall try to be worthy of your love.'[27] This ending is blatantly lifted from Henry Byron's hit, *Uncle Dick's Darling*, staged at the Gaiety in 1869. The play also echoes one by an earlier Jewish playwright, C. Z. Barnett (real name:

Charles Zachary), *The Dream of Fate; or, Sarah, the Jewess* (Sadler's Wells 1838). Barnett's play, safely set in Frankfort, also appropriated plotlines from English melodrama. Behind all these dream plays lies the French source, *Victorine*. What's new in E. Manuel's play is that key central characters are *English* Jews: Rachel, her father Abraham Levy, and her would-be husband Reuben Meyer. These characters lack the usual visual and verbal cues that denote 'un-Englishness'. Their speech is standard, their appearance not marked in the text as particularly exotic. E. Manuel's Jews wear the masks of generic, rather than racial, types. Paradoxically, Rachel's impending marriage within the faith bestows upon her the happy ending suitable to the English heroine of melodrama.

While some of the scenes in *Rachel's Penance* take place in London, we mostly move between the West End (site of villainy) and a village outside the city (home of pastoral English virtues, represented here by Abraham Levy). E. Manuel's next play, *The Rabbi's Son; or, The Last Link in the Chain* (Britannia, April 1879), is set in the East End, as the play opens and concludes in a Jewish rooming house in Spitalfields. While *Rachel's Penance* was modelled on the melodrama of the fallen woman, *The Rabbi's Son* draws on urban melodrama, telling the familiar story of the young man going astray in the city, living beyond his means and falling for the wrong woman. Young Raphael Miewski, not noticing the attentions of the loving and deserving Miriam (the daughter of his landlady), is smitten with the deceptive and calculating Theodora, a supposed Polish countess. Like many a young man, in such plays as Charles Selby's *London by Night* (Strand 1848) and Paul Merritt and G. F. Rowe's *The New Babylon* (Duke's 1879), Raphael succumbs to two of the familiar dangers of London: Jews and foreigners. For, in addition to the lure provided by the Polish Theodora, Raphael faces the temptation presented by the mysterious Moses Samuel, keeper of a curiosity shop near the docks (a marvellously well-stocked shop, which contains original Titians and precious jewels). A despondent Raphael enters the shop only to kill time as he waits for an opportune moment to throw himself into the Thames, for Theodora has discovered his poverty and cast him off. Solomon offers Raphael a mysterious talisman, a chain bearing the seal of Solomon, that grants wishes – at a cost. With each wish a link vanishes, and shortens the life of the chain's owner.

What does everyone wish for in the East End? Wealth. Gabriel grasps the chain, crying, 'what e'er I wish, I have! I would be rich!'[28] E. Manuel is here playing with both the conventional desire of the poor man of London and the stereotypical Jewish attachment to money. He then proceeds systematically to invert the stereotypes he invokes. Raphael's obsession with wealth turns to disgust. The mystically powerful Jew – here the curiosities man, Moses – does not ultimately control the fate of the hero. And Mrs Moss and her daughter Miriam, far from pressing Raphael for his overdue rent, attend to him assiduously. Miriam does his laundry and sits up at night doing needlework to save money for him: 'I used to work until three or four o'clock in the morning. I gave half the money to mother and the rest was for you.'[29] During Raphael's sojourn in West London as a man of wealth, they keep his rooms for him in Spitalfields, and he finds himself drawn back to their home. Finally, for the curse of the chain to be revoked, acts of self-sacrifice are required (here the fairy-tale elements of melodrama are clear). Someone must agree to die in Raphael's place. That someone, of course, is Miriam. But E. Manuel loved the 'dream plays', and once again the central character awakens from a nightmare to find that a second chance awaits him. Miriam's sacrifice also manipulates the tradition of the Jewess dying for her gentile lover, redirecting the effort towards saving the straying Jewish man. 'I will die happy in the thought that he will perhaps mourn for me,' she cries.[30] But, as with Gemea, the apparent loss and sacrifice turn, miraculously, into an opportunity to get things right.

Raphael's path through temptation and redemption is a familiar one to heroes of domestic melodrama. Low rooming houses, London street scenes, London docks, West End villas by moonlight all figure in his trial and transformation. Critics commented on the authenticity and effect of the scenery (especially noting that the Britannia nailed the depiction of an opulent party at the villa). E. Manuel here juggles two opposing traditions: the depiction of the Jew as foreigner, and the imperative to localize, to tell stories of London life. In the year *The Rabbi's Son* was produced, the critic Thomas Purnell, writing in the *Athenaeum*, would wearily concede the power and prevalence on stage of the local and familiar:

> Formerly the remote in time and place was most agreeable to the public. The novelist found profit in describing feudal times, or painting the scenery of distant lands, or sketching the manners of the high nobility with whom only a few of his readers were acquainted. And the dramatist resembled him. He was successful when he depicted life elevated, intellectually or socially, above his audience. What was heroic was received with applause. In our day 'stagey' has become a word of reproach. An audience no longer enjoys the representation of what is beyond its reach. The present and the near now best satisfies it. In the drama, as in prose fiction, realism is wanted. Every man judges what is laid before him by his own experience. Resemblance to what he is acquainted with is the measure of excellence. Truth to current existence is the criterion of merit he applies to a drama.[31]

If the City of London's version of *l'affair Mortara* relied on the audience's taste for miraculous transformation to pull off the trick of resurrecting the Jewish family, *The Rabbi's Son* manipulates audience expectations of urban melodramas. Raphael's story is shaped as much, if not more, by earlier plays of London life as by the tradition of the stage Jew (here a nightmare from which the central character awakens). The setting determines the story, while giving the old story a new twist. The doubleness at work, the interplay of 'Jewish' and 'English' types and stories, is observed even in the playbill, which gives the title in Hebrew and the subtitle in English. For *Rachel's Penance* the playbill used Hebrew for the title, but also offered a translation. For *The Rabbi's Son*, no translation to the title is given, on the one hand evoking a sense of exotic foreignness for non-Jewish theatregoers while on the other unifying two previously conflicting identities for Jewish playgoers.

Something different is going on here, a change in the pattern of assimilation and Anglicization seen in Taylor's *Payment on Demand*. E. Manuel anglicizes with a

Illustration 23 Playbill for E. Manuel's *The Rabbi's Son; or the Last Link of the Chain*, with main title in Hebrew. Courtesy of the Harvard Theatre Collection.

vengeance, but provides a new version of the happy ending that requires assimilation. Like the heroine in *Rachel's Penance*, Raphael learns that 'happiness is close to home'.[32] The adoption of domestic English theatrical types, London locations, and standard plot lines in which the hero or heroine spurns the 'wrong path', requires that these characters fit their melodramatic roles by *remaining* Jews. The happy endings of *Rachel's Penance* and *The Rabbi's Son* demand the turning away from marriages with gentiles – which is made natural and inevitable by making the gentile lovers highwaymen and continental gold-diggers (again, known stage types). Non-Jewish theatregoers can find these Jewish characters reassuringly familiar and 'English', while Jews can enjoy the spectacle of survival. Jewish audience members might also link E. Manuel's visions of continuity of family and community to his punning pen-name (Emmanuel means 'God is with us').

A 1908 *Pall Mall Gazette* article entitled 'The East End Jew at His Playhouse' by Anthony Ellis clearly links the theatre to the project of assimilation: 'If you observe closely the young men and women of the newer generation, you will see that already the Semitic appearance of their for[e]bears is modified in them, and that in feature and complexion they approximate more to the English physical type.'[33] E. Manuel has anticipated this fiercely assimilationist notion of approximation. The usual Britannia actors played these roles, as they had played precisely the same character types in other melodramas, and without the accents and dialect of the stage Jew. The result is a strange kind of 'stealth Jewish' identity. In an inversion of the kind of nightmarish transformation described by *Figaro in London*, in which the Victoria Theatre was made over into a lockup house by Jewish influence, here the London scenes on the stage seem inevitably to anglicize the central character. The 'escape into fantasy' found by Michael Booth in East End melodramas[34] serves a very particular point here: E. Manuel finds a way to localize his Jews while avoiding the seemingly inevitable 'foreign' cast given to such figures in domestic drama. Just like more obviously 'English' heroes and heroines of urban melodrama, descendants of Egan's Tom and Jerry, they move through the familiar theatrical landscape of England and cityscape of London (Raphael can in fact fit neatly into London's world of wealth). And in the larger drama of London's theatrical life, the East End houses have recast their own parts, playing the role at last of 'real' theatres, capable of acts of recreation and authentification crucial to their audiences; it is not only the Jews on stage that claim insider status, but the very venue itself. The East End theatres undeniably demonstrate an ability to make use of a kind of dramatic mode – urban realism – so often used to define and display the peoples of their neighbourhoods. E. Manuel's characters have a forceful double image: thorough 'English' types who are also, irrevocably, Jewish. And not the Jew-at-arm's-length, the biblical, continental or historical Jew, but the local product, the Jew next door.

Notes

1. Pierce Egan, *Life in London, or the Day and Night Scenes of Jerry Hawthorn, Esq., and his elegant friend Corinthian Tom . . . on their rambles and sprees through the metropolis* (New York: Appleton, 1904), iv.

2. Jane Moody, *Illegitimate Theatre in London, 1770–1840* (Cambridge: Cambridge University Press, 2000), 51.

3. *Illustrated London News*, 19 September 1885.

4. The working-class theatres of London were located primarily in the East End and Surrey-side of the city. In the east were the Britannia, Standard, Effingham (later East London), City of London, Garrick and Pavilion Theatres (joined by the Grecian to the northeast); on the south side of the Thames were the Victoria, the Surrey and the Bower Saloon.

5. *Knight's Cyclopaedia of London* (London: C. Knight, 1851), 827.

6. 'Karl', 'Travels of Thespis: the Bower Saloon on Boxing Night', in *The Thespian and Dramatic Record*, 5 August 1857.

7. Cited in Moody, 157.

8. *Figaro in London*, 27 October 1838, 170.

9. BL Add MS 53032L, J. B. Johnstone, *London Highways and Byeways*, f. 26.

10. George Rowell, *The Old Vic: a History* (Cambridge: Cambridge University Press, 1993), 35.

11. *Figaro in London*, 13 August 1836, 135–6.

12. *Figaro in London*, 19 November 1836, 192.

13. For an example see my discussion of the Standard Theatre's production of *Glad Tidings* in 1883. The play featured a spectacular scene in Hyde Park's fashionable 'Rotten Row', and some reviewers were doubtful that this theatre could accurately recreate the site and its wealthy visitors. Heidi J. Holder, 'Outcast London on the Victorian and Edwardian Stage', *Theatre History Studies*, 23 (2003): 49–64.

14. See the chapter, 'Orientalism and Social Condescension: Constructing London's East End Audiences', in Jim Davis and Victor Emeljanow, *Reflecting the Audience: London Theatregoing, 1840–1880* (Iowa City: University of Iowa Press, 2001). Davis and Emeljanow pay particular attention to the ubiquitous fascination with Jews described by visitors – from outside the neighborhood – to the East End theatres.

15. Grace Aguilar, 'The History of the Jews of England', in *Grace Aguilar: Selected Writings*, ed. Michael Galchinsky (Peterborough, Ontario: Broadview Press, 2003), 312.

16. Richard Cumberland, *The Jew*, in *The Plays of Richard Cumberland*, ed. Roberta F. S. Borkat (London: Garland, 1982), 6–7.

17. Ibid., 73.

18. Tom Taylor, *Payable on Demand* (London: Samuel French, c.1875), 5.

19. For a comprehensive account of Mortara's kidnapping and the response of the international community, see David Kertzer, *The Kidnapping of Edgardo Mortara* (New York: Knopf, 1997).

20. See, for example, the report of a possible abduction entitled 'Another Mortara Case' in the *Jewish Chronicle*, 19 September 1879, 11.

21. J. Stirling Coyne, *The Woman in Red*, Sergel's Acting Drama no. 136 (Chicago: Dramatic Publishing Co., c.1880), 38.

22. Ibid., 56.

23. BL Add MS 52995M, *The Fortune Teller; or, The Abduction of the Jew's Daughter*, f. 9v.

24. Ibid., 21–21v.

25. Ibid., 23–4.

26. Reviewers identify the playwright as the son of Johnny Gideon, a bookmaker (the sporting kind); Allardyce Nicoll, for reasons I have been unable to recover, has attributed the plays to Johnny himself. See Nicoll's *History of Late Nineteenth Century English Drama, 1850–1900* (Cambridge: Cambridge University Press, 1946), vol. 2.

27. E. Manuel, *Rachel's Penance*, microform in *The Popular Stage: Drama in Nineteenth Century England: the Frank Pettingell Collection of Plays in the Library of the University of Kent at Canterbury*, Series 1 (Sussex: Harvester Press, 1985–), 42.

28. E. Manuel, *The Rabbi's Son; or, The Last Link in the Chain*, microform in *The Popular Stage: Drama in Nineteenth Century England: the Frank Pettingell Collection of Plays in the Library of the University of Kent at Canterbury*, Series 1, 13.

29. Ibid., 30.
30. Ibid., 42.
31. 'Q' [Thomas Purnell], *Dramatists of the Present Day*, 1871 (repr. New York: Garland, 1986), 80–1.
32. Manuel, *The Rabbi's Son*, 45.
33. Anthony Ellis, 'The East End Jew at His Playhouse', *The Pall Mall Gazette*, new series, 41.78 (February 1908): 174.
34. Michael Booth, 'East End Melodrama', in *Theatre Survey*, 17.1 (May 1976): 65. Special issue on *British Theatre 1800–1900*.

6

Theatre History and Capital on the Victorian Stage

Jane Moody

The nineteenth-century British theatre was a cultural institution dependent on and intensely preoccupied by the growth of capitalism. The plays of this period feature a dizzying range of shares and dividends, delusive promoters and rapacious bankers, hopeful investors and new millionaires. With the exception of Shaw's dramas, however, critics have paid little attention to these plays. Indeed, this argument starts from the proposition that the virtual silence surrounding capital drama in the Victorian age marks a significant faultline in theatre historiography.

Stage representations of capital in other periods, by contrast, have been the subject of frequent discussion. Jean-Christophe Agnew, for example, famously interpreted the early modern theatre as 'a laboratory of and for the new social relations of agricultural and commercial capitalism'.[1] As Douglas Bruster points out, the late sixteenth century was the historical moment when the exchange value of plays first came to be recognized: the far-reaching cultural implications of this new marketplace became an important dramatic subject for playwrights such as Ben Jonson, Thomas Dekker and John Marston.[2] In the eighteenth century, too, the significance of the British theatre as a site for the exploration of capital is now starting to be acknowledged.[3]

In the nineteenth century, however, the history of stage capitalism has become narrowly identified with the characters and conventions of melodrama. Many critics have emphasized the eloquence with which melodrama's perilous dramaturgy speaks on behalf of the disenfranchised members of a capitalist society, embodying the anxieties, pain and injustice of the powerless and dispossessed.[4] One of the central subjects of melodrama, as Ben Singer observes, is 'the relentless victimization of innocents' under capitalism.[5] According to some critics, melodrama may actually represent an early form of radical or socialist theatre, a dramatic protest against the aggressive and destructive dynamics of the market.[6]

The central position of melodrama in nineteenth-century theatre historiography perhaps reveals more than the ubiquity of these plays on the British stage. Arguably, the social and political values of melodrama provided a foundational narrative or ideological counter-structure for the emerging discipline of theatre history. Melodrama's care for the common man or woman, its idealistic celebration of human community and deep suspicion of power and privilege offered an influential discourse through which to differentiate the collective ethos of performance from the ostensibly 'elite' texts of literary criticism.[7] If it seems that some critics have been too ready to make common ideological cause with the victims of capitalism, then those sympathies need to be interpreted in relation to the birth of theatre history.

Yet the critical tendency to interpret stage capitalism through the lens of melodrama has fundamentally distorted our understanding of the period's theatre.[8] As a result, scholars have neglected representations of capital in other theatrical forms and ignored the generic hybridity of many plays about capital, their complex mixtures of melodramatic and realistic modes. Too often, too, the ideological loyalties of a play, and its capacity to 'resist' capitalism, have dominated theatrical analysis. The dominance of this melodramatic history may also help to explain a pervasive reluctance to consider how nineteenth-century markets shaped the economy of theatrical institutions and the making of performance.[9]

This essay sets out to explore stage capitalism against the grain of theatrical history. My argument attempts to reorient our critical and ideological perspectives in a number of ways. Rather than concentrating on plays which depict the experiences of working-class labour, I have chosen to focus on dramas preoccupied by the alternately exhilarating and bewildering effects of capital on the middle and upper classes. The essay starts from the hypothesis that capital created a commercial and psychological need for new kinds of theatrical characters and stage plots, and indeed a distinctive dramatic language for the risks, liabilities and moral conflicts which this transformation brought into being.

Capitalism, as Shaw explained, 'breaks through every barrier, rushes every frontier, swallows every religion . . . and sets up any code of morals that facilitates it'.[10] The theatre proved to be an art form fascinated by and curiously well adapted to representing this ubiquitous force and for evoking its crashing barriers and collapsing certainties. Performance lent itself to the investigation of capital because the illusions of the stage provided an evocative corollary for the dark operation of this intangible new market. One notable feature of these plays is their use of religion as a language through which to explore the social psychology of capitalism. Though the relationship between religion and capitalism has long been the subject of debate amongst prominent social theorists, critics have not previously acknowledged the stage's importance as a public site for dramatizing the nature of economic belief.

One of the most striking, tangible and deceptive features of theatrical capital is its bourgeois materiality. Part of the commercial and aesthetic attraction of these dramas was the realist precision and care with which they reproduced the domestic worlds of Chislehurst and Brompton. Many Victorian and Edwardian plays about capital take place in elegant suburban villas furnished with ottomans and a piano; conservatories are stocked with flowers and the garden produce might win prizes at the local horticultural show. But the solidity of the furniture and the apparent sanctity of a household's domestic and social routines are both a literal and a metaphorical illusion. What marks out the world of theatrical capital is the certainty that things will fall apart.

As audiences discover, part of the settlement on a daughter's marriage has been invested in a company promising a dubious form of galvanic transport or corrupt solicitors have embezzled their clients' trust funds. These plays depict the financial – and often the sexual – liabilities incurred through naiveté, inattention and criminal action. Invariably, the crisis threatens not simply the financial stability of a family but its moral foundations. Characteristically, protagonists have to confront this combination of sexual and financial liabilities in order to restore domestic and financial order.

Some plots ostensibly present capital speculation as a temporary means to a greater sentimental end. George Henry Lewes's play, *The Game of Speculation* (1851), adapted from a French play based on Balzac's *Le Faiseur*, is a good example. In the opening scene, the handsome furnishings of Hawk's house conceal its impending financial disintegration: the servants have been waiting for their wages for a year and Dimity deceives visitors by pretending that her master ' "is gone to Manchester, about some new speculation . . . a splendid affair, I hear – discovery of a copper mine" '.[11] As the servants observe, Hawk keeps his creditors at bay with a succession of magnificent promises: 'I have seen him with creditors around him like hornets, till I have said to myself – "Well, at last he's done for!" Not a bit of it! He has received reams of writs, tons of protested bills – Basinghall Street has gasped for him – when, hey presto! he bounds up again, triumphant, rich!' (Act I, 52). But what prevents the audience from condemning Hawk as a charming but immoral swindler is that his game of speculation is expressly designed to provide a dowry for Julia, his daughter.

Hawk, a character written for the comedian Charles James Mathews, has perfected the virtuosic art of playing one creditor off against each other. During the play, having borrowed money, shares and plate from Prospectus, Hardcore and Earthworm, he decides to solve all his financial problems at one fell swoop by arranging for the pretended return of Mr Sparrow, his absconded business partner. Through this ruse, Hawk outwits his creditors by driving up the price of shares acquired in the Emerald Mine Company and then selling them at a profit of £20,000. As Hawk points out to his creditors, it is they who 'first taught me to handle the dangerous weapons with which I have kept you at bay'. At the end of the play, it is significant that Hawk presumes to offer his creditors and the play's spectators a moral, encouraging them to 'play your game boldly and steadily, till some good card turns up – then reap the reward of your courage and your toil – burn the cards, and eschew for ever, as I shall do – the game of speculation' (Act III, 102). The moral end of Hawk's speculation is thus seen to legitimate its ingenious deceits.

The Game of Speculation was hugely successful on the London stage and the name Affable Hawk became a byword for speculative genius. Indeed, the spectators' awareness of the alloy between the character and performer was an essential part of the entertainment. During his managerial career, Mathews had become famous for his skill at pacifying enraged creditors. In April 1851, however, just six months before his appearance as Hawk, Mathews had petitioned the Bankruptcy Court for protection against arrest under the Debtor and Creditor Private Arrangements Act. His financial predicament was partly a result of his extravagance (he and his fellow manager Eliza Vestris were notorious spendthrifts) and partly a consequence of the perilous character of theatrical entrepreneurship in this period. Since banks regarded theatres as ventures too risky for the investment of their own capital, actor-managers had no choice but to depend on various expensive forms of private credit.

So comic was the description Mathews offered at the Bankruptcy Court of his financial circumstances that it went down in financial history. As David Morier Evans commented, 'it is much to be questioned if he ever brought down heartier peals of laughter on the mimic stage, than did he when he was recounting the story of his career in discounting before the supposed prosaic audience in the rooms of Commissioners Holroyd and Fonblanque.'[12] In his memoirs, Mathews ruefully reflected on the comic contrasts between the dilemmas of theatrical and managerial credit: 'How many times have I gone upon the stage to act, with a merry face, the very part in jest that I was playing behind the scenes in earnest!' What amused and frustrated Mathews was the spectators' willingness to take these illusions for the truth: 'everyone seemed to believe that I revelled in it, and every allusion I had to make to duns and bailiffs was hailed by the audience as the emanation of a light heart, and the most unctuous enjoyment.'[13] At the heart of *The Game of Speculation*, then, was the ironic correspondence – and the pleasurable complicity – between Hawk's financial crisis and Mathews's managerial sleights of hand.

The Game of Speculation disconcerted critics because it came so close to condoning illegitimate speculation. One reviewer objected to the transformation of Balzac's tragic speculator into the mischievous, playful Hawk; others expressed anxieties about the idea of a speculator as a light-comedy hero.[14] But as one critic insisted, Hawk is 'almost, but not quite, a heartless schemer: he has still in him enough stuff o' the conscience for you to sympathize with him, and you relish his successes.'[15] This interest in reassuring audiences about Hawk's conscience underlines the mixture of fascination and unease surrounding the hero in *The Game of Speculation*. Lewes's play produced a new kind of speculative hero for the nineteenth-century stage and also broke new ground by presenting speculation as an activity which depends on forms of belief analogous to both religious faith and theatrical illusion.

The threat of adultery is one of the most powerful tropes in this period for the dangers of capital. The connection between capital and sex in these plays is not in itself new: early modern dramatists had often presented adultery as 'a kind of metonymic double for the cash marketplace'.[16] In the nineteenth-century theatre, this trope returns as a means by which to explore what we might call the social psychology of capital. In *Still Waters Run Deep* (1855), Tom Taylor's melodramatic comedy, the capitalist bounder Captain Hawksley has insinuated himself and his Galvanic Navigation Company (a 'magnificent' speculation, allegedly guaranteeing 8 per cent interest), into Mildmay's Brompton household. As the play reveals, 'the man of business' is a dangerous new figure in suburban life. The play opens on the eve of Emily and John Mildmay's first wedding anniversary: the contretemps about Emily's choice of piano music that evening alerts us to the explosive tensions which lurk within the elegant drawing room. Having won the romantic attentions of Mrs Sternhold, Hawksley is now on the point of seducing Mildmay's naive young wife.

The age of capital produces a need for new and perhaps unexpected dramatic heroes. At the beginning of the play, the family regards Mildmay almost as a figure of fun: 'sluggish', dull and apparently incapable either of chivalry or of decisive action. Certainly, the action of the play forces Mildmay to realize that the principles of laissez faire are a dangerous guide to the conduct of married life. The defining characteristic of Mildmay's heroism is that he understands the moral and financial conditions of capitalism. What makes Mildmay such an effective opponent of Hawksley's speculative villainy is his shrewd interpretation of risk.

The scene where Mildmay visits Hawksley's apartment, ostensibly to buy additional shares in the crook's unexplodable galvanic boats, reveals the conditions of this new heroism. Hawksley tells his client that the galvanic boats will create an extraordinary international network, uniting Ireland, the United States, Mexico, West India and Brazil and destroying the great profits of cities such as Liverpool and Bristol. He even attempts to demonstrate this innovation by blinding his client with algebraic equations: 'let $Y = A$ plus B/x be the formula for profit in the case of steam, then $Y(1) = A$ plus B/x, divided by 2, will be the formula for profit in the case of galvanic transport'.[17] Unknown to Hawksley, however, Mildmay is a banker who has spent his professional life calculating financial risk. What is more, Mildmay has discovered that the forger of a bill presented at his City counting house, allegedly drawn by the bank's Brazilian associates, was none other than Hawksley himself.

When Mildmay discloses this information, and threatens to inform the police, Hawksley has no choice but to buy back the Galvanic shares and to return his collection of Mrs Sternhold's love letters. Throughout this skilfully constructed scene, Taylor contrasts Hawksley's melodramatic menace and his opponent's cool, understated rationality. When Hawksley grinds his teeth and threatens to murder his opponent, Mildmay dismisses such a denouement as improbable: 'For a man who can snuff a candle at twenty paces to call out another who never fired a pistol in his life is no great piece of heroism; but to commit a murder requires some pluck. You've defied transportation, but I don't think you're the man to risk the gallows!' (Act II, 49). Similarly, when Hawksley arrives at the Brompton villa demanding his 'satisfaction' as a gentleman, Mildmay deploys the contemporary language of risk to expose the proposed duel as nothing less than an assassination, and promptly delivers Hawksley into the hands of the police. Throughout this dark comedy, the shadow of melodrama evokes the dangerous proximity of Mildmay's household to financial and moral disaster.

In *Still Waters*, the traditional figure of the impostor appears in new and threatening forms: thousands of pounds, not to mention the moral respectability of two women, are at stake. Hawksley endangers the Brompton household precisely because he promises both romance and capital accumulation. In many plays of this period, women are highly susceptible to this heady combination. Unlike Mildmay, they are too naive, or, in Mrs Sternhold's case, too hungry for domestic power, to estimate the risks of speculation.

The commercial potential represented by Britain's expanding empire introduced a new twist to nineteenth-century plots about the sexual risks of capital. In Anthony Hope's play, *The Price of Empire* (1896), members of a syndicate formed to develop a mysterious territory called Omofaga discuss Ruston's demand to provide £70,000 for acquiring the rights to develop a railway from a rival German speculator.[18] The elusive promoter of this scheme is a shadowy figure, full of smooth words about certain profits and the investors' moral duty to risk their capital in the name of empire. In return for their 'faith' – a repeated metaphor in the play – Ruston promises them what he calls 'a kingdom'. But the syndicate members fear that they are now at the mercy of a Juggernaut. The play highlights the fears of a group of people at once transfixed by the appeal of capital and yet at the same time intensely afraid of losing their money and even their lives under the crushing weight of an inexorable capitalist machine.

As in *Still Waters*, sexual transgression becomes a metaphor for the risks of speculation. The illicit relationship between Ruston and Mrs Denison, the wife of one of the syndicate members, is an open, explosive secret. During a misty night at the family villa in Dieppe, the threat of an elopement hangs in the air. When Ruston is suddenly recalled to London, the threat of moral catastrophe recedes: alarmed by his wife's mysterious illness, Denison decides to withdraw from the syndicate. Significantly, however, the project of developing Omofaga continues. Is Ruston another criminal promoter who has duped these individuals into parting with thousands of pounds for investing in a territory which does not even exist? Or are these uncertainties no more than the necessary risks of empire? Hope's play uses the image of a casino to evoke the risks and rewards of imperial speculation. But in this drama, no one knows what the price of empire will be, in money or in the destruction of human lives.

Dramas of capital did not always present women as victims of ingenious fraudsters and dubious promoters. Crucially, some plays focus on capital's invention of new kinds of economic and moral agency for women. In Taylor's *Settling Day* (1865) Miss Hargreaves is a woman of business who claims to understand trusts and takes pride in her knowledge of dividends. When the West End bank jointly owned by her husband and his business partner is on the point of collapse (Meikland has fiddled the books in order to cover up his misguided investments in foreign stock), Miss Hargreaves decides to put her fortune at her husband's disposal. From one perspective, this play exemplifies the moralization of capital which is typical of the period: the threat of financial ruin now provides an opportunity for a wife to demonstrate her virtue. As Miss Hargreaves sententiously observes, 'money is never so well ventured as in aid of those we love'.[19] Whereas Mrs Vernon's opinion that speculation offers 'all the excitement of passion without its punishment' is presented as a fantasy which leads in the direction of moral disaster, Mrs Hargreaves's action represents an uxorious model of joint stock capital in action.

Gilbert's burlesque, *Engaged* (1877), brilliantly travesties these sentimental pieties.[20] In this ludicrous and yet disturbing piece of theatre, Gilbert mocks the conventional moralization of capital on stage. In particular, the play debunks the illusion, propagated by playwrights and duly applauded by spectators, that romantic love naturally transcends financial self-interest. The absurdities begin in a picturesque cottage near Gretna on the border between England and Scotland where the inhabitants periodically derail the trains in order to extract payment from hapless travellers for food and refreshment. In the wake of one such derailment, Cheviot Hills, a quixotic young man of property, proceeds to declare his love for three women: Minnie, a girl whom he claims to love 'madly, passionately, irresistibly' (Act I, 143), Maggie (who promptly persuades her fiancé Angus to accept 'twa pound' in order to abandon his own, prior claim) and Belinda Treherne, a woman to whom he has spontaneously pledged his troth in order to save her from marriage to the terrifying Major McGillicuddy.

Throughout the play, Gilbert highlights the characters' cynical self-interest and their 'incessant craving after money' (Act III, 165). As the protagonists are fond of reminding each other, 'this is business' or 'business is business'. The fact that Cheviot's marriage would have immediate financial consequences for both his friend Belvaney (who would lose £1,000 a year) and his uncle Symperson (who would gain £1,000 a year, either on his nephew's marriage, or upon his death) compounds the risks involved. At one point Symperson arrives in mourning clothes, having resigned himself to the financial benefits of allowing his lovesick nephew to commit suicide. The hypocrisy of the young women is a frequent motif in the play: Maggie, Minnie and Belinda take up and abandon their partners at lightning speed, according to their estimates about the man's financial value in the romantic marketplace. Whilst proclaiming their ignorance of money, these women are quick to demand 'some definite idea of your pecuniary position' or 'the very clearest proof that your position, is, in every way, assured' (Act III, 169).

Having secured the attentions of a man said to have £2,000 a year in shares in the Royal Indestructible Bank, Minnie is triumphant. But as soon as she hears the (erroneous) news about the collapse of the Royal Indestructible Bank, Minnie gives up her plan to marry Cheviot, telling her father:

> Dear papa, I am sorry to disappoint you, but unless your tom-tit is very much mistaken, the Indestructible was not registered under the Joint-Stock Companies Act of Sixty-two, and in that case the shareholders are jointly and severally liable to the whole extent of their available capital.
>
> (Act III, 165)

Minnie's rejection of Cheviot as an unlimited commercial risk confirms the utter cynicism of her romantic protestations. *Engaged* appropriates the self-conscious discontinuities of burlesque, the genre's fascination with incongruity and contradiction, to mock the predatory individualism of Victorian capital. But Gilbert is also appropriating the absurdities of burlesque to mock the deceptive platitudes surrounding the theatrical representation of capital.[21]

For George Bernard Shaw, the public's willingness to deceive itself about the true nature of capitalism was indeed one of the most pressing problems of the age. In his essay, 'The Illusions of Socialism' (1896), the playwright offered a trenchant analysis of this phenomenon.[22] At the heart of socialism, Shaw argued, is a 'dramatic illusion': that ubiquitous narrative which 'presents the working class as a virtuous hero and heroine in the toils of a villain called "the capitalist"'. The features of this narrative, he explained, are all too familiar. After terrible suffering and struggle, the villain faces 'fearful retribution' whilst the hero and heroine are rewarded with 'a future of undisturbed bliss'. According to Shaw, these are the 'illusions' ceaselessly propagated on 'the stage of the Adelphi Theatre' and on socialist platforms as well. What seemed to be so dangerous about these plays were that their forms of moral 'assurance' had come to be taken as political truths.[23] In this paradoxical essay, Shaw sets out to explain both our indispensable need for such illusions and, at the same time, the political and social urgency of liberating ourselves from their deceitful power. The image of the capitalist as a 'stage villain' becomes the most dangerous example of that 'crude drama of villain and hero' from which Shaw hopes to extricate both the theatre and socialism.

As the introduction to this essay made clear, nineteenth-century theatre history has not escaped the ideological deadlock described by Shaw. On the contrary, our interpretations of stage capital are still dominated by the villain-and-hero psychology of melodrama. For Shaw, such a theatre represented a major obstacle to the creation of a genuinely critical socialism. Stage capitalism, he argued, is alluring, deceptive and complacent: a world of synthetic pictures and false promises which deceives spectators about the nature and operation of capitalism. The precondition for a genuinely socialist theatre, then, was the transformation of melodramatic anti-capital. In the last section of this essay, I present Granville Barker's drama, *The Voysey Inheritance* (1905) and Shaw's *Major Barbara* (1905) as theatrical investigations of these pervasive illusions.

Granville Barker's play explores the moral dilemma of a man whose father, a solicitor, has embezzled his clients' trust funds. On discovering this news, Edward Voysey's first, horrified impulse is to reject this inheritance entirely. But eventually he decides to take on the business in the hope of retrieving some of the lost capital and so protecting the financial interests of the firm's most vulnerable clients. Like *Widowers' Houses* and *Mrs Warren's Profession*, Barker's play turns on the individual's response to 'tainted money'. What distinguishes the dramaturgy of *The Voysey Inheritance* is the fantasy of a melodramatic restoration.

In *The Voysey Inheritance*, the hero yearns for a catastrophic event. 'The smash has come', Edward tells Alice at the end of the play, with an air of what the stage direction calls 'sudden exaltation' (Act V, 155). The apocalyptic language of the stage direction seems curiously at odds with the emotional dryness of Barker's play. But from another point of view, the phrase helps alert us to that uncomfortable blending of surface realism and melodramatic causality which one commentator vividly summed up as the drama's 'lack of nitrogen, a disconcerting quality of dream'.[24] For most of the play, Edward feels himself to be living in a moral limbo, an undefined period of moral suspension which will end when 'the next smash comes' (Act IV, 141). At various moments, he imagines that the arrival of the police, a trial and his own imprisonment will free him from the burden of this outlaw existence. The world of Edward's dreams is of course the world of melodrama, a dramatic environment which characteristically ignores such ethical impurities and murky choices.

The Voysey Inheritance presents capitalism as a system predicated on such illusions and the willingness of an entire society to collude in the production of immoral profit. As Mr Voysey informs his son, '[b]usiness nowadays is run on the lines of the confidence trick' (Act II, 111).[25] This buccaneering character has devoted his public and private life to the successful production of confidence. Having gambled with his clients' capital, Voysey dies leaving behind a deficit of between two and three hundred thousand pounds.

The scene in which Edward breaks this news to his family brilliantly dramatizes the habits of moral complicity on which capitalism depends. The idealistic Edward is shocked by his family's refusal to take moral responsibility for his father's crimes. His mother, he now realizes, has been aware of these illegal speculations for years. The dry, acerbic Trenchard refuses to see the matter in anything other than purely legal terms, and the tedious and asinine Major is 'far less concerned about the clients' money than . . . at the terrible blow to the Family' (Act III, 124). Beyond the household, employees and investors alike presume that they represent the exceptions to Edward's plans for financial reparation. Peacey, Voysey's clerk, cites precedent and the expenses of keeping his son at Cambridge as indisputable reasons for the continued payment of his annual hush money whilst Booth and the vicar propose an elaborate scheme for having their own capital repaid more quickly than anyone else's. Through the repeated clashes between hypocritical rationality and Edward's 'brutally humorous' reactions, Barker creates some of the most damningly ironic and uncomfortably comic indictments of capitalism in English drama.

When Desmond MacCarthy reviewed the first production of *The Voysey Inheritance*, he complained that the audience never learn whether or not Edward is to be prosecuted for his violation of the law.[26] To be sure, the proleptic language of the smash encourages the audience to expect some kind of legal jurisdiction of Edward's decision. But Barker's play invokes such melodramatic conventions only to abandon them. In this play, as Edward starts to realize, 'nothing [will] ever happen to set me free' (Act V, 158). Eric Salmon rightly comments that the absence of legal jurisdiction highlights Edward's need to renounce 'the personal, private idealism which longs for an absolute right'.[27] But whilst offering shrewd interpretations of Edward's dilemma, such arguments seem to miss the significance of its underlying cause. Capitalism, Barker's play seems to suggest, has changed the conditions in which individuals are obliged to make moral and ethical decisions. One of the problems about the capital is its ingenious skill in defying the intervention of the police or the judiciary.

Barker's decision to make ambiguous Voysey's account of his swindling is crucial to the play's subtle engagement with the dynamics of capitalism. Though in a more hesitant way than Shaw, Barker uses the experience and insights of women to explore the amorality of capital. 'I'm lawless by birthright, being a woman,' declares Alice, a young woman who has learned from her uncle about the vulnerability of her own capital. Alice's marginal position in this society also enables her more easily to 'see beyond the letter of the law' (Act I, 91) and so to make ethical decisions on the basis of an instinctive morality which acknowledges the systematic complicity on which capitalist society is built.

Beatrice's attitude towards Voysey complements as well as contrasts with Alice's opinions. A woman resolutely intent on divorce from her husband and the pursuit of writing as a career, Beatrice is one of the 'new women' of late nineteenth-century drama, a character determined to seek self-fulfilment on her own terms. This rebellious, contrary sensibility enables Beatrice to see Voysey as 'a man of imagination and a great financier'. Through Beatrice, the play explores the public's irrational willingness to be enthralled by the dark energy of the robber-baron. And it is this anarchic energy of capital which evocatively connects *The Voysey Inheritance* and Shaw's *Major Barbara*. Having experimented with a full-scale attack on capitalism in *Mrs Warren's Profession*, Shaw seems to have decided to make the diabolical appeal of capital, its irrepressible, almost ecstatic power, the starting point for a socialist drama.

In the final act of *Major Barbara*, the heroine witnesses the irresistible perfection of industrial capitalism: a beautiful town almost devoid of smoke, full of 'clean workshops, and respectable workmen, and model homes', plentifully supplied with schools, libraries, financial institutions and even restaurants. As Cusins declares with evident perplexity, 'it's all horribly, frightfully, immorally, unanswerably perfect'.[28] For Barbara, the shock of visiting Perivale St Andrews evokes the memory of an earthquake she experienced as a child: again, the world seems to reel and crumble beneath her. Whereas in melodrama such apocalyptic events presage the defeat of villainy and the restoration of providential order, Barbara's earthquake marks the beginning of her conversion to the gospel according to capitalism.

Though there have been many fine readings of Shaw's remarkable play, none has analysed the way in which *Major Barbara* confronts and transforms the stage history of capitalism.[29] Most interpretations treat the play in isolation, as if Shaw's dramatization of capital had no theatrical precedents. The one exception to this general rule is Martin Meisel whose argument turns on Shaw's appropriation of melodramatic characters (the villainous 'heavy' and the innocent, virtuous heroine) and recapitulation of familiar plots (the heroine's capture and destruction and the motif of the foundling heir); he also suggests that Undershaft's mesmeric power recalls that of ruthless theatrical bankers such as Bloodgood in Boucicault's notorious melodrama, *The Poor of New York* (1857).[30] However, Meisel's ground-breaking interpretation neglects the political and social issues which might be at stake in the creation of these generic anti-types. In this short discussion, I want to present *Major Barbara* as an unprecedented intervention in the staging of capital.

In Victorian drama, the millionaire must be stripped of his riches. Perhaps a financial panic will destroy his fortune; perhaps his criminal activities will be finally discovered. In any case, the risks and liabilities of capital prove to be their own moral undoing. Crucially, millionaires such as Matthew Ruddock in Henry Arthur Jones's *Wealth* (1889) or Bloodgood in *The Streets of New York* must discover that sentimental loyalties to a wife or a daughter override the brutal, destructive logic of capital. By the end of the nineteenth century, the theatre had become a stage for repeated rehearsals of capitalism's moral defeat. For Shaw, the ideological fraudulence of these anti-capitalist dramas represented one of the most urgent and distinctive challenges for realist theatre.

Paradoxically, the dynamics of capitalism – its bursting of frontiers, destruction of moral boundaries and swallowing up of religions – seemed to require a kind of dramaturgy which broke the boundaries of realism. What distinguishes *Major Barbara* from Shaw's earlier explorations of capital is the mythopoeic clash of forms taking place in the drama and the play's disconcerting closeness to parable. The drama self-consciously conflates Wildean high comedy, the grim social realism of the Salvation Army's depot at West Ham and fabulous, utopian allegory. This compendiousness clearly recapitulates the spectacular scenic contrasts between the worlds of capital and labour which Boucicault's melodrama had made famous. But in Shaw's case, this disjunction between ostensibly conflicting forms of dramaturgy seems to highlight the resistance of capital to political and social control, its almost supernatural energy. What Shaw sets out to find through *Major Barbara* is a dramatic form which can embody the moral anarchy and sheer lawlessness of capital.

Barbara's conversion to the gospel of capital is one of Shaw's most daring inversions of Victorian dramatic conventions. As we have seen, it is axiomatic in the plays of the period that a capitalist villain obtains financial power through his sexual attractiveness to women. In this tradition, women must be rescued from the dangers of capital. But Shaw's drama invokes these expectations only to turn them on their head: Barbara needs to be rescued not from capital, but from the melodramatic morality of the Salvation Army, with its fake representations of peril and tantalizing promises of safety. Having started from the comic cliché of the woman seduced by capital, Shaw makes the dynamic attraction between an innocent heroine and the destructive capitalist not a moral lapse but a shocking ideological necessity, a symbol, indeed, of the fusion of beliefs and values necessary for the socialist transformation of society.

The creation of Andrew Undershaft, a self-created millionaire who not only escapes retribution but emerges with a degree of immoral triumph, is a highly calculated intervention by Shaw in the theatre of capital. It is as if Shaw unearths the capitalist thrills dishonestly hidden in so much of Victorian theatre and, with an almost perverse delight, brings to the surface their dark unconscious drives. Undershaft is a man of capital who has already performed the villain in countless roles: he knows his lines so well that he plays against type for the sheer diabolical pleasure of the entertainment. Whereas the rhetoric of speculative villains in earlier plays was always demonstrably suspect and transparently deceptive, Undershaft's 'passionate and even poetical conviction' is, as William Archer reluctantly acknowledged, 'intensely dramatic and thrilling'.[31] As in the case of Milton's Satan, the munitions maker speaks some of the best and most unanswerable lines in the play, as when he argues that capitalism is the most effective system yet invented for the destruction of poverty. And in a mischievous riposte to that theatrical tradition which summoned the police to punish the man of capital, Undershaft makes it clear that governments and empires are merely puppets of capitalist power.

Shaw's theatre of capital is designed to reveal that '[t]he faults of the burglar are the qualities of the financier'.[32] Such a paradox confirms not only the circumstantial nature of character but also the success of capitalism in bypassing codes of morality. As Shaw had argued in his essay on 'The Illusions of Socialism', socialism, both on the stage and on the public platform, is stubbornly reluctant to tolerate such heretical revelations.[33] The originality of *Major Barbara* lies partly in the way in which Shaw turns religion into a weapon of ideological heresy in order to produce a vision of capital's spiritual power. As we have seen, several Victorian playwrights had used the language of religion to evoke the beliefs on which the system of capitalism depends. Not only does Shaw's play present the fervour of Salvationism as a delusive shadow of these beliefs but the drama also polemically confuses pagan worship and Christianity, the promises of capital and those of eternal life. Above all, through a range of allusions to Greek tragedy, *Major Barbara* suggests that the most authentic precedents for a theatre of capital might be found in the ecstatic frenzy of *The Bacchae* rather than in the sentimental ethics of melodrama.

This essay has questioned the undisputed position of melodrama in the stage history of capital. Such a narrative, I have claimed, privileges melodrama's own anti-capitalist vision. My argument has tried to break out of this pattern by exploring a number of plays which license and moralize capital in ambivalent and contradictory ways. As I have demonstrated, many of these dramas blend realist and melodramatic conventions in ways which challenge the 'evolutionary and adversarial narratives' which have dominated theatre history.[34] The question of how to come to theatrical terms with the nature and operation of capital presented the nineteenth-century British stage with one of its most urgent and fruitful challenges.

Notes

1. Jean-Christophe Agnew, *Worlds Apart: the Market and the Theatre in Anglo-American Thought, 1550–1750* (New York: Cambridge University Press, 1986), xi.
2. Douglas Bruster, *Drama and the Market in the Age of Shakespeare* (Cambridge: Cambridge University Press, 1992).
3. Daniel O'Quinn, for example, has highlighted Samuel Foote's depictions of colonial capital in plays such as *The Nabob*. See O'Quinn, *Staging Governance: Theatrical Imperialism in London, 1770–1800* (Baltimore: Johns Hopkins University Press, 2005), 61–7. For a powerful interpretation of the effects of capitalism on nineteenth-century American theatre, see Bruce A. McConachie, *Melodramatic Formations: American Theatre and Society, 1820–1870* (Iowa City, IA: University of Iowa Press, 1992).
4. Martha Vicinus, '"Helpless and Unfriended": Nineteenth-Century Domestic Melodrama', *New Literary History*, 13 (1981): 127–43.
5. Ben Singer, *Melodrama and Modernity: Early Sensational Cinema and its Contexts* (New York: Columbia University Press, 2001), 11.
6. See, for example, Harmut Ilsemann's discussion of melodrama's 'emancipatory potential' in 'Radicalism in the Melodrama of the Early Nineteenth Century', in Michael Hays

and Anastasia Nikolopoulou, eds, *Melodrama: the Cultural Emergence of a Genre* (New York: St. Martin's Press, 1996), 191–207. Many critics, however, have tended to question both melodrama's social radicalism and its capacity to rehearse forms of emancipation. See Jeffrey Cox's argument in this volume and, for a different approach, see Elaine Hadley, *Melodramatic Tactics: Theatricalized Dissent in the English Marketplace, 1800–1885* (Stanford, CA: Stanford University Press, 1995) who argues that the 'melodramatic mode' could 'both cannily subvert and unwittingly adopt some of the emerging values of institutionalized capitalism' (12).

7. On nineteenth-century liberal humanism blocking melodrama's access to the canon, see Thomas Postlewait's important essay, 'From Melodrama to Realism: the Suspect History of American Drama', in Hays and Nikolopoulou, eds, 39–60.

8. For an exception, see Michael R. Booth's brief but illuminating comments on the drama of business crime in *Theatre in the Victorian Age* (Cambridge: Cambridge University Press, 1991), 164–7.

9. Tracy C. Davis makes a series of bold and far-reaching challenges to this historiography in *The Economics of the British Stage, 1800–1914* (Cambridge: Cambridge University Press, 2000). Recent scholarship in the period suggests a new willingness to explore theatrical markets. See, for example, the wide-ranging chapter on 'Money' in Katherine Newey, *Women's Theatre Writing in Victorian Britain* (Basingstoke: Palgrave Macmillan, 2005) and the arguments put forward by contributors to Mary Luckhurst and Jane Moody, eds, *Theatre and Celebrity in Britain, 1660–2000* (Basingstoke: Palgrave Macmillan, 2005).

10. Bernard Shaw, *The Intelligent Woman's Guide to Socialism and Capitalism* (London: Constable and Co., 1929), 314.

11. Lewes, *The Game of Speculation*, Act I, 51. The play is conveniently reprinted in *The Lights O'London and Other Victorian Plays*, ed. Michael R. Booth (Oxford: Oxford University Press, 1995).

12. David Morier Evans, *Speculative Notes and Notes on Speculation*, first published 1864 (New York: Augustus M. Kelley, 1969), 187.

13. *The Life of Charles James Mathews, Chiefly Autobiographical*, ed. Charles Dickens, 2 vols (London: Macmillan, 1879), 2: 96.

14. See Percy Fitzgerald's anonymous remarks, published in the series, 'Players of our Day', *Gentleman's Magazine*, 1872.

15. *Leader*, October 1851, 949.

16. Bruster, 59.

17. *Still Waters Run Deep*, reprinted in *Plays by Tom Taylor*, ed. Martin Banham (Cambridge: Cambridge University Press, 1985), Act II, 45.

18. BL Add MS 53594R, Anthony Hope, *The Price of Empire*.

19. Tom Taylor, *Settling Day* (London: Lacy, 1865), Act I, 16.

20. *Engaged* in *Plays by W. S. Gilbert*, ed. George Rowell (Cambridge: Cambridge University Press, 1982).

21. For critical hostility to *Engaged*, see Jane W. Steadman, *W. S. Gilbert: a Classic Victorian and his Theatre* (Oxford: Oxford University Press, 1996), 151.

22. The essay was first published in 1896 and is reprinted in *Selected Non-Dramatic Writings of Bernard Shaw*, ed. Dan H. Laurence (Boston: Houghton Mifflin, 1965), 407–26.

23. On 'assurance' as a central function of melodrama, see Peter Brook, *The Melodramatic Imagination: Balzac, Henry James, Melodrama, and the Mode of Excess* (New Haven: Yale University Press, 1995), 43.

24. Article in *The Bookman* (1914), cited in Eric Salmon, *Granville Barker: a Secret Life* (London: Heinemann Education, 1983), 95.

25. *The Voysey Inheritance* in *Plays by Harley Granville Barker*, ed. Dennis Kennedy (Cambridge: Cambridge University Press, 1987).

26. Desmond MacCarthy, *The Court Theatre, 1904–1907* (London: A. H. Bullen, 1907), 28–9.

27. Salmon, 83. On the play's search for a moral code 'untrammelled by received notions of religious, legal or social attitudes', see further, Jan McDonald, *The 'New Drama' 1900–1914* (New York: Grove Press Inc., 1986), 70.
28. George Bernard Shaw, *Major Barbara* (London: Penguin, 1957), Act III, 141; 130.
29. The interpretation which follows builds on the insights of Shavian scholars including Margery M. Morgan, *The Shavian Playground: an Exploration of the Art of George Bernard Shaw* (London: Methuen, 1972); Alfred Turco, Jr., *Shaw's Moral Vision: the Self and Salvation* (Ithaca, NY: Cornell University Press, 1976); Tracy C. Davis, *George Bernard Shaw and the Socialist Theatre* (Westport, CT: Greenwood Press, 1994); and Stuart E. Baker, *Bernard Shaw's Remarkable Religion: a Faith that Fits the Facts* (Gainesville, FL: University Press of Florida, 2002).
30. Martin Meisel, *Shaw and the Nineteenth Century Theatre* (Princeton, NJ: Princeton University Press, 1963), 296–300.
31. Archer, from a notice published in the *World*, 1905, cited in *Shaw: the Critical Heritage*, ed. T. F. Evans (London: Routledge, 1976), 153.
32. Preface to *Major Barbara*, 35.
33. On the idea of melodrama as a pulpit in which 'there is no heresy' see 'The Decay of Melodrama', in *The Nation*, 5 March 1910, cited in Singer, *Melodrama and Modernity*, 135.
34. Postlewait, 44.

7
Modernity, Geography and Historiography: (Re)-Mapping Irish Theatre History in the Nineteenth Century

Mark Phelan

> But the nineteenth century, with its moral zeal, its insistence upon irrelevant interests, having passed over, the artist can admit that he cares about nothing that does not give him a new subject or a new technique.[1]

> To explain the work is to show that, contrary to appearances, it is not independent, but bears in its material substance the imprint of a determinate absence which is also the principle of its identity.[2]

The nineteenth century presents Irish theatre historians with an immense lacuna and the inherent limitations of our discipline. Beyond brief historical surveys,[3] some studies of Boucicault,[4] and recent scholarship on the late Victorian era,[5] it is a veritable *tabula rasa* which vividly contrasts with British theatre history. So, when asked to contribute to a book series dedicated to nineteenth-century theatre and designed to interrogate 'the methodological . . . and theoretical bases on which theatre history has been or might be constructed',[6] an enveloping sense of anxiety understandably overwhelmed me. First of all, as one hapless historian declared a decade ago, 'there was no such thing as Irish drama' in the nineteenth century; an apparently self-evident fact he finds 'worth repeating that for nine tenths of the nineteenth century, there was no such thing as an Irish drama'.[7] Other historians are equally adamant, 'It may be said boldly as a fact that all drama in Ireland until the beginning of the twentieth century was English drama.'[8] However, such sweeping, simplistic statements in fact describe the 'determinate absence' of Irish theatre history of the nineteenth century rather than the absence of Irish drama.[9] Given this historiographical void, the tradition of 'archaeo-historical' fieldwork of British theatre history, which frustrates historians like Jacky Bratton given its positivist purview of the theatrical past,[10] actually provides a methodological process and product that one could get positively nostalgic about, not to mention envious of, as a historian working in Irish theatre in the same period.

135

Secondly, the wider remit of this Palgrave book series in fomenting discussion about the methodological, philosophical and epistemological approaches to theatre history – the meta-language of our discipline – is a debate in its infancy in Irish theatre studies[11] given the debilitating, continuing emphasis on examining theatre in national terms, merely as a 'mirror up to nation'.[12] This approach remains the primary conceptual and organizational modality of Irish theatre historiography. Ironically, this is in the putatively post-modern, post-*national* context of the Peace Process and Celtic Tiger Ireland, and the no less illustrious context of Dennis Kennedy's decommissioning – with all that term connotes – of the category of national theatre from the *Oxford Encyclopedia of Theatre and Performance*: an editorial elision recounted by an unrepentant Kennedy in the inaugural book of this series.[13] Kennedy's 'Confessions of an Encyclopedist' poses profound, provocative questions for theatre historians, the implications of which for Irish historians I will unpack towards the end of this essay.

Both these problems – the lack of research in nineteenth-century Irish theatre and the limited disciplinary debate within Irish theatre studies as a whole – are inextricably linked. Indeed, archival research on this 'barren' period reveals a wealth of material available, whether related to local commercial theatres, stock companies, national touring circuits, or the virtually unexplored world of music halls, 'free and easies', singing saloons, variety theatres and vaudeville.[14] Beyond this is the hybrid, heteroglossic plenitude of theatrical activity outside of the urban, institutional and professional sphere in the diversity of popular traditions, forms and practices: from the nomadic performances of strolling players and travelling fit-up companies to the folk traditions of mummers,[15] wren boys,[16] straw boys,[17] Biddy boys,[18] rhymers,[19] street balladry against the background of an underlying, miasmatic Gaelic culture that was inherently performative with its *seannachies*,[20] dances, christenings, wakes, weddings,[21] 'patterns',[22] holy healing wells,[23] *Samhain*,[24] *Imbolc, Beltaine*[25] and *Lughnasa*, not to mention the rhizomic, ritualized performances associated with fairs, faction fights, folk plays, parades, pageants, codified rituals of secret societies, political demonstrations and commemorations.[26]

With this realization comes recognition of how extraordinarily successful the father of modern Irish drama, W. B. Yeats, has been in shaping the modernity of Irish theatre as evidenced by the hegemony of the national(ist) meta-narrative of Irish theatre history which hails the inauguration of the Irish *Literary* Theatre (ILT, my italics) in the final year of the nineteenth century as *the* founding moment of Irish drama. Yeats's *haute bourgeois* dismissal of popular theatre and his modernist privileging of 'literary' drama along with Lady Gregory, Edward Martyn et al. is vividly, visually manifest in an ink and pen drawing by his brother Jack Yeats, entitled: ' "Hellfire": Drawing of a People's Theatre', which depicts an East-End London theatre audience. Yeats's portrayal perhaps self-consciously reverses *Punch* magazine's racist depictions of the Irish as simianized savages with brutish British spectators instead appearing as an ungovernable, wild and unruly audience.[27] In this chaotic playhouse, what Joyce elsewhere excoriated as the 'Day of the Rabblement' is vividly manifest and the presence of prostitutes, food and drink further accentuates the Dionysian energy and activity of the scene that was anathema to its author (and his brother), who decried such ritualized rowdiness as the debased behaviour of the 'mob'. However, the title refers to this institution as the 'People's Theatre'; all the more ironic given Stuart Hall's definition of the people as 'the working people, the labouring classes, and the poor',[28] precisely the audience-citizen constituency that were beyond the pale of Yeats's putatively 'national' theatre project.

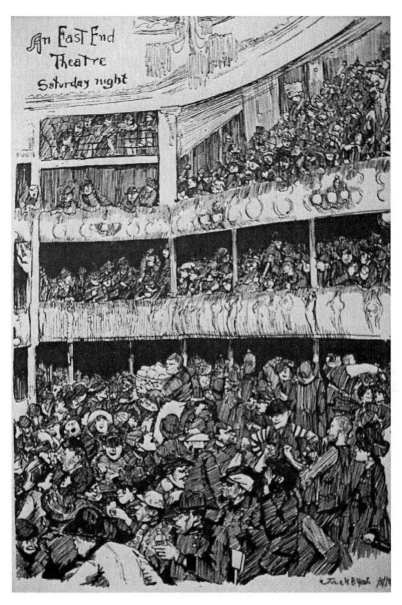

Illustration 24   Jack B. Yeats, ' "Hellfire": Drawing of a People's Theatre', from *Bric-a-Brac*, 1891.

In *Beltaine*, the journal of the ILT, Yeats opined that his model audience for its 'remote, spiritual and ideal'[29] drama comprised people, 'who read books, and do not go to the theatre'.[30] This inaugural issue also contained an article by his co-founder of the ILT, Edward Martyn, entitled, 'A Comparison Between Irish and English Theatrical Audiences', which reports the 'steadily growing belief' that England is a 'half-civilised country',[31] and declares that the decadence of its audience is 'irrevocable and complete'.[32] In contrast to the 'brutish and imbecile parade' of British theatre Irish drama was 'founded upon the ancient genius of the land', as its audiences are 'people uncontaminated by false ideals'.[33] Martyn, evidently, had never attended the Queen's Theatre in Dublin, let alone any of the infernal temples of Thespis in the black North!

In the light of all this it is quite extraordinary the extent to which theatre historians have been consistent in reproducing Yeats's metropolitan version of the theatrical past. They are also complicit in the replication of Yeats's modernist privileging of institutional, literary theatre over and above popular forms and traditions, to the extent that a whole century of dynamic theatrical activity can be instantly erased:

> Until the last years of the [nineteenth] century there was no such thing as Irish Drama . . . the Act of Union put an end to this . . . The repertoire of the Dublin Theatre Royal, the playhouse that dominated the Irish theatre for most of the nineteenth century was practically indistinguishable from that of the leading London theatres.[34]

It is a telling statement, with regards to what exactly constitutes 'drama' and 'Irish': both of which are configured and conjugated on reductive, essentialist terms. Drama is something that is *textual*, takes place within an *institutional* context, in a *metropolitan* location. Irish is defined in contradistinction to London and in terms of the 'nationality of the literary works, not simply by the birthplace of their authors'.[35] It is emblematic of how nationality and textuality are imbricated in a defining double helix which has generated a debilitating network of relations between literature and drama, national identity and a theatrical institution that have become normative in Irish theatre studies, to the detriment of both scholarship and practice.

Lionel Pilkington has pointed out how Irish theatre history and criticism has remained largely unaffected by seismic methodological and ideological shifts that 'revisionism' – 'an intellectual movement that defines itself as an objective critique of the orthodoxies of pietistic nationalism'[36] – has brought about in Irish historiography. As he observes, no 'parallel movement may be detected in relation to Irish theatre'[37] where scholarship continues to focus on the national(ist) narrative of the Abbey.[38] I would take Pilkington's critique a little further by adding that this cyclopean, thematic fixation of historians on 'national' theatre can be concomitantly mapped onto its historicist methodology, as Irish theatre historiography is also theoretically dominated by a temporal/historical epistemology, at the expense of any examination of space and geography. This absence seems particularly paradoxical given that Irish drama is axiomatically acclaimed as the decolonizing ideological apparatus of a nascent state-in-waiting. Moreover, every post-colonial scholar from Wole Soyinka to Edward Said emphasizes how the imperial encounter involves a territorial struggle over space and geography, through the way in which it is mapped and represented, controlled and contested.

Perhaps this is partially due to the fact that until recently, the regional sphere has always been subordinate to the national, as historian Alon Confino observes, 'the nation acts as a context within which the region can be intelligibly understood'.[39] Several seminal figures in post-colonial studies have articulated the 'National Longing for Form',[40] not the regional, nor the local. However, this paradigmatic relegation of the regional in relation to the national axiomatically assumes that the provincial is regressive, whereas the nation is progressive: a territorial teleology that needs to be challenged. Indeed this turn is underway as post-colonial histories and geographies reverse the privileging of metropolitan centres over colonial peripheries by decentring Europe through writing its history 'from and for the margins'.[41] The same approach could productively be applied internally to an examination of the geographies of nationalist discourse in the decolonizing context by examining its formation 'from and for' its own margins, such as the North of Ireland, as Ulster was imaginatively occluded from the nationalist mapping of the nation. The Irish Revival failed to recognize the regional realities of the North and was unable and unwilling to accommodate Ulster within its theatrical imaginary of the nation: an elision that was soon followed by (and helped facilitate) the empirical exclusion of the North through the political reality of Partition.

Yeats's vitiating influence on Irish theatre historiography has been recently challenged by a number of scholars. Christopher Wheatley, Alan Fletcher and Helen Burke's[42] pioneering work establishes the existence of indigenous theatrical traditions in the sixteenth, seventeenth and eighteenth centuries especially; Cheryl Herr, Mary Trotter and Stephen Watt have examined Irish melodrama at the Queen's Theatre in Dublin; and Christopher Morash's landmark study, *A History of Irish Theatre 1601–2000* reconfigures the diachronic and synchronic axes of conventional Irish theatre history to vividly reconstruct three centuries of a vital theatrical culture predating the advent of the Abbey. In spite of the apparent vitality of Irish theatre historiography two problems remain: the continuing neglect of the nineteenth century (outside of the late Victorian period), and the fact that all of these histories, bar Fletcher, are primarily Dublincentric and examine theatre and performance largely 'within the pale', the phrase used to delimit the boundaries of the capital of colonized Ireland beyond whose borders the imperial control was much more precarious.

This continuing neglect of the nineteenth century contrasts strikingly with the extraordinary proliferation of social, economic, political, literary, cultural, revisionist and counter-revisionist histories of this period, known as the 'long century' as it opens in the bloody wake of the 1798 Rising with the 1801 Act of Union and closes in 1921 with the Partition of Ireland and the formation of two states. Numerous diachronic studies of the 'long century' characterize this period as struggle for conformity over conflict;[43] however, a post-structuralist distrust of such teleological grand narratives has fragmented this field in favour of local studies and micro-histories, most notably Jim McLaughlin's work which argues the need for a 'place-centred' approach to the study of history and nationalism, one that includes the role of geography in the formation of local, regional and national identities.[44] This methodological *segue* seems ideally suited to theatre scholars as the very subject of our study is always local, given the temporal-spatial contingencies of live performance. It then follows that theatre historians are perfectly positioned to articulate these disciplinary developments.

This essay will examine how the introduction of a geographical hermeneutic to the traditionally historicist study of Irish theatre can help displace the singularity of the master narrative of nation that Yeats and successive historians have helped author(ize), with a diffuse plurality of marginalized histories and practices. I will examine a number of case studies of discrete dramatic performances in non-institutional and institutional contexts and the more discursive theatricality of popular politics in the mid to late nineteenth century in order to explore the complex interplay between theatre, performance and theatricality in Belfast.

'The Northern Athens'

Late eighteenth-century Belfast was an enlightened, progressive, civic city, where the egalitarian ideals of the French and American revolutions radicalized local Presbyterian intellectuals who founded the United Irishmen (1791), a separatist, republican society which uniquely espoused its nationalist ideology in civic, secular terms and sought to the establish an ecumenical alliance between Protestants, Catholics and Dissenters. It was in this culturally dynamic period that Belfast was known as the 'Athens of the North', an appellation which originated from the opening prologue to the new playhouse at the Rosemary Street theatre. Indeed, as the political upheaval and nationalist unrest increasingly destabilized the wider *mise-en-scène* of the city, the theatre became a critical site of conflict where the hegemony of state was contested on a regular, riotous basis.[45] In this volatile period of 'gunpowder law',[46] Martha MacTier's letters document the deleterious effect that such disturbances had on a hitherto thriving theatrical scene, especially given the brutal extent of government repression and reprisal which both provoked and crushed the 1798 Rising.[47] The impact of these events even forces itself centre stage in W. J. Lawrence's account of theatre in this period, a historian who is otherwise infuriatingly impervious to the influence of political events and contexts on theatrical production. The 'minute book' methodology that under-pins – or undermines – his unpublished manuscript *The Annals of the Old Belfast Stage 1731–1831* grinds to a halt when he reaches the year 1796 as

> a remarkable blank occurs in local records. For considerably over three years, the *Newsletter* (our one great source of information) is utterly silent regarding dramatic doings at Arthur Street. Not the modestest paragraph chronicles the opening of the theatre, and no advertisements appear, as heretofore, calling the patrons of benefits to arms.[48]

This 'blank' silence is suggestively filled as the pedantic historian is propelled into a poetic register entirely at odds with the dully data-based, positivist-chronological approach that dessicates his normal mode of writing:

> Throughout the dark days of the rebellion, the inhabitants of Belfast took their pleasures sadly and somewhat desperately; but they took their pleasures. At the time when the gallows in the Market House was seldom without its grisly tenant; when public flagellation grew so common that the onlookers remained unmoved by the groans and cries of the victims; an affected gaiety took possession of the town. There was feasting in the Exchange; balls and routs; and even playgoing had its votaries. Laughter and Death sauntered arm in arm together, Laughter, perhaps, the ghastlier of the two. But martial law was not fruitful or good for the theatre, and Northern players felt the force of the old mazarinade:
>
> > 'Comedians[sic], c'est un mauvais temps
> > La Tragédie est par les champs.'[49]

It is an extraordinarily evocative passage which hauntingly records the slaughter unleashed by the Rising and its subsequent repression, during which Belfast's theatres went dark as public performances of a different kind were enacted in the city in the gruesome spectacles of pitch-cappings, half-hangings, public executions and flagellations which crushed the Rising. The activity of the United Irishmen, an organization founded in Belfast and whose members swore separatist oaths on the slopes of Cave Hill overlooking the city, ironically culminated in the 1801 Act of Union, legislation which strengthened rather than severed the colonial link with England.

In spite of the complete victory of the governmental forces, Belfast wasn't entirely quiescent in the early nineteenth century. Repeated disturbances resulted from disputes over the playing of National Anthems during performances; the theatre continued to be a contested space wherein soldiers garrisoned in the city and the victorious yeomanry clashed violently with those vestigial elements who remained sympathetic towards the defeated insurgents of '98. Advertisements for the theatre regularly sought to reassure audiences, 'The Public may rest assured that such precautions are taken as will prevent all further disturbances in the Gallery.'[50] Robert Emmet's attempted rising in 1803 in Dublin led to further disturbances in Belfast and the reimposition of martial law, and indeed when the newly refurbished theatre in Arthur Square reopened on 15 January 1806, advertisements carried the statement:

> To prevent any unpleasant consequences which may arise from Airs being called for not advertised in the Bills, Mr Bellamy deems it necessary to inform the public that 'God save the Queen' will be performed by the band at the end of the fourth act of the Play, 'Patrick's Day', prior to the farce, & 'Rule Britannia'

between the 1st and 2nd Acts, and on no account whatever will they be played at any other period of the evening.[51]

Such advertisements signalled what was to become an ongoing struggle by different theatre managers in Belfast throughout the nineteenth century to discipline unruly audiences and to curtail, or at least contain, the political agency of highly partisan audiences. This was especially evident in the wave of Irish political melodramas popular from the 1880s which were known in Belfast as 'Irish Nights'.

'Irish Nights'

Belfast underwent vast changes in the nineteenth century as the rapid development of its manufacturing industries, its factories, foundries, mills and massive shipyards, linen and tobacco industries attracted an immense influx of agricultural workers, particularly after the famine of 1845–9, when starving peasants fled the blighted countryside for the city. Belfast was the fastest growing city in the British Isles from 1841–1901 and its population outstripped that of Dublin: a radical demographic change confirmed in the 1891 census which established Belfast as the largest city in Ireland, its population having increased from 20,000 in 1801 to 350,000 by 1901. Popular entertainment for the city's new urban population was much the same as other industrial cities in Britain. However, the 'Victorian or Edwardian social consensus'[52] manifest on the mainland was undercut in Belfast by sectarian conflict and territorial struggle for supremacy given rapid Catholic immigration into what had been a securely Protestant city. Little wonder then that local audiences were distinguished by a certain toughness that caused performers to remark that 'if you could survive Belfast and Glasgow, you could survive anywhere'.[53] One theatre critic recalls how a journalist colleague from Dublin requested he be brought to the gallery of Belfast's Theatre Royal, an institution 'which had no parallel in the United Kingdom', and, after visiting the aforementioned establishment, 'he considered there was nothing like it between a certain warm quarter and Connaught.'[54] The considerable reputation of Dublin's theatres for riots and ructions[55] makes his description of the infernal atmosphere of Belfast's playhouses especially significant. As with Britain, Dublin's social (and nationalist) consensus was also undercut by Belfast's sectarian geography and the particularly heated horizon of expectations shared by the 'Montagues and Capulets of inflammable Linenopolis'.[56]

For instance, in a Belfast playhouse in 1819, a stone, rather than a thunderbolt, hurled from a local divinity in the gods, seriously injured an actress, and in the Grand Opera House the fourth wall literally had to be materialized in the form of a giant net installed to catch 'Belfast confetti' (steel rivets from the shipyards) and (empty) porter bottles hurled from the gallery. However, whilst such violent *fracas* frequently occurred in theatres throughout the British Isles, the unique in-house ructions associated with what became known as Irish Nights can be distinguished from other theatre disturbances as they were precipitated by performances of Irish political melodramas on the public stage. The popular subgenre of Irish political melodrama in the mid-to-late nineteenth century was partly due to the recrudescence of nationalist feeling in this period and the recognition of its commercial potential by Hubert O'Grady, Dion Boucicault, John Baldwin Buckstone and J. W. Whitbread.[57] Irish Nights, however, were unique to Belfast given the city's context as a crucible of inter-communal conflict throughout the various Home Rule crises. On 'Irish Nights', audiences in the city attended the theatre equipped with flags, instruments, oranges and other paraphernalia. Little wonder then that one play-goer referred to Irish Nights as 'melodramas within melodramas',[58] and certainly they can be seen as plays within plays, with multiple roles being performed both on and off the stage by the Catholic and Protestant audiences. One of the best accounts of an Irish Night is recorded in the memoirs of the Ulster actor, Whitford Kane, who recalls performing Boucicault's *The Shaughraun* in the 1890s:

> The play was generally turned into a battle between the religious factions. Naturally, it was a nervous play for the actors . . . especially the priest and young Fenian hero . . . they often looked with anxious eyes at the gallery knowing that the climax at the end of the first act would cause a hullabaloo. This occurred when the young Irish rebel was in hiding. The gallery patrons would point out to the English captain where he was concealed for they believed this was their duty as true British subjects, and when the priest refused to disclose it, they hurled rivets and bottles at the actor. Luckily this scene happened just before the intermission and the asbestos curtain served as a timely shield for the players . . . and the gallery policeman would conveniently turn his back and see nothing if an odd rivet should find its way there. Cracking the skull of a fellow citizen during a performance of *The Shaughraun* was hardly a misdemeanour.[59]

This colourful account reveals the sense of ritualized theatre both on and off the stage and the symbolic, strategic and sectarian segregation of the audience with the added symbolism of the asbestos curtain which, in protecting the stage, reflected the poisoned fabric of Belfast society before it.

In the subgenre of Irish political melodrama written by O'Grady, Boucicault and Whitbread, the nationalist eponymous heroes of *Wolfe Tone*, *Robert Emmet*, *Sarsfield*, *Lord Edward* and *Father Murphy* arrived on stage in Dublin to deafening cheers of 'patriotic sentiment' whilst the villains (informers, soldiers and police) were catcalled and 'hissed'.[60] Belfast, however, had little of the capital's political homogeneity – this demographic difference undermined the dramaturgical dialectic of the play by disrupting this hero–villain hierarchy, so that when the Kennedy Miller Company toured from Dublin to Belfast with *Lord Edward*, loyalists and nationalists lauded their own representatives and lambasted those of their 'Other' simultaneously. Take for example the different reactions described by Belfastman Hugh MacCartan, to the hero Lord Edward Fitzgerald and the villain Magan:

> the Shankill hurled oranges at Tyrone Power [who played Lord Edward], and the Falls shared its hatred of Frank Breen's informer by fierce hisses and catcalls . . . Now and then a scuffle would break out at the points of junction between the two.[61]

Lord Edward dealt with the life of Lord Edward Fitzgerald, a nationalist hero of the 1798 rebellion. However, it attracted audiences equally from the Catholic Falls and the Protestant Shankill, who were seated to the left and right respectively. Both camps attended with instruments, flags, oranges and, more ominously, rivets purloined from the shipyards, a setting deemed unsuitable for the young dramatist, St John Ervine, by his aunt who refused to take her curious nephew to an Irish Night for 'she was fearful there may be a row in the gallery between the Papist and the Orange corner boys who congregated there . . . .to make a demonstration of their religious beliefs.'[62]

Again, the drama of these occasions was well underway before the curtain had even been raised, with cries of 'Up the Celts' and 'Go on the Blues' and as the first bars of 'The Wearing of the Green' opened the play, the collected Catholic choirs of the Falls and the Markets roared along. In response, a similarly enthused Shankill replied with a loyalist broadside of the 'The Protestant Boys' and when Lord Edward entered onstage to reveal his plans to free Ireland from English tyranny, St Peter's Brass Band, from the heart of Falls, subsequently 'marched round the boards playing "The Boys of Wexford"'[63] in carnivalesque support of their patriot hero's revolutionary speechifying, a nationalist demonstration which prompted the Protestant gallery to stage 'a melodrama of their own'.[64] This synchronous, symbolic and ritualized interaction between text, performance, actors and audience(s) was an anticipated and integral part of the theatrical event and created a somewhat intimidating atmosphere which leaves MacCartan wondering:

> What the Kennedy Miller company – straight from the applause of the Old Queen's theatre in Dublin – thought of their noisy prelude, I could only guess; probably they were prepared for it, possibly they enjoyed it.[65]

It is significant that in spite of the voluminous scholarship exploring the process of political polarization which led to the sectarian segregation of Belfast, the theatre has been completely neglected in all historical, anthropological, cultural, sociological and political research, though it remained virtually the singular, secular meeting place in the whole of Belfast! Catholics and Protestants, separated, residentially, religiously, socially and spatially, attended the theatre together in droves and mixed freely together, with the notable exception of Irish Nights, when audiences self-consciously replicated the religious and political segregation extant outside the theatre within it. Whilst the segregation of audience members served to minimize points of contact and conflict between the two communities it also had a deeper structural effect in that it served to regulate and reinforce each community's reading of the performance text and the history enacted on the physical stage before them and its significance in the wider political stage outside the theatre.

In spite of the perfervid political atmosphere of these occasions, I have been unable to find any records of serious disturbance either in or outside theatres in Belfast on Irish Nights, suggesting that these in-house ructions were an accepted part of the theatrical experience. The fact that the audience corralled themselves in different areas and brought 'ammunition' with them, suggests a local familiarity with and popular anticipation of the likelihood of offstage dramatics. This supposition is supported by Whitford Kane's acknowledgement that Irish political melodramas were 'always a draw in Belfast, not so much for its dramatic value, but as the audience knew it would get a chance to participate in the performance'.[66]

Para-theatrical performance: street theatre and mass politics

Such para-theatrical performances associated with 'Irish Nights' may also be examined in relation to the more discursive context of participatory/spectactorial dynamics of political meetings and demonstrations in this period. Theatre historian Andrew Malone states that:

> throughout the nineteenth century, when the countries of Europe were turning to realism in the theatre, the only form of drama with which the people of Ireland were generally too familiar was that supplied by the dramatisation of political conditions in the speeches of politicians.[67]

Another historian, Gary Owens, notes that 'public assemblies became increasingly familiar forms of public expression'[68] in the mid-to-late nineteenth century. Indeed, the massive campaigns for Catholic Emancipation and repeal of the Act of Union spearheaded by Daniel O'Connell, which prepared the grounds for later pro- and anti-Home Rule movements, politicized and polarized nationalists and unionists on a spectacular scale with millions mobilized: a popular involvement in politics unparalleled in Britain. Only recently it has been asked how 'these mass phenomena can be read as texts that might tell us something about the popular and political culture that produced them'.[69] Perhaps it is more meaningful to reverse this question and to investigate how popular culture and theatre shaped these political performances? One fascinating aspect to researching theatre in the mid to late nineteenth century is how frequently music halls, theatres and other performative venues were used for political meetings. Indeed, from the stage of Belfast's Theatre Royal, 'innumerable political addresses in previous times had been delivered on almost every political and religious subject'.[70] In the space of a few weeks in 1846 the Music Hall hosted a nationalist meeting of 'the repeallers of Belfast and friends of O'Connell',[71] the loyalist Belfast Protestant Operatives, the Belfast Anti-Slavery Society and the Society for the Education of Native Irish in their own Language. Even the firebrand pastor Dr Henry Cooke who blasted the 'Sabbath breaker' as 'one degree lower than a theatregoer'[72] and gave blistering sermons against the ungodly theatricals which combined 'Scripture, satire, wit, denunciation, invective, appeal... in such an onslaught as must have brought terror even to the spirit of poor old Thespis, for all his years in Arcady or Hades',[73] preached to his congregation at Batty's Equestrian Circus to celebrate his successful 'Repulse of the Repealer', Daniel O'Connell, after the latter's disastrous visit to Belfast in 1842.

Illustration 25 'View of the CIRCUS as it appeared at the Great Protestant Meeting held in Belfast, 21st Jan., 1841', from *The Repealer Repulsed!: A correct narrative of the rise and progress of the repeal invasion of Ulster: Dr. Cooke's challenge and Mr. O'Connell's declinature, tactics, and flight. With appropriate poetical and pictorial illustrations.* Courtesy of Linen Hall Library.

This convergence in the performative modes of popular theatre and mass politics has remained largely unexplored and untheorized, yet a more detailed study of the way in which specific theatrical spaces codified and conditioned these political exchanges, and the process whereby the 'horizons of expectation' of the public were co-ordinated, or calibrated, according to their experiences of the music hall and theatre, could help our understanding of both the production and reception of these political performances.

A vivid example of this mutually constitutive relationship is evident in Daniel O'Connell's much mooted first visit to Belfast as part of the Repeal campaign. In the weeks preceding his visit, unionist papers were filled with febrile speculation as to the exact date of his visit and the threat it posed to the union. What is interesting about the newspaper reports of the period is the way in which theatrical metaphors, references and conventions provide a meta-theatrical narratological framing device, 'This is the time for pantomimes and pantaloons, harlequins and basty speeches, wonderful changes and working the chances, frieze coats and fruitless talk. Following close upon the heels of the laughing moving hero at the theatre . . . we find the Mighty O, hastening to Dublin.'[74] Moreover, O'Connell's appearances before his supporters from the balcony of his hotel, the Music Hall, and Batty's Equestrian Circus, and were all elaborately staged 'theatre events'.

At the latter venue the 'Liberator' appeared before an enthused audience on a stage bedecked with busts, banners, bunting and flags. In the background was a bust of O'Connell with two female figures representing Peace and Fame, the latter depicted crowning O'Connell with a wreath of laurels with the motto, 'The triumph of the peaceful conqueror', whilst stage left was an 'allegorical painting of Erin weeping over a harp encircled with wreathes of shamrocks', with another motto, presumably for the semiotically illiterate, 'Erin, the victim of misrule'.[75] Another bust of O'Connell and Erin, with a harp in her right hand and wolfhound at her feet, was placed at the front of the stage, whilst a portrait of Darrynane Abbey flanked by further busts of O'Connell and Napoleon and the Queen and her consort 'on the opposite "scenium" – added their attraction to the *tout ensemble*'.[76] This lavish nationalist scenography was further enhanced by numerous laurel branches,[77] banners belonging to the Tailors' Union, the Sawyers' Union, and the Belfast Reform Society that show this political meeting to be a contemporaneous form of medieval processional, with guilds replaced by unions. As a final, finishing touch, a flag to the right of the Chair declared, 'The public will be our guide – the public good our aim.'[78]

The visual grammar of this stage setting symbolically framed the Liberator's political performance and had an important dramaturgical function in aesthetically connecting his high politics with the plebeian moving picture world of melodrama and the visual culture of the popular stage. This seems to be part of a wider development of the 'scenography' of Irish nationalist popular politics which managed to successfully appeal to all sections of Irish society in this period, from the 'sophisticated' audiences of the middle classes through to the skilled trades and artisans and, crucially, the urban working-class audiences who frequented playhouses, were familiar with these aesthetic forms, and thus susceptible to their ideological function.

However, working-class engagement with such stage-managed politics could take place in more dissonant, disruptive ways, as the participatory performance licensed in nineteenth-century playhouses extended to the political stage. A fascinating example of such an encounter is the chaotic meetings held in 1847 in the Music Hall and the Theatre Royal Belfast by the Young Irelanders (a faction who split from O'Connell's movement over the issue of using physical force). Their own paper, *The Nation*, optimistically opines, 'We have no doubt that the representatives of the Irish Confederation will be received courteously, and listened to attentively, in the chief town of Ulster';[79] however, the unionist *Newsletter* delights in describing how the 'Confederates' were confronted by an 'anti-audience':

> the pit's anti-audience produced a number of watchmen's rattles, which they twirled about making a great noise, while they also cheered as lustily as they could . . . then a quantity of powder was ignited which exploded with a great flame, and caused considerable confusion . . . [as] mingled with the tobacco smoke . . . it was difficult to discern the front of the boxes from the stage.[80]

The gloating correspondent goes on to relate how the rest of the meeting proceeds in a dumb show pantomime as handkerchiefs were waved by friends, fire rockets were ignited by enemies and the 'Old Ireland' Repealers knowing of no better organised method of putting down all attempts at speech making and hostile vociferation, than the Kentish-fire sunk their hatred of this Protestant species of applause by unitedly using it to the utter discomfiture of the confederation . . . gave the scene the appearance of the imps of Pandemonium rebelling against their leaders.[81]

On this occasion 'Belfast confetti' was replaced by more carnivalesque ammunition as delegates were pelted by pig bladders filled with blood, leaving the bespattered speakers Bakhtinian spectacles. Nevertheless, in spite of the 'horrid smell of sulphur and brimstone'[82] the meeting was hailed by its organizers as a success.

In spite of the seemingly extreme violence of these reactions there is a sense that much of this was ritualized and regulated as the theatre building itself disciplined and controlled the audience's agency and actions from spilling over into very real rioting.[83] More often than not this occurred as a result of political street theatre held outside of theatre buildings, such as O'Connell's next appearance in Belfast in 1864. Long dead at this stage, O'Connell's posthumous presence was manifest in the form of an enormous effigy:

A few tradesmen constructed a colossal figure of O'Connell . . . clothed in garments like those in which the Irish Agitator, when in the flesh, was wont to encase himself. A wallet, characteristic of his lifelong mendacity, was suspended by his side. An emblem, indicative of Popery, was placed upon his breast; and a large supply of combustible material was secreted in the hinder parts of the prodigious effigy . . . and borne away to the Boyne Bridge.[84]

This 'surrogate victim'[85] was then ritually burned by 10,000 loyalists at the appositely named Boyne Bridge to taunt buoyant nationalists returning from Dublin where they had attended the 'seditious'[86] ceremonial laying of the foundation stone for a monument to O'Connell. At first, this provocative spectacle did not trigger major unrest; however, the mock funeral of the effigy's ashes attempted by loyalists the following day when they marched *en masse* with a 'rudely constructed'[87] coffin across the city to the Catholic cemetery of Friar's Bush, almost inevitably culminated in conflict, as the 'funeral' train was attacked by incensed nationalists, a prelude to five days of rioting which concluded with very real wakes and funerals.

More people were killed during such sectarian rioting in Belfast than in all the rebellions of the nineteenth century. Such unrest was often sparked by national events such as the one described above, but was more often triggered by territorial tensions resulting from the contiguity of both communities. Increased Catholic immigration meant that the sectarian geography of the city, the 'seismic zones' in Frankfurt Moore's memorable description, began to slip their spatial co-ordinates as, to borrow Friel's phrase, the city's communities found themselves increasingly 'imprisoned in a linguistic contour that no longer matches the landscape of fact'.[88]

Ulster as 'Other': regional modernity vs. revivalist modernism

Belfast was a scientific, industrial and technological city; yet one of the defining aspects of the Irish Revival and of a great deal of Irish nationalist culture and politics in the late nineteenth to early twentieth century, was its profound antipathy to science and modernity.[89] John Wilson Foster's work has done much to recuperate and re-evaluate the cultural history of Irish science[90] and he makes an incisive and important connection between industrial 'aesthetics' of the late nineteenth century and one avant-garde strain of modernism: the Futurism propounded by Marinetti, and its celebration of speed, technicism and the 'reign of the machine'[91] as the touchstones of the new modern age. Indeed, essayist and Ulsterman, James Winder Good described Belfast as 'a Futurist fantasia that would have delighted Marinetti'.[92] Futurism's celebration of the interdependence of man and machine, combined with Marinetti's advocacy of technology, speed and war, which underpinned the cultural and nationalist politics of Italian imperialism, also had a certain purchase in Belfast. After all, the city, which in manufacturing the *Titanic* made what many cultural critics later hailed as *the* iconic symbol of modernity the manifest apotheosis of 'the machine age', established Belfast as the scientific, mechanical, modernist capital of Ireland, qualities wholly inimical to nationalist discourse promulgated in Dublin. What was formerly described as 'the Northern Athens' was now defined as a 'monument to Victorian self-help',[93] inhabited by the 'economic man' of Victorian textbooks where, Good describes, 'there is probably no city of the same size in the Three Kingdoms which retains so much of the spirit of the early Industrial Revolution, with its childlike faith in the gospel of salvation by machinery and its glorification of the man of business as the real saviour of society.'[94]

However, the North's commercial, materialist modernity was anathema to Yeats and inimical to the profoundly anti-modern, anti-material and anti-urban precepts of the Revival, so much so that John Wilson Foster caustically classifies 'contempt of Ulster' as one of four structuring principles of the Revival's paradigmatic construction of Irishness.[95] Foster's description of Yeats's 'disdain for Ulster ... with its nasty undisguised urbanism of Belfast, its filthy industrialism, its contemptible Protestant low-church non-conformism', certainly resonates with Sam Hanna Bell's description of Yeats's 'antipathy for all things Ulster',[96] and is further reinforced by an unpublished letter written to Maud Gonne in 1938, in which he mocks Northerners as 'a horrid lot. Who, within our borders, would sour all our tempers.'[97]

Robbie Meredith alleges that leading architects of the Revival like Lady Gregory and Yeats endured a troubled relationship with the North and notes how both sought to decouple the 'geographical signified'[98] from folklore so that Yeats could claim that 'a woman from the North would probably be a fairy woman ... and certainly not necessarily at all a woman from Ulster.'[99] Thus fairies were more amenable to Revivalist rhetoric than Nordies. Similarly Lady Gregory opined that 'knowledge of charms has usually come from the North, but the North may be taken to mean any strange unfamiliar place.'[100] Certainly, such a description of a 'strange unfamiliar place' seems apposite as this was often the experience of Belfast shared by many Southerners, and is particularly evident in popular travel literature of the period. For example, the alienation and antipathy to Belfast of ardent nationalist William Bulfinn, who recorded his experiences of cycling across Ireland, are made abundantly clear in *Rambles in Erin* (1902):

> Belfast . . . repelled me. As I stood within it I asked myself was I in Ireland . . . I saw churches of all denominations, Freemason and Orange lodges, wide streets, towering smokestacks, huge factories, crowded traffic. And out of the water, beyond the Custom House, dimly seen through the smoke and mist, rose some huge shapeless thing which I found to be the shipbuilding yard where some 10,000 men were hammering iron and steel into great ocean liners . . . in the shadow of a great vibrating towering clanging factory I stood once more and looked for some signs of Ireland . . . it is not an Irish city . . . simply the creation or the outgrowth of a state of things completely un-Irish . . . it seemed to have a foreign complexion. Its methods, its enthusiasms, its outlook . . . its idealism was anything but Irish . . . There is no Irish geniality about Belfast street life. It is cold, austere, rigid, grim.[101]

This profound sense of dislocation and estrangement must have, in part, stemmed from the brutal reality of Belfast's alterity from the Revival's ideological and aesthetic representations of 'Irishness'. Belfast's accents, architecture, atmosphere and outlook, let alone its deviant political unionism and different religious demography, made it incompatible with the Revival's essentialized and simplistic counter-hegemonic narrative of nationhood.

Belfast's scientific, industrial and technological modernity operated as an internal Other to the southern-based Irish Revival's self-fashioning of 'national identity' whilst concomitantly shaping the discourse that proved equally indispensable to political unionism's ideological self-fashioning. Belfast's manufacturing prowess and proficiency, in an age underpinned by the *telos* of technological accomplishments and scientific progress, made it a symbolic city of the modern period. Inventions such as the internal combustion engine, pneumatic tyres (invented by an Ulsterman), kinetoscopes, celluloid film, radio, box cameras, automobiles, aircraft and ocean liners, transformed the modern world.[102] In this 'machine age', scientific qualities of size, speed, power and efficiency were transmuted into cultural values, becoming 'cultural imperatives and not just technical ambitions'.[103] In Belfast, such cultural imperatives were imbricated within the mythology of the Protestant work ethic, and were crucially important in the formation of unionist identitarian paradigms in this period: the pragmatic, industrious, rational 'Ulsterman', as opposed to the Celticized 'Irishman'.

Against this seismically different cultural *mise-en-scène*, I would like to finally examine a spectacular form of theatrical event unique to Belfast. In the late Victorian period, the city's unionist authorities developed extraordinary expertise in stage-managing massive, public performances of Belfast's industrial supremacy through huge civic ceremonies celebrating the launch of Harland & Wolff's largest ships. These spectacular performances enacted and enforced, in the public sphere, Belfast's modernity, its material progress, its Protestant work eth(n)ic, and its British, imperial identity. In arguing the importance of synthesizing geographical and historical materialism in (re)considerations of the theatrical past, it is fitting to finish with a final, *fin-de-siècle* performance in Belfast, albeit of a non-dramatic variety: the launch of *Oceanic II* on 14 January 1899.[104]

This titanic, stage-managed spectacle 'performed' Belfast's civic pride and industrial prowess before the world's press and the local population. Six hundred and eighty-six feet in length and 17,274 gross tons, *Oceanic II*'s twin screws, powered by four-cylinder triple expansion engines, provided 28,000 horsepower and propelled it at a top speed of twenty-one knots: it was the first ship to exceed Brunel's *Great Eastern*. For its launch, a special stand, eight hundred feet in length, was constructed at Victoria Wharf to accommodate an elite audience of 5,000 spectators (3,000 seated with 2,000 more provided 'a comfortable standing view').[105] This was an exclusive, ticketed event with the revenue philanthropically donated to local charities. Special trains were laid on to transport spectators from all over Ireland and indeed visitors from all over the world. As for the ordinary vulcanites who constructed the ship, they thronged in multitudes on the roofs of warehouses and along the shore, behind barriers erected to prevent deaths from the massive displacement of water expected from the launch. The Irish Temperance League Dining Rooms, promoted in unionist *Newsletter* editorials, opportunistically opened so that 'Visitors to the Launch may procure Coffee and other refreshments', obviously of the non-alcoholic variety, speaking of which, police and infantry were stationed in certain parts in 'the neighbourhood of the yard'.[106]

The fetishized object of all this scopophilic attention, *Oceanic II*, replete with 1,704,000 rivets, a lot of Belfast confetti, was painted bridal white for the occasion: 'She has been temporarily painted in hues which will afford every opportunity to the cinematic and photographic artist on the occasion of the launch',[107] many of whom studded the shores or were perched in a special crow's nest built above the viewing stand to provide the perfect photograph of the largest ship in the world, and the first to be launched by hydraulic power. As the clock counted down to the sounds of salvoes of gunfire to the 11 a.m. launch, some of the old war cries 'were trotted out and banded about freely, the antiphonal chorus of "Go on the Blues" being the principal method'.[108] When the moment arrived and the Leviathan slipped from the Lagan into the Lough, 150,000 spectators – almost half the city's overall population – cheered, clapped and celebrated as the Union Jack, the Stars and Stripes and the White Star Flags were simultaneously unfurled. A local, satirical publication, *The Magpie*, acidly lampooned this excessively jingoistic pageantry:

It was in all senses a triumph in stage management... There was only one thing necessary, perhaps, and with the jingo atmosphere everywhere at present, I wonder how it came to be overlooked. The absence of a military band to strike up 'Rule Britannia'... is the only fault I have to find... otherwise the arrangements were perfection out-perfected.[109]

However, the *Newsletter* was more patriotically fulsome:

> the people of Belfast, and the people of Ulster, are proud of the notable fact that this great vessel has been built ... on the shores of the Lagan, and that wherever she may go she will not only be a monument to British Enterprise, but also an incontrovertible witness to the mechanical ingenuity and ability of the men who designed her and the artisans who ... carried out those designs ... But the *Oceanic* is much more than this. She is another of the gifts of commerce to the cause of humanity – another important link in that chain of intercourse which binds together men of different, yet of kindred races. The century that is now rapidly drawing to a close ... has witnessed many changes, but perhaps none have been more striking or more noteworthy because of their influence on the world at large than those which have taken place in the means of communication between one country and another. Nations that were once, to all intents and purposes far as the poles asunder have been brought near to each other through the triumphs of science. Distance has been well nigh annihilated ... old time jealousies are being forgotten and the people of the British Empire and the mighty Western Republic are beginning to remember their close relationship and to manifest the affection which should spring from a common parentage and a common heritage.[110]

The gap between this unionist imperial modernity and the nationalist revivalist modernism is crystallized beautifully by the fact that, two days later, Yeats and Edward Martyn urged the foundation of an Irish Literary Theatre at a meeting of the Irish National Theatre Society.

Conclusion

Finally I would like to finish with a confession, well at least one belonging to Dennis Kennedy, as in his account of the prodigious process of editing the *Oxford Encyclopedia of Theatre and Performance* he states that, 'Convinced that entries on national theatre traditions were inevitably oversimplified and misleading we made what is probably the most controversial decision and eliminated them.'[111] His proposition is all the more jarring when juxtaposed with the other framing figure of this essay, W. B. Yeats, who declared, 'All art is national',[112] although it nevertheless remains that theatrical performance is always local for it is dependent on the spatial and temporal contingencies of live performance.[113] In decentring the 'nation' in favour of 'cities and regions that are theatrical centres'[114] Kennedy maps the critical contours of a geographical hermeneutic that can enable Irish historians to slip the epistemological yoke of a national, modernist historiography that privileges texts over performance, high art over popular culture, professional praxis over amateur activity, institutional theatre over non-institutional drama, and the national sphere over the local.

Notes

1. W. B. Yeats, 'Literature and the Living Voice', *Samhain* (1906): 7.
2. Pierre Macherey, *A Theory of Literary Production*, translated from the French by Geoffrey Wall (London: Routledge & Kegan Paul, 1978), 79–80.
3. Peter Kavanagh, 'Dramatic Trends, 1800–1900', *The Irish Theatre: Being a History of the Drama in Ireland from the Earliest Period up to the Present Day* (Tralee: The Kerryman Limited, 1946), 395–401; and Christopher Fitz-Simon, *The Irish Theatre* (London: Thames and Hudson, 1983), 82–104.
4. Richard Pine, ed., *Dion Boucicault and the Irish Melodrama Tradition as Prompts*, 1, no. 6 (special edition, 1983); J. M. Nelson, 'From Rory to Paddy in Boucicault's Myles, Shawn and Conn, the Irishman on the London Stage, 1830–1880', *Éire-Ireland*, 13.3 (1978): 79–105; Stephen M. Watt, 'Boucicault and Whitbread: the Dublin Stage at the End of the Nineteenth Century', *Éire-Ireland*, 18.3 (1983): 23–53; and John P. Harrington, ' "Rude Involvement": Boucicault, Dramatic Tradition and Contemporary Politics', *Éire-Ireland*, 30.2 (Summer 1995): 89–103.
5. Cheryl Herr, *For the Land They Loved: Irish Political Melodramas, 1890–1925* (Syracuse: Syracuse University Press, 1991); Mary Trotter, *Ireland's National Theaters: Political Performance and the Origins of the Irish Dramatic Movement* (Syracuse: Syracuse University Press, 2001), 25–72; and Stephen Watt, *Joyce, O'Casey, and the Irish Popular Theater* (Syracuse: Syracuse University Press, 1991).
6. Peter Holland, 'Series Introduction: Redefining British Theatre History', in *Theorizing Practice: Redefining Theatre History*, ed. W. B. Worthen with Peter Holland (Basingstoke: Palgrave Macmillan, 2003), xvi.
7. Heinz Kosok, 'The Image of Ireland in Nineteenth-Century Drama', *Perspectives of Irish Drama and Theatre*, ed. Jacqueline Genet and Richard A. Cave (Gerrards Cross: Colin Smythe, 1991), 50. This neglect is also evidenced in *The Field Day Anthology of Irish Writing*, ed. Seamus Deane (Derry: Field Day, 1991). This enormous three-volume study (excoriated for ignoring women writers) also evacuates the nineteenth century in its purview of Irish theatre over four centuries, which is classified under the following four categories: Christopher Murray, 'Drama 1690–1800', vol. 1, 500–657; D. E. S. Maxwell, 'Irish Drama 1899–1929: the Abbey Theatre', vol. 2, 562–719; Terence Brown, 'The Counter-Revival: 1930–60'; D. E. S. Maxwell, 'Contemporary Drama: 1953–1986', vol. 3, 171–231; 1137–1307.
8. Andrew E. Malone, *The Irish Drama* (London: Constable & Co Ltd., 1929), 12. Una Ellis-Fermor makes a similar claim, 'The history of the English drama (with which the Irish was, until the end of the nineteenth century, for practical purposes identical)'; *The Irish Dramatic Movement* (London: Methuen & Co. Ltd., 1939), 2.
9. Kosok states that the nineteenth century represents, 'a large, and largely uncharted, territory' ('Nineteenth Century Drama', 66) and Morash in his superb study, points out that the 'early nineteenth century has long been something of a blind spot for Irish theatre historians' (Christopher Morash, *A History of the Irish Stage 1601–2000* [Cambridge: Cambridge University Press, 2002], 307). Morash's history, along with Fitz-Simon's and Ophelia Byrne's historical survey, *The Stage in Ulster from the Eighteenth Century: Selected from the Theatre Archive of the Linen Hall Library* (Belfast: Linen Hall Library, 1997) are the only works which cover, albeit briefly, the nineteenth century beyond the late Victorian period.
10. Jacky Bratton, *New Readings in Theatre History* (Cambridge: Cambridge University Press, 2003), 3–6.
11. At an IASIL conference (Galway 2004) I participated in a panel with colleagues from Queen's addressing this specific problem and proposing alternative theoretical paradigms of class, geography and gender to reconfigure Irish theatre studies. More significantly, Lionel Pilkington's recent essay in a special edition of *Modern Drama* on Irish theatre critiques the current state of play of Irish theatre historiography and declares the need for new theoretical and methodological approaches to be deployed if

the field is to flourish ('Recent Developments in Irish Theatre History', *Modern Drama*, 47.4 [2004]: 721–31). At present, discussions are also ongoing on the establishment of an Irish Society for Theatre Research (ISTR): an organization which will have as part of its remit the specific objective of engendering disciplinary debate/development within Irish theatre studies.

12. See Christopher Murray's seminal book, *Twentieth Century Irish Drama: Mirror up to Nation* (Syracuse: Syracuse University Press, 1997).

13. Dennis Kennedy, 'Confessions of an Encyclopedist', in *Theorizing Practice*, 36.

14. This neglect starkly contrasts with the proliferation of British studies, notably Peter Bailey, ed., *Music Hall: the Business of Pleasure* (Milton Keynes: Open University Press, 1986); Jacky Bratton, ed., *Music Hall: Performance and Style* (Milton Keynes: Open University Press, 1986); Dagmar Kift, *The Victorian Music Hall: Culture, Class and Conflict* (Cambridge: Cambridge University Press, 1996); Michael Kilgarriff, *Beauty and Banjos: Peculiar Lives and Strange Times of Music Hall and Variety Artistes* (London: Oberon Books, 1998). The only publication in the Irish field is Eugene Watters and Matthew Murtagh's *Infinite Variety: Dan Lowrey's Music Hall, 1879–97* (Dublin: Gill and Macmillan, 1975), although this particular publication is written more as homage than history.

15. A composite form of Anglo-Saxon folk culture and indigenous Irish traditions, mummers toured house-to-house in rural areas performing their set play which depicted the life cycle of death and revival using iconic nationalist and unionist political and religious figures (St Patrick, St George, Daniel O' Connell, Cromwell, etc.). These characters fought one another with victor varying according to the political persuasion of the household in which the mummers were performing.

16. The wren has long been bound up in superstition in Ireland and wrenboys throughout the country traditionally 'hunt the wren' on St Stephen's Day: a medieval tradition possibly imported from England, but customized by Irish costumes of straw masks, animal skins and horns, and musical accompaniments played on home-made tambourines. The wren was killed beforehand and in a noisy, carnivalesque procession was carried on a holly bush from house to house where wrenboys demanded food and drink. Earlier versions of these performances involved men dressed as women and were linked to fertility rituals.

17. Strawboys, so named because of their straw masks and clothing, appeared at weddings and wakes where they were involved in dancing, music and games which were often sexual in nature.

18. The 'Biddy boys' wore straw masks like the mummers, wrenboys and strawboys and were associated with the feast day of St Briget, during which they would carry a doll made of straw from one house to another, singing songs in honour of the saint. These practices were common in the south-west of Ireland.

19. Christmas rhymers performed Yuletide plays in late December and toured from house to house collecting money and food.

20. Gaelic term for a traditional storyteller.

21. For descriptions of some of the folk rituals and performances associated with weddings and wakes see E. Estyn Evans, 'Weddings and Wakes', *Irish Folk Ways* (London: Routledge & Kegan Paul, 1967), 282–94.

22. Feast days of parish patron saints celebrated at sacred sites connected with the saint and often with the local topography of a more ancient, Gaelic, pagan tradition. These respectful, religious devotions were invariably followed by carnivalesque celebrations involving excessive drinking, dancing, music, feasting, courtship, sports, and faction fighting. See Diarmuid Ó Giolláin, 'The Pattern', in *Irish Popular Culture 1650–1850*, ed. James Donnelly Jr. and Kerby Miller (Dublin: Irish Academic Press, 1988), 201–21.

23. Over three thousand holy wells have been identified in Ireland. The symbolism of water as a source of purification, fertility and healing made them equally amenable to pagan and Christian rituals and they provide a fascinating point of convergence between both cultures.

24. *Samhain*, or all All-Hallows Eve, was the largest festival in Ireland during which the dead were commemorated through myriad performative customs, games, amusements and rites: from processions to the ritualized smashing of pots, and cattle being driven through fires.

25. The May festival, which remained remarkably free from Christian influence, featured a variety of superstitious rituals and performances: bonfires were lit, fertility rituals known as the parade of the May Babies were held, cattle were driven into old raths and forts where fairies were believed to dwell. Here the animals were bled and their blood poured on the earth to protect them from evil spirits.

26. See Pilkington, 'Recent Developments', 725.

27. See L. P. Curtis, *Apes and Angels: the Irishman in Victorian Caricature* (Newton Abbot: David and Charles, 1971). Jack Yeats later regularly worked as a contributor to *Punch*.

28. Stuart Hall, 'Notes on Deconstructing "The Popular"', in *People's History*, ed. Raphael Samuel (London: Routledge & Kegan Paul, 1981), 227.

29. W. B. Yeats, 'Theatre', *Beltaine*, 1.1 (1899): 21.

30. Ibid., 20.

31. Edward Martyn, 'A Comparison Between Irish and English Theatrical Audiences', *Beltaine*, 1.1 (1899): 11.

32. Ibid., 12.

33. Ibid.

34. Kosok, 'Nineteenth Century Drama', 50.

35. Ibid.

36. Lionel Pilkington, 'Theatre History and the Beginnings of the Irish National Theatre Project', in *Theatre Stuff: Critical Essays on Contemporary Irish Theatre*, ed. Eamonn Jordan (Dublin: Careysfort Press, 2000), 27.

37. Ibid.

38. Shaun Richards also notes that Irish theatre is 'haunted' by 'the idea of "nation"', a framework that has defined (and distorted) theatre history and criticism. Shaun Richards, 'Plays of (Ever) Changing Ireland', *The Cambridge Companion to Twentieth-Century Irish Drama*, ed. Shaun Richards (Cambridge: Cambridge University Press, 2004), 1.

39. Alon Confino, 'On Localness and Nationhood', *Bulletin of the German Historical Institute* 23.2 (2001): 9.

40. Timothy Brennan, 'The National Longing for Form', in *Nation and Narration*, ed. Homi K. Bhabha (London: Routledge, 1990), 44–70; and Declan Kiberd, 'The National Longing for Form', *Inventing Ireland* (London: Vintage, 1996), 115–32. Salman Rushdie also refers to 'the national longing for form' in his post-colonial novel, *Midnight's Children* (New York: Penguin Books, 1980), 375.

41. Dipesh Chakrabarty, *Provincializing Europe: Postcolonial Thought and Historical Difference* (Princeton: Princeton University Press, 2000), 16.

42. Christopher J. Wheatley, *Beneath Iërne's Banners: Irish Protestant Drama of the Restoration and Eighteenth Century* (Notre Dame, IN: University of Notre Dame Press, 1999); Alan J. Fletcher, *Drama, Performance and Polity in Pre-Cromwellian Ireland* (Cork: Cork University Press, 2000); Helen M. Burke, *Riotous Performances: the Struggle for Hegemony in the Irish Theatre, 1712–1784* (Notre Dame, IN: University of Notre Dame Press, 2003).

43. Theodore K. Hoppen, *Ireland Since 1800: Conflict and Conformity* (London: Longman, 1989).

44. Jim MacLaughlin, *Reimagining the Nation State: the Contested Terrains of Nation Building* (London: Pluto, 2001).

45. See Martha McTier's (sister of William Drennan, the founder of the United Irishmen), account of a night at the theatre (27 February 1793): 'I sat in a box with three officers at the opening of our elegant new theatre on Monday who appeared as if they were sent to Coventry. *God Save the King* was the first tune. The officers clapped, *all* the house did the same, but the gallery and a few voices in the pit for the second music called *Ça*

Ira, this was silenced and they contented themselves with obtaining and clapping the *Volunteer March*; thus this much feared first night ... was happily got over.' *The Drennan Letters: Being a Selection from the Correspondence Passed between William Drennan, M. D. and his Brother-in-Law and Sister Samuel and Martha McTier During the Years 1776–1819*, ed. D. A. Chart (Belfast: His Majesty's Stationery Office, 1931), 138.

46. Ibid., 139.
47. 'Our playhouse, it is probable will be shut up, as last night two officers jumped over the box while *God save the King* was playing and horsewhipped a captain of a ship sitting in the pit with his hat *off*. Most of the ladies left the house, except Mrs. Mattear, who cried out, but in vain, to the whippers that she saw the man take off his hat. The answer was, he was, he was not on his feet ... The man proves to be a most loyal subject, a stranger here, not, perhaps, blessed with a quick ear', a defect, 'paid for' in Belfast with a thick one (*Drennan Letters*, 299).
48. W. J. Lawrence, *The Annals of the Old Belfast Stage 1731–1831*, unpublished manuscript (Linen Hall Library, Belfast, 1896), 186–7.
49. Ibid., 187–8.
50. Cited in Lawrence, *Annals*, 227.
51. *The Belfast Newsletter*, 14 January 1806. Martha McTier also records some of these disturbances; in October 1804 she writes of 'a great riot in the playhouse on Friday about *God Save the King* and the military prevailed ... for the future *God Save the King* is to be played every night, and *Rule, Britannia, when convenient*' (*Drennan Letters*, 341). In August 1806 she describes how she was 'much more diverted by the spirit of the audience', as the gallery and elements of the pit demanded *Patrick's Day*, 'but the box would not', and its officers 'damned them for croppies' (*Drennan Letters*, 349).
52. Bratton, ed., *Music Hall*, xi.
53. Cited in John Grey, 'Culture and Arts in the North of Ireland Since 1891', in *A Century of Northern Life*, ed. Eamon Phoenix (Belfast: Ulster Historical Foundation, 1995), 165.
54. 'Some Personal Reminiscences of an Old Belfast Pressman. No. VIII: Old Players and Playgoers', *Evening Telegraph*, 1 August 1887.
55. See Burke, *Riotous Performances*.
56. W. J. Lawrence, *Barry Sullivan* (London: W. & G. Baird, 1893), 65.
57. Whitbread's melodramas were usually staged as part of an Irish season at his Queen's Theatre; however, he also sold the performing rights to small fit-up theatre companies which then toured town and countryside throughout Ireland. See W. G. Fay and Catherine Carswell, *The Fays of the Abbey Theatre* (London: Rich & Cowan Ltd., 1935), 39.
58. Hugh McCartan, 'Some Backward Glances', *The Capuchin Annual* (1943): 175.
59. Whitford Kane, *Are We All Met?* (London: Elkin, Mathews and Marrot, 1931), 46–7.
60. Joseph Holloway, 'Extract from a Paper Read to the National Literary Society', *The Irish Playgoer*, 12 April 1900, 13.
61. McCartan, 175. McCartan's account relates to performances in Belfast circa 1898–9.
62. St John Ervine, *The Theatre in My Time* (London: Rich & Cowan Ltd, 1933), 14.
63. McCartan, 175.
64. Ibid.
65. Ibid.
66. Kane, 46.
67. Malone, *Irish Drama*, 8.
68. Gary Owens, 'Nationalism Without Words: Symbolism and Ritual Behaviour in "Monster Meetings"', in *Irish Popular Culture*, 242.
69. Ibid., 242.
70. 'Recollections of an Old Belfast Reporter', *English Telegraph*, 25 August 1886, in the John J. Marshall Scrapbooks, vol. 4 (Linen Hall Library, Belfast), 22.
71. *The Belfast Timeline*, ed. Joe Baker, Glenavel Local History Project, http://www.glenravelonline.com/_downloads/glenravelonlinesite/Belfast_Timeline_1840s.pdf (11 January 2006).

72. Cited in J. W. Good, *Ulster and Ireland* (Dublin: Maunsel & Co., 1919), 128.
73. Hugh A. McCartan, *The Glamour of Belfast* (Belfast: Talbot Press, 1921), 112. Anti-theatrical prejudice was particularly virulent in Belfast where pastors regularly preached and published theological tirades against theatricals; see Anonymous, *Lectures and Conversations, Expressive of Character and Sentiment etc.* (Belfast: William Ferguson, 1837) which takes as a central moral question, 'Let us enquire have theatrical entertainments a greater tendency to promote virtue or vice, religion or profaneness?', to which the author decides that all temples of Thespis are 'school[s] of vice . . . profanity, irreligion and wantonness' (16–17).
74. *The Northern Whig*, 7 January 1841.
75. *The Northern Whig*, 19 January 1841.
76. Ibid.
77. *The Belfast Newsletter*, 22 January 1841. Owens notes that laurel branches represented amity, peace and regeneration (252) but were also subversively symbolic: surrogate signifiers of nationalist resistance.
78. Ibid.
79. *The Nation*, 13 November 1847.
80. *The Belfast Newsletter*, 16 November 1847.
81. Ibid.
82. Ibid.
83. Guy Debord describes how urbanism and architecture in modern capitalist societies 'safeguards class power' (172) and suppresses workers, *Society of the Spectacle* (Detroit: Black and Red, 1983), 169–73.
84. Henry Thomas, *History of the Belfast Riots* (Belfast and London: James Reed Hamilton and Adams, 1864), 4.
85. Joseph Roach, *The Cities of the Dead: Circum-Atlantic Performances* (New York: Columbia University Press, 1996), 40.
86. Thomas, *Riots*, 3.
87. Ibid., 4.
88. Brian Friel, *Translations*, in *Modern Irish Drama*, ed. John P. Harrington (New York: W. W. Norton & Co., 1991), 351.
89. See Greta Jones, 'Catholicism, Nationalism and Science', *Irish Review*, 20 (1997): 47–61; Gordon Herries Davies, 'Irish Thought in Science', in Richard Kearney, ed., *The Irish Mind: Exploring Intellectual Traditions* (Dublin: Wolfhound Press, 1985), 295–310; and John Wilson Foster, *Recoveries: Neglected Episodes in Irish Cultural History, 1860–1912* (Dublin: University College Dublin Press, 2002), 7.
90. Significantly, two-thirds of *Recoveries*, Foster's superb reappraisal of the history of Irish science, is (necessarily) Belfastcentric in focusing on this aspect of nineteenth-century cultural history.
91. See J. W. Foster, *The Age of Titanic: Cross-Currents in Anglo-American Culture* (Dublin: Merlin Publishing, 2002), 26, 30–1, 35, 167, 169.
92. Good, *Ulster*, 253.
93. A. T. Q. Stewart, *The Ulster Crisis* (London: Faber & Faber, 1967), 44.
94. Good, *Ulster*, 256.
95. J. W. Foster, *Colonial Consequences: Essays in Irish Literature and Culture* (Dublin: Lilliput Press, 1991), 253.
96. Sam Hanna-Bell, *The Theatre in Ulster: a Survey of the Dramatic Movement in Ulster from 1902 Until the Present Day* (Dublin: Gill and Macmillan, 1972), 2.
97. This is one of 400 letters owned by Anna MacBride White (Maud Gonne's daughter) drawn from a fifty-year correspondence between Yeats and her mother Maud that were sold to Emory University, Atlanta, Georgia, in 2003. This particular fragment was quoted by John Harlow, 'Letters Reveal the Pain of Yeats's Platonic Love', *The Sunday Times*, 9 February 2003.

98. Robbie Meredith, '*The Shan Van Vocht*: Notes from the North', in *Critical Ireland: New Essays in Literature and Culture*, ed. Aaron Kelly and Alan A. Gillis (Dublin: Four Courts Press, 2001), 174.

99. W. B. Yeats, *Visions and Beliefs in the West of Ireland*, 2 vols (New York and London: G. P. Putnam's Sons, 1920), 2:343, cited Meredith, 'Notes', 174.

100. Lady Gregory, *Poets and Dreamers: Studies and Translations from the Irish Including Nine Plays by Douglas Hyde* (Gerrards Cross: Colin Smythe, 1974 [1903]), 274.

101. William Bulfinn, *Rambles in Eireann*, vol. 1 (London: Sphere Books Limited, 1981), 89, 94.

102. See John Wilson Foster's superb account of how the 'Mechanical Age' which changed utterly the modern world culminated in the manufacture of the *Titanic*, the sinking of which signalled the opening of the twentieth century as the collapsing of the Twin Towers closed it (*The Age of Titanic*, esp. chapters 1 and 6: 1–38, 166–207). See also Foster's *Recoveries*, 49–138.

103. Foster, *Recoveries*, 67.

104. Other launches like that of the *Olympic* on 20 October 1910 were equally massive civic occasions. Dennis Ireland notes the formality of these performances, recalling how his father would take these days off and 'appeared at launches in the same uniform that served for funerals – that is, in frockcoat and top hat'. Dennis Ireland, *From the Jungle of Belfast: Footnotes to History 1904–1972* (Belfast: Blackstaff Press, 1973), 28.

105. *The Belfast Newsletter*, 14 January 1899.

106. Ibid.

107. Ibid.

108. Ibid.

109. *The Magpie*, 21 January 1899.

110. *The Belfast Newsletter*, 14 January 1899.

111. Dennis Kennedy, 'Confessions', 36.

112. W. B. Yeats, *Uncollected Prose by W. B. Yeats*, ed. J. P. Frayne and C. Johnson, vol. 2 (New York: Columbia University Press, 1975), 141.

113. See my article, 'The Critical "Gap of the North": Nationalism, National Theatre, and the North', *Modern Drama*, 47.4 (2004): 594–606.

114. Kennedy, 'Confessions', 36.

Part III
Repertoires

8
The Death of Tragedy; or, the Birth of Melodrama

Jeffrey N. Cox

A standard history of early nineteenth-century drama and theatre, still quite powerful despite the work of many of those included in this volume to contest it, discovers the romantic drama as a version of the melodrama, with both contributing to an overall decline of serious theatre in the late eighteenth and early nineteenth centuries. In this particular version of that long-running scholarly history play, the 'death of tragedy', melodrama is cast as a Brutus, the bastard offspring of high literature, joining the murderers of the most august form of drama, with the romantic drama appearing in a minor part, perhaps as Cinna the Poet, seen by the crowd as part of the conspiracy but in the end torn apart for its 'bad verses'. Scholars, playing Antony straight, come to the romantic period to bury its theatre and drama, not to praise it, as they await the rise of those theatrical Octavians, Ibsen and Shaw, who will create the empire of modern drama – though, as we will shortly see, some scholars are of Brutus's party and find in the outcast melodrama the progenitor of much in modern theatre and drama.

Such accounts of romantic period drama and theatre deploy a number of binaries – echoing behind my own title – that Jacky Bratton has found structuring standard theatrical histories: text vs. context, high literature vs. low theatre, the written drama vs. the material stage.[1] But such histories of romantic-era drama engage these oppositions in order to dismiss both poles, with the 'low', physical, collective theatre, when not simply ignored, being seen as one cultural context for the creation of high, visionary poetry written in solitary splendour as one reaches the mountain top or listens alone to the nightingale, far in any event from the crowded pits of Covent Garden and Drury Lane, and with romanticism's 'high', literary, written drama being understood, exactly because it was created by men chasing birds on mountaintops rather than learning the secrets of the stage, as deeply untheatrical, unstageable, and thus uninteresting. The drama celebrated as high literature here is that of the early modern period or perhaps of the modern period, not the plays of Baillie and Coleridge, Byron and Hemans.

As a result, when we work to rescue the theatrical side of this reductive account, we replace the tragic story of the death of tragedy with a melodramatic tale of the victory of melodrama, where the drama and theatre have fallen on bad times, enabling that decadent aristocrat, poetic tragedy, to continue its degradation of the virtuous but rough, and sometimes mute, popular theatre, until the day is saved by the miraculous emergence of a realistic drama later in the century. While, again, some theatrical histories discover realism in the rejection of all of nineteenth-century drama, the arrival of realism is dependent, in this second account, upon developments within the theatre that include the melodrama, the well-made play, and the Adelphi drama, but not the poetic drama of romanticism. Realism can be victorious when the drama, following the melodrama, sets aside such 'un-modern', 'un-theatrical' subjects as Cain's battle with Lucifer, the siege of Valencia, the unbinding of Prometheus, or the Faustian struggles of Manfred to take up naval mutinies, factory conditions, alcohol abuse, and absentee landlordism in order to move towards the serious treatment of everyday life, the goal, according to Erich Auerbach, of Western mimetic art.[2] Melodrama here is revealed as a vital, popular, subversively 'illegitimate' form opening up new vistas in a theatrical landscape dominated by the patent theatres royal, seen as pursuing a dead and deadening traditionalism to which even the innovative romantic poets paid homage in eliza-bethanizing tragedies that could never command the stage. Melodrama shadows forth, however darkly, the forms of modern drama, whether those of the realists and naturalists, those of the expressionists, or those of Brecht and other creators of a modern political drama.[3] In both versions of theatrical history that I have been simplifying here, one dismissing and one celebrating the melodrama, the plays of the romantic poets take a backward step in the grand march of theatrical intellect.

To escape from the binary oppositions that have crippled histories of early nineteenth-century theatre and drama, we cannot simply invert the traditional hierarchy of terms; we must dissolve such simplifications in a more complex account of early nineteenth-century drama and theatre that is both intertextual and intertheatrical, to use Jacky Bratton's phrase.[4] For there was not so much an opposition in the period between performance and poetry – roughly between the stage of the 'illegitimate' drama and the page of the so-called closet drama – as there was a juxtaposition of different kinds of performances, including 'perform-ances' in poetry and fiction that have been usefully studied by scholars such as Judith Pascoe and Peter Brooks.[5] For example, Catherine Burroughs has shown us the complexity of the idea of closet drama – that includes real performances in private spaces, imagined performances in reformed theatres, and dramas simply waiting to be performed in theatres less subject to government control – and Jane Moody among others has revealed to us the range of theatre sites in the period where one could sample different kinds of performances – from tragedy to circus acts – at different kinds of theatres.[6] When Wordsworth, Coleridge, Baillie, Hemans or Byron thought about writing for the stage, they did not write one kind of play but instead engaged the entire dramatic and theatrical tradition, nor did they face a monolithic theatrical institution, but a complex range of performance spaces, genres and styles. The mistake is to separate poetry from the stage, or for that matter circus acts from stage tragedy. We need to see the array of perform-ances in London as part of an interlocking system, not least because they were in competition with one another for audiences and thus needed to be concerned with what rival establishments were offering. Much as we think of radio, broadcast television, cable, videos and DVDs, movies, the internet and pod-casts as all part of a media system in which each outlet bids for our attention, so should we see the major theatres offering tragedies and comedies, pantomimic stages, circus rings, street fairs, and even poetic plays in print as all connected in a performance system that helps shape each part: so that, when we read Byron's *Manfred*, we must, as Philip Martin has shown, think of contemporary spectacular stage practices that Byron knew well and drew upon in creating the atmosphere of his poetic play, or when we delight in the Christmas pantomime *Harlequin and Humpo*, we need to recall that on many nights it was preceded by Coleridge's *Remorse*.[7] We should neither delegitimatize forms such as the melodrama nor detheatricalize the dramatic works of the romantic poets.

The melodrama and romantic tragic drama both played a role in the formation of the dramatic/theatrical complex of their moment and thus in the ongoing lived processes that continue to shape plays and their performances. While the melodrama may have been dismissed by some as merely theatrical, and while romantic tragic drama may have been set aside by others as unfit for the stage, at the time they both contended for the attention of that portion of the public that cared about the theatre and the drama. We should not collapse romantic drama into the melodrama or celebrate the romantic drama as the hero of some self-defeating conflict between high literature and materialist theatre, but we do need to read the melodrama and romantic drama together to see how, confronting a shared literary, cultural, social and political moment, they offered competing visions and drew on differing literary and theatrical tactics that are still usefully defined in relation to one another. We need, as Edward Ziter puts it, to adopt a phenomenological approach to the drama and theatre of the day to reveal the romantic drama and melodrama as differing, even opposing responses to the same epistemological shift found in the era's theatrical representation and shaping of the experience of space and time.[8] In order to begin the mapping of the theatrical landscape to include both the melodrama and the romantic drama, I will first outline the presence of the melodrama in the patent theatres royal (where the romantic poets hoped to triumph), as it presented one key popular way to deal with the aesthetic, cultural, social and political tensions of the Napoleonic era; I will then suggest how we might understand the kind of realism offered by the melodrama as 'sensationalist', before more briefly considering how the romantic drama offered competing forms and visions that create a 'virtual' rather than 'realistic' theatre.

Patent house melodrama in the era of Napoleon

Any attempt to equate romantic drama and the melodrama faces the opposition of the 'father' of the melodrama, Charles Guilbert de Pixérécourt, and his great defender, Charles Nodier. In the preface to Pixérécourt's *Théâtre choisi*, Nodier would first seem to agree that the romantic drama is a mere subset of the melodrama, for he says of the 'new school' of romanticism that it is 'scarcely anything other than the melodrama adorned with the artificial pomp of lyricism', but he immediately adds the wish that romantic playwrights had been 'as faithful to the first aim of the melodrama as to its form', that is, to the moral vision of melodrama as created by Pixérécourt.[9] While Nodier finds romantic drama celebrating the 'poetic beauties of crime',[10] he argues that Pixérécourt's plays actually reduced the crime rate: in his account, the melodrama, treating the extremities of danger and fear that the people confronted under the Revolution, asserts that those trials issue within the theatre in a clear moral order, as the melodrama serves a profound moral, even sacred function in a period during which, Nodier argues, Christianity was banned from public life. Pixérécourt himself located, as he put it, 'religious and providential' ideas at the heart of the melodrama and wanted to be sure that the melodrama was distinguished from romanticism, which he found to be 'dangerous, immoral, destitute of interest and truth'.[11] We certainly can find romantic plays borrowing devices, motifs, characters from the melodrama, but Nodier and Pixérécourt make it clear that Hugo, Dumas, Vigny and Musset offer an opposing vision.

Nodier's fascinating if somewhat fawning essay on what he calls classic melodrama defines a particular phase in that form's development, for, in introducing a playwright who was still active in the 1830s alongside of Hugo and Dumas, Nodier sees the central works of the genre being penned during the years of the Consulate and the Empire – that is, the melodrama, at least in its classic form, is a product of the age of Napoleon. He dates the birth of the genre from Pixérécourt's staging of *Cœlina* on 2 September 1800 (Théâtre de l'Ambigu-Comique), even though Pixérécourt's *Rosa, ou L'Ermitage du Torrent* had been offered as his first 'mélodrame' the month before (9 August 1800, Théâtre de la Gaîté); it was, of course, Thomas Holcroft's translation of *Cœlina* as *A Tale of Mystery*, premiering at Covent Garden on 13 November 1802, that first brought the label of 'melodrama' to the London stage,[12] so, while there clearly are earlier plays by Kotzebue or Colman or Morton that possess melodramatic features, this international hit offers the rare opportunity to discover the birth date of a literary form. I want to follow Nodier to locate the 'classic' melodrama in England in the years between Holcroft's innovative drama and the fall of Napoleon, that is between the Peace of Amiens and Waterloo, with the two key phases of dramatic writing by the romantic poets bracketing these years, the initial efforts of Baillie, Wordsworth and Coleridge coming before 1800 and the striking turn to the drama by the younger writers occurring during the post-Napoleonic restoration.

A focus on the melodrama of the decade and more of war that followed the Peace of Amiens enables us to see how the melodrama in England first arose, as Frank Rahill long ago noticed, as a patent house form.[13] A rough accounting of melodramas during the war years indicates their strong presence at the theatres royal of Covent Garden, Drury Lane and the Haymarket: for example, Covent Garden staged not only Holcroft's play but such works as Thomas Dibdin's *Valentine and Orson* (3 April 1804), Matthew Lewis's equestrian *Timour the Tartar; a Grand Romantic Melo-drama in Two Acts* (29 April 1811) and Isaac Pocock's *The Miller and his Men* (21 October 1813); Drury Lane during the same period offered

Frederick Reynolds's *Caravan; or, The Driver and his Dog*, with Carlo the Wonder Dog performing a daring rescue (5 December 1803), Elliston's *Venetian Outlaw*, taken perhaps from Pixérécourt (26 April 1805), Theodore Hook's *Tekeli; or, The Siege of Montgatz*, another adaptation from Pixérécourt (24 November 1806), later revised down to two acts for performances at the Haymarket in 1809, and Samuel Arnold's *The Woodman's Hut* (12 April 1814); the Haymarket not only recycled melodramatic works, including *A Tale of Mystery* and *Tekeli*, but also offered new melodramas such as Hook's *The Fortress* (16 July 1807) and William Dimond's *Foundling of the Forest* (10 July 1809), a rare case where a melodrama during these years was offered as a mainpiece. James Kenney had the distinction of having melodramas at both patent theatres royal at the same time when *Ella Rosenberg* was premiered on 19 November 1807 at Drury Lane while his *Blind Boy* opened a few weeks later at Covent Garden (1 December 1807).[14] Matthew Lewis may have tried his hand repeatedly at tragedy during the first decade of the nineteenth century, but he had a series of successes with major house plays labelled as melodramas. Melodrama at the major theatres rapidly became pervasive and flexible enough that it could be used for everything from patriotic spectacles such as Cumberland's *Victory and Death of Nelson* staged at Covent Garden on 11 November 1805 to the satire of Thomas Dibdin's 'mock' melodrama, *Boniface and Bridgetina; or, The Knight of the Hermitage; or, The Windmill Turret; or, The Spectre of the North-east Gallery* (Covent Garden, 31 March 1808).

Beginning this trend, Holcroft's play opened at a key moment in the history of the London stage and of that other stage, what John Wilson Croker called 'the theatre where the great European tragedy is now performing',[15] for the 1802–3 season witnessed both the Peace of Amiens, a brief respite in the war between England and Napoleonic France, and the continuing hostilities between John Philip Kemble and Drury Lane that would lead to his defection, and that of his even more brilliant sister, Sarah Siddons, to the rival house at Covent Garden. The melodrama, as we will see, is a form particularly suited to a public anxiously balanced between war and peace, but its appearance first makes sense as a response to the anxious condition of the patent theatres royal, glimpsed in Kemble's move to Covent Garden that has been configured by theatrical historians such as Boaden and Genest as the moment in which Drury Lane as the main home to the high literary drama and particularly tragedy 'sunk into a state of inferiority', in Genest's words;[16] Kemble's move would also, as we all know, lead in a few years to the O. P. Riots at the time of the reopening of Covent Garden, when audiences contested the significant changes occurring in the physical space of the London theatres, in modes of acting and stage presentation, and in the kinds of drama capable of pleasing a changing public, a public which the prologue to Elliston's *Venetian Outlaw* imagines as a monstrous centaur divided between man and beast and unable to decide what theatrical fare it will find nourishing.[17]

At a moment when the hierarchy of dramatic genres seemed threatened (Leigh Hunt would proclaim that 'There is no such thing as modern comedy, tragedy, nor even farce, since Mr. Colman has left off writing it'),[18] when the patent theatres royal felt themselves threatened by competition from the 'minor' theatres that were redrawing the map of what Jane Moody calls 'the theatrical city',[19] and when the nation faced the threat of a European axis of evil devoted to revolutionary terror, the melodrama offered Covent Garden and Drury Lane a new form of serious drama, capable of importing the tactics of their rivals onto their legitimate stages and able to stage and to manage the fears and desires of their audience.[20]

Recognized as the innovative work of its season, Holcroft's *Tale of Mystery* received thirty-eight performances as an afterpiece at Covent Garden, with additional performances being offered during the summer at the Haymarket, so that it was seen more often than even that year's successful Christmas pantomime of *Harlequin's Habeas; or, The Hall of Spectres*. While appearing after several of Shakespeare's tragedies and Addison's *Cato*, Holcroft's melodrama most often followed comedies or comic musical works, either war-horses such as Macklin's *Man of the World* of 1781 or new works such as Thomas Dibdin's controversial *Family Quarrels* (18 December 1802), Frederick Reynolds's *Delays and Blunders* (30 October 1802) – with that pairing being staged by royal command on 25 November 1803 and generating over £500 in receipts – and Colman the Younger's most financially lucrative play, *John Bull; or, an Englishman's Fire-Side* which opened on 5 March 1803. This matching of *A Tale of Mystery* with comic works suggests the kind of balance we often note in the scheduling of plays in the period. It also points to the generic threat that the melodrama was seen by some to pose: Holcroft's play appeared as one of very few new serious dramas among the twenty-seven plays premiered at the patent theatres during the 1802–3 season. While there were two other plays we might label as melodramas, most importantly William Dimond's *Hero of the North* (19 February 1803), and while one finds an adaptation of Shakespeare's *King John* (20 May 1803), the overwhelming majority of new works were comic: there were six new five-act comedies, three farces, the two Christmas pantomimes, and a mixed gathering of comic musical pieces.

The only new plays staged during the year of Amiens that might be thought of as tragedies were both by Matthew Lewis, and it is thus perhaps not surprising that during the prior season, his tragedy, *Alfonso, King of Castille* (Covent Garden, 15 January 1802), had offered a prologue that, recognizing Joanna Baillie's *De Monfort* staged in 1800 as the only notable recent tragic drama, looked forward to the peace with France then being negotiated and hoped it would open a new era for British tragedy:

> While ruthless War his thunders hurl'd around,
> The *laugh* might *soothe*, the sigh, tho' just, might wound.
> For reason mourned such tragic Scenes to view,
> Each grief too probable, each pang too true:
>   . . .
> Britons, a fairer hour awaits us now;
> Lo! peaceful Olive binds each manly brow
>   . . .
> Such kindness may the tragic Muse restore.[21]

Lewis, finding tragedy to be realistic at an emotional level ('Each grief too probable, each pang too true'), believes that audiences in the midst of the horrors and sorrows of war will have little tolerance for the terror and pity of tragedy. With peace now at hand, Lewis hopes that the theatre can offer less escapist fare.

While Lewis sought to fulfil his own prophecy through his adaptation of Schiller's *Kabale und Liebe* as *The Harper's Daughter* (Covent Garden, 4 May 1803) and his 'tragic scene', the monodrama of *The Captive* (22 March 1803), both failed after one performance. Instead of traditional tragedy, there was Holcroft's *Tale of Mystery*, playing as the serious counterpoint to comic mainpieces. It is this slot offered to the melodrama in the nightly generic programming of the patent theatres royal that gives rise to the worry that this new, hybridized literary form posed a threat to the legitimate, regular drama.

The phrases 'legitimate' and 'regular' drama are wonderfully adaptable during the period, referring now to the legal control the patent theatres had over the drama of the word, now to canonical status, now to modes of performance, as can be seen in the responses to questions about these terms in the 1832 parliamentary investigation into dramatic literature. We, of course, need to remember that those who testified had interests to defend, so that we get the wonderfully inclusive definition of James Winston, a stage manager for the Haymarket and Drury Lane theatres which were vested in protecting the monopoly on the drama, who claimed, 'The regular drama I consider to be tragedy and comedy, and everything on the stage.'[22] More useful is the testimony of David Edward Morris, the proprietor of the Haymarket in 1832, who calls the 'regular' drama 'All the plays of Shakespeare, and all other classical authors; all plays that are licensed by the Lord Chamberlain'; the illegitimate drama is found in a work 'where you require scenic effect and music'.[23] For Morris, plays can become 'regular' either by being in the canon of dramas penned by 'classical' authors or by being licensed by the Lord Chamberlain and his Examiner of Plays; the illegitimate drama is not, however, the illegal or the uncanonical but the sensational. The confusion that might arise can be seen when Morris was asked if Fielding's *Tom Thumb* – which some considered formally to be a burletta and thus a proper piece for the minor theatres – is a legitimate drama: he answered, 'Yes; because it was written by a classical author, and produced at a regular theatre.'[24] Still, it was the sensational nature of these plays that was the key, as in Douglas Jerrold's attempt to distinguish between the legitimate and the illegitimate drama by considering the nature of their dramatic appeal: 'I describe the legitimate drama to be where the interest of the piece is mental; where the situation of the piece is rather mental than physical. A melo-drama is a piece with what are called a great many telling situations'; when asked if he meant a distinction between a 'piece rather addressed to the ear than to the eye', Jerrold replied, 'Certainly.'[25] Again, Genest, in writing of Dimond's *Foundling of the Forest*, which we need to remember was offered as a mainpiece, argues, 'it would have been a very good piece, if it had not been degraded from a place in the legitimate drama by the introduction of 6 or 7 songs, without any good reason.'[26]

The mere appearance of music cannot be the cause of Genest's complaint: musical scores were featured throughout the drama of the period in comic operas, ballad operas, musical entertainments, ballets, operatic farces and burletta.[27] Drury Lane and Covent Garden claimed a right not only to the spoken drama but also to all opera except the Italian ones given at the King's Theatre in the Haymarket, so that during the 1813–14 Drury Lane season, for example, one hundred nights were devoted to musical drama.[28] At another point, Genest defines the melodrama as a 'mixture of dialogue and dumb show, accompanied by music',[29] but again the presence of pantomime alluded to here cannot alone be the source of melodrama's 'illegitimacy': while a staple of the 'minor' theatres, pantomime both lies behind a patent theatre form – the holiday harlequinade – and travels through many forms of theatre, as the dumb show in the play-within-a-play in *Hamlet* suggests. While the mixture of forms involved in the melodrama might alone offend those interested in preserving the purity of genres, what is specifically disturbing, I believe, is the introduction of instrumental music, extensive pantomime and powerful spectacle into what was in the first instance a form of patent house serious *spoken* drama – Boaden calls the melodrama 'an *opera* in prose, which is merely *spoken*; and in which music discharges the duty of a *valet de chambre*, because her office is simply to announce the actors'.[30] What I will want to explore shortly is that the innovation that gives the form melo-drama its name – the introduction of near continuous music behind the action rather than as the accompaniment to sung words – is an example of a new deployment of existing theatrical practices that created a different kind of theatrical experience, a different relationship between audience and the 'reality' it watches on stage.

The irregular, illegitimate nature of the melodrama, then, arises from aspects of its stagecraft. Its illegitimacy, of course, might have been linked to its moral and political vision.[31] Barry Sutcliffe has shown how the notion of 'legitimacy' can be seen as moving from artistic merit to legal right to moral worth, and finally, in the era of Burke and Paine, not to mention the rise of the 'illegitimate' political authority of a Napoleon, legitimacy must also carry an ideological valence.[32] The linked defence of 'legitimate' theatre and government is perhaps best seen in the *Anti-Jacobin*'s satire on the German or Gothic drama, *The Rovers; or, The Double Arrangement*, where German dramatic innovations are linked to French political ones in what Coleridge would label as the 'modern, jacobinical drama'; when Coleridge argues that the return of Shakespeare, Jonson and Otway to the centre of the dramatic repertoire would constitute the 'redemption of the British stage' and the restoration of traditional drama in its 'rightful dominion over British audiences', we engage a political and a moral as well as a cultural register of values.[33] While the 'German' drama, identified with the Gothic, with Kotzebue, with the moral complexities of the plays of Schiller and Goethe, rang up short on those registers, the same was not true of the classic melodrama inspired, ironically enough, by models coming from Revolutionary France. Again, as Pixérécourt and Nodier argued, the classic melodrama is moral, providential, patriotic. To take one quick example from the British drama of the period: Reynolds's *The Caravan* might at first seem to stage challenges to 'legitimate' political authority, for figures such as Arabbo, an Algerian pirate, and Blabbo, a worker on a Caravan, protest the oppression dealt out by the Spanish government. However, we rapidly learn that the problem arises because there is a Napoleon-like 'Usurper' running the country, not the rightful king who is too young to rule. The key act of tyranny by the grasping regent is, typically enough, a domestic and sexual one, for he has ordered the execution of the Marquis of Calatrava in order to force his wife to give in to his lustful demands. Vowing to die rather than violate her marriage vows, the Marchioness links domestic security with political legitimacy: 'the Patriot Monarch knows the proud boast of reigning in the heart; and mothers then shall clasp their children in their arms; and not like me, be victim of a Tyrant.'[34] While at moments Arabbo can seem like a precursor to a Byronic pirate-rebel, and while it might appear that Blabbo follows Lazarillo de Tormes in celebrating the body's needs over society's regulation, in the end everyone works for the restoration of familial and political order, as the dog Carlo saves the Marchioness's son at the very moment her husband is freed and the king is restored. Everyone can join in a final chorus that celebrates the kind of legitimate authority embodied in the British monarchy and not in that upstart Napoleon:

> Since Heaven's restor'd our much lov'd King,
> The tyrant's pow'r no more we own,
> . . .
> We'll scorn the pale usurper's sway,
> Our King we'll love and still obey, –
> Then ev'ry one, with joy to day,
> Your monarch's rights aloud proclaim![35]

Imported from Napoleonic France, the melodrama becomes a key form for reaffirming the legitimacy of the British monarchal and patriarchal orders, with Revolutionary and especially Napoleonic France being depicted as a threat to both sexual morality and political stability.

The 'illegitimate' nature of the classic melodrama, then, arises neither from its pedigree – it was born in a patent theatre house – nor its legal status – it was a licensed form of spoken drama offered at the theatres royal – nor its moral and political vision – it was, if anything, ultra-legitimate. It is, I want to argue, the stagecraft of the melodrama that was new, even though these innovations could be used to defend the old order. It is the sensational nature of the 'irregular' or 'illegitimate' melodrama that I want briefly to consider, but I want to make it clear that I do not want to view such sensationalism as some set of cheap, stagey tricks but instead as an array of theatrical devices that define a melodramatic realism, with these theatrical tactics being usefully understood in relation to the architect and theorist Paul Virilio's analysis of a poetics and politics of speed.[36]

Sensational realism

While we tend to think of the melodrama as involving a kind of exaggeration of character, movement and action at odds with realism, at the moment

Holcroft's *Tale of Mystery* reached the stage, *The Times* found it 'natural and characteristic... There is no extravagance of idea – no elaborate research after simile and metaphor, no display of pomp and inflated expression: the thought seems to arise from the moment, the words appear to be suggested by the circumstances which pass under the eye of the spectator.'[37] Compared to what the reviewer saw at the theatre on other nights, Holcroft's melodrama appeared true to life.

Such claims to literary 'realism' always arouse suspicion, and, of course, 'realism' in the theatre is essentially a matter of stage conventions: there is finally nothing more 'real' about small theatrical movements, conversational speaking tones, and sets designed to make the audience believe they are seeing into real middle-class rooms than there is about large gestures, oratorical styles of delivery, and spectacular sets designed to make the audience believe they are viewing exotic locales. There is a new realism in the early nineteenth-century theatre, but it does not have so much to do with the accurate portrayal of the day-to-day lives of everyday people as it has to do with a set of techniques developed to make the audience feel as if it is experiencing along with the characters the tensions, fears and joys evoked by the situation on stage. It is not a pictorial but an experiential realism, proved upon our pulses, that is won by early nineteenth-century theatrical techniques. The music, dumb show and spectacular effects in the melodrama (and Ziter reminds us to include changes in acting styles, developments in lighting and the creation of *in situ* displays) that worried traditional critics were of concern because they were capable of overwhelming an audience's sense of distance and judgement, but it is exactly this ability to transport the audience that gave melodramatic theatre its sense of reality: people felt the action on stage in a visceral way. As the advertisement to the second edition of *Tale of Mystery* put it, Holcroft's play seeks 'to fix the attention, rouse the passions, and hold the faculties in anxious and impatient suspense'. These three objectives offer us a schema for the tactics of a sensational realism.

Fixing attention was not necessarily an easy task in a theatre fully lit, with an evening programme that might move from Shakespeare to music to animal acts, and with an audience as interested in watching itself as the play before it. The melodrama, arising within theatres filled by spectators talking to one another and talking back to the actors on stage, works to form the kind of audience we are used to from movie theatres, where we quiet our neighbours and try to block out everything that surrounds us in the dark so that we can be absorbed in the images presented to us. Accounts of performances from the period repeatedly refer to great sensationalist moments – the sudden appearance of the ghost in Lewis's *Castle Spectre* or the incantation scene in Coleridge's *Remorse*, for that matter[38] – where the audience's attention, often wandering, is firmly arrested and fixed on the action. Melodramatic sensationalism was already creating the artistic machine needed to mould the quiet spectator.

In Holcroft's programme, we are quieted in the theatre and focused upon the stage so that our passions may be aroused, our affective response engaged. When our attention is fixed, we become susceptible to the manipulations of the action in front of us – seen most simply in the tactic found from the Gothic theatre to horror movies of having something jump out at us that makes us flinch in turn. We might later discount our reaction, even be embarrassed by it, but at the moment we do not just watch someone in terror but sitting in the theatre we are terrified: at the only performance of Lewis's *Captive*, the audience was so horrified that people screamed aloud and panicked.[39] We do not merely see someone experiencing passion but we are overwhelmingly moved, so that, as Jane Moody reports, audiences for *Luke the Labourer* shuddered with 'alarm and dismay'; Byron fainted with emotion during a performance by Kean as Sir Giles Overreach in Massinger's *A New Way to Pay Old Debts*, where we see the greatest actor of the theatre of sensation forging a 'melodramatic' role within a 'classic' play.[40] Nineteenth-century sensationalist theatre created a mode of presentation that relied less upon what some have seen as a conventional sense of artificiality and theatricality shared between actor and audience, than it did upon a sense of illusion and an overwhelming of one's disbelief – one way of earning its suspension. Melodramatic realism worked on its audiences the way our powerfully sensationalist movies work on us: we come away having had a 'real' experience, having 'really' felt something while we were in the theatre, but the experience is closer to that of an amusement park ride – as movies are repeatedly referred to as putting us on an emotional roller-coaster – than to that of traditional drama.

As we again know from the movies, music is an important aspect of this rousing of the passions, but music, a strongly temporal, forward-moving art, also increases the speed of the experience, with the structure of the plot being another important contributor to what Holcroft calls 'anxious and impatient suspense', that is, a desire to get to the end of the play so as to resolve the tension in the storyline. We might find an emblem of such suspense in our attention to the lit fuse at the climax of *The Miller and his Men* which must reach the powder and blow up the mill before the villains succeed in their plot. Any number of theorists of the melodrama have explored the ways in which the melodrama raises situations of threat, terror or frustration which suspend the audience in an anxious state that demands a resolution: one role of the innocents, the mutes, the children in melodrama is to heighten our anxiety for the unprotected and thus our desire for the relief of a sense of an ending. While all plays look to their end – after all, we could certainly speak of anxiety and suspense in *Oedipus* – melodramas such as *A Tale of Mystery* – where the very title sets up a problem we desire to see resolved – strive for that end at a more frantic pace, with what French critics called 'the breathless style' (*le style haletant*),[41] urged on by the music, supplemented by the telegraphic impact of pantomime and the ability of spectacle to draw in and draw on the spectator. Melodrama is built for speed.

This is not to suggest that melodramas proceed at one pace, but it is to argue, with the philosopher of speed, Paul Virilio, that speed is always present, even when we are moving in a lower gear, at a slower speed; or, to use another Virilian formulation, an engine built for speed must have a brake, so that breaks in the forward movement of the plot are brakes on the action's speed, but the plot's motor keeps running. Great dramatists are masters of pacing, and great melodramatists are masters in particular of speed, but that in part means using various retarding devices to give greater force to the final drive to a conclusion. As Winton Tolles puts it in his account of mid-century melodrama, where he sees the plot as defined as a struggle between two forces or figures, 'A' and 'B': 'The action . . . leads the opposing forces through a series of artfully contrived crises, each more exciting and piquant than the last. Suspense is constantly present, and surprise occurs repeatedly as first A and then B gains the supremacy . . . As the play develops the pace with which the commanding position changes accelerates, until in a whirlwind climax one force attains final victory.'[42] There are clearly many things within early nineteenth-century presentations of melodramas that worked against the forward movement of plot, from the applause that might stop the action at the end of a great speech or the unveiling of a new set design (not to mention less polite audience interventions); to the use of dramatic tableau as moments of frozen action examined by Martin Meisel[43] or the power of great language to arrest thought; to the intervals between acts and scenes. In many ways, early nineteenth-century theatre created a drama of moments, where individual scenes, speeches, songs can break free from the overarching control of aesthetic plot or political ideology. Some have found such moments providing an opening for radical critique in the midst of what might seem a traditional plot and a conventional vision. Some, and I include myself, have seen spectacular moments as being so overwhelming as to draw attention to themselves as moments of self-reflexive theatricality that, in Tracy C. Davis's understanding of the term, can grant the audience 'the self-possession of a critical stance'.[44] While such moments are surely there to be exploited by a particular playwright, in general the melodramatic plot is designed to drive us through those moments to a conclusion, with the very speed of the plot threatening the powers of reflexivity.

Melodrama's use of comedy in the form of comic relief, where the relief is presumably from the urgent forward thrust of the serious plot, might seem to offer a particularly strong resistance to the speed of melodrama. In Holcroft's *Tale of Mystery*, for example, the maid Fiametta's constant interruptions of the report of Signor Montano are, like those of many other humorous servants in the melodrama and the Gothic drama, meant to be funny, but they also increase suspense as we, along with the characters on stage, await the revelation Montano promises. Such devices may modulate the speed of the scene, but they still contribute to it. Again, the servant Fiametta's stance as the voice of reason within the play might suggest a critique of the play's patriarchal, hierarchical order, but her oppositional role surely comes to an end when, as Bonamo repents his harsh treatment of Francisco, she proclaims, 'You're my master again' and kisses his hand.[45] Larger comic structures – such as the love plot in *Tale of Mystery* that seems to be headed towards a conclusion in the wedding of the first scene of Act II – also seem to stand outside or in opposition to the serious plot involved in unravelling the mystery of the title, as the act opens upon comic gardeners and pauses for the music and dance of the Italian peasants. One might even want to argue that this scene – filled with peasants, laughter, erotic promise and 'dancing, which should be of the gay, comic, and grotesque kind'[46] – serves as a kind of anti-masque to the central plot with its drive towards the reassertion of conventional familial and social orders.

However, the moment of comic possibility is literally a moment, bounded by a temporal marker, as 'In the midst of the rejoicing the clock strikes; the dancing suddenly ceases; the changing music inspires alarm and dismay.'[47] There is simply no time for comedy, as the evil Malvoglio stalks on stage to dissolve the comedic marriage back into the mystery of parental and familial relations at the core of the serious plot. Fun gives way to fear. Terror itself, clearly part of the tension contributing to melodrama's suspense, might also provide emotional moments of arrest. Bernard Sharratt, for example, finds in melodrama a tension between moments of fear and a plot ending in order.[48] Moments of terror – like any other instance of intense emotion – might be seen as retarding the forward plunge of the plot, but here the function of speed is to move us through the fear quickly enough that it can be enjoyed; if the moment of tension is too intense, it would not be pleasurable, and so there must be patterns of tension and release in the melodrama just as there are in thrill rides, as one seems to pause on the upward course of the roller-coaster before plunging back into the experience of pure speed.

The melodrama – with its two or three or four acts rather than the five of conventional tragedy and comedy of manners – seems to suggest that there is no time for the development of traditional comic or tragic plots – in Holcroft's play, for either the comic resolution promised by the interrupted marriage of Selina and Stephano or for an exploration of the sad career of Francisco that Fiametta calls 'quite a tragedy'.[49] *The Times* review of *Tale of Mystery* makes this point in giving Holcroft's play a backhanded compliment: 'This kind of composition, which is unequal to the province of Tragedy in producing pity or terror, and inferior to that of Comedy in calling forth pleasantry and amusement, has given birth to the *Melo-Drame*, which strengthens the mixed composition we have noticed, by the powers of music, imitating at once both passion and action, and its success is the best proof of its influence over the human mind.'[50] The 'powers of music', the most audible sign of melodrama's forward movement, help drive the melodramatic machine which can only glance at comedy and tragedy as it speeds towards a resolution that is marked neither by the clarifying terror and pity of tragedy nor the satisfying, pleasing and amusing resolution of comedy but instead by melodrama's own tempered reassertion of threatened family and social orders hedged round by fear.

It is in this context that Paul Virilio's analysis of speed and the militarization of culture proves useful for understanding the melodrama. Virilio explores the ways in which modernity has collapsed space into time to create not so much a Wordsworthian spot of time – where the past is preserved at a particular spatial point – as a time spot – where distance is erased by techniques of speed that enable us to experience different places as part of a simultaneity: the whole world watches planes crash into the Twin Towers at the same instant. While Virilio is mainly thought of as an analyst of how the contemporary media and now particularly the internet accelerate culture, of the close connection between the developments within military technology and the formation of a global, simultaneous culture, and of the contemporary 'accident' as a kind of false apocalypse as seen in May 1968, various limited wars from Bosnia to Iraq, and the events we now call 9/11, he repeatedly locates an early moment of the processes he analyses in the period of the revolutionary and Napoleonic wars, that is in the era of the first phase of melodrama. For example, on a number of occasions and perhaps most extensively in *The Art of the Motor*, he argues that we witness the coming collapse of time and space under the aegis of military innovation when in 1792 Claude Chappe proposed the creation of an optical telegraph system for command and control of the French army; Chappe himself argued that 'The telegraph shrinks distances and in a way joins an entire, huge population *into a single point.*'[51] The British military rapidly imitated the enemy and set up between 1796 and 1806 a shutter semaphore version of the optical telegraph that used the data compression of shortened words to relay information within fifteen minutes between London and the coast with lines running to Deal and Portsmouth. The goal was at first to be able to relay orders rapidly to the fleet, but it also became a way of alerting the government if the feared French invasion was taking place. This invasion, real enough in its way in Ireland, was itself a false apocalypse for Britain, but this general atmosphere of terror, which reached a new pitch at the end of the Peace of Amiens and which resulted in an unprecedented mobilization of the country as a whole, is a particularized locus for the fear that Sharratt, as we have seen, finds as central to the melodrama. From the perspective of Virilio, we can read the moment of melodrama's arrival on the London stage as one marked by the optical telegraph's symbolic conversion of the country from disparate, localized communities separated by space into a unified body all straining to collapse in time the distance between them and the threatened coast. Again, in 1794, the same year as Chappe's optical telegraph system was completed in France, the French military also put to use balloons at the Battle of Fleurus, providing another key Virilian moment when one begins to gain a simultaneous view of wide spaces through elevation, the kind of view to be provided in the theatre by panoramas and other spectacular effects. When we remember that the Napoleonic wars were global in nature, when we note the importance of a growing media in the war years, when we look at advances in transportation that also concern Virilio, we can begin to see the era of the Napoleonic wars as creating the first Virilian culture of speed or what he calls, from the Greek word for 'race', dromocracy.

Melodrama, I want to suggest, is a key form of serving and managing this early nineteenth-century accelerated culture and its war on sociability, instanced by how theatrical sociability was undermined by a different pace and a different relation between audience and stage. One might here pursue various Virilian themes, thinking, for example, about the globe-trotting nature of the melodrama in the era of the Napoleonic world war – taking us from the mines of Poland (Pixérécourt's *Les Minges de Pologne*, Théâtre de L'Ambigu-Comique, 3 May 1803; adapted for the Royalty on 14 January 1822) to the desert sands of Africa (William Dimond, *The Aethiop; or, The Child of the Desert*, Covent Garden, 6 October 1812), from the Caucaucus (Lewis's *Timour the Tartar*, Covent Garden, 29 April 1811) to the cataracts of the Amazon (Charles Isaac Mungo Dibdin, *The White Witch; or, The Cataract of Amazonia*, Sadler's Wells, 18 April 1808) only to discover the same basic plots in all contexts – as part of an earlier globalization-as-levelling that Virilio sees as a kind of planet-wide incarceration, or exploring the 'mediatization' of the theatre through reviews, prints, toy theatres and the like; but I want to remain with the stage devices we identify with the melodrama which from a Virilian perspective contribute to an experience of speed. Music becomes a means of emphasizing the temporal aspect of the theatre, to control its tempo, most often to increase it or at least to increase our experience of it as moving forward, seen for example in musical moments from Holcroft such as 'Quick march' and 'Music of hurry'.[52] The rapid, staccato speech found so often in melodrama – here's a snippet from Elliston's *The Venetian Outlaw*: 'When?'/'This night.'/'Where?'/'Contrive by some means to lead him towards the grotto at the close of the entertainment.'/'Will you be there?'/'I must'[53] – creates a sense of breathless urgency. Gesture serves as its own form of data compression, seeking to express immediately through the body emotional states that might require a considerable amount of speech to convey, as when Holcroft's mute Francisco, being offered money, 'rises with a sense of injury', as he 'Expresses gratitude, but rejects the purse'.[54] Spectacle provides the theatre a means of providing a simultaneous image of what are sometimes large spaces, as in the recreation of battle scenes such as we find at the end of Hook's *Tekeli* or of entire landscapes, such as the one that opens Dibdin's *Valentine and Orson*: 'A long Perspective of the Suburbs of Orleans, terminating with the ancient City Gates – On one Side a Convent, the Windows of which are illuminated from within – The Stage is at first dark, which gives Effect to the Transparency of the Windows – As the Curtain rises slowly, the following choral Chaunt, accompanied by the Organ, is heard from the Interior of the Monastery.'[55] Sometimes one finds stage directions that explicitly evoke an overall emphasis upon speed, as in Holcroft's instruction that 'The whole scene passes in a mysterious and rapid manner' or Elliston's that 'The ensuing scene ought to be conducted with much haste and mystery.'[56]

Gillian Russell, who herself mentions Virilio's analysis of the connections between a culture of speed and the militarization of modern life, has reminded us of the centrality of war to romantic-era theatre and of theatrical images to the representation of warfare.[57] What I want to suggest is that the melodrama gains its initial power as perhaps the key means of both representing and creating the accelerated culture of perpetual war during the Napoleonic era, by which I do not mean that we should read each melodrama as an allegory of the battle with Napoleon but rather that the theatrical tactics of the melodrama begin to organize the audience to see the militarized world that they come to inhabit. The melodrama appeared on the British stage during a temporary peace, and if Matthew Lewis in the passage quoted earlier argued that comedy was the form for war and tragedy that for peace, then the melodrama appears as the form for the temporary and tense cessation of official hostilities that can be the continuation of war by other means and then for a sense that one is engaged in perpetual war, whether the war England and its allies would continue to wage even after Napoleon's defeat, when on the same day as that they signed the second Treaty of Paris in November 1815, Austria, Britain, Prussia and Russia created the Quadruple Alliance, suggesting there was something to be allied against, even in peace; or the war at home against those who sought to change the British government that would in the next few years lead to the Spa Field Riots of late 1816, the March of the Blanketeers in March 1817, the Pentridge Rising of June 1817, and then the Peterloo Massacre of 1819 and the Queen Caroline Affair and the Cato Street Conspiracy of 1820; or other unending wars we are familiar with such as the war on drugs or the war on terror; or less political wars, such as the struggles against immorality or secularism. The rhythm of the melodrama – its welding together of individual moments of threat and fear into an engine hurtling towards an anticipated moment of moral, domestic safety – creates a world of violent struggle issuing in a peace that always seems challenged by new violence; it is a world in which a seemingly universal moral and providential order is obscured again and again by a fall into particularized moments of deception, violence and destruction: more precisely, the melodrama offers a world in which a supposedly transcendent order of church, state and family, of God, King and Father, is repeatedly challenged by the energies unleashed during the age of democratic revolutions, with the defeat of these energies on stage being offered as an assertion that the time of revolutionary war is over, that the peace of providential, hierarchical and patriarchal order has returned. Of course, the Peace of Amiens lasted only a year, and this false ending is an appropriate sign to preside over the birth of the melodrama; for like the sense that the war was over, the assertion that the Revolution was over was false, and thus it had to be asserted on stage over and over again, night after night. The melodrama depicts the threats to nation or family or morals in apocalyptic terms only to settle for domestic ones. In an emblematic moment from Holcroft's *Tale of Mystery*, the villainous Romaldi enters the last scene near a waterfall, pelted, we learn from the stage directions, by the 'increasing storm of lightning, thunder, hail, and rain', 'pursued, as it were, by heaven and earth'. He is, in fact, only pursued by human archers who refrain from shooting him as Selina pleads on familial grounds, 'Oh, forbear! Let my father's virtues plead for my uncle's errors.'[58] The melodrama finally rejects an apocalyptic solution that would offer an end to the struggle against evil, individual or political, sexual or 'Jacobin'. To adapt the phrase of Ira Chernus from the completely different context of nuclear war and deterrence, as the drama of reaction in an era of revolutionary war, the melodrama finally offers 'apocalypse management'.[59] Or to put it another way, the melodrama, intent on speed and never stopping, operates under the slogan 'Apocalypse Never'.

Romantic drama's virtualities

While my argument may seem headed towards an account of the theatre's contribution to the hegemony of the imperial liberal state, I in fact would want to celebrate the various sites of opposition within the dramatic/theatrical complex of the romantic era, and I would want, if I had world enough and time, to make the argument that, within a theatrical scene increasingly dominated by the melodrama, romantic tragic drama created one particularly important site of resistance by offering a different set of theatrical tactics issuing in a different vision. In recognizing the power and the pervasive influence of the melodrama as creating a new kind of theatrical experience and a sensationalist realism, we can then see how romantic dramatists created a counter-theatre of 'virtuality'.

It is easy to recognize how the romantic drama set itself, at times self-consciously, against the moralism of the classic melodrama – we need only look at Maturin's *Bertram* where critics found a 'jacobinical' embrace of a villain hero and adultery, or Byron's *Manfred* where a Faustian figure proclaims his ability to live beyond the good and evil Nodier finds reasserted in the melodrama, or Shelley's *The Cenci* where the triumvirate of God, Pope and Cenci as father and lord is seen to create not order but an anarchy of oppression and violence, or Hemans's *Siege of Valencia* where Elmina seeks a feminine vision opposed to a masculinist world of religious hypocrisy and death. We need to see how romantic drama also drew upon theatrical sensationalism in order to contest the stagecraft of the melodrama. Coleridge's *Remorse* (Drury Lane, 23 January 1813), the most successful stage play by a major romantic poet, is perhaps closer to the tactics of the melodrama than most romantic plays, but when – in the first scene of Act III – Coleridge draws upon all the powers of spectacle, music and lighting for his incantation scene, he creates a moment which, as Barnes reported above, enthralled the audience, only to let us know that all this powerful stagecraft is actually a staged hoax, as he releases his audience from its fixed attention into contemplation. Baillie, in seeking to create a theatre of character, resisted the tyranny of plot and speed because she felt that the focus on action did not allow time for the play to investigate or the audience to experience the emotional life of characters: such plays offer 'events . . . of such force and magnitude that the passions themselves are almost obscured by the splendour and importance of the transactions to which they are attached'.[60] The turn to classical and neo-classical models in Byron's history plays and in a different way in Shelley's *Hellas* can be read as a different attempt to discover alternatives to an accelerated dramatic form. In perhaps the most systematic response to the melodrama, Shelley in *Prometheus Unbound* offers as a counter to a Virilian theatre of speed and continual, global war a new theatre of reimagined space and time to create a cosmopolitan community of peace and art; Shelley demands an experimental theatre realized in part through a performance by the Rude Mechanicals that, strikingly, stretched over three days (across as well multiple modes and media) in Austin in 1998, as time was found to discover a way beyond the poetics of violent speed.

I want to suggest that these plays proffer 'virtualities' rather than staged realities. As Jennifer Jones's ongoing work suggests, current debates over 'virtuality' can be seen to re-enact romantic-era discussions of realism and the imagination, as they move between a fear of the 'virtual' – a concern that the 'virtual' is so powerful that it will overwhelm the 'real' – and a sense that the 'virtual' opens up a space from which we can imagine and perhaps re-make the 'real', a space which might, in the words of Geoffrey Hartman writing about Wordsworth, 'revive in us the capacity for the virtual, a trembling of the imagined on the brink of the real, a sustained inner freedom in the face of death, disbelief, and fact'.[61] A Virilian theatrics of speed threatens the kind of overwhelming of the real feared here, and I want to suggest that romantic drama, while consciously engaging such a theatre, moves us towards the imaginative version of 'virtuality'. Romantic drama does not claim to hold a mirror up to nature, nor does it seek to displace the 'real' with a 'virtual' theatre of simulated sensations; rather it offers visions 'on the brink of the real' – and not just a reality that already exists but one that these dramas might help to create. Taken together, the melodrama and romantic drama can help us better understand the complex development of modern devices for depicting the 'real' on stage, and modern drama, I would want to argue, learned as much from these virtual visionary works as it did from melodrama's sensationalist realism, so that, say, Ibsen's titanic visionaries such as Solness and Borkman are the inheritors of Faust and Manfred, the now playful, now critical stance towards realism found in Strindberg's Chamber Plays or in Pirandello or Brecht explore ground already opened up by Tieck, Kleist or Shelley, and modern drama's prolonged engagement with the history play – from Strindberg's Vasa Trilogy to Stoppard's *Arcadia* – owe something to the reimagining of historical tragedy by writers such as Schiller and Byron. Finally, romantic drama can only be understood in relation to the melodrama, not because it is melodrama but because it developed its own tactics as a response to the melodrama and the world it both helped to represent and to forge.

Notes

1. Jacky Bratton, *New Readings in Theatre History* (Cambridge: Cambridge University Press, 2003), 5–10.
2. Erich Auerbach, *Mimesis*, trans. Willard Trask (Princeton: Princeton University Press, 1953), particularly the chapter on naturalism, 493–524; Auerbach argues for the naturalist novel, rather than the great novels of mid-nineteenth-century realism, as in some sense the culmination of the West's pursuit of mimesis, and one could imagine a parallel argument being made for the melodrama.
3. See, for example, Hartmut Ilsemann, 'Radicalism in the Melodrama of the Early Nineteenth Century', in *Melodrama: the Cultural Emergence of a Genre*, ed. Michael Hays and Anastasia Nikolopoulou (New York: St. Martin's Press, 1996), 191–207. He argues: 'one might even go so far as to say that . . . [the melodrama addressing contemporary social problems] constitutes the beginning of a series of developments that, toward the end of the century, will lead to both realistic and naturalistic drama' (101). Simon Shepherd and Peter Womack, in *English Drama: a Cultural History* (Oxford: Blackwell, 1996) see the melodrama leading to modern cinema (218), and there is a great deal of scholarship on melodrama and film. My position is closer to that of Thomas Postlewait, 'From Melodrama to Realism: the Suspect History of American Drama', in *Melodrama: the Cultural Emergence of a Genre*, where he argues that melodrama should be considered 'its own expansive generic form, as artistically whole or complete as any other genre' and not 'like a child or a rudimentary organism' that 'grew or developed into realism' (55).
4. Bratton, 36–8.
5. Peter Brooks, *The Melodramatic Imagination* (New Haven: Yale University Press, 1976); and Judith Pascoe, *Romantic Theatricality: Gender, Poetry, and Spectatorship* (Ithaca: Cornell University Press, 1997).
6. Catherine B. Burroughs, *Closet Stages: Joanna Baillie and the Theater Theory of British Romantic Women Writers* (Philadelphia: University of Pennsylvania Press, 1997); and Jane Moody, *Illegitimate Theatre in London, 1770–1840* (Cambridge: Cambridge University Press, 2000).
7. See Philip W. Martin, *Byron, a Poet Before His Public* (Cambridge: Cambridge University Press, 1982); and Jeffrey Cox, 'Spots of Time: the Structure of the Dramatic Evening

in the Theater of Romanticism', *Texas Studies in Literature and Language*, 41.4 (1999): 403–25.

8. Edward Ziter made this observation in his response to my essay delivered at The Romantic and Victorian Theatre Workshop held in conjunction with the 2006 NASSR Convention. I am indebted to Ted for sharpening a number of points in this essay.

9. Charles Nodier, 'Introduction', Charles Guilbert de Pixérécourt, *Théâtre Choisi*, 4 vols (1841–3; rpt. Geneva: Slatkine Reprints, 1971), 1: vii.

10. Nodier, v.

11. Pixérécourt, *Dernière réflexions sur le mélodrame* (1843), included in *Théâtre Choisi*, 4: 493, 498.

12. The *OED* does cite an earlier use of the word in *Sketches of Paris* (1802), 2: lxx: 390, but Holcroft is the British writer first to use the term to identify his play on a title page.

13. See Frank Rahill, *The World of Melodrama* (University Park: Pennsylvania State University Press, 1967), 111–19. I will be focusing on melodrama in the major theatres where it first took hold in London rather than in the so-called minor or illegitimate theatres; David Worrall has suggested that there is a working-class melodrama beyond even those 'minor theaters' in his 'Artisan Melodrama and the Plebeian Public Sphere: the Political Culture of Drury Lane and its Environs, 1797–1830', *Studies in Romanticism*, 39 (Summer 2000): 213–27.

14. On Kenney, an interesting but under-studied playwright, see Terry Robinson, 'James Kenney's Comedic Genius: Early 19th c. Character, Commerce and the Arts in *Raising the Wind*, *The World!*, and *Debtor and Creditor*', *Literature Compass*, 3 (http://www.blackwell-compass.com/subject/literature/section_home?section=lico-romanticism).

15. John Wilson Croker, Review of Barbauld's *Eighteen Hundred and Eleven*, *The Quarterly Review*, 14 (June 1812): 309.

16. John Genest, *Some Account of the English Stage from the Restoration in 1660 to 1830*, 10 vols (1832; rpt. New York: Burt Franklin, 1965), 7: 564–5. See also James Boaden, *Memoirs of the Life of John Philip Kemble*, 2 vols (1825; rpt. New York: Benjamin Blom, 1969), 2: 325.

17. See the prologue by Hart in R. W. Elliston, *The Venetian Outlaw* (London: London: C. and R. Baldwin, 1805); licensing manuscript held at the Huntington Library, LA 1449. On the O. P. riots, see Marc Baer, *Theatre and Disorder in Late Georgian London* (Oxford: Clarendon Press, 1992).

18. Leigh Hunt, *Examiner*, 5 January 1817.

19. Moody, 148–77.

20. I make a similar argument in '*Manfred* and the Melodrama', in *Poetic and Dramatic Forms in British Romanticism*, ed. Franca Dellarosa (Bari, Italy: Laterza and Figli, 2006), 17–38.

21. Lewis, 'Prologue', *Alfonso, King of Castille* (London, 1801).

22. *Report from the Select Committee Appointed to Inquire into the Laws Affecting Dramatic Literature* (1832), Irish University Press Series of British Parliamentary Papers (Shannon: Irish University Press, 1968), 20.

23. Ibid., 138.

24. Ibid., 139.

25. Ibid., 158.

26. Genest, 8: 151.

27. For the importance of music to the melodrama, see, for example, David Mayer, 'Nineteenth Century Theatre Music', *Theatre Notebook*, 30.3 (1976): 115–22; and David Mayer, 'The Music of Melodrama', in *Performance and Politics in Popular Drama: Aspects of Popular Entertainment in Theatre, Film and Television 1800–1976*, ed. David Bradby, Louis James and Bernard Sharratt (Cambridge: Cambridge University Press, 1980), 49–64.

28. Rahill, 125.

29. Genest, 7: 579.

30. James Boaden, *Memoirs of the Life of John Philip Kemble*, 2 vols (1825; rpt. New York: Benjamin Blom, 1969), 2: 331–2.

31. For varying accounts of the political valence of the melodrama, see Michael Booth, 'East End and West End: Class and Audience in Victorian London', *Theatre Research International*, 2 (February 1977): 98–103; Elaine Hadley, *Melodramatic Tactics: Theatricalized Dissent in the English Marketplace, 1800–1885* (Stanford: Stanford University Press, 1995), esp. 34–76; Marvin Carlson, 'He Never Should Bow Down to a Domineering Frown: Class Tensions and Nautical Melodrama', in *Melodrama: the Cultural Emergence of a Genre*, 147–66; Islemann; and Jane Moody, 'The Silence of Historicism: a Mutinous Echo from 1830', *Nineteenth Century Theatre*, 24 (Winter 1996): 61–89.

32. See Barry Sutcliffe, 'Introduction', *Plays by George Colman the Younger*, ed. Barry Sutcliffe (Cambridge: Cambridge University Press, 1983), 1–7; and Moody, *Illegitimate Theatre*, 1–10.

33. *The Rover* was run in *The Anti-Jacobin; or, Weekly Examiner* on 4 and 11 June 1798. George Colman used some of this satire in his burlesque of melodrama and the hippodrama, *The Quadrupeds of Quedlinburgh; or, The Rovers of Weimar* (Haymarket, 26 July 1811). Coleridge's remarks come in his attack upon Maturin's *Bertram*, reprinted in his *Biographia Literaria*, ed. James Engell and W. Jackson Bate (Princeton: Princeton University Press, 1983), 2: 221. See also, Michael Gamer, *Romanticism and the Gothic: Genre, Reception, and Canon Formation* (Cambridge: Cambridge University Press, 2000), 127–62.

34. Reynolds, *The Caravan; or, The Driver and his Dog. A grand serio comic romance, in two acts* (London: G. and J. Robinson, 1803), Act II, scene 3, p. 43; the licensing manuscript is held at the Huntington Library, LA 1394.

35. Ibid., Act II, scene 3, p. 45.

36. Paul Virilio (1932–) studied at the L'École des Métiers d'Art in Paris and then at the Sorbonne with Merleau-Ponty. He formed the *Architecture Principe* group with Claude Parent in 1963. After participating in the events of May 1968, Virilio was made Professor by the students at the École Spéciale d'Architecture; he retired from teaching in 1998. His major works include: *Speed and Politics: an Essay on Dromology*, trans. Mark Polizzotti (New York: Semiotext(e), 1986); *War and Cinema: the Logistics of Perception*, trans. Patrick Camiller (London: Verso, 1989); *The Art of the Motor*, trans. Julie Rose (Minneapolis: University of Minnesota Press, 1995); *The Information Bomb*, trans. Chris Turner (London: Verso, 2000); and *Desert Screen: War at the Speed of Light*, trans. Michael Degener (London: Continuum, 2002).

37. *The Times*, 15 November 1802.

38. See Boaden's account of the ghost's appearance in *Castle Spectre* in *Kemble*, 2: 206; Thomas Barnes, future editor of *The Times*, reported on the incantation scene in Coleridge's *Remorse*: 'We never saw more interest excited in a theatre than was expressed at the sorcery-scene in the third act. The altar flaming in the distance, the solemn invocation, the pealing music of the mystic song, altogether produced a combination so awful, as nearly to overpower reality, and make one half believe the enchantment which delighted our senses.' He also makes a comment similar to Holcroft's on capturing the audience's attention through surprise and speed: the 'Fable is managed and developed with a rapidity which never languishes, an intelligibility which a child might follow, and a surprise which would keep awake the most careless attention' (*The Examiner*, 31 January 1813: 74).

39. See Lewis's own account of the performance of *The Captive* in a 23 March 1803 letter to his mother, where he notes that 'two people went into hysterics during the performance & two more after the curtain dropped', in Louis F. Peck, *A Life of Matthew G. Lewis* (Cambridge, MA: Harvard University Press, 1961), 221–2.

40. See Moody, *Illegitimate Theatre*, 84–5. On Byron's fit while watching Kean perform Sir Giles Overreach, see Thomas Moore, *Letters and Journals of Lord Byron: with Notices of His Life*, 2 vols (London: 1830), 1: 553; Robert Ball, *The Amazing Career of Sir Giles Overreach* (Princeton: Princeton University Press, 1939); and the account in J. Fitzgerald Molly, *The Life and Adventures of Edmund Kean*, 2 vols (London, 1888), which states 'Byron . . . was seized in his box by a convulsive fit; whilst women went into hysterics, and the whole house burst into a wild clamour of applause' (1: 248).

41. See Barbara T. Cooper, 'French Romantic Tragedy', in *A Companion to Tragedy*, ed. Rebecca Bushnell (Oxford: Blackwell Publishing, 2005), 455.

42. Winton Tolles, *Tom Taylor and the Victorian Drama* (New York: Columbia University Press, 1940), 115; quoted in J. O. Bailey, 'Introduction', *British Plays of the Nineteenth Century* (New York: Odyssey Press, 1966), 33–4.

43. Martin Meisel, *Realizations: Narrative, Pictorial, and Theatrical Arts in Nineteenth-Century England* (Princeton: Princeton University Press, 1983), esp. 38–51.

44. Tracy C. Davis, 'Theatricality and Civil Society', in *Theatricality*, ed. Tracy C. Davis and Thomas Postlewait (Cambridge: Cambridge University Press, 2003), 153.

45. Holcroft, *Tale of Mystery: a Melo-drama* (2nd ed, London: Richard Phillips, 1803), 2.2; p. 40.

46. Ibid., 2.1; p. 29

47. Ibid., 2.1; p. 29.

48. Sharratt, 277–81.

49. Holcroft, 1.1; p. 5.

50. *The Times*, 15 November 1802.

51. Quoted in Virilio (1995) 40; see also Virilio (1986).

52. Holcroft, 2.3; pp. 46, 49.

53. Elliston, 2.2; p. 30.

54. Holcroft, 2.1; p. 32.

55. Theodore Hook, *Tekeli; or, The siege of Montgatz. A melo drame, in three acts* (London: C. and R. Baldwin, 1806), 3.3; pp. 45–7. Thomas Dibdin, *Valentine and Orson, a Romantic Melo-Drame* (London: Barker and Son, 1804), 1.1; p. 5.

56. Holcroft, 2.3; p. 49. Elliston, 2.2; p. 30.

57. Gillian Russell, *The Theatres of War: Performance, Politics, and Society, 1793–1815* (Oxford: Clarendon Press, 1995), 74–5.

58. Holcroft, 2.3; p. 50.

59. Ira Chernus, *Eisenhower's Atoms for Peace* (College Station, TX: Texas A & M University Press, 2002), 9. I also make this point in my essay, '*Manfred* and the Melodrama', cited above, n. 20.

60. Baillie, 'Introductory Discourse', *A Series of Plays: in which it is attempted to delineate the stronger passions of the mind – each passion being the subject of a tragedy and a comedy* (London: T. Cadell Jun. & W. Davies, 1798), 39. See also Jeffrey Cox, 'Staging Baillie', in *Joanna Baillie, Romantic Dramatist: Critical Essays*, ed. Thomas Crochunis (London: Routledge, 2003), 146–67.

61. Geoffrey Hartman, *Wordsworth Poetry 1787–1814* (New Haven: Yale University Press, 1964), 11. See also Jennifer Jones, 'Absorbing Hesitation: Wordsworth and the Theory of the Panorama', *Studies in Romanticism* (forthcoming); her book-in-progress is entitled *Virtual Romanticism*.

9

Fitting the Bill: Acting Out the Season of 1813/14 at the Sans Pareil

Gilli Bush-Bailey

If the London theatrical season of 1813/14 is noted in British theatre histories it is because it marks a moment of hope for the legitimate drama in the arrival of the tragedian Edmund Kean on the stage of the Theatre Royal, Drury Lane. The playbill for Wednesday, 25 January 1814 announces the performance of *The Merchant of Venice*, noting merely that Shylock will be played by 'Mr. Kean, from the Theatre Royal, Exeter (His First Appearance at this Theatre)'. The fare also includes an afterpiece, the standard addition to an evening's entertainment, in this case a revival of Arthur Murphy's eighteenth-century farce, *The Apprentice*. The playbill further serves as an advertisement for forthcoming attractions, here, for the '(26th time) the Grand Oriental Spectacle of *Illusion or, The Trances of Nourjahad*', with a promise of the imminent arrival of 'A New Farce . . . in rehearsal and will be produced immediately'.[1] Within weeks, Kean has added the title role in *King Richard the Third* to his repertoire and the Theatre Royal is enjoying a roaring trade at the box office, sufficient to add to the bill of 12 February 1814 that 'No Orders will be admitted'.[2] The restriction is apparently extended to include the musical farce *Turn Out* which follows the main piece of the evening. This Saturday night bill goes on to advertise forthcoming performances to include revivals of stock comedies, a new ballet, a pantomime, a farce, and the promise of 'A New Melo-Drame' to be 'produced in a few days'. The whole is wrapped up with an assurance to the audience that 'Due Notice will be given of Mr. Kean's next performance of Shylock'.

My purpose here is not so much to dwell on Kean's arrival on the London stage as to draw attention to the theatrical context in which his innovations in acting style were generally welcomed and, central to the purpose of this chapter, to emphasize the wider context of the theatre bill upon which performances were announced. To borrow from Joseph Roach: 'the pursuit of performance does not require historians to abandon the archive, but it does encourage them to spend more time in the streets.'[3] The theatrical playbill provides the link between the archive and the street: between the information on past performance the historian seeks and an insight into the expectations of that ever-elusive group, the audience, who bought their tickets on the *promise* of performance contained there.[4] But my interest in the bills for the theatrical season of 1813/14 extends further than Drury

Lane and the other theatres royal at Covent Garden and the Haymarket. The bills from these theatres bear witness to the real and vibrant presence of those suspect, visceral theatrical forms, melodrama and, a key component in this discussion, the farces, which are central to theatrical competition and criticism in the patent houses and the licensed theatres.

The minors are generally thought of as occupying the Surrey side. Theatres like the Olympic and the Sans Pareil were, however, a great deal closer, snapping at the heels of Drury Lane and seeking to poach its audience from the uncomfortably close proximity of the Strand. For while the minors were, of course, prohibited from providing the kind of dramatic vehicle upon which Kean made his entry to London, much of the comic stuff of an evening's entertainment at the theatres royal was being emulated or, more dangerously, newly minted by their rivals on the illegitimate stages. Performers too were central to the ongoing battle for audiences in the fast-changing business of theatre. The star system that recruited and fashioned Kean the tragedian also created comics Liston and Mathews; and then there is Elliston who, like some others, moved between the theatres on both sides of the legitimate divide to the benefit of his pocket but also to the detriment of his reputation. Contemporary responses to performance are, on the whole, reserved for those acting in the theatres royal but my interest here is in the less well-documented star system at work in the minor houses. From the considerable archival evidence relating to comedy and comic performance at Drury Lane, Covent Garden and the Haymarket and the more fragmentary but, nonetheless, important documentary evidence of the playbills for the Sans Pareil, this chapter will investigate the range of comic performance promised at that minor house on one particular evening and, more crucially, the virtuosity of the performers who made up the Sans Pareil company.

The story so far

New theatre histories have been largely successful in recovering that much maligned dramatic form, melodrama, from the reductive mire of historical criticism that preceded the theoretical perspectives admitted by the rise of cultural studies. Concomitant with this work has been a growing realization that contemporary resistance to the appearance of melodrama in all its gaudy colours in the theatres royal was rather more to do with the abhorrent idea that the audience in the boxes wanted spectacle just as much, if not more, than the lower orders in the gallery. Curiously, rather less attention has been paid to that other staple of an evening at the theatre in the early nineteenth century – the farce. Allardyce Nicoll, one of the chief players in the historical act of denigrating the early nineteenth-century stage, notes that 'with the melodrama naturally goes the farce... [the] audience wanted to laugh; it wanted its comic friend in the melodramatic spectacle'.[5] As Nicoll's comprehensive accounts have worked to justify the binary that separates and privileges the legitimate over the illegitimate, the tragedian over the comic, the poetry of drama over the melodrama/farce double-act, it is not surprising to find that he has been cited in new histories more for his invaluable cataloguing of plays of the period than for his critical commentary on the stage and its performers. But he sometimes makes unexpected asides that render his works worth revisiting. While Nicoll is immovably convinced that the unstoppable spread of melodrama and farce mark the decline of the drama, he acknowledges that they also represent 'all that was vital and popular in the theatrical world of the time', leading him to offer an unexpected personal admission:

> Gazing drearily on the long array of 'unacted' dramas and of 'poetic' dramas put forward by well-meaning litterateurs of the age, I personally feel convinced that, had I lived in these decades, I should have loved better the struggling actors at the minor theatres than the lordly potentates legitimately wedded at Drury Lane and Covent Garden.[6]

Nicoll clearly envisages a journey across the river to the minors of the Surrey side for 'an evening's treat'[7] where a rich diet of spectacle interlarded with pantomime and burlesque was always on offer.

The Times for Monday, 17 August 1812 advertises 'the Spelling Dog' as well as the expected 'Equestrian Troupe' in the attractions on offer at Astley's. On the same night at the Surrey, the actor/manager Elliston promises 'a new Operatic and Melo-Dramatic Burletta in Three Acts, founded upon and called The Honey Moon',[8] clearly a steal from Tobin's *Honeymoon* first performed at Drury Lane on 31 January 1805 and regularly revived at the patent houses. Elliston had made his name in the Duke of Aranza, a triple role, and here he had recruited at least one of his company directly from the theatres royal. Elliston's twentieth-century biographer notes that Mrs Edwin, 'was of immense value, for she was admired as an imitator of Dora Jordan, and thus made an excellent partner for Elliston in the plays in which he had starred with Jordan'.[9] Such connections between the plays and players of the theatres royal and their transpontine rivals did not go without notice by contemporary critics. Leigh Hunt was vociferous in his criticism of Elliston's performances in the minors:

> We remember the time when his Duke Aranza in *The Honey Moon* was one of the few performances that might absolutely be termed complete; but between this and his present style of acting it, we understand there is now as much difference as between a nobleman himself and a noisy fellow in front of a booth.[10]

The polarized positions occupied by the legitimate actor on one side and the illegitimate performer on the other is accentuated here: the annual fairs were increasingly seen as sites of depravity and, for Hunt at least, the association with the booth-actor makes this connection clear.[11]

The performer and the performance

Elliston was among the few actors who moved between the legitimate and illegitimate stages, albeit uneasily, and he also moved between dramatic genres. Generally performers at the theatres royal were expected to perform in either tragedy or comedy. The playbills show that only the lesser actors and actresses in the company appear in both the main piece and the following farce or afterpiece. But, to return to Kean for a moment, the performer's destiny in one genre or the other was a far from predetermined matter. *The Satirist* for May 1814 endorses the enthusiastic welcome given to Kean's 'original, vigorous [and] energetic' innovations as a tragedian but adds:

> we are informed that his talents are not confined to this walk. On the contrary, he is the very 'admirable Crichton' of performers, sings divinely, plays Comedy with the utmost spirit and ease, and in the nimble Harlequin is among the best leapers of the day.[12]

The writer's desire to convey 'the extraordinary versatility of this new Roscius'[13] is not immediately apparent in Kean's almost instant rise to fame as a tragedian, and versatility of this kind is certainly at odds with the general critical perception of the quite different spheres of dramatic performance that mark the early nineteenth-century stage. The fear that the appetite for melodramatic spectacle will overwhelm the dramatic stage makes it quite unthinkable that a leading tragic actor such as Kean might appear in the Drury Lane pantomime as Harlequin. Cross-overs from tragedy to comedy were rarely successful, as demonstrated by Leigh Hunt's firmly delineated profiles of 'Comic Actresses', 'Tragic Actresses', 'Comic Actors' and 'Tragic Actors', published in *The Theatrical Examiner* between January and February 1815.[14] Hunt's critical comments are interestingly polarized. He bemoans the 'exceeding barrenness which the stage has exhibited of late years in everything that concerns the tragic department'[15] but is much more enthusiastic in his discussion of comic actors and actresses. Hunt's approbation is of comics Dowton and Bannister as 'excellent in sailors and other hearty, unaffected characters', and Liston's 'face of irresistible drollery . . . [that makes one] doubt whether to call him an actor at all, and whether the part which he pretends to act is not rather a vehicle for Liston than Liston for the part'.[16]

I would like to probe further the gap in Hunt's critical perceptions of performance. The binary of high (tragedy) and low (comedy) extends not only to the class, or social level, of the performer but also to the very nature of performance itself – and its connection to perceptions of the real. While the tragedian or tragic actress is praised for their power to *act* the part, the comic performer is commended for his/her power to *imitate* or, as in the obvious case of Charles Mathews, his specific capacity for mimicry:

> Mr. Mathews sometimes appears in rustic characters, and does them very well after the usual nature of his style of acting – that is to say, as pieces of mimicry;

for all his performances are more or less of this description . . . Mr. Mathews is excellent in a hey-day song, and has latterly, among his other mimicries, shewn himself a great adept in the slang of our fashionable coach-drivers, the cut of whose intellects and greatcoats he imitates with equal felicity.[17]

The tragic actor *represents* the higher emotions of the tragic character and his skill in being 'genuine' – or 'natural' – in expression is commended, while the comedian *illustrates* the type of character performed and it is his ability to present the real, the 'fashionable coach-driver' which elicits the critic's praise. The tragedian then enables his audience to *feel with* the character, while the comedian enables his audience to *see through* the stage character to the 'real' man. The difficulty here is that the 'real' in this case is seen as undesirable – a pandering to the lower tastes of the audience.

The critical fear, expressed by Hunt and others, is of an increasing vulgarity and coarsening in the public appetite – an appetite whetted by the lower pleasures offered by the illegitimate stage. This contamination, as Hunt argues, is what has turned Elliston's virtuosity to mere rant and cant:

> He had always a tendency to overdo his part; and the consequence of his Circus vagaries, added to the flattery of those who could not distinguish between any species of success and the best species, is that he is become little better than a mere declaimer in tragedy, and degraded an unequivocal and powerful talent for comedy into coarseness and vulgar confidence.[18]

Elizabeth Inchbald also warns against declining standards in her introductory remarks to the many-volumed *British Theatre* (1808). In discussing the decline of the five-act comedy she suggests that 'the extravagance of farce has given to the Town a taste for the pleasant convulsion of hearty laughter, and smiles are contemned, as the tokens of insipid amusement.'[19] And she does not spare the rod where, in her opinion, writers are being lazy. In her introductory remarks to the popular and much-revived comedy *Heir at Law* (1797), by George Colman the Younger, she notes that he has presented 'true pictures of common life' but that the dialogue is 'deformed by dialect' and thus inaccessible to the reader – a fault she does not forgive. Inchbald concedes that the play displays Colman's talents as a playwright but the depiction of the real in character and dialogue leads her to conclude that '*taste* seems wanting', a charge she lays at Colman's feet, damningly asserting that it is 'evidently not an error in judgement, but an escape from labour'.[20] The easy depiction of characters from real life is, for Inchbald, a direct result of the decline in poetic drama – and comedy's slide towards farce is decried as forcibly as the decline of tragedy towards melodrama.

When is a comedy not a farce?

The defence of the old, literary forms of comedy places a certain pressure on the definition of the various kinds of writing for performance being played out on both legitimate and illegitimate stages. Allardyce Nicoll notes the 'break-down of the original "kinds"' in the 'movement towards novelty of form' that resulted in a range of new names such as the 'comedietta, or *petite comedie*' that 'marks the endeavour of the playwrights to indicate at what precise stage or level their particular works stood'.[21] Leigh Hunt was less troubled by these definitions, advocating the importance of the comedy in the dramatic diet and arguing that, 'a good social comedy or farce we hold to be a most refreshing and virtuous thing'.[22] Hunt and *The Theatrical Examiner* appear to make little distinction between the full-length comedy and the farce and, indeed, many stock comedies were performed in shortened versions, often as afterpieces, in a bid to return them to the repertoire of the theatres royal. It is interesting to note that in her *Collection of Farces and Afterpieces* (1815) Elizabeth Inchbald does not see fit to include any of her usual 'remarks' in the seven volumes of mainly older plays contained there.[23]

Attempts by the theatres royal to produce new comedies were frequently disastrous. *The Satirist* for 1 March 1814 includes a lengthy description of the first performance of a new farce, *Rogues All, or 3 Generations* after which Elliston appealed to the audience for a fair hearing – an affront, in the view of the writer for *The Satirist*, who declares that 'it was patiently heard through the first act, and deservedly hissed in the second'.[24] Genest makes no comment other than to note that 'this F[arce], in 2 acts, was acted but once'.[25] Even the popular Elliston could not rescue the piece for the unknown author, or the Committee of Management at Drury Lane, where the general problem seems to have been that the promise of 'new' comedies was more often than not realized in reworkings of old plays and old plots, as a review in *The Times* confirms:

> Last night a new Comedy was produced at this Theatre, [Drury Lane] called 'Recrimination, or, a Curtain Lecture'. Its author is understood to be a Mr. Clarke, who wrote, or rather put into a new form, with a new name, the piece called 'The Kiss'. As it was doomed, like so many other modern plays, for a most unfavourable reception, it is unnecessary to dwell much upon its merits or defects.[26]

The critic goes on, of course, to detail *all* its faults with the main complaint being that 'the plot was meagre. There was no trait of novelty or originality in any of the characters.' Critical responses to 'new' comedy in the following summer at the Haymarket are much the same, with a review of Barrett's three-act comedy *My Wife – What Wife?* being utterly damning. 'His characters are worse than old; they are corruptions of old and worn out models . . . This paltry production must die speedily. It is an indulgence shewn by the public, if its death is natural.'[27] This critic has nothing but praise for the performances, especially Tokely's creation of the character, Paddeen O'Callaghan: 'if you wish to meet the Paddy of real life, unexaggerated, unpruned in all his raciness, but with no adventitious or fanciful peculiarities, Mr Tokely is the specimen we would produce.'[28]

The theatres royal increasingly depended upon a few key performers to please their audience. Mathews and Liston moved between the summer season at the

Haymarket to Covent Garden while Elliston, De Camp and Palmer filled the comic bills at Drury Lane, with Fanny Kelly notable among the actresses making their mark with the audience. But while the received wisdom of the period placed an emphasis on the talents of individual performers, *The Satirist* for January 1814 makes the following interesting remarks on the state of things at Drury Lane:

> we need not be surprised . . . at the listless ineffectiveness which attends most of the plays which have been performed at this theatre. The obvious truth is, that, with many admirable performers, Drury Lane does not possess a COMPANY; and the wretched hacks destroy and swallow up the merits of the deserving: so much so indeed, that there is scarcely one of their comedies, or even farces, moderately well cast, or in which the preponderance of villainous bad acting does not overshadow and ruin the portion that is good.[29]

If, then, the plays and players at Drury Lane were deemed lifeless, and the Surrey-side minors decried for being full of cheap imitation and even cheaper spectacle, where else might the theatregoer of 1814 venture?

A stroll to the Sans Pareil

There is, of course, another route that takes the reader of *The Times*'s theatrical advertisements away from the theatres royal: towards the Strand. To pick up once more on Roach's notion of the historian and the street: a short walk in one direction up the Strand will take the theatregoer to the Olympic, for an evening of typical mixed-bill minor theatre fare,[30] while a short walk in the other direction will take the theatregoer to the Sans Pareil, where Jane Scott had been providing her own particular mix of melodrama, spectacle and farce since first receiving a licence to perform burletta in 1807.

The 1813/14 season marks a mid-way point in the rising fortunes of the Sans Pareil, a theatre built by John Scott but co-managed with his playwright/actress daughter, Jane Scott.[31] The season opened on 22 November 1813 and ran through to 2 April 1814, a shorter season than usual, but the Scotts' success is born out by the fact that the ensuing nine-month closure was in order to enlarge and refurbish the auditorium in time for a grand opening in the new season.[32] The Sans Pareil is a regular advertiser in *The Times* during this season, their offerings most usually placed between adverts for the two theatres royal and the Olympic. Unlike Drury Lane and Covent Garden, the adverts for the Sans Pareil and Olympic identify the acting company by name, enumerating the pieces they will appear in during the evening, with special emphasis on featured appearances in additional, incidental specialities. In its advertisement for 1 February, the Sans Pareil is unique in also advertising the name of the writer for two of the pieces to be performed: the 'Farcical Comic Burletta' and the concluding piece, 'an entire new Comic Pantomime', are both 'written by Miss Scott'.[33]

The 1813/14 season contained nine pieces written by Jane Scott, four of which were new and untried. A key member of the company in this season was the dancer, Gabriel Giroux, who created five new pieces, including *Love in the Grove*, the second piece for the evening advertised on 1 February. Giroux, along with his wife and daughters, are familiar names on the Sans Pareil bills, along with Villiers, the Dalys, Scruton and the Widdicombs, who frequently returned to work with Jane Scott season after season. There were twenty-four actors and seventeen actresses listed on the bills for the 1813/14 season. Some, like Andrew Campbell, specialized in imitations of famous actors from the theatres royal, as well as appearing in a number of different named roles. Others, such as Meredith, Huckel and Stebbing, were familiar comics to the Sans Pareil audience. Jane Scott most usually played the leading female characters in her own plays but she was supported by company stalwarts such as Mrs Daly and Mrs Widdicomb.

There is relatively little documentary evidence concerning the acting talents of Scott's company. Occasionally, a performer such as Richard Flexmore is identified beyond the minors when, as in this case, his son Richard Flexmore rises to prominence in the patent houses. Scott also recruited her company from other theatres, as this report for the season of 1815/16 attests:

> it is pleasing to observe also, that due attention has been paid to the selection of performers of ability both male and female, from whose merits the most sanguine expectations of success may fairly be entertained. In the course of the piece [a farce] two new performers were introduced to a London audience, namely, Mr and Mrs Weston from the Theatre Royal Dublin, both of who [sic] possess intrinsic merit.[34]

This unattributed newspaper cutting is most likely to be a 'puff' for the new season but it is clear that Scott places as much emphasis on the company she writes for as the plays they perform in. A more secure source of evidence for the range and abilities of her company can be found in a careful study of the playbills on which they appear. By tracing the patterns of performance in the 1813/14 season, it becomes clear that the Sans Pareil had exactly the kind of Company that is deemed to be missing at Drury Lane.

The promise of the new

The Adelphi Calendar provides us with the materials for such a study. It records in detail the versatility of the company and the novelty of their offerings across an extraordinary mix of genres performed at the Sans Pareil in the 1813/14 season: 'Melo-dramatic Burlettas'[35] of various kinds, ranging from 'Naval Romances' to 'Grand New Eastern Melo-dramas', 'Pastoral Ballets', 'Scotch ballets', 'Comic Pantomime' and the usual incidental entertainments. There is an emphasis on 'difference' here (which goes beyond Nicoll's argument around the desires of the playwright) as each piece is identified with an implicit expectation that it must appeal to the audience. The sense of audience expectation of difference – of variety – can be seen in the kinds of materials offered in the four new pieces, authored and performed by Scott in this season.

Raykisnah the Outcast; or The Hollow Tree was premiered on 22 November 1813 and is described as an 'eastern new grand melo-dramatic burletta' in three acts. Scott played Luxima, the daughter of the titular hero in a typically exotic melo-drama that pits the innocent against the tyranny of the Brahmins who wish to enforce a law that insists upon all female offspring being sacrificed to their gods. Giroux and his daughters offered suitable incidental dances and the cast included Stebbing as the Brahmin leader, Meredith as the outcast father, intent on saving his daughter, and Huckel as a shipwrecked European and unwilling witness to such heathen goings-on. The newly worked plot for a popular and predictable exotic setting was successful enough for the piece to be repeated at least thirty-three times in the season. Similarly, the 'Comic Pantomime', *The Magicians; or The Enchanted Bird*, first performed 23 December 1813, would have delivered the expected seasonal fare with company comic Huckel playing at least two roles, including a 'Cockney sportsman'.

Indian Hunters; or, The Inscription, first performed on 28 February 1814, combines the old with the new in an interesting way. This 'Melo-Dramatic Naval Romantic Burletta' is an overtly patriotic romp, taken from Arthur Murphy's 'dramatic poem' *The Desert Island*, a three-act piece performed at Drury Lane in 1770.[36] Scott's innovation is not only to add all the 'vulgar' ingredients that Murphy was advised to include if he wanted to make it more audience-friendly, but she also makes it topical.[37] Jane Scott played the central character of the young midshipman Sidney Nelson (one of many cross-dressed roles she wrote for herself), named after the two naval heroes of the day. With Meredith playing the central comic role of Dan Dock, the jack tar with a 'wife' in every port, Scott's piece had all the crowd-pleasing ingredients to flesh out the central tale of the abandoned mother and daughter, reunited with the husband she thinks has deserted her. The presence of contemporary concerns, including attitudes at home to the returning and victorious navy, does not, of course, make this adaptation a wholly new piece of work.

Scott's fourth, and most successful production of this season is, however, quite new – and very modern. *Whackham & Windham; or, The Two Wrangling Lawyers* was one of the most successful pieces of the season. Advertised in *The Times* on 1 February 1814 as 'a new Farcical Comic Burletta', it was first produced on 24 January 1814 and performed thirty-seven times and closing the season on 2 April. Uniquely among Scott's new works, this seems to have attracted some critical attention. The Adelphi Calendar includes a most favourable review from *The Theatrical Inquisitor* published on 14 February 1814:

> It does infinite credit to the literary talents and scenic skill, of its fair writer, Miss Scott, and we augur that had it been acted at either of the Winter theatres, it would have placed her in the first class of our modern dramatic authors; as it is, she must be content to know, that it is by far the best production we have witnessed this season; and that the treasury of her father has greatly profited by her exertions.[38]

Scott's originality as a 'modern dramatic writer' was, inevitably perhaps, doubted but the proof of her success lies in another theatre's attempt to poach the play for the following season. When *Whackham & Windham* was revived in the 1815 season, the bill for 20 February is headed with a fervent defence against

Plagiarism!
As it is rumoured that this celebrated Burletta is an Apology for the PLAGIARISM to be brought forward in ANOTHER THEATRE, as a *Translation from the French*, – Miss Scott, in justice to herself, thus publicly affirms – the Piece of WHACKHAM and WINDHAM never was a French piece, *but wholly* ORIGINAL; the Plot, Incidents, and Dialogue, *the Fabrication of her own Imagination*, founded on Domestic Occurrences within the Circle of her own Family and Friends.
The character of Thomas Thresher was drawn from that of a Man Servant in the Family.[39]

This, then, is a new piece, a domestic comedy focusing on the old story of thwarted young love pitted against parental wishes but it is modern in its depiction of London life, not least in the way Scott sets the activities of the Whackham family in the very specific location of the Strand. In Act I, the lovers (Maria Whackham, played by Jane Scott, and Henry Windham played by Andrew Campbell) send the maid, Rebecca (Mrs Daly) off on an errand in order to secure some time alone together. Henry presses money into the servant's hand, insisting: 'Don't hurry yourself Mrs Becky, I entreat/If you can't suit yourself in the Strand, there/Is great variety in Oxford Street.'[40] This is a very 'middle-class' family, created to be recognized and identified with by its audience. These are the streets they know, and the shops they visit – in what we now call the West End. The meta-theatrical self-consciousness of the contemporary setting is matched by the inter-theatrical expectation of the audience. The heroine/actress/playwright Jane Scott is, at one point at least in the licensed text, referred to as 'Miss Jane' by the doltish country servant Thomas Thresher (played by Huckel). This is the familiar delight of the television sit-com, the recognizable face of middle-class living that Ayckbourn makes his own in the late twentieth century and is perhaps prescient of the moves by that social group to dominate the output of the West End theatres for decades to come.

The pattern of performance across these four, quite different new plays by Jane Scott, demonstrates that the Sans Pareil repertoire demanded a company of performers that could be versatile – the kind of versatility that actors such as Kean evidently brought with him to the London stage but, in the theatres royal at least, did not expect to exploit to the full. If, like Elliston, a performer moved between genres, they were rarely expected to do so on the same night. This was far from the case at the Sans Pareil. By narrowing the focus on the 1813/14 season to one particular night in the season, a far greater depth of versatility than is usually expected in an early nineteenth-century acting company is revealed.

Fitting the bill

There is no extant bill for Thursday, 10 March 1814 but the list of performances recorded in the Adelphi Calendar allows us to create a vivid picture of the evening's entertainment. Here is my own reconstruction of the missing playbill:

Strand Theatre, *Sans Pareil*, opposite the Adelphi,
Under the authority of the Right Hon the Lord Chamberlain

This Present Thursday, March 10th 1814, and To-Morrow FRIDAY 11th
When will be presented the Highly-Popular Comic Burletta, written by Miss Scott called

Whackham And Windham!

Wilford Whackham, Esq. *(Attorney at law)* ———— Mr MEREDITH
Worrit Windham, Esq. *(Attorney at law)* ————— Mr STEBBING
Henry Windham, *(his Son)* ———————————— Mr CAMPBELL

Thomas Thresher *(Whackham's Servant Man)* — Mr HUCKEL
Quilldrive *(Whackham's Clerk)*—Mr Haughton   *Rebecca*—Mrs Daly
And Maria Whackham, by Miss SCOTT

Mr Campbell will give his *Imitations and Peculiarities of several distinguished Dramatic Performers*

After Which *(the last time this season)* Will be Added the Melo-drama of legendary and historic figures

The Forest Knight; or, The King Bewildered
Henry *(King of England)*———————————————Mr MEREDITH
Lord Lurewell———————————————-Mr WIDDICOMB
Robin of Ryland———————————————-Mr HUCKEL
John Cockle *(the miller and one of the keepers of Sherwood)*—Mr STEBBING
Margery *(the miller's wife)*—Mrs DALY   Kate— Miss GARCIA
Ellen of Mansfield—Miss Browne
And Richard (the miller's son), by Miss SCOTT

A new comic descriptive address, written by Miss Scott will be spoken by
Mr Widdicomb
In the course of the evening two songs by Mr Huckel and a dance by
Miss Giroux

To Be Followed by

THE 27th BURLETTA WRITTEN BY MISS SCOTT AND PERFORMED IN THIS THEATRE

The Admired Melo-Dramatic Romantic Naval Burletta

INDIAN HUNTERS!
Or, The Inscription
EUROPEANS

Captain Maitland—Mr Campbell,   Dan Dock *(an old sailor)*—Mr Meredith,
Herbert *(or Henry)*—Mr Villiers   Styptic *(Ship's Doctor)*—Mr Stebbing
Sailor – Mr HUCKEL

And SIDNEY NELSON — (A Midshipman) – By Miss SCOTT
Matilda—Miss BROWNE   Rosa (her daughter)—Miss F. GIROUX

INDIANS

Hunter—Mr WIDDICOMB, Quashee – Mr CAMPBELL, Wowski – Mrs DALY

At The End of The First Act

A Grand Characteristic Dance by Mr Giroux and Miss C. Giroux
WITH A BROAD SWORD COMBAT BY MR GIROUX & MISS SCOTT
The Finale by the Corps de Ballet

In the Course of the Evening a NATIONAL GLEE for Four Voices written by
MISS SCOTT
Mr HUCKEL, Mr BARCLAY, Miss WATLEN and Miss SCOTT

Doors open at half-past 5, and begin at half-past 6. Boxes 4s. Pit 2s. Gallery 1s. Second Price at half-past 8. No Money returned. Places to be taken of Mr Stuck at the Box-office of the Theatre, from 10 to 3. Places cannot be kept later than half-past 7. Vivant Rex et Regina.
[with apologies to] Lowndes, Printers, Marquis Ct., Drury Lane.

Two of the new plays mentioned above are included here: *Whackham & Windham* and *Indian Hunters* are performed either side of a revival of the 'Melo-drama of legendary and historic figures', *The Forest Knight; or The King Bewildered*, first performed on 16 January in the previous season and, once again, attributed to Jane Scott, who plays Richard, the heroic miller's son, in a tale of a disguised king, villainous lords and honest subjects. What is extraordinary is to find that on this night, most of the leading members of the company appear in all three pieces. But how did they deliver such different roles in quite different pieces? And how might this event contribute to new understandings about acting styles and skills in this period?

We have no personal commentary on any of these minor-house actors; but we can make some inferences and deductions from Leigh Hunt's profiles of comic actors.[41] He includes, for example, a detailed description of Munden's 'complic-ated grin' that evolves through a series of moves to a 'general stir round and grind of the whole lower part of his face' which, accompanied by a good line, brings the house down 'but' as Hunt is eager to note, 'he is a genuine comedian nevertheless, with a considerable degree of insight into character as well as soph-isticated humour for five or six minutes together, scarcely speaking a word the whole time.'[42] We might conjecture that Huckel, who plays Thomas Thresher in *Whackham & Windham*, Robin of Ryland in the middle piece and then a sailor in the spectacular melodrama, *Indian Hunters!* was the same kind of comic as Munden and able to deploy his own particular mix of physical and characterized comedy. Huckel also sang in various incidental songs and, for this evening, I have taken the liberty of including two of his better known performances, including his part in singing a 'National Glee' to conclude the evening's offering.

Meredith has a rather different trajectory on this bill. He begins by playing Wilford Whackham, the crusty London lawyer, moves on to play Henry, King of England, and finally creates the comic jack-tar Dan Dock in the *Indian Hunters*. These three quite different roles suggest the need for accepting a greater range of performance than is expected in the course of one evening by a single player. Stebbing also moves from creating the warring and aptly named Worrit Windham in the first piece to honest John Cockle, 'the miller and one of the keepers of Sherwood', finally appearing as the character of Styptic, the fussy and fearful ship's doctor. In this role, Stebbing acts as the feed to the Scott/Meredith double-act, a role which requires a high level of physical comedy, while as John Cockle, he needs a different approach in order to convey this open and honest character. Worrit Windham is more challenging still, requiring a quick, fast delivery of the brief but (sometimes) wittily written rhymes.

Of the women, only Jane Scott and Mrs Daly play in all three pieces. Mrs Daly plays the chirpy and romantically inclined maid, Rebecca, in *Whackham & Windham*, Margery, the miller's wife, in *Forest Knight* and Wowski, an 'Indian' in the final piece. The central female 'Indian', Quashee (who in a parallel plot to the main storyline, was once married to the jack-tar, Dan Dock, and now seeks him out to return him to the Indian village), is played by Andrew Campbell. This cross-dressed pantomimic performance is in stark contrast to his appearance in the first piece as the modern-day heroic lover, Henry Windham. Campbell was renowned for his 'Imitations and Peculiarities of several distinguished Dramatic Performers', an incidental appearance performed during the season and which I have included in my mock bill for the evening. Campbell appears sixty-four times in this season as an actor and it is not hard to imagine that his capacity for imitation enabled him to produce a wide range of 'straight' and comic characters – including the absurd patois patter of the native woman Quashee.

Jane Scott's own characters also suggest a range of acting skills in performance as well as in writing. Two of her roles on this night were cross-dressed but the more serious miller's son, Richard, would demand a greater sincerity than is needed for the playful young midshipman, Sidney Nelson. As Maria Whackham, Scott creates and plays the modern young woman dealing with the old problems of love and duty with a sharp line in quick fire repartee. She also frequently addressed her audience in verses that were both serious and, as with the incidental piece I have included here, comic.

Putting it into practice

Exactly how the performers move between the emotionally vivid gestural language required by the melodrama and the comic romp that makes up most of the new material found in *Indian Hunters*, and then onto the depiction of the 'real', recognizable family clashes in the London families of *Whackham & Windham* is yet to be uncovered. The sense of the ephemerality of performance is inescapable – all one can say is 'you should'a been there!' Written descriptions are usually incomplete and point, inevitably, to the need to take such a study beyond the confines of the library to the practical space of the rehearsal and performance. And even then, the findings can only be a starting point for the vexed but fascinating questions around acting and performance in this period.[43] But Scott's company, as evidenced by this bill and others, demonstrates that there is much more complexity and depth to the early nineteenth-century performer than has been accepted in traditional histories of the period.

The reductive binaries between tragedy and comedy, comedy and farce, the drama and the melodrama, legitimate and illegitimate, patent and Surrey-side, have served to polarize historical responses and demand a kind of categorization of the theatre, in writing, performance and reception. Theatres such as the Sans Pareil (and, later, Vestris's Olympic) defy this polarization as they occupy a different theatrical (and geographical) space to either the theatres royal or the Royal Circus.

Drury Lane had the patented 'right' to the dramatic text but, at times, it was this very right that militated against the possibility of producing anything really new or topical. The bill for 8 December 1813 advertises a 'comic divertissement', *Orange Boven; or, More Good News*, but as Genest confirms, the piece was 'obliged to be put off as the license was not obtained . . . there seems to have been some political strokes improper for the stage'.[44] It was produced two days later on 10 December but most likely the offending passages were expunged. Scott and her company, however, regularly serve up a remarkable array of new productions at the Sans Pareil on London's Strand. The received judgement of the creative descent into rhymed burletta could be seen to work as a cloak for an array of topical references and political ideas, shielded from the Licensor's attention by their packaging in fabulous 'melo-dramas' and 'comic burlettas' in the modern world of commercial theatre. The work of the Sans Pareil company, playing across several pieces in the course of one evening, and across successive seasons, offers new ways of seeing the repertoire of the early nineteenth-century performer – who had, above all things, to fit the bill.

Notes

1. *Playbills and Programmes from London Theatres 1801–1900, Theatre Royal, Drury Lane, 6 December 1813 to 12 February 1814* (microfiche publication; London: Chadwyck-Healey, 1983).
2. Ibid., Saturday, 12 February, i.e. none of the writers, actors etc. who had the right to free entry to the theatre would be admitted to any part of the performance free of charge.
3. Joseph Roach, *Cities of the Dead: Circum-Atlantic Performance* (New York: Columbia University Press, 1996), xii.
4. For more on the playbill and its uses in theatre history see Jacky Bratton, *New Readings in Theatre History* (Cambridge: Cambridge University Press, 2003), 38–40.
5. Allardyce Nicoll, *XIX Century Drama 1800–1850*, 2 vols (Cambridge: Cambridge University Press, 1930), 1: 120.
6. Ibid., 119–20.
7. Ibid., 120 where Nicoll quotes from H. S. Leigh's doggerel in praise of the Surrey theatres.
8. *The Times*, Monday, 17 August 1812, p. 2.
9. Christopher Murray, *Robert William Elliston Manager* (London: Society for Theatre Research, 1965), 45.
10. Lawrence Huston Houtchens and Carolyn Washburn Houtchens, eds, *Leigh Hunt's Dramatic Criticism 1808–1831* (New York: Columbia University Press 1949), 96.
11. See Bratton, *New Readings*, 142–50 for an account of performances and the eventual closure of the annual Bartholomew Fair in the nineteenth century.
12. *The Satirist*, 1 March 1814, 263.
13. Ibid.
14. See Houtchens and Houtchens, 87–106.
15. Ibid., 103. Hunt first saw Kean perform in February 1815, noting in his criticism of *Richard III*, that he was 'disappointed'; see Houtchens and Houtchens, 112
16. Ibid., 99.
17. Ibid., 101.
18. Ibid., 96.
19. Elizabeth Inchbald, *The British Theatre*, 25 vols (London: Longman, Hurst, Rees and Orme, Paternoster Row, 1808), 21: 3, *John Bull or, The Englishman's Fireside*.
20. Ibid., 21: 3.
21. Nicoll, 133–4.
22. *The Theatrical Examiner*, 20 July 1817, quoted in Houtchens and Houtchens, 315, n. 3.
23. Mrs Inchbald, *A Collection of Farces and Afterpieces*, 7 vols (London: Longman, Hurst, Rees, Orme and Brown, 1815).
24. *The Satirist*, 1 March 1814, 213–16, p. 214.
25. John Genest, *Some Account of the English Stage from the Restoration in 1660 to 1830* (Bath: H. E. Carrington, 1832), 10 vols, 8: 407.
26. *The Times*, Friday, 23 April 1813, p. 3
27. *The Times*, 27 July 1815, p. 3.
28. Ibid.
29. *The Satirist*, 1 January 1814, p. 96.
30. Elliston was taking up the reins of management at the Olympic from 1814, having decided not to renew his lease on the Surrey.
31. For more on Jane Scott as playwright, actress and manager see Jacky Bratton, 'Miss Scott and Miss Macauley', *Theatre Survey*, 37 (May 1996) and Jacky Bratton and Gilli Bush-Bailey, 'The Management of Laughter', in Catherine Burroughs, ed., *British Women Romantic Playwrights* (Cambridge: Cambridge University Press, 2000), 178–204.
32. *The Times*, 26 December 1814 includes an advertisement for the reopening announcing that the theatre has been 'Rebuilt, considerably enlarged, and elegantly embellished', p. 3. For more on the reopening of the refurbished Sans Pareil see Bratton and Bush-Bailey, 'An Evening with Jane Scott', forthcoming in Thomas Crochunis and Michael

Oberle-Smith, eds, *19th Century British Romantic Playwrights* (Ontario: Broadview Literary Texts).

33. *The Times*, 1 February 1814. p. 3. All further references to the bills and seasonal information for the Sans Pareil (later the Adelphi) have been derived from *The Adelphi Theatre 1806–1900*, Calendar for 1813–14, ed. Frank McHugh, a publication of the Adelphi Calendar Project, Alfred L. Nelson and Gilbert B. Cross, General Editors, Theodore J. Seward, Jr., Systems Analyst, 1992 accessed at http://www.emich.edu /public/english/adelphi_calendar unless stated otherwise.

34. Unattributed newspaper cuttings, Adelphi file 1815–16, Theatre Museum, London.

35. See Nicoll, 137–41 for definitions of the much vexed term 'burletta', its legal status as a condition of the licence issued to theatres such as the Sans Pareil and Nicoll's inevitable deduction that the minors flouted this at all opportunities in order to rework legitimate dramatic fare.

36. Arthur Murphy, *The Desert Island* (London, 1760).

37. The play text includes an advertisement in which a 'friend' is said to have advised Murphy as follows: 'throw in something here and there to season it more to the public Appetite? – Suppose you were to change the Title, and fix the Scene among the *Anthropophagi* . . . a few of those extraordinary Personages exhibited on the Stage, will prove very acceptable: – What think you of an *Irish* servant in it? . . . add some aerial beings, and conclude the Whole with a drunken Song by the tars of Old England' (ibid., sig. A2r).

38. *The Theatrical Inquisitor*, February 1814, 128, quoted in the Adelphi Calendar, 1813–14, 'The Season', 3.

39. See *Playbills and Programmes from London Theatres 1801–1900, Adelphi Theatre, 3 April 1810 to 30 December 1818*, microfiche publication (London: Chadwyck-Healey, 1983).

40. Jane Scott, *Whackham & Windham, The Wrangling Lawyers*, Act I, ed. Jacky Bratton in *British Women Playwrights Around 1800*, www.etang.unmontreal.ca/bwp1800/ plays/scott_whackham

41. Andrew Campbell's 'Forty Years' Recollections of a London Actor' (*Bentley's Miscellany*, 28, London: Richard Bentley, 1850, 481–6) is disappointing for its lack of reference to either his or others' actual performance. The anecdotes included here are largely concerned with management, the professional status he eventually took up as manager of the Grecian in London's East End.

42. Houtchens and Houtchens, 101.

43. For more on practice-based approaches to the work of Jane Scott and her company at the Sans Pareil see *Nineteenth Century Theatre & Film*, 29.2 (2002), ed. Jacky Bratton and Gilli Bush-Bailey. This special issue of the journal is accompanied by a CD-ROM which, with the journal essays, chart an AHRC Innovations Grant workshop undertaken at Royal Holloway, University of London, 2002, in which a group of academic experts worked with a professional company on two plays, including *Indian Hunters; or The Inscription*.

44. Genest, 8: 404.

10

Charles Mathews, Low Comedian, and the Intersections of Romantic Ideology

Edward Ziter

Like other British low comedians of the romantic period, Charles Mathews the elder inspired detailed analysis from many of the principal writers of the day. Sir Walter Scott, George Gordon, Lord Byron, Samuel Taylor Coleridge, Leigh Hunt and Henry Crabb Robinson all praised Mathews for grasping the abstract nature of character, for inducing thought in spectators, and for the ability to articulate contrasting emotions – abilities that are also indicated in paintings and prints of the actor at work. Critics and artists translated comic acting – a highly visual entertainment form – into an example of, and spur to, abstract thinking. Despite this fact, Mathews is little studied today; in the minds of most scholars, it would appear, comic acting was incidental if not irrelevant to the artistic movements of the early nineteenth century.[1] I will argue, to the contrary, that Mathews, as low comedian, is a particularly rich site for understanding romantic ideology. Charles Lamb wrote of another comic actor, Joseph Munden, 'a tub of butter, contemplated by him, amounts to a Platonic idea.'[2]

The discovery of a rich noumenal world from the contemplation of familiar objects makes such low comedians apt case studies in romantic aesthetic theory. However, my purpose in reclaiming Mathews as an object and example of romantic thinking is not simply to extend the term romantic to an understudied performer. Instead, I am interested in what can be revealed through an integrated analysis of early nineteenth-century print, performance and visual cultures – elite and popular. Elsewhere, I have argued that racialization in the Victorian period developed through a symbiotic relation between the entertainment industry and scholarly institutions such as the British Association;[3] since processes of racialization were (and are) dispersed across cultural venues, their analysis must be similarly disparate. Because Mathews's performance style focused on human difference, and since he was analysed and reproduced in various print and visual media, he is a particularly rich figure for such analysis.

Charles Mathews (1776–1835) was a character actor whose forte was the rapid transition from one character to the next in full view of an audience. He first demonstrated this skill in a London theatre in a role written for him, Buskin in

Killing No Murder (Haymarket 1809) by Theodore Edward Hook. In one scene, Buskin (an out of work actor) convinces a travelling aristocrat that he is at a well-staffed inn by pretending to be a drunken boot-catcher, a waiter, a French hair-dresser and a cook. Mathews had performed one-man shows as early as 1808 before coming to London, but he first attempted the format on a London stage in 1817 at the English Opera House. The show, the *Mail Coach Adventures*, was a popular success and he continued to give one-man performances, which would become known as 'At Home with Charles Mathews', until just before his death. He performed the At Homes in London in the winter and then throughout the provinces in the summer. In these hugely popular shows, Mathews created as many as thirty characters in a series of songs and monologues, culminating in a short farce in which he played all the characters. The At Homes relied on Mathews's ability to rapidly create dissimilar characters though changes in expression and voice, and demonstrated his skill as a ventriloquist. As some of the characters were reportedly drawn from observation, the shows also demonstrated his mimicry.

Popular prints and portraits, as well as published memoirs, essays and reviews recorded Mathews's performances. Paintings and prints of Mathews replicate aspects of romantic writing on the theatre; specifically, this iconography depicts Mathews in a performance that necessarily takes place in the mind's eye. Performance in such images emerges as a remembered event or alternately an imagined event. In either case, playgoing is transformed into an act of creative engagement with an art that is, by definition, passing. Lamb and Hazlitt wrote of 'Old Actors' in the *London Magazine* with the same longing and pleasure that mark Wordsworth's expectation of future memories as he stands on the banks of the Wye, north of Tintern Abbey.[4] By working between iconographic and literary reproductions of the actor, I hope to delineate a new visual mode of being in the world, one that was indebted to the entertainment industry and that helped shape romantic writing. I will further argue that this new visual mode helped shape emerging conceptions of race. I will examine representations of Mathews in the writings of romantic essayists and in painting and prints, while referencing his ethnic and racial impersonations. The goal is not to assert that romantics universally accepted the stereotypes presented by Mathews as accurate. To the contrary, William Hazlitt criticized Mathews's one-man shows for 'caricaturing the most common-place and worn-out topics of ridicule'.[5] Rather, I would like to demonstrate that Mathews and several romantic writers shared a fascination and anxiety in the face of a new sense of the range of human diversity, and conceived of similar strategies for responding to the spectacle of human difference.

Essayists in the early nineteenth century repeatedly described Mathews's process of observation and embodiment in terms that paralleled their own process of writing. Mathews is shown to observe, transform, adopt and then shed ethnic, racial and social characteristics – presenting and playing with the traits of highly delineated characters so as to comment on classes and ethnicities. In much the same way, essayists rapidly moved across elite and popular examples of visual and performance culture, extracting significance that would appear to exceed the external qualities of the specific objects and individuals described. Both Mathews and these essayists produced virtuosic displays, presenting themselves as empirical observers, who – through the juxtaposition of unlike materials – create unique depictions of their world. Furthermore, illustrations of Mathews attempted to capture this mix of observation and imaginative invention. Such strategies of reproduction, I will argue, delineate a new observing subject who extracts abstraction from spectacle (whether that be a world or a stage teeming with ethnic and class differences) and whose genius resides in the ability to create composite pictures through the idiosyncratic handling of disparate objects and people. As such these performances, writings and illustrations not only take a position on the represented object, they take a position on what can be known about an object and how such knowledge can be communicated to audiences, readers and viewers. In short, the new performance, print and visual cultures form part of a single epistemological shift.

Several nineteenth-century commentators asserted that Mathews's performances revealed abstract aspects of character. Lady Blessington recounted that Lord Byron commented that when Mathews personified an individual, he gave not only the 'looks, tones, and manners' of a person, but the 'very trains of thinking and the impressions they indulge in', and that Byron recalled Sir Walter Scott observing that 'Mathews's imitations were of the mind', and that rather than a mimic he should be understood as 'an accurate and philosophic observer of human nature; blessed with the rare talent of intuitively identifying himself with the minds of others'.[6] The quotes suggest an ability to trace out invisible internal processes, embodying an active interior and then linking this embodiment to a perfect external reproduction. Henry Crabb Robinson's depiction of Mathews transforming himself 'as if by magic' into an old Scottish lady in one of his At Homes with only the addition of a hood and tippet makes clear that such transformations relied on more than external changes alone.[7] The question of imitation versus mimicry was a complex issue for critics of the romantic period, and the topic was given full analysis in Leigh Hunt's essay on Mathews (first published in the *News* and republished in 1807 in *Critical Essays on the Performers of the London Theatres*) and in Samuel Taylor Coleridge's letter to Mathews from 1814. Both essayists examine whether, as Leigh Hunt explains, Mathews is to be considered an actor of 'habits' or 'passions'.[8] The distinction takes on considerable significance for the two, as it indicates an ability to transcend the mimicry of superficial details so as to discover internal human processes enabling the actor to invent a unique work.

For Hunt it only recently became clear that Mathews had attained this level of art. Hunt begins by explaining that he had long marvelled at Mathews's skill in acting national types. Hunt asserts that few can even recognize Mathews after his 'transformation into the French-man' in *Catch Him Who Can* (an 1805 comic opera by Theodore Edward Hook). It is not simply that Mathews adopts an accent; rather his 'alteration of manner, tone, and pronunciation' (68–9), rivals that of the greatest comedians of the day. According to Hunt, Mathews is no less successful in his frequent depictions of old age. Mathews disappears into his elderly characters; 'the appearance of years he manages so well, that many of his admirers, who have never seen him off stage, insist that he is an elderly man' (69). Hunt connects the fullness of this illusion to Mathews's understanding of the process of ageing and the responses of human vanity to the decay of the body. Other actors adopt and drop external characteristics, forgetting on occasion their 'tottering knees and bent shoulders'. By contrast, Mathews gives us the psychology of age: 'Mathews never appears to wish to be old; time seems to have come to him, not he to time, and he never, where he can avoid it, makes a show of feebleness which the vanity of age always would avoid.' In particular, Hunt praises Mathews for his understanding of the infinite variety in human experience. 'Our old men of the stage', Hunt complains, 'are in general of one unvarying age in all their various characters.' By contrast, Mathews creates old men of different ages and abilities; in one role he 'exhibits all the gradations of the strength and weakness of declining years' and then in another role 'settles himself into a confirmed and unresisting old age' (70–1).

Despite this praise, Hunt explains that until recently he did not think that Mathews exceeded mere mimicry. Hunt is convinced of Mathews's skill by his performance as Sir Fretful Plagiary in Sheridan's afterpiece *The Critic*, in a scene in which the character – a playwright – projects an air of amused indifference while listening to the pillorying of his play. Hunt explains: 'We are generally satisfied when an actor can express a single feeling with strength of countenance; but to express two at once, and to give them at the same time a powerful distinctness, belongs to the perfection of his art' (71). Hunt goes on to describe, at considerable length and in minute detail, Mathews's depiction of intense rage at war with a calm demeanour. The description, about a page long, completes Hunt's essay – an impressive display of invention masquerading as simple description. While many of Hunt's details presumably reproduce actor choices – 'the closing thrust of his buttons, which [Mathews] fastens and unfastens up and down his coat' – other details are much more impressionistic – 'the rage in his eyes' contrasting with the 'drawing of air to and fro through his teeth'. Hunt concludes his essay with a call for other actors and playwrights to attain similar excellence: 'If our farcical performers and farcical writers could reach this refined satire, ridicule would vanish before them, like breath from a polished knife.'

Through this complicated closing image, Hunt imagines a theatre that – like Mathews's performance – has been wiped down such that ridicule has nowhere to lodge. It is at first glance a conservative figuring: Mathews is used to imagine a cleansed theatre that has been returned to its original pristine state. However, the image is also menacing. The ideal to which farcical performers and writers should strive is 'refined satire', and once it is attained the theatre will become, once again, 'a polished knife'. The image of vanishing air explicitly refers to the fact that when one breathes on silver, fingerprints and other residues become momentarily visible and soluble; moisture quickly evaporates from polished silver. However, the image carries aggressive connotations – it is the breath of criticism that has disappeared before this now polished knife. The impotent rage of Plagiary against calumny shades into the productive rage of a new theatre whose biting satires would silence critics like a knife. Unable to fully describe the rage Mathews suggests, Hunt enacts it while calling for the renovation of theatrical comedy. Here we see Hunt modelling the inventive imitation for which he praises Mathew: literal description of physical choices becomes subjective description which concludes with the figurative evocation of a new satirical theatre. As Hunt demonstrates, the creative mind does not simply imitate but invents through imitation.

The most salient features that inform Hunt's analysis of Mathews – the emphasis on variety, the elevation of invention over mimicry, and the distinction between outward display and inward passion, as well as the self-reflective turn in the writing – are evident in Coleridge's letter to Mathews from 1814. Whereas Hunt was writing for a public audience and took this as an opportunity to call for changes in the theatre, Coleridge wrote an impassioned fan letter with the hopes of aiding a fellow man of the theatre; while apologizing for the intrusion, Coleridge is careful to identify himself as one who 'has had already some connection with the stage, & may have more' (presumably referring to *Remorse* which had been staged the year before at Drury Lane). Coleridge praises the 'astonishing effect' of Mathews's performance of Sir Archy Macsarcasm in Charles Macklin's *Love à La Mode*, a performance that 'on the whole was almost *illusion*' (500). However, Coleridge goes on to distinguish between such perfect mimicry of behaviour and

> *Profound* Comedy (i.e. that which gives us the *passions* of men & their endless modification and influences on Thoughts, Gestures, & c. modified in their turn by Circumstances of Rank, Relations, Nationality & c., instead of transitory manners – in short, the inmost man represented on the superficies, instead of the Superficies merely representing itself). (500–1)

Great comic acting makes internal processes apparent and links internal processes to outward signs. Passion is made discernible, as well as passion's transformation of thought and gesture. Social factors such as class and nationality are not displayed for their own right, but are evident in their modification of thoughts and gesture as well. All visible factors lead to a non-visible order: 'the inmost man represented on the superficies, instead of the Superficies merely representing itself' (501).

In a move common to romantic essayists, Coleridge passes from the particular (Mathews) to the universal (art). I quote at length:

> A great Actor, comic or tragic, is not to be a mere *Copy*, a *fac similie*, but an imitation, of Nature. Now an *Imitation* differs from a Copy in this, that it of necessity implies & demands *difference* – whereas a Copy aims at *identity*. What a marble peach on a mantelpiece, that you take deluded, & put down with pettish disgust, is compared with a fruit-piece of Vanhuysen's [sic], even such is a mere *Copy* of nature compared with a true histrionic Imitation. A good actor is Pygmalion's Statue, a work of exquisite *art, animated* & gifted with motion; but still *art*, still a species of *Poetry*. (501)

At the same time that the audience consumes the performance, the audience also notes a difference between what is seen on stage and what would be seen in life.

One effect of this difference is to enable the audience member to recognize the artistry of the performer and the superiority of the actor over the mimic. This is not to suggest that Coleridge is calling for something later known as a Brechtian bifurcation of actor from role so as to create a space for commentary. Instead, the actor aspires to wholeness, to fully *be* Pygmalion's statue – an animated work of art, a species of poetry, and, as such, greater than the real. The actor is the real plus a difference.

Hunt similarly praised Mathews for prompting detached contemplation in his audiences. In Hunt's essay on Mathews, the critic noted that the actor did not try to 'amaze [his audience] like many inferior actors with sudden bursts of broad merriment' but instead inspired a 'cheerfulness' that was 'more agreeable to reason, because it leaves room for thinking' (68). In short, through performance audiences are estranged from the everyday so that they may contemplate it anew. Shelley provides an eloquent elaboration on this idea when he explains that art 'reproduces the common universe of which we are portions and percipients, and it purges from our inward sight the film of familiarity which obscures from us the wonder of our being'.[9] Similarly, profound comedy, as Coleridge termed it, is drawn from the habits of the everyday, reproducing the 'common universe' so that we may see the truth of our being: the Platonic idea in the tub of butter, as Lamb would say.

Whereas Hunt completes his argument by invoking the image of Mathews on stage, Coleridge turns to painting. Coleridge's reference to the still-lifes of Jan van Huysum, the eighteenth-century Dutch artist, further clarifies the relation the author imagines between actor and audience. While the most notable feature of Van Huysum's fruit and flower still-lifes is their striking illusionism, it is not this illusionism (or at least not this illusionism alone) that prompts Coleridge's praise – simply tricking the eye would only inspire 'pettish disgust'. While the profusion of tiny insects and carefully drawn rain drops in these still-lifes is remarkable, it is the composition that holds the viewer's attention. Asymmetrical groupings and frequent serpentine lines give the effect of spontaneity, especially when grapes or other fruit appear about to spill off a table or flying insects are frozen in motion. The exuberant colours often against light backgrounds lend a dynamic sense of depth. The frequent inclusion of flowers in various states of bloom and decay gives these compositions a sense of organic vitality and unfolding time. Overall, the effect is to draw the viewer in, overcoming what Michael Fried has described in reference to eighteenth-century French painting as 'the estrangement of the beholder from the objects of his beholding'.[10] Simple reproductions, according to Coleridge, do not draw the viewer in but repel them because reproductions such as a marble peach temporarily trick rather than engage the imagination. Imagination was instrumental in Van Huysum's compositions. They are evidently imaginary compositions as they feature flowers that bloom at different times of the year. Van Huysum regularly composed his paintings from individual studies completed earlier of flowers in season or waited until a particular plant was available – a practice that meant that he sometimes took years to complete a single work.

Comic acting similarly juxtaposes diverse details so as to replicate organic processes rather than 'superficies'. The result is a sympathetic engagement with

Illustration 26   Jan van Huysum (1682–1749), *A Basket of Fruit*, 1744.

the work of art – in this case, character wrought from the actor's body. We are, after all, portions and percipients of a common universe, which is to say the object of our own observation. As such, the actor is the perfect object for the aesthetic criticism of the romantic period. George Henry Harlow's 1814 portrait of Mathews in various characters – popularly reproduced in engravings – provides a visual corollary to that idea (Illus. 27). The portrait depicts Mathews in his study, looking with inward eye at roles he has created. It is an image of solitude literally crowded with the debris of memory, as four additional figures extend beyond the frame and crowd Mathews against the wall. The caption to prints of the painting identifies the roles: an idiot amusing himself with a fly; the aforementioned Buskin as a drunken boot-catcher in *Killing No Murder*; Mr. Wiggins from the farce *Mrs. Wiggins*; and Fond

Barney, a familiar character from the York racecourse. The caption then explains that 'the intention of the artist is to present a portrait of Mr. Mathews as studying those characters for imitation preserving at the same time his likeness as varied in the representation of each.' In a solipsistic chain worthy of Wordsworth, Mathews studies himself in past roles so that he may imitate them in future performances. While Harlow 'preserves' Mathews's likeness in the successive iterations of character, Mathews engages in a project of preservation and transformation; he studies his own past creations so that he may create them anew – an activity that leaves him engrossed in his own creation of the idiot. The effect of this image, and arguably the effect the image ascribes to Mathews's acting, is of total absorption in an idea of character. The central figure is gleefully fixated on a fly, oblivious of those around him. Mathews watches himself with an expression of surprised disbelief, as do his other manifestations. The fact that Buskin seems to acknowledge the presence of the viewer makes the other characters' full engagement in the world of the portrait all the more striking, to adapt Michael Fried's analysis of Greuze. It is this refusal to acknowledge the viewer that paradoxically draws the viewer into the frame just as the apparent disorder and spontaneity of a Van Huysum still-life prompts the viewer to linger and explore its composition.

Paradoxically, the painting both undermines and underlines the distinction between actor and character. These concentric rings of absorption – the idiot absorbed in examining the fly and the other figures (excluding Buskin) absorbed in examining the idiot – intensify the viewer's focus on the idiot, which constitutes a final ring of absorption. The other characters, and Mathews himself, are so taken by the idiot's intense focus that they seem to have forgotten that he is simply a character created by Mathews, that this is in fact Mathews pretending to be absorbed. Even the viewer is susceptible to such a lapse of memory, which is particularly striking given the image's composition. But lest the viewer linger too long like one 'deluded' by a marble peach, Harlow has included additional clues that this is a painting of a representation and not a painting of the thing in itself. As Jim Davis points out in his analysis of the portrait, the idiot is dressed in rehearsal clothes and holds a wire between his hands on which a fly is mounted.[11] However, Harlow then undermines the latter device, as the idiot is clearly staring at something above the mounted fly. The scene of the idiot and the fly might be staged, but the idiot's absorption is apparently not. In short, the image repeatedly slips back and forth between drawing attention to the artifice of the composition and inducing the viewer to share in 'real' states of absorption.

Every theatrical portrait is obviously a representation of a representation. However, the Mathews portrait is unusual in the degree to which it both disavows and highlights the conventions of the genre; it asks the viewer to both see and disregard the theatricality of theatrical portraiture. Harlow is not depicting absorption in the manner of rococo painting, rather he is employing the conventions of rococo painting in order to comment on the methods by which absorption is induced and art is created. You may be enthralled by the apparent absorption of these figures, the portrait whispers to the viewer, but look and see the theatrical techniques by which absorption is staged. Harlow undermines distinctions

Illustration 27 Charles Mathews as four different characters: Fond Barney, Mr Wiggins, Buskin and idiot. By George Henry Harlow (1787–1819).

between art and commentary, just as romantic essayists routinely did. And like romantic essayists, Harlow has fastened on Mathews's performances as an opportunity to explore the complexities of mimesis. A Van Huysum still-life asserts the illusion of life with its realism only to undermine this illusion with blooms that cannot share the same time frame, multiple insects frozen in motion, and precariously balanced objects. Harlow uses less subtle means, depicting the same individual five times. More significantly for this essay, Harlow reminds the viewer that the actor is never what he appears to be, he too is art, 'a species of poetry' as it were. Coleridge wrote Mathews in May of 1814, and Harlow exhibited his portrait of Mathews at the exhibition of the Royal Academy later that summer.

Mathews owned the portrait and very likely commissioned it, suggesting that he may have been giving thought to the nature of mimesis at the same time that Coleridge penned his letter to the comedian. Far from an insubstantial entertainment, Mathews's performances may have been conscious experiments in theatrical representation, meriting the analysis they inspired.

Mathews, in any case, was an appropriate subject for a mimetically complex portrait. This visible conjoining of the real and the represented – which is a necessary element of the theatre – was heightened in Mathews's repertory, or at the very least in the plays that most attracted the attention of essayists and artists. The production that transformed Hunt's opinion of Mathews, Sheridan's *The Critic*, is filled with allusions to the theatre business. In its original production, the play disparages the theatre in which it was performed and a character named Puff insincerely praises the very actor who originated that role. Similarly, the play that prompts Coleridge's qualified praise of Mathews – Macklin's *Love à la Mode* – manipulates theatrical convention, setting up the audience to expect a stock Irishman (to complement a cast of derogatory ethnic stage-types) only to produce a patriotic and sincere Hibernian hero. The play ends happily with the observation of the Irishman and his father-in-law to be: 'This is something like the catastrophe of the stage play, where knaves and fools are disappointed./And an honest man rewarded.' This is not Brechtian alienation, but rather art's embrace of the real as the world of the play extends to include the world of the playhouse. In such a context, Mathews's highly delineated performances drew attention to the theatre's reproduction and manipulation of human behaviour through the actor to the suturing of theatrical artifice to a real body.

In Mathews's repertory, this juxtaposition of actor and character frequently served to accentuate the actor's apparent mastery of diverse social, ethnic and national types. This was particularly true of his one-man shows, first performed in 1812 and performed in London from 1817 until the year before his death in 1835. However, this layering of types was prominent in Mathews's London repertory even before the Harlow portrait of 1814. The figure in the portrait that looks out to the viewer, Buskin, was a role that highlighted Mathews's ability quickly and convincingly to adopt and inhabit behaviours associated with widely divergent classes and ethnicities. In *Killing No Murder*, when an aristocrat – a recently returned nabob – stays at the same inn as Buskin, the out of work actor obliges the humble inn keeper by impersonating a full staff associated with more opulent accommodations. Over the course of the scene Mathews rapidly creates a drunken boot-catcher, a French hairdresser, the hairdresser's young son, a cook and a waiter. By the end of the scene most of Mathews's creations are on stage simultaneously, as Mathews darts behind the confused nabob. In the play, the display of difference was staged for an imperial administrator, the butt of the joke but the individual whose wealth and importance commands the performance in the first place. However, the nabob only stands in for a higher authority – the audience – that actually commands Mathews's/Buskin's protean display. As Buskin looks to a nineteenth-century viewer from Harlow's painting, that viewer is made complicit in Buskin's joke and interpolated into the place of power that is the audience.

Romantics like Hunt and Coleridge valued the theatre for its ability to make available the tremendous range of human diversity, and to do so in a manner that demonstrated the actor's mastery and manipulation of the source material. Otherwise the actor would become indistinguishable from his source material and become a part of London's 'thickening hubbub', as Wordsworth described it in *The Prelude*: a city displaying 'all specimens of man' in 'all the colours which the sun bestows' (*Prelude* VII 211, 221–2). Without the 'difference' Coleridge ascribes to imitative genius, the actor would become little more than a human display, like those crowding Piccadilly. Pygmalion's statue could be confused with the Hottentot Venus. The creation of this difference was a function of the actor's knowledge of internal processes. As Coleridge explained, 'profound comedy' not only 'gives us the passions of men and their endless modifications on thoughts [and] gestures' but also shows how these thoughts and gestures are in turn modified by 'rank, relations, [and] nationality'. One's class, one's circle and one's nation of origin shaped one's bearing as well as the very thoughts of which one was capable. Grasping social and ethnic diversity as somatic processes distinguished the mimic from the artist. According to Hunt, there is a great difference between the actor of 'habits' and the actor of 'passions', which is to say the actor who masters representative external characteristics and the actor who fully understands the internal proclivities of character.

Mathews's performance of social, ethnic and national diversity grew more pronounced in the At Home, a format that particularly underscored the actor's manipulation of his source material. Mathews began the At Homes as himself and then, using a simple narrative, introduced a series of characters, effecting the changes in full view of the audience with the addition of a few properties or accessories. The narratives asserted or implied that Mathews had encountered these varied characters in life, then culled from and reshaped their behaviour to produce a suitable performance, demonstrating the process as he shifted in and out of character. This spectacle of transformation attained a frenzied pace in the final act, a short farce called a 'monopolyogue', in which Mathews performed all of the roles. Here one sees the layering of social, ethnic and national types, which had been a feature of Mathews's repertory, in extreme form. Taken as a whole, Mathews's At Homes form an international catalogue of human diversity comprised of Europeans and Americans of multiple classes, ethnicities and races including Scots, Irish, African-Americans and English Jews, as well as Chinese and Indian jugglers. While the At Homes prompted less comment from romantic critics, these shows were a natural culmination of Mathews's performance style. In the At Homes, the quality that Coleridge considered essential in art – the clear differentiation between the representation and the thing represented – is presented in extreme form; Mathews's rapid transformation between characters keeps the actor in view just as in Harlow's portrait Mathews is clearly seen next to his creations. Similarly, the variety that Hunt valued in Mathews's depictions of old men is taken to an extreme form in an At Home such as 'A Trip to America' in which Mathews depicted several distinct Yankee characters as well as a slew of characters of different ethnic and racial backgrounds.

One can only guess at why there is so little comment by major essayists on the At Homes (though they were praised by Hunt). It may be due to the fact that they were not classified as legitimate drama. Or it may be the quality of their composition, or even the quality of Mathews's performance. Or it may be that as a performance form premised on the exaggerated presentation of difference and variety, the At Homes function almost as a lampoon of romantic aesthetic theory. Here difference is not the additional quality that prevents the audience from mistaking the representation for the thing represented; difference is instead the very essence of the spectacle. And the audience enjoys the spectacle of difference precisely because it is so masterfully controlled by an actor who – by comparison – is very much akin to the audience. Regardless of why the At Homes were not a favourite object of romantic examination, their exaggeration of elements praised by romantics makes these shows a rich site for the analysis of romantic ideology.

Limitations of space do not allow for a detailed discussion of the At Homes and the criticism they prompted. Instead, I will examine selected images depicting Mathews in the At Home that has prompted the most interest among theatre scholars: *A Trip to America*, which Mathews performed in 1824 after his first theatrical tour of the United States. First it should be noted that the various texts of *A Trip to America* (and all of the texts of the At Homes are pirated transcriptions as Mathews refused to publish the At Homes)[12] make clear that the performance is prompted by a complex commingling of ethnographic and economic interest. One typical (though more detailed) transcription of *A Trip to America* starts by noting that Mathews explained that

> Some Tourists travel to find *black men* and *brown women*, but though one of the *generation* of the Tourists, his object in crossing the Atlantic was to find and secure the *yellow boys* [slang for guineas], being like his great prototype Columbus, lured to the new world by the yellow fever, the '*auri sacra fames*' [the holy lust for gold].[13]

Mathews contrasts his trip, which was prompted by a desire for theatrical receipts, with the tourist's trip, which is prompted by the desire to see black bodies. However, the two projects are clearly one and the same for the audience is attending the profitable performance precisely to witness Mathews's presentation of the black bodies he encountered; black men and brown women do in fact spell 'yellow boys' for the performer. He further connects his thirst for gold to a history of exploration dating back through Columbus (or to Rome, through the quote from Virgil). Later in the show, Mathews appears as a slave owner lamenting the loss of sixty dollars and twenty-five cents of human flesh with the escape of a newly purchased slave; the figurative connection between black bodies and yellow boys is made literal – an implicit reminder that guineas were first coined for use in trade with Guinea, the European name of a portion of West Africa. (Guinea-man was a common term for 'slave ship' until at least the last quarter of the nineteenth century.)

This conjoining of the ethnographic and the economic was also a benefit to illustrators who provided numerous cheap etchings. However, before taking up one such example, it is useful to consider an oil portrait in which Mathews simultaneously appears as two characters that he first created in *A Trip to America*. George Clint's 1832 portrait of Mathews, which is clearly indebted to the 1814 Harlow portrait, similarly emphasizes the actor's powers of transformation and imaginative composition. The portrait is based on William Thomas Moncrieff's play *Monsieur Mallet or My Daughter's Letter* (Adelphi 1829), which was inspired by a short scene in the monopolyogue in *A Trip to America*. In that scene a French immigrant to the United States repeatedly attempts to retrieve his daughter's letter from a Boston post office. Mathews appears as Mallet at the centre of the canvas and as the post-office keeper at the left. Clint, it has been argued, had earlier emulated Harlow's portrait of the Kembles in *The Court for the Trial of Queen Katharine*.[14] It would appear that with the portrait of Mathews as Mallet, Clint again took inspiration from Harlow. The year after the portrait was completed it was donated to the Garrick Club, where it was joined two years later by the Harlow portrait of Mathews.

Illustration 28 Monsieur Mallet or My Daughter's Letter by W. T. Moncrieff with Charles Mathews as Mallet, oil on canvas by George Clint (1770–1854).

Considered side by side, the portraits of Mathews by Clint and Harlow would appear as mirror images, with the two seated Mathews gazing up at their own standing likenesses at the centres of the compositions. In both paintings, the absorption of the examined character is signalled by upward-cast eyes and a light delicacy in the hands that signals the figure's distance from the material world – these are not hands meant for grasping objects (though in the Harlow portrait the position of the hands also reveals a stage trick, signalling the artifice of the pose). Most significantly, in both images, we do not witness an actual event but the act of memory. While Harlow clearly depicts Mathews's memory of his own roles, Clint also represents memory. When Moncrieff's play was staged several years earlier, Mathews played Mallet and James P. Wilkinson played the post-office keeper. The image, then, draws on the viewer's knowledge that Mathews had in fact originated the role of the post-office keeper in an At Home dating five years prior to Moncrieff's play. Clint, like Harlow, paints a history of performances rather than a single performance, and so relies on the viewer's own playgoing experience. Memory is also signalled through the sitting figure of Mathews, for while he occupies the place of the post-office keeper his ordinary costume – compared with that of Mallet – prompts the thought that this might in fact be Mathews in his own persona once again entering into memory for the purposes of self-observation.

While Harlow and Clint painted for elite audiences (an audience ultimately limited to the 'actors and men of refinement and education' accepted by the Garrick Club), their strategies of representation were widely copied. Harlow's portrait circulated in a 1817 mezzotint, but even the At Home etchings play with the mimetic complexities of Mathews's performances. These etchings are no less visualizations of the mind's eye than the oil portraits. For example, etchings that accompanied published versions of the At Homes show Mathews in a sequence of roles (often in a fold-out strip) and in each character Mathews appears in an entirely different costume. However, contemporary accounts describe only the most minor costume changes. Far from 'bringing a fine vision to the standard of flesh and blood' (Lamb's infamous indictment of the stage), Mathews's one-man shows apparently induced visions that exceeded his highly visual performance style as evident in an iconography of imaginary performance. Abstract and ephemeral, performance is now relegated to the realm of the imagination. Theatre is the art that most fully demonstrates the subjective nature of vision, as evident in the deep sense of nostalgia that inflects so many of the essays on theatre by Hazlitt and Lamb and in cheap prints of low comedians.

All of these etchings clearly depict Mathews under the costumes, even when he appears in drag. The one exception to this rule are the etchings illustrating *A Trip to America*. Scholars of American theatre history have given considerable attention to this show because of Mathews's depiction of black characters (notably a black tragedian at the African Theatre in New York). The complexity of the work's racial representations can hardly be addressed here. Instead I will simply note that of the five different etchings of scenes or series of characters that I examined, the one figure who appears in all – the run-away slave Agamemnon – bears no resemblance in any of the illustrations to Mathews. The radical difference of this figure is especially striking in a Cruikshank etching, entitled 'The Mathew-Orama for 1824'. Like the Harlow portrait, the Cruikshank etching presents Mathews in his own person accompanied by his creations. Mathews sits at the centre table, his features evident in the characters' faces, except for that of the grotesquely obese Agamemnon. The repeated source of wonder in images of Mathews, from Harlow portrait to the At Home etchings, is that each profoundly distinct character is fashioned from the same body. The images celebrate Mathews's artful doubling, his ability to be both a part of, and apart from, his creations no matter how similar or different these characters are from his own person. With Agamemnon we encounter the limit case, the moment at which the character is seen as so different – such a different register of humanity – that he blots out any memory of Mathews.

The manipulation of difference, according to Coleridge, is the essence of art and when art too closely mimics its object, we respond with 'pettish disgust'. Coleridge developed this idea in response to Mathews's depiction of a Scotsman making his way in London society, a depiction, which Coleridge complained, bordered on illusion. Romantic acting theory repeatedly denigrated mimicry, demanded that actors demonstrate mastery of the ethnic and class difference that divided humanity, and asserted that mastery of such differences allowed the actor to exceed the original. The true artist shows his manipulation of

Illustration 29 'The Mathew-Orama for 1824', published by G. Humphrey, 1824 (coloured etching). By Robert Cruikshank (1789–1856) and George Cruikshank (1792–1878).

his sources, heightens the distance between the real and the represented, and demonstrates that what is written on the skin springs from internal processes. This acting theory developed at the same time that the diversity of the human species was coming into new focus for anthropologists. The stakes for acting were high in early nineteenth-century Britain. Fear of a thickening hubbub could, at any time, blot out the artist and leave in his place a grotesquely different body. Analysis of romantic writing's engagement of visual and performance culture allows one to imagine genealogies linking the racial impersonations of the Victorian and Jacksonian periods to romantic theatre criticism and reveals the relation of a romantic ethos to evolving conceptions of race. Such a project hinges on the recovery of the acting body, and here theatre historians can make an invaluable contribution.

Notes

1. An important exception to this absence of scholarship is Jim Davis's two excellent articles: 'Self-Portraiture On and Off the Stage: The Low Comedian as Iconographer', *Theatre Survey*, 43.2 (November 2002): 117–98; and 'Representing the Comic Actor at Work: the Harlow Portrait of Charles Mathews', *Nineteenth Century Theatre and Film*, 31.2 (2004): 3–15. The latter essay provides a detailed reading of a Harlow portrait that will figure prominently in my argument.
2. Charles Lamb, 'The Old Actors', *The London Magazine* (October 1822): 351.
3. Edward Ziter, *The Orient on the Victorian Stage* (Cambridge: Cambridge University Press, 2003).
4. William Hazlitt, 'On Play-going and On some of Our Old Actors', no. 1, *London Magazine* (January 1820). Charles Lamb's three-part essay, 'The Old Actors', appeared in the February, April and October issues of the *London Magazine* in 1822. From this essay, Lamb prepared the better known essays 'On Some of the Old Actors', 'On the Artificial Comedy of the Last Century', and 'On the Acting of Munden', which he published in the 1823 volume commonly known as *Essays of Elia*.
5. William Archer and Robert Lowe, eds, *Hazlitt on Theatre* (New York: Hill and Wang, 1957) 168.
6. *Lady Blessington's Conversations of Lord Byron*, quoted in Ann Mathews, *Memoirs of Charles Mathews Comedian*, 4 vols (London: Richard Bentley, 1838), 3:156.
7. *The London Theatre, 1811–1866: Selections from the Diary of Henry Crabb Robinson*, quoted in Jim Davis, 'Self-Portraiture On and Off the Stage', 181.
8. Samuel Taylor Coleridge, 'To Charles Mathews', Earl Leslie Griggs, ed., *Collected Letters of Samuel Taylor Coleridge. Vol. 3. 1807–1814* (London: Oxford University Press, 1959), 500–1; and Leigh Hunt, 'Mr. Mathews', *Dramatic Essays*, ed. William Archer and Robert W. Lowe (London, W. Scott, 1894), 71.
9. 'A Defense of Poetry', *English Essays: Sidney to Macaulay*, vol. 27, The Harvard Classics (New York: P. F. Collier & Son, 1909–14); Bartleby.com, 2001. www.bartleby.com/27/ (18 October 2006).
10. Michael Fried, *Absorption and Theatricality: Painting and Beholder in the Age of Diderot* (Berkeley, CA: University of California Press, 1980), 132.
11. Davis, 'Representing the Comic Actor', 7.
12. On the complexities of reconstructing Mathews's performances from these pirated texts, see John A. Degen 'Charles Mathews' "At Homes": the Textual Morass', *Theatre Survey*, 28.2 (November 1987): 75–88.
13. *Sketches of Mr. Mathews' celebrated Trip to America: comprising a full account of his admirable lecture on the peculiarities, characters, and manners: with the most laughable of the stories and adventures, and eight original comic songs* . . . (London: J. Limbird [1824?]), 2.

14. According to Geoffrey Ashton, Harlow's *The Court for the Trial of Queen Katharine* (exh. RA 1817) made a huge and lasting impact on Clint after he produced a mezzotint of the painting: 'Harlow's attempt to create a history painting out of a theatrical scene haunted Clint during his subsequent artistic career and inspired his most important painting *The Last Scene in 'A New Way to Pay Old Debts'* (exh. RA 1820).' 'Clint, George', Grove Art Online. Oxford University Press (22 August 2007), http://www.groveart.com/.

11
The Persistence of Closet Drama: Theory, History, Form

Catherine Burroughs

I

By featuring the closet drama revival of the Romantic period and its women practitioners – most notably Joanna Baillie's lone closet play, *The Martyr* (1826) – this essay offers a formulation of the state of scholarship on closet drama and a programme for future research. It is structured by several questions: how does the periodic revival and persistence of closet drama[1] affect our construction and reading of theatre history and the canons of drama that this history produces, and what has the closet play enabled writers to express at different points in time? Certainly the corralling together of 'unperformed drama' sheds light on the ways in which theatrical practices, regulations and conventions have changed over time and reminds us that one way of marking the divide between pre- and post-twentieth-century theatre[2] is to consider that no subject or topic is regarded as 'unperformable' in the current age. Though the 'too horrible' or 'holy' were considered especially unsuited for the stage before 1900,[3] no one would suggest so today, even as these categories might prevent a play from being commercially produced.

As this essay will show, however, there are sometimes significant dramaturgical differences between a play that has been 'unperformed' – for whatever reasons – and a play written solely to be read. It is this latter tradition that interests me: the consciously constructed closet play. Through the years, much attention has been paid to the more than twenty closet dramas by Wordsworth, Byron, Percy Shelley, Coleridge and Keats. But what do we make of the fact that, after Aphra Behn had demonstrated that women could find commercial success with performed playscripts, male and female writers would continue to compose closet dramas throughout the eighteenth century and beyond – following and adapting modes first established in Great Britain during the Renaissance?[4] What factors caused women writers during the Romantic period to turn with increasing frequency to this genre forged in Classical times, and how does a study of this phenomenon cause us to revise narratives of theatre history?

While Romantic scholars have made fewer advances than Renaissance critics in analysing closet drama's unique form and its relationship to gender, Michael Simpson and William Jewett have done much to deepen our understanding of the ways in which the dramaturgy of closet plays functions to critique accepted paradigms.[5] Their books demonstrate that, if Romantic closet dramas are studied not as *failed* plays (or ones that happened *not* to have been produced) but – instead – as intentional responses to their historical moment, then one can come to understand more precisely the ways in which the closet play has emerged at different moments in history to comment on theatre as a medium. Martin Puchner's recent book on modernist closet drama – though it neglects the theorizing by Renaissance and Romantic scholars – does a brilliant generic analysis, dividing the closet play into two types (the 'restrained' and 'exuberant'),[6] in the process of arguing the need for a more sustained investigation of closet drama as a discrete form.

Yet the current state of closet drama scholarship presents us with something of a paradox: spurred by Queer Studies to investigate 'the closet' as both an epistemological and architectural space that has shaped historical and cultural practices, critics have tended to redefine 'closet drama' not so much as a genre but as *a mode of reception*. In recent years, the phrase 'closet drama' has been used to refer to two types of plays that do not necessarily share any formal properties: (1) plays written for reading; (2) those that have never been staged. Some plays have both of these features, but there is nothing intrinsically – generically – similar about these categories of texts; the only links occur in a shared history of non-performance. To make the issue of definition more complicated, the term 'closet play' has also recently been used to describe dramas about sexual 'closeting' created by (gay) playwrights.

At the definitional level, the term 'closet drama' is sometimes used interchangeably with other related, but distinct, terms. For example, in *English Drama 1900–1930* (1973), Allardyce Nicoll uses the term 'poetic play' to denote 'fundamentally unactable' dramas and connects this mode to 'dramatic poems'.[7] He also charts the persistence in the Modern period of the 'poetic and literary drama' – plays that were often acted and written in an anti-realist mood. But these are not really the same as 'closet play', a term more effectively reserved for the deliberate writing of works in playscript form for reading (perhaps aloud) rather than staging. Closet drama is also distinct from 'chamber dramas', plays like Yeats's in *Scenes and Plays* (1929), which were written for any 'room large enough for a gathering place',[8] done by amateur groups who were attracted to 'choric speaking'.[9] One sees the confusion in terminology persisting into the closet drama revival of the 1970s with – for instance – Om Prakash Mathur's definition, who described the closet play as 'drama which, on account of an undue prominence of the "literary" element, "reads" much better than it acts (if it is at all intended to be produced), and communicates its full characteristic pleasure in reading and not in a theatrical performance'.[10] This cumbersome, albeit ecumenical, explanation – blending form ('the "literary element" ') with questions of context and intent (is the play written to be 'read' or 'produced'?) and aesthetics (it 'pleases' 'fully' when read) – also characterizes definitions from the 1990s, as suggested by the following in the third edition of *The Penguin Dictionary of Literary Terms and Literary Theory* (1992): a closet play '(sometimes called a dramatic poem)' is 'designed to be read rather than performed. The term may also apply to a play which was intended to be performed but hardly ever is, and yet has survived as a piece of worthwhile literature.'[11]

A quick look at the issue of reception encapsulates some of the challenges facing those theorists of closet drama who insist upon thinking more critically about the history of the term itself. John Gay's *Polly*, published in 1729, was 'not allowed to be acted' by the Lord Chamberlain until the late eighteenth century – and only then in a cut version of George Colman the Elder's at the Haymarket on 19 June 1777. Yet, as Gay writes in his preface, *Polly* was 'principally designed for representation . . . I hope when it is read it will be considered in that light.'[12] That *Polly* was unstaged for such a long period of time – to the point where it became largely a 'read piece' rather than a performed one – belies the fact that Gay intended the play be a staged sequel to *The Beggar's Opera* (1728).

Polly's circumstances forecast the reception history of other 'closet plays', such as Percy Shelley's *The Cenci* (1819), which, along with Milton's *Samson Agonistes* (1671), is still likely to be cited as the most famous example of the genre. *The Cenci*, according to Shelley, was never intended to reside in the closet; he wrote it specifically for Eliza O'Neill, the successor to Sarah Siddons, and only the squeamishness of theatre management kept it from O'Neill's consideration. (The play's incest victim-heroine was regarded as too indecorous a part for a reputable stage actress.) Not until the late nineteenth century did *The Cenci* receive its first public performance. But even though it has been staged sporadically in the twentieth century (and inspired Artaud's sparer version espousing the tenets of his Theatre of Cruelty), *The Cenci* continues to be referred to as a 'closet play'.

The move to make the genre of closet drama more inclusive is tempting because it allows us to ignore the circumstances of a play's creation as well as to bypass the issue of 'intent' – the author's perception of her own process. The result, however, is that not enough attention is paid to the fascinating tradition of deliberately crafting a play written for readers only. Moreover, if we expand the term 'closet drama' to include those plays that were never staged or never produced until many years after composition (for reasons ranging from public to self-censorship), we bleed the term into another category – that of 'the historically closeted' or, to use John Galt's phrase from the periodical he briefly edited in 1814, 'the rejected theatre'.[13]

The tradition of closet drama should be framed not only apart from 'the rejected theatre' but also from a category that we can derive from eighteenth-century playwright, Mary Latter, in her remarkably vituperative rant against the rejection of her 1763 tragedy, *The Siege of Jerusalem*. This is the category of 'disappointed authorship'.[14] Latter's phrase is useful for highlighting the practice of playwrights who have aspired to theatrical success and failed – and who then published their work so that it might be assessed anew, perhaps even eventually performed, an option increasingly available to playwrights in the late eighteenth and early nineteenth centuries.

For instance, in 1799 Jane West echoes the gist (but not the tone) of Latter's complaints when she writes in the preface to her four-volume *Poems and Plays* that, because several of her dramas were rejected by Drury Lane and Covent Garden, she is 'soliciting attention of the public to her works through another channel'.[15] 'It has been said,' West writes, 'that with very few exceptions, the dramatist who would prefer pleasing through the medium of understanding, [compared] to the construction of eye-traps, must appeal to the press as the only vehicle by which they can hope to escape from total oblivion.'[16] 'In the present state of the drama,' she concludes, she has chosen to submit her plays 'to the public with a conviction, that they will prove as agreeable *closet companions as some compositions* which have been seen with admiration'[17] – that is, uncritical adoration. (West's case is the reverse of Fanny Burney, who, when she replaced a play that she had composed for the stage and which had been accepted by Drury Lane in 1793 – *Hubert de Vere* – with another play – *Edwy and Elgiva* – she subsequently revised the former *as a closet drama*, 'a Tale in Dialogue . . . readable for a fireside'.)[18]

That West makes clear that 'the present state of the drama' has caused her to turn her plays into 'closet companions' invites us to revisit the question of the extent to which intentionality matters as we theorize closet drama anew. Are closet plays 'closet' because their authors say they are? Of course not. And yet, while a broad swathe of twentieth-century theory would have us ignore intentionality, when playwrights telegraph that their dramas have been crafted for the closet (or for the stage), they not only acknowledge that certain formal traditions and generic expectations lie behind their choices but they also indicate a *willingness* to engage with the specific structural demands dictated by that choice. It is this consciousness that can trigger us to pay more attention to the discoverable formal features that may align particular playscripts with the closet – even as we are also spurred to look more carefully at dramaturgical alignments with the stage. Furthermore, those documents that convey a writer's conscious decision to craft a closet play – as this conceptualization shapes the practice – can make a difference in how we receive a particular playscript. Thus, statements of intention direct us to look for generic features particular to closet drama, even though such statements will not necessarily result in our finding them or indicate that the intent has been formally realized.

Whether or not a closet play can ever be performed may be less a factor in constituting its generic identity than its 'desire' – or rather, its author's desire – to use dramaturgical elements for a purpose that lies outside of the traditional stage. What Keir Elam has written about the 'performed text' is helpful in thinking about the closet play: 'in order to be genuinely *performable*, the dramatic text will leave space for the movement and self-display of the body and its accessories on stage, pointing to them explicitly through direct reference or calling upon them implicitly through the "gaps" left by incomplete linguistic references.'[19] Closet drama does not always do this – or rather, sometimes it chooses *deliberately* to shun concerns with bodies in space. That is, in contrast to a playscript written with a performance in mind or created through imagining a performance in a theatrical arena, many closet plays – even those that may eventually be staged – do not yearn for 'the performed text'; there is no 'incompleteness' as the result of the fact that the written and performed text each 'bears the other's traces'.[20]

In his published and unpublished work, Jonas Barish's discussion of the formal features of closet drama underscores the fact that the closet play represents neither a failed nor 'incomplete' endeavour but rather a generically specific tradition honed over hundreds of years. As Barish observes in contrasting 'the language of the study' with that of 'the stage', 'we can detect degrees of what we might call closetness even among closet plays.'[21] For instance, the performance of rhetorical moves often takes precedence over bodily movement (including exits and entrances) to the point where speech-making is *the* central action; monologues and soliloquies dominate, and, when dialogue appears, it often resembles stichomythia. Interiority is privileged. Rarely does a closet play contain scenes among more than three characters, since the focus is usually an argument or a debate, the action being the working out of a philosophical problem or the advocacy of a moral position. And, even in the debate format that is so characteristic of the genre, the dialogic nature of such an exchange is predominately monologic. Moreover, the intellectual appeal and the architectural 'austerity' that Barish identifies in the form (simple plots, for instance, characters that speak at length) result in the dramaturgy's comfort with, indeed a relishing of, 'sententiae' – that is, prescriptions for social behaviour that moralize and/or advocate. These didactic moments function like the choral passages in Greek drama – when the action is summarized, reflected upon, and offered as a 'product' for intellectual and spiritual consumption – and which also lend themselves to memorization and quotation. In short, the *intentional* closet play is primarily a tool for learning, rehearsing, reflection and re-reading. It posits a reader who, if not analytically inclined, has time enough (if not the patience) to study both the closet play's content and form.

II

Closet playwrighting has a long history that dates back to Greece and Rome, the ten plays that have been attributed to Seneca establishing the genre to which Italian and later English Renaissance writers became attracted. While it is not certain the extent to which Seneca's plays were written for the stage or for private recitation in small audiences, by the Renaissance they 'were assumed to be meant for performance, and were sometimes performed at universities'.[22] Around 1550, Lady Jane Lumley composed *Iphegenia at Aulis* – the earliest extant English translation of a Greek play (from Euripides) – and arguably the first English closet drama. But not until the early 1590s did closet drama have its first major period (lasting until around 1607) when the Pembroke Circle, led by Mary Sidney, crafted plays for reading that were preoccupied with the topic of 'Antony and Cleopatra'.[23] The second major period of closet drama occurred during the Interregnum – which also saw 'political dialogues' multiply, a mode of politically charged closet play.

In considering the history of closet drama criticism, I should note that those of us who have studied this subject through the years have yet to determine precisely when the label 'closet drama' was first employed in a critical context.[24] In his excellent dissertation on closet plays and the Interregnum, Jonathan Heawood observes the following: while a a critical vocabulary for discussing the textuality of plays was emerging by the 1630s – giving closet drama 'a nascent identity, in the decade before the closure of the theatres' – as late as 1841 'critics were still grasping after a term just out of reach'.[25] This is obviously problematic for the field, for even as it is well-documented that – by the latter quarter of the eighteenth century – the opposition between 'closet' and 'stage' had become firmly part of the critical discourse, the history of closet drama's reception is far from clear.

As a number of critics (myself included) have pointed out, Stephen Larrabee's 1941 essay still resonates for its identification of two documents – Edward Young's *Conjectures on Original Composition* (1759) and Oliver Goldsmith's *An Enquiry into the Present State of Polite Learning* (1759) – that mark the rise of the closet/stage opposition in the middle eighteenth century – one more vehement and schematic than during the seventeenth (as Straznicky has persuasively argued). Young's *Conjectures* contains a critique of Addison's *Cato* (1713) that associates 'the closet' with coldness, stasis, unnaturalness, artifice, the sculptural, the poetic, the didactic, the virtuous and the moral. By contrast, the stage is all 'nature' and 'warmth'.[26] Goldsmith goes so far as to assert: 'I think it would be more for the interests of virtue, if stage performances were read, not acted . . . for all must allow, that the reader receives more benefit by pursuing a well written play, than by seeing it acted.'[27]

Scholars have also noted the importance of William Mason's dramatic prefaces and letters for establishing the growing closet/stage schism in the 1750s. Allardyce Nicoll writes that the 'tendency towards the purely poetic play is to be traced' to Mason's *Caractacus*, which was written 'on the plan of Aeschylean tragedy' to feature a 'theme . . . taken from Druidic Britain'.[28] While Mason's *Caractacus* was performed several times (in Dublin in 1764 and London in 1776), the date of its publication – 1759 – emerges as the pivotal date for sowing the seeds of the closet drama revival in the Romantic era, for this is the year when the 'closet/stage' dichotomy gains currency in the critical discourse. Jonathan Heawood also draws attention to Mason (particularly his criticism of Milton's closet drama, *Samson Agonistes*), observing that, in the 1750s, there was 'for the first time . . . a sense that a published text might remain in the closet – and that in fact it might be intended for the closet. This is a crucial shift towards the formulation of closet drama: in arguing that *Samson Agonistes* is in the closet because of Milton's refusal to gratify his audience, Mason draws a distinction between public and private texts.'[29] And, in the handwritten notes that he left for his planned book on closet drama, Jonas Barish cites Mason in order to make the point that, between 1750 and 1770, closet drama became 'regarded seriously as a species of lyric poetry, entitled to be criticized & commented on in the same way, quite irrespective of its lack of connection with the stage'. In a letter to Walpole on 3 March 1775, Mason wrote: 'However, when you send me the tragedy itself, perhaps I shall be able to fill a page with *closet* criticism, for that power has not quite left me, and I distinguish it from *theatrical* criticism widely.'[30] In short, after 1750 and particularly around 1759, there is a growing culture for both the publication and critical reception of closet drama leading to the closet drama revival of the late eighteenth and early nineteenth centuries.

While closet drama has historically attracted a large number of female practitioners – for reasons that I do not have time to rehearse here – a relatively large gap in closet playwrighting by women appears between 1700 and 1760.[31] We can link this gap, in part, to the first wave of female playwrights after Aphra Behn. (Catharine Trotter, Mary Pix, Delariviere Manley, and Susannah Centlivre debuted a large body of work on the British stage between 1695 and 1722.) Conversely, the *rise* of closet drama written after 1760 can be framed, in part, as a response to the Stage Licensing Act of 1737, which – by restricting the performance of Britain's canonical theatre to Covent Garden, Drury Lane, and to the summer Haymarket, and by institutionalizing the Lord Chamberlain's role as censor – limited what performed playscripts could do. But just as had happened after the theatres closed in 1642, playwrighting did not abate (it actually proliferated), and alternative venues and modes emerged to accommodate the differing needs of writers who were drawn to the drama. One of these alternative modes was the closet play.

Marta Straznicky has observed – in reference to Anne Finch's closet plays from the 1680s in which the reader 'experiences no lapse in "seeing" the represented action' – that 'a play on the page is in no *intrinsic* way identifiable as a closet drama.'[32] This is true to an extent. But, by 1800, closet playwrights seem more fiercely self-conscious about the historical, theoretical and generic underpinnings of their enterprise and, for this reason, may be seen as embracing the closet play as a form with which to effectively express everything from disaffection with the limits of the stage to interest in what a drama for reading enables.

Indeed, with increasing intensity, from 1770 onward, as the Age of Sensibility segues into Romanticism – with its embrace of the emotional capacities provided by the lyric – and as writers struggle against the limits imposed by licensing, closet drama offers an outlet for a simultaneous deployment of three generic impulses: the lyrical, the dramatic and the narrative. Paul Hunter locates a shift in generic dominance – from drama to novel – in the 1740s and attributes this shift to 'the Puritan fear of theatre as a force of immoral infection, the growing cultural distrust of village festivals, the proscription of the telling of traditional tales, the court terror of nonconformist assemblies that led to laws such as the Conventical Act, and the political fears that produced the Licensing Act of 1737'.[33]

Certainly the historical reasons for the re-emergence of the closet play in the 1780s require more space than this essay can offer. But what is important, as we retheorize the genre, is to note that, although the closet play has specific generic expectations, it does not 'police' these modes in the same way as do the poem, the stage play and the novel. Elizabeth Inchbald compared drama unfavourably to the novel, writing that 'The Novelist is a free agent . . . whilst the Dramatic Writer exists but under a despotic government' as the 'very slave of the audience'; he 'must not speak of national concerns . . . [h]e must not allude to the feeble minister of state, nor to the ecclesiastical coxcomb.'[34] But, as other women writers of this period make clear, when one writes *closet* drama, one can craft a play without having to deal with the politics or economics of theatrical production; one can act, direct and design without having to be reviewed; one can read – in silence or aloud – without having to accommodate a paying audience, although one can invite an audience in. Furthermore, closet drama allows writers (and readers) to fantasize a theatre without consequence – without real people, without real bodies – and the result is a discrete form that pays homage to a theory of playwrighting but not to a practice; to the idea of a staged play but not to its gritty reality.[35]

III

The flurry of closet drama publication in the 1790s set the stage for Joanna Baillie's creation in the early nineteenth century of a single play intended to reside solely in the closet – one that culminates the third major period of closet drama in Great Britain.

It is something of a paradox that, though devoted to creating a three-part dramatic series now referred to as the *Plays on the Passions* (1798, 1804, 1812), Baillie turned to closet drama to vent one of her greatest passions in the early 1800s: her belief that Christianity was a vitally civilizing force for inducing what she famously called 'sympathetic curiosity'. But precisely because closet drama posits a readership that will respond intellectually (as much as emotionally) to its subject matter, it was an ideal form for Baillie's attempt to disseminate her theology.

Indeed, *The Martyr* is a product of that important but understudied period of Baillie's life (between 1815 and 1836) when she seems to have been most intent not only on reading religious philosophy but also on sharing with readers her thoughts about Protestantism. The topic of religion had always engaged her – her father was a Professor of Divinity at Glasgow University before his death in 1778 – but it was not until the 1820s that Baillie began to use publication as a means of 'instructing' a readership conceptualized as alternately uneducated and intellectual through projects ranging from the missionary drama, *The Bride* (1828),[36] and the essay, *A View of the General Tenour of the New Testament Regarding the Nature and Dignity of Jesus Christ* (1831), to the closet drama, *The Martyr*, which Baillie tells us was 'written for a long time' (512)[37] before its publication in 1826.

In my earlier work – in an attempt to draw attention to the spatial and sexual components of Joanna Baillie's dramaturgy – I made much of her as a 'closet dramatist'.[38] But subsequent research has caused me to concur with Isabella Imperiali[39] that Baillie, the author of twenty-seven plays, wrote only one work that can generically be categorized as closet drama – that is, a 'play never intended to be acted', and this is *The Martyr* (1826). (*The Bride* [1828], while also a play of religious instruction, was written to be performed for the natives of Ceylon or modern-day Sri Lanka.)

In Baillie's preface to the *Dramas* of 1836, she states that, though she intended 'not to have them published in my lifetime', she still hoped that 'after my death ... they should have been offered to some of the smaller theatres of our metropolis'.[40] *The Martyr*, reprinted with these plays, is different because – as she tells us in the preface written ten years earlier – she would only have dared to have 'venture[d], with diffidence and awe, to make' Religion the subject of a play if she knew it would never be performed.[41] 'I need scarcely observe to the reader,' she writes,

> that the subject of the piece is too sacred, and therefore unfit for the stage. I have endeavoured, however, to give it so much of dramatic effect as to rouse his [the reader's] imagination in perusing it to a lively representation of the characters, action, and scenes, belonging to the story; and this, if I have succeeded will remove from it the dryness of a mere dramatic poem. Had I considered it as fit for theatrical exhibition, the reasons that withold me from publishing any other manuscript plays, would have held good regarding this.[42]

In contrast to 'the dryness of a mere dramatic poem', closet drama allows Baillie to dramatize the culturally unstageable (the 'too sacred') even as it permits her to 'rouse' the reader's imagination. The form is liberatory in the sense that Baillie could subtly register protests against social practice and counter theatrical convention even as she obliquely complied with cultural pressures. For if one wanted to challenge those who, in the words of Romantic closet playwright, Ann Wilson, 'are so tenacious of scripture, that they think any thing which bears the resemblance of a play, a profanation of it',[43] then a dramatic form that slides between a number of modes in its aim to subordinate the sensual to the intellectual might seem especially well-equipped to negotiate a cultural taboo.

Like the dramaturgy of the play itself, the preface to *The Martyr* is both a polemic and a scholarly document, alternating between impassioned assertion and footnotes that cite the sources of Baillie's reading (from Stewart's *Elements of the Philosophy of the Human Mind* to Pope's *Odyssey* and a sermon by Samuel Clarke). At one point in the preface, Baillie bursts forth: '[C]an we conceive mingled feelings of gratitude, adoration, and love, more fervent, and more powerfully commanding the soul and imagination of man, than those which must have then been excited by this primitive promulgation of the Gospel?'[44] But although 'primitive promulgation' is her topic, the central action is the rhetorical passion of the play's main character, a Roman soldier named Cordenius Maro, who converts to Christianity during the Age of Nero. There is little debate per se, for the play assumes the superiority of Christianity, and the important moments of conversion and martyrdom, which take place offstage, are all reported by characters that function like the messengers in Senecan drama. But, as analysts have demonstrated in reference to classical tragedy, these moments of reporting encourage a reader of *The Martyr* to focus on the import of the acts being described rather than become sidetracked by watching actual bodies struggle with persecution and death. Thus, the characters' act of describing their experiences serves not only as a textual stage for their rhetorical innovation but also as a subject for the reader's rhetorical analysis, as the following passage from *The Martyr* suggests.

In 2.1, Cordenius Maro, entrusted by Nero with persecuting the Christian converts in his empire, has himself converted near the start of the play – offstage.

To the Christian father's concurring with Maro that he is 'alter'd' as a result, he responds with this rhetorical flight:

> I am, methinks, like one who, with bent back
> And downward gaze – if such an one might be –
> Hath only known the boundless azure sky
> By the strait circle of reflected beauty,
> Seen in the watery gleam of some deep pit:
> Till on a sudden roused, he stands erect,
> And wondering looks aloft and all around
> (Granting again that such an one might be)
> Who hath but seen the element of fire
> On household hearth or woodman's smoky pile,
> And looks at once, 'mid 'stounding thunder-peals,
> On Jove's magnificence of lightning. – Pardon,
> I pray you pardon me! I mean *His* lightning
> Who is the Jove of Jove, the great Jehovah.[45]

More so than in verse plays written for performance, this act of simile-making – so central to narrative poetry – is characteristic of the kind of action that *The Martyr*, as a closet play, makes central. The extended simile above serves not only to convey what being a Christian is 'like' but also to show how 'unlikely' (in Baillie's view) it is for Christians in the early nineteenth century to emulate the 'simplicity', 'nobility', 'purity' and 'innocence' of the earliest martyrs. This passage, like many in the play, is designed to 'rouse' the reader until she, like Maro, 'stands erect' in attentiveness to the reasons for exploring, and celebrating, early Christian history.

Given the play's emphasis on rhetorical action, it is not surprising, then, that the climax of the play occurs during Maro's three major monologues in Act 3. Pretending to be a Christian prisoner he has rescued from prison and 'throwing off his Grecian cloak',[46] Maro advances towards Nero and engages in a linguistic performance given force not only through his rhetorical competency and the space that this rhetoric occupies but also through the fact that, traditionally, the genre of the closet play posits an audience released from concerns with stageability. Thus, while the dramaturgy of *The Martyr* permits its characters to indulge in – among many rhetorical moves – apostrophe, sententiae, description, lyricism and prescription (as one might do if teaching a class, instructing a pupil, or giving a sermon), it also creates a space for the play's *readers* to indulge themselves in the activity of analysis. Moreover, Baillie's consciously constructed closet play – the only one she wrote – pushes readers to engage in a variety of emotional and intellectual ways with her contention in her preface that Cordenius Maro's conversion represents 'the simplest and most perfect state' of 'a class which' she believes 'to have been very rare, except in the first ages of Christianity'.[47] Whether through the acts of rereading, meditation, rhetorical analysis, or committing passages to memory and voicing others aloud for elocutionary purposes, the implied reader of *The Martyr* is a studious Christian and an active intellectual.

IV

When Mary Russell Mitford looked back in 1854 on her 'dramatic scenes' from several decades earlier and observed that '[t]heory, right or wrong...forms the ground-work of most dramatic Prefaces',[48] she pointed to the fact that prefatory material affixed to closet plays – advertisements, dedications, introductory essays – contains a body of theory about closet drama that differs from our current age, one which was powerfully shaped by women during the Romantic period and which requires our attention today. As Martin Puchner has suggested, when a writer creates a play that consciously eschews the stage, he or she can be said to theorize – through dramaturgy – the state of the theatre at a particular moment in history. Karen Raber makes a related observation in her book on women and sixteenth- and seventeenth-century closet drama: the genre's deliberate 'distance' 'detachment' and 'dissociation' from the stage, she writes, 'produces reflection, investigation, and theory'.[49]

Baillie's preface to *The Martyr* and the play itself remind us that drama written for the closet has, since its early appearances in England, often been crafted not only for entertainment but as a teaching tool. This 'Theatre of Education' (Elizabeth Pinchard's phrase in *Dramatic Dialogues, for the use of young persons* [1792]),[50] resembles what Anne Mellor – in reference to the major performed plays by Romantic women – has described as the concept of 'Theater as the School of Virtue'.[51] But late eighteenth-century instructional closet drama – particularly its biblical closet plays – springs less from the commercial stage than from the tradition of creating dramas designed to encourage intellectual growth or spiritual development. While this essay cannot sufficiently address the growing trend from the 1790s and into the early nineteenth century for women to translate French and German plays that had attained a large measure of stage success, it is important to note that many of these translations were undertaken not so much with the expectation that they would be staged but in order to provide the translator with a chance to learn or improve in another language and/or to participate in a humanistic tradition of education that valued Classical training. Some of the earliest closet plays by women had been undertaken for these very reasons, such as Jane Lumley's *Iphegenia at Aulis* (c. 1550).

Whether through recitation, translation and/or the act of rereading, closet dramas of the Romantic period are often constructed to encourage a careful study of their content, if not their rhetorical strategies, and, in this sense, they anticipate the deliberate distancing effect – if not the parable-telling and political focus – of Brecht's 'Lehrstücke', or 'learning/teaching plays'.[52] Straznicky has observed that studying closet drama necessarily causes us to think about 'the history of reading',[53] which inevitably focuses our attention on the 'word "closet" in "closet drama"' – 'the most efficient way,' she writes, 'of signalling that the cultural position of these plays is formed by the same ideology of privacy that structured the paradoxical conceptions of domestic and theatrical space'.[54] In a related comment, J. Paul Hunter notes that, as the physical space of 'the closet' became associated with the growing trend of secular reading in the eighteenth century, moralists worried about the fact that 'books unfit for public rooms may be found in the closets of even the most devout families.'[55]

But because a number of Romantic women writers describe the closet play as licensing what we might call a 'theatre of contemplation', they point to the long tradition in closet playwrighting of using form to facilitate spiritual, moral or intellectual growth. Richard Lovell Edgeworth's comments about the plays of his daughter, Maria Edgeworth – *Comic Dramas* (1817) – are useful for highlighting some of the ways in which the perceived formal differences between closet drama and staged plays affected closet drama composition in this period. Urged by friends and theatre professional Thomas Sheridan to write for the stage, Maria Edgeworth was, in her father's words,

> aware of the wide difference that there is between the exhibition of a character in a Tale and circumstances, and for that gradual development of sentiments and incident, which make us acquainted with the persons whose adventures are related, and which insensibly interest us in the fable.
>
> On the contrary, in the Comedy, the characters must be shewn by strong and sudden lights, the sentiments must be condensed; and nothing that requires *slow reflection* can be admitted. The audience must see, hear, feel, and under-stand at once. Overawed by these considerations, Miss Edgeworth has declined to risk a bolder flight. But encouraged by her father, without venturing on the stage, she publishes the following little Comic Dramas, to feel her way in this new career. Her failure in such an humble attempt cannot be attended with much disgrace, as it is made with real humility.[56]

As Richard Edgeworth condescendingly suggests, a play written for the stage is the antithesis of 'slow reflection' – one of the key attractions of the closet play – and that publishing a play as a means to 'feel one's way' in a 'new career' was (and perhaps still is) an advantage of closet playwrighting, since the form provided a low-risk apprenticeship or training ground for becoming an eventual playwright – or not. Edgeworth also implies that, while the staged Comedy requires that 'the characters must be shewn by strong and sudden lights, the sentiments must be condensed; and nothing that requires *slow reflection* can be admitted', comic dramas published for a reading audience show the writer's 'humility' and 'cannot be attended with much disgrace'. A female practitioner who might inevitably feel 'overawed' by the requirements and pressures of the five-act classical form that dominated the late eighteenth- and early nineteenth-century stage – in both comedy and tragedy – might be drawn to the closet play because plays published to be read would often be received as studious and educational documents in which both reader and playwright were engaged in learning. Paradoxically, even as a closet playwright might teach or prescribe, she could inhabit the position of someone who is a student, rather than an expert, of dramaturgical craft.

When, for example, the author of *The Carthusian Friar, or the age of chivalry* (1793) – identifying herself only as a 'Female refugee' from the French Revolu-tion – tells her readers that her five-act tragedy 'was written long previous to the

Author's coming to this hospitable and blessed country, and without any idea of committing it to the press', she also clarifies that, in publishing it so many years later – during the Reign of Terror – '[h]er aim, her desires, are confined to the narrower circle of the *studious* and, above all, the *compassionate!*' 'It is in the silent recess of the closet, that she [the playwright] dares to court the eye of sensibility!'[57]

This idea of a thoughtful, reflective readership (often constructed as children, teenagers, friends or relatives) undergirds a significant portion of closet drama by women, and, for this reason, especially after the 1780s, 'the dialogue' emerges as an increasingly useful form for focusing on what closet playwright Ann Wilson calls 'edification'[58] or what Charlotte Smith refers to (after Madame de Genlis) as '*les petites morales*'.[59] This edification is the aim of Elizabeth Subthorpe Pinchard in her preface to *Dramatic Dialogues, for the use of young persons* (1792): '[W]ell aware that the length of the scenes, in some places, and the simplicity of the Plot in all, would render them flat and heavy in representation', Pinchard tells readers that she has found herself motivated 'to throw her stories into Dialogue', believing that 'young people are easily captivated and interested [as in 'involved' or 'invested in'] by this manner of writing'. Embracing 'the dialogue' ensures Pinchard 'the convenience of avoiding the "*said she*," and "*replied she*," which becomes so fatiguing in a narration of any length'.[60]

Similarly, in the preface she affixed to the series of dialogues called *Rural Walks . . . Intended for the use of young persons* (1795), Charlotte Smith explains: 'I wished to unite the interest of the novel with the instruction of the school book, by throwing the latter into the form of dialogue, mingled with narrative, and by giving some degree of character to the group.' When Smith confesses that it was 'less easy than I imagined' to write 'stories which are attractive to children, yet not uninteresting to others farther advanced in life',[61] she implicitly targets some of the structural advantages offered by closet playwrighting when distilled into dialogue form. In her first dialogue, for instance, called 'The Sick Cottager', one finds nine pages of narrative establishing the characters and their circumstances. This narration is shortly followed by a soliloquy by Caroline, the main character, and then a dialogue between several others – written with character names as in a play and containing stage directions for how the lines should be voiced – such as '(sighing)' and '(dejectedly)'. Narrative continues to intrude throughout the text, sometimes as many as two prose pages, in past tense. But, on occasion, Smith switches to the present, as if more closely to resemble the directions in stage scripts. For example: 'The breakfast passes with little conversation. Mrs. Woodfield makes tender inquiries after her niece's health. Caroline appears cold and dejected.' And Smith also incorporates moments of dialogue into the narration, as in a novel: ' "Ah! madam," said she [the wife of the sick cottager], "how good it is in you to come again!" '[62]

Yet however much dialogue and present-tense narration structure her text, occasionally Smith's stage directions appear in the past tense – a reminder that closet drama, as Jonas Barish has observed, 'relishes *telling* more than *showing*'.[63] This is a point that Puchner underscores when he writes that stage directions 'are located at the heart' of (Modernist) closet drama;[64] its 'diegetic' features – 'the descriptive and narrative strategies' – convey the closet play's effort 'to channel, frame, control, and even interrupt what it perceives to be the unmediated theatricality of the stage and its actors'.[65] Thus, the tension between narrative and the formal elements of playwrighting – dialogue, monologue and soliloquy – are underscored in the hybridity of the stage directions that sometimes emerge from Smith's dialogue, as in this example: '[Mrs. Woodfield and Elizabeth were at work – Caroline was drawing at a table near the fire].'[66]

The flexibility with genres that the dialogue form has consistently encouraged throughout British history helps explain why some critics have recently laced their discussions of closet drama with words like 'resistance',[67] 'ambivalence' and 'deviance'. Thomas Crochunis, for example, has described Baillie's dramaturgy as 'ambivalent' because it 'uses mixed media – stage and page – to give complex performances for the public'.[68] Crochunis also notes that the 'ambivalent desires underlying Baillie's dramaturgy ... resemble those described in recent theories of sexuality'.[69] For 'closet drama (like bisexuality) might more resourcefully be seen as the product of a meta-orientation toward the not-here – toward the "both/and" – that always keeps part of its apparel offstage (or in the closet), and is best understood through the particulars of its practices rather than through the various objects of its desires.'[70] This assessment of Baillie as closet dramatist would suggest that the experience of reading *The Martyr* – chocked full of large crowds and more than the usual amount of songs that appear in Baillie's plays – positions one schizophrenically between imagining a real stage (and staging) and embracing the play as a text that serves to persuade others of its doctrine through careful study of the rhetoric.

Certainly this is the case. But I want to underscore that, when we contemplate those formal features of the closet play that attracted women writers of the Romantic period and what they believed this form enabled them to do, one answer emerges from the word 'simplicity'. That is, when this word recurs in prefaces (and, with some frequency, in the text of *The Martyr*), it suggests that the closet play permitted authors to worry less about plot or dramaturgy while homing in on a single intellectual issue, a moment of high emotion, or a scene of instruction. Released from worries about brevity or length – from the challenges posed by the typical five-act structure of eighteenth-century comedy or tragedy – the closet playwright could focus on a single structural element in the drama such as character, dialogue, monologue, soliloquy or scene. 'Simplicity' is also, paradoxically, a code word for closet drama's preference for rhetorical display – the ability to persuade readers of a particular perspective through the marshalling together of specific figures of speech, as Baillie's *The Martyr* is clearly designed to do.

In her preface to *Sacred Dramas* – so popular that they went through nineteen editions after their publication in 1782 – Hannah More foregrounded anticipated objections to her plan to dramatize stories from the Bible in the process of describing some of the 'readerly'[71] or 'literary' elements typical of the closet play:

I AM as ready as the most rigid Critic, to confess, that nothing can be more *simple* and inartificial than the plans of the following Dramas... Some of the speeches are so long as to retard the action; for I rather aspired after moral *instruction*, than the purity of Dramatic Composition. The very terms of Act and Scene are avoided, because I was unwilling to awaken the attention of the Reader to my deficiencies in critical exactness.[72]

This anti-dramaturgical stance is one of closet drama's main attractions for women writers in the Romantic period and one of the reasons that, from the sixteenth century onward, the form was employed to facilitate elocutionary exercise in domestic circles and educational environments.

When they serve elocutionary development, such 'academic dramas'[73] – whether labelled 'dramatic scenes', 'dramatic poems', 'dramatic verses', 'poetic dramas' or 'dramatic entertainment' – are performance pieces. Barish, in his notes, reminds us that this genre has historically been used to 'teach deportment, elocution, poise, etc. Closet drama [was] a way of circumventing the vulgarity of the playhouse while keeping the dramatic poetic essence.' Likewise, Straznicky emphasizes the differences between sixteenth- and seventeenth-century closet dramas and those that came later: the closet dramas of that period were 'not understood as antithetical to the stage, regardless of performance history or authorial intention, nor was it [closet drama of the period] in any fixed sense a private mode. Rather, closet drama or "dramatic poetry," the nearest equivalent Renaissance term, was a label that could be applied to *any* play – whether performed or not – that was or sought to be inscribed in literary culture, a culture that, informed as it was by ideas of reading as social practice and print as engagement with the public sphere, was not in stable opposition to "public" forms of theatricality.'[74] And, as Anne Mellor has shown, the 'leading women playwrights of the Romantic era – Joanna Baillie, Hannah More, Hannah Cowley, and Elizabeth Inchbald – consciously used the theater to re-stage and thereby revise both the social construction of gender and the nature of good government', functioning 'as a public school for females, one that could be used to correct the inappropriate or inadequate education many good girls received at home'.[75]

And yet, while some Romantic closet plays resemble private theatricals and household drama in their semi-public and intimate contexts, the rehearsing of rhetorical mastery nevertheless takes precedence over action. As the female author identified only as 'C. Short' explains in *Dramas for the use of young ladies* (1792), long prose passages figure prominently in her two plays because they 'were written for a Society of young ladies, in whose welfare and improvement I am warmly interested; and as they have proved beneficial to this small circle, *in promoting the habit of speaking with grace and propriety*, I conceived they might be useful to others in similar situations, and therefore determined to present them to the public.'[76] Hannah More had a similar aim in *A Search after Happiness*, the very popular pastoral in three dialogues that she wrote in 1763 at the age of eighteen and published ten years later and which would have been widely available to women writing into the nineteenth century. This closet drama, she tells us, was originally written 'to be recited . . . by a party of young Ladies' – at the Bristol girls' school founded by her three older sisters (1758). Moreover, one of the main characters, named Euphelia – a young lady 'of distinction in search of happiness' – voices an introductory address that contains a pithy description of a large strand of women's closet drama during this period: Euphelia tells us that 'No deep-laid plot adorns our humble page,/But scenes adapted to our sex and age':

> Simplicity is all our author's aim,
> She does not write, nor do we speak for *fame*,
> To make amusement and instruction friends,
> A lesson in the guise of play she sends.[77]

This phrase, a 'lesson in the guise of play', underscores the fact that Baillie and her contemporaries saw closet drama – when defined as a text for reading only – as a powerfully enabling tradition that ultimately encourages readers to study its arguments, ideas and rhetorical moves. It is a tradition that can also encourage critics today to 'reflect' 'slowly' on the ways in which parallel traditions – 'the historically closeted play', 'the rejected theatre', 'disappointed authorship' – affect readings of theatre history. Indeed, a pressing project for theatre historians in the early twenty-first century is to acquire a fuller understanding of the generic landscape that writers of closet drama have traversed in the past in order to more accurately navigate its rich historical terrain.

V

I end with a comment meant to be a tribute to Jonas Barish whose *The Anti-Theatrical Prejudice* (1981) is essential reading for theatre historians and who died in 1998 before he could write the book he was planning on closet drama.[78] Barish's would have been a major contribution to theatre scholarship, as his notes suggest. In both his published and unpublished work, it is clear that Barish was wrestling with the extent to which closet plays can be distinguished from stage drama at the formal level. As I have tried to show, the kind of work that Barish was interested in doing at the end of his life marks an important step towards forging a more rigorous analysis of an under-theorized and under-historicized phenomenon. In his significant 1994 article on Italian closet plays by men, Barish poses the question of why it should matter to us that, in the case of many plays throughout history, we cannot know whether they have been intended for performance or not. Here is his answer:

> Because in the first place the theater is an exceptionally social and public art, no doubt the most public and social of all the arts, whereas reading is by nature one of the most isolating of activities, yet the boundaries between what we might expect to find between two wholly incompatible forms are often hard to establish. And there is a puzzle in the very quantity of plays apparently written over the centuries with no performance in mind or even with active antagonism to it. Why should so many talented authors, some of them authors of genius, write plays and not wish to see them played? The mere existence of

a large body of such apparently anomalous work presses questions on us, and the whole matter of the relations between text and performance, between plays as theater and plays as literature becomes, on closer inspection, complex and enigmatic.[79]

Notes

1. I am thinking of Erik Ehn, who crafts poetic plays that consciously explore Catholicism's mystery (see *The Saint Plays* [Baltimore and London: Johns Hopkins University Press, 2000]). While a number of his dramas have been staged, implicit in his plan to write a drama about each of Catholicism's more than 10,000 saints – what he calls 'his saint's plays project' – is the acknowledgement that many of these works will be read rather than performed.
2. I appreciate my conversations with Marvin Carlson through the years, especially those we have had on closet drama.
3. I extend my gratitude to Millie Barish, who (in 2003) entrusted me with her husband's handwritten notes for his planned project on the closet play (see note 71 below). As Jonas Barish observes in one of these notes, in a postscript to *The Mysterious Mother* (1768), Horace Walpole writes: 'From the time that I first undertook the foregoing scenes, I never flattered myself that they would be proper to appear on the stage. The subject is so horrid, that I thought it would shock, rather than give satisfaction to an audience.' And, in the introduction to his play, *Anne Boleyn* (1826), Henry Montague Grover, who had clerical ambitions, explains: 'It may appear almost superfluous to add, that the manner in which the Poem is written, as well as the religious nature of the interest, must for ever preclude it from public representation.'
4. This question echoes Marta Straznicky's in reference to seventeenth-century women closet dramatists (in *Privacy, Playreading and Early Modern Women's Closet Drama, 1550–1700* [Cambridge: Cambridge University Press, 2004], 3): 'why did women continue to write plays for readers even after the professional theatre began to stage their work?'
5. See Michael Simpson, *Closet Performances: Political Exhibition and Prohibition in the Dramas of Byron and Shelley* (Stanford: Stanford University Press, 1998); and William Jewett, *Fatal Autonomy: Romantic Drama and the Rhetoric of Agency* (Ithaca and London: Cornell University Press, 1997).
6. Martin Puchner, *Stage Fright: Modernism, Anti-Theatricality, and Drama* (Baltimore and London: Johns Hopkins University Press, 2002), 15.
7. Allardyce Nicoll, *English Drama 1900–1930: the Beginnings of the Modern Period* (Cambridge: Cambridge University Press, 1973), 218.
8. W. B. Yeats cited in Nicoll, 302.
9. Nicoll, 302.
10. Om Prakash Mathur cited in Mary A. Waters, *British Women Writers and the Profession of Literary Criticism, 1789–1832* (Basingstoke: Palgrave Macmillan, 2004), 189, n.35.
11. J. A. Cuddon cited in Alison Findlay, Gweno Williams and Stephanie J. Hodgson-Wright, ' "The Play is ready to be Acted": Women and Dramatic Production, 1570–1670', *Women's Writing*, 6.1 (1999): 129–48; 146, n.7.
12. John Gay, 'Preface' to *Polly*, in *John Gay: Dramatic Works*, vol. 2, ed. John Fuller (Oxford: Clarendon Press, 1983), 70.
13. In their introduction to *Drama by Women to 1900: a Bibliography of American and British Writers* (Toronto and Buffalo: University of Toronto Press, 1992, vii–xxi), Gwenn Davis and Beverly A. Joyce directed my attention to John Galt's project 'to print works that were not produced' (xiii). See Galt's four volumes of *The New British Theatre* (London: Henry Colburn, 1814).
14. Mary Latter, *The Siege of Jerusalem, by Titus Vespacian; a tragedy. To which is prefixed, by way of introduction, an essay on the mystery and mischiefs of stage-craft* (London: C. Bathurst, 1763), xix.

15. Jane West, 'Preface' to *Poems and Plays. By Mrs. West*, 2 vols (London: C. Whittingham, 1799), 1:vi.
16. West, 1:vii.
17. West, 1:xv.
18. Frances Burney cited in Peter Sabor, 'General Introduction', *The Complete Plays of Fanny Burney: Comedies*, vol. I, ed. Peter Sabor (London: William Pickering, 1995, xi–xlviii), xvii. Unfortunately, according to Peter Sabor, 'no fair copy of the play seems to have been made, and no publisher approached' (xvii).
19. Keir Elam, *Shakespeare's Universe of Discourse: Language-Games in the Comedies* (Cambridge: Cambridge University Press, 1984), 5 (my emphasis).
20. Keir Elam, *The Semiotics of Theatre and Dance* (London: Routledge, 1980), 208–9.
21. Jonas Barish, 'Language for the Study; Language for the Stage', in *The Elizabethan Theatre*, 12, ed. A. L. Magnusson and C. E. Mcgee (Toronto: Meany, 1993), 43.
22. Andrew Brown, 'Seneca', in *The Cambridge Guide to Theatre*, ed. Martin Banham (Cambridge: Cambridge University Press, 1995), 974–5; 975.
23. Mary Sidney Herbert's translation of French dramatist Robert Garnier's *Marc-Antoine* – under the title of *Antonius* – inaugurated the vogue in 1592. (She also published this play under the title of *Antonie* in 1595.) Dramatists in the Countess of Pembroke's circle included Thomas Kyd, and Samuel Daniel, who wrote *Cleopatra* in 1594 as a response to Mary Sidney's play. Fulke-Greville also wrote a play on Antony and Cleopatra but destroyed it because it was considered too topical (Geoffrey Bullough, ed., *Poems and Dramas of Fulke Greville, First Lord Brooke*, 2 vols [London and Edinburgh: Oliver and Boyd, 1939], 2:6). Samuel Brandon (*Tragi-Comedy of the Virtuous Octavia*, 1598) and William Alexander are other practitioners of the genre.
24. Karen Raber addresses this issue in *Dramatic Difference: Gender, Class and Genre in Early Modern Closet Drama* (Newark: University of Delaware Press, 2001), 293, n. 28: 'Among all the articles and other works on closet drama this project includes in its bibliography, only Burroughs in *Closet Stages* gives a full discussion of the term's origins' (180–1, n. 29). Raber is forced, as am I, to acknowledge that the term cannot be historically pinned down; numerous handbooks and literary dictionaries include the term, and some mention the early modern plays as examples of the category, but it is clear (at least to me) that these are retroactive associations. As Raber points out, there are abundant examples of the term 'closet' used flexibly from the sixteenth century on, but I have been unable to find any instances of the terminology applied to drama before the nineteenth century.
25. Jonathan Heawood, ' "Never Acted But . . . ": English Closet Drama, 1625–1685' (unpublished dissertation. Cambridge University, 2003).
26. Stephen Larrabee, 'The "Closet" and the "Stage" in 1759', *Modern Language Notes*, 56 (1941): 282–4; 283–4.
27. Goldsmith cited in Larrabee, 284.
28. Allardyce Nicoll, *A History of Late Eighteenth-Century Drama, 1750–1800* (Cambridge: Cambridge University Press, 1927), 221.
29. Heawood, ' "Never Acted But . . . ": English Closet Drama, 1625–1685'.
30. This quotation is from Barish's handwritten notes; thus, there are no pages to cite. See note 3 above.
31. These gaps, as best I can discern them from my research, occur during the following years: 1714–24; 1726–31; 1734–46; and 1748–51.
32. Straznicky, *Privacy, Playreading and Early Modern Women's Closet Drama, 1550–1700*, 95.
33. J. Paul Hunter, 'The World as Stage and Closet', in *British Theatre and the Other Arts, 1660–1800*, ed. Shirley Strum Kenny (Cranbury, NJ: Associated University Presses, 1984), 271–87, 285–6.
34. Elizabeth Inchbald, 'To the Artist', in *Nature and Art*, ed. Shawn Lisa Maurer (Peterborough, Ontario: Broadview Press, 2005), 165–6.

35. Jonas Barish puts these ideas in another way in 'The Problem of Closet Drama in the Italian Renaissance', *Italica*, 71 (1994): 4–30, when he writes: 'If this hasty survey [of Renaissance Italian closet drama] has demonstrated anything, it is first of all that however public an activity theatergoing may be, and however private the act of reading, the two can come together in unexpected ways, and that theatrical form – the imagined projecting of one's ideas, images, and ruminations – into the throats of third persons can exert an irresistible spell even over authors with no interest in performance or actively hostile to it. It [theatrical form] offers not only a well-defined structure for rendering matters of weight and scope in fictional form, a function ultimately taken over by the novel, but also a chance to confer immediacy and excitement on material that[,] expounded systematically or methodically[,] might risk overloading the minds and dulling the attentiveness of readers' (28).

36. Catherine Burroughs, *Closet Stages: Joanna Baillie and the Theater Theory of British Romantic Women Writers* (Philadelphia: University of Pennsylvania Press, 1997).

37. Joanna Baillie, 'Preface to *The Martyr*', in *The Dramatic and Poetical Works (1851)* (Hildesheim and New York: Georg Olms Verlag, 1976), 509.

38. See my 'The Erotics of Home: Staging Sexual Fantasy in British Women's Drama', in *Women's Romantic Theatre and Drama*, ed. Lilla Maria Crisafulli and Keir Elam (Ashgate Publishing Ltd., forthcoming).

39. This point appears in Isabella Imperiali's unpublished essay, 'Joanna Baillie's Last Phase', which she presented at the conference, 'Il teatro romantico inglese (1760/1830: Testi, teorie e pratiche sceniche' ('British Romantic Theatre and Drama 1760/1830: Text, Theory, and Stage Practice') in Bertinoro, Italy (November 2004).

40. Joanna Baillie, 'Preface to *Dramas*', in *The Dramatic and Poetical Works (1851)* (Hildesheim and New York: Georg Olms Verlag, 1976), 312.

41. Baillie, 'Preface to *The Martyr*', 512.

42. Ibid.

43. Ann Wilson, 'Preface' to *Jephthah's Daughter: a Dramatic Poem. By Mrs. Ann Wilson* (London: printed for W. Flexney, 1783).

44. Baillie, 'Preface to *The Martyr*', 512.

45. Baillie, *The Martyr* in *The Dramatic and Poetical Works (1851)* (Hildesheim and New York: Georg Olms Verlag, 1976), 516.

46. Baillie, 'Preface to *The Martyr*', 509.

47. Baillie, *The Martyr*, 523.

48. Mary Russell Mitford, 'Preface', in *The Dramatic Works of Mary Russell Mitford*, 2 vols (London: Hurst and Blackhurst, 1854), 1:vii.

49. Raber, *Dramatic Difference*, 26.

50. Elizabeth Subthorpe Pinchard, 'Preface' to *Dramatic Dialogues, for the use of young persons. By the author of The blind child*, vol. 1 (London: Printed for E. Newbery, 1792).

51. Anne K. Mellor, 'Theater as the School of Virtue', in *Mothers of the Nation: Women's Political Writing in England, 1780–1830* (Bloomington: Indiana University Press, 2000), 39–68, 39–40.

52. For a discussion of the Lehrstücke in the context of the closet play, see Michael Evenden's 'Inter-mediate Stages: Reconsidering the Body in "Closet Drama"', in *Reading the Social Body*, ed. Catherine B. Burroughs and Jeffrey David Ehrenreich (Iowa City: University of Iowa Press, 1993), 244–69.

53. Straznicky, *Privacy, Playreading and Early Modern Women's Closet Drama, 1550–1700*, 113.

54. Straznicky, 120.

55. J. Paul Hunter, 'The World as Stage and Closet', 282.

56. Richard Lovell Edgeworth, 'Preface' to *Comic Dramas. By Maria Edgeworth* (1817), no pages, emphasis mine (Kroch Cornell Library).

57. *The Carthusian Friar, or the age of chivalry. A tragedy, in five acts, founded on real events. Written by a female refugee* (London, 1793), v–vi.

58. Ann Wilson, 'Preface' to *Jephthah's Daughter*, vii.

59. Charlotte Smith, 'Preface' to *Rural Walks; in dialogues. Intended for the use of young persons. By Charlotte Smith*, 2 vols (London: T. Cadell jun. and W. Davies, 1795), 1:iii.

60. Elizabeth Subthorpe Pinchard, 'Preface' to *Dramatic Dialogues*, vi.

61. Charlotte Smith, *Rural Walks*, v.

62. Ibid., 12.

63. Jonas Barish, 'Language for the Study; Language for the Stage', 31.

64. Puchner, *Stage Fright*, 27.

65. Ibid., 21–2.

66. Charlotte Smith, *Rural Walks*, 29.

67. Katherine Acheson highlights *resistance* as a key element with which to analyse closet drama's formal properties; see ' "Outrage your face": Anti-Theatricality and Gender in Early Modern Closet Drama by Women', *Early Modern Literary Studies*, 6.3 (2001): 7–16 (http://purl.oclc.org/emls/06-3/acheoutr.htm). Her argument is that Mary Sidney's *The Tragedie of Antonie* (1592) and Elizabeth Cary's *Mariam* (c. 1603) 'can be seen as protests against, or resistances to, the ways in which women of the period were contained and determined by being seen, and challenge the assumption that performative notions of gender were uniformly regarded as liberatory by the culture' (para. 9).

68. See Thomas Cruchunis, 'Joanna Baillie's Ambivalent Dramaturgy', in *Joanna Baillie, Romantic Dramatist: Critical Essays*, ed. Thomas Crochunis (London and New York: Routledge, 2004), 169.

69. Ibid., 175.

70. Ibid., 173.

71. In 'Closet Drama', in *A Companion to Renaissance Drama*, ed. Arthur F. Kinney (Oxford: Blackwell Publishing, 2002, 416–28), Marta Straznicky characterizes 'the intellectual elite drama' of the sixteenth and seventeenth centuries – which included 'academic translations, plays of moral or religious instruction, and the kind of topical political drama written by the Sidney circle' – as marked by ' "readerly" devices, orienting the reader as they do in the process of moving through the text or being particularly well suited to the intellectual focus that reading affords: an introductory argument outlining the context and action of the play, a list of speakers, division into acts, lengthy sententious speeches typographically represented in continuous text columns, and a chorus serving to prompt and guide interpretation' (422). During the seventeenth century, she writes, 'reading aloud was a familiar *alternative* to performance, perhaps even the normal mode in which plays were enjoyed' ('Reading the Stage: Margaret Cavendish and Commonwealth Closet Drama', *Criticism*, 37.3 [1995]: 355–90, 380).

72. Hannah More, 'Preface' to *Sacred Dramas: chiefly intended for young persons: the subjects taken from the Bible. To which is added, Sensibility, a poem* (London: T. Y. Cadell, 1782), v–vi (my emphasis)

73. Straznicky, 'Closet Drama', 426.

74. Ibid., 417.

75. Mellor, 'Theater as the School of Virtue'.

76. C. Short, *Dramas for the use of young ladies* (Birmingham: Swinney & Walker, 1792), no page numbers (emphasis mine).

77. Hannah More, *A Search after Happiness: a pastoral. In three dialogues. By a young lady* (Dublin: R. Wilson, D. Graisberry and J. Black, 1773), no page numbers.

78. In their online tribute to Jonas Barish after his death ('In Memoriam, 1998: Jonas A. Barish'), Paul Alpers, Frederick Crews and Donald Friedman wrote: 'Barish's last major project was a study of closet drama, i.e., plays intended to be read rather than performed. He was uniquely qualified to undertake such a study, both because his zestful patience enabled him to work through such behemoths as Victor Hugo's *Cromwell*, not to mention tiresome works by lesser figures, but also because his vast comparative knowledge enabled him to raise questions fundamental to this project – e.g., whether what looked unperformable to 19th-century scholars was in fact thought to be so by 16th-century writers. He first investigated closet drama as a kind of follow-up to *The*

Antitheatrical Prejudice, and he worked steadily on the project after his retirement, in 1990. One can regret his only having published a few pieces of it – articles on Renaissance drama in France, Italy, and England, with a few tantalizing glances at the 19th-century material that was so important a part of the story he had to tell. But he never rushed into print, and he would not have wanted to have published anything which he had not fully considered, in respect to its argument, and polished, in respect to its style' (a publication of the Academic Senate of the University of California-Berkeley, 13 November 2000. http://sunsite.berkeley.edu/uchistory/in_memoriam/mem98barish.htm).

79. Jonas Barish, 'The Problem of Closet Drama in the Italian Renaissance', 4.

12
Shakespeare and the Music Hall

Richard Schoch

On 28 February 1866, Parliament formed a Select Committee to examine the laws for licensing and regulating places of entertainment.[1] The issue at stake was the increasing frequency of comic sketches, ballet, pantomime and operatic selections being performed in London music halls. Though popular with audiences, such performances were illegal, because music halls, licensed by local magistrates, were not authorized to present theatrical entertainment. Only the Lord Chamberlain could authorize that, but he had no jurisdiction over the music halls.

In 1843, when the Theatres Regulation Act was passed, London had a population of one and a half million, the Lord Chamberlain had licensed twenty-four theatres, and music halls had yet to be invented. By 1866, the number of Londoners surpassed three million – the population doubled in but a generation – and twenty-five licensed theatres operated in the metropolis, along with thirty music halls.[2] Thus, while the number of theatres remained virtually unchanged (in real terms they declined, because the population was growing) the number of music halls steadily increased. Merely to maintain the 1843 ratio of theatres to Londoners – twenty-four theatres for a million and a half people – *thirty* new theatres should have been built by 1866.

Nearly all licensed theatres, from Drury Lane in the fashionable West End to the Standard in most unfashionable Shoreditch, stood in united opposition to music halls. Theatre managers struggling to turn a profit complained that music halls stole the gallery sections of their audience. The music halls were frustrated that their advancement was checked by unfair licensing laws. Certainly the laws were ambiguous, and open conflict was unavoidable. As Sir Richard Mayne, Chief Commissioner of the Metropolitan Police, dryly observed: 'persons who are licensed for theatrical performances are naturally anxious to report unlicensed performances'.[3] In this atmosphere of accusation and recrimination, the Committee called its witnesses.

But long before that day, the Committee knew what everyone in the theatrical world knew: the licensing laws were a mess. Subsequent to the Act of 1843, all London theatres were licensed by the Lord Chamberlain, who also censored the content of performances by requiring that the script be approved in advance by the Examiner of Plays. The Act was silent on the matter of regulating music halls, because in 1843 they did not exist. Once, however, music halls arrived on the scene, they were licensed by local magistrates under the Disorderly Houses Act of 1751.

Under the terms of the 1751 Act, a music hall licence permitted 'public dancing, music, or other public entertainment of the like kind'. The Act entailed no censorship, for it was limited to defining, however inadequately, the kinds of entertainment that were permissible. Like the several hundred licensed saloons and singing taverns, music halls were free to put on the bill whatever they liked in terms of content, as long as the form did not exceed the bounds of the licence.

The question as to whether London music halls were being properly licensed arose from an ambiguity in the 1843 Theatres Regulation Act. The notorious paragraph twenty-three stipulated that 'every Tragedy, Comedy, Farce, Opera, Burletta, Interlude, Melodrama, Pantomime, or other entertainment of the stage, or any part thereof' constituted a theatre play – and thus had to be licensed by the Lord Chamberlain. The problem was that by the early 1860s music halls were regularly presenting 'entertainments of the stage', most especially pantomime and opera. Indeed in 1854, when music halls were still in their infancy, Parliament acknowledged that '[t]he imperfect definition of the term stage-play, given in the [1843] act, enables persons to have performances, some of them of a very inferior and demoralizing character, in places that are not licensed [by the Lord Chamberlain]'.[4]

Certainly these stage performances were illegal, for they violated the music hall's licence. Yet there was no way to make them legal because magistrates could not license stage plays and the Lord Chamberlain could not license music halls. In an article printed a month before the Select Committee began its hearings, the *Era*, the main theatrical trade paper, summarized this chaotic state of affairs:

> the whole Licensing System is an incoherent absurdity, and a positive insult to the common-sense of the age. Act of Parliament is made to oppose Act of Parliament, Lord Chamberlain is made to contradict the County Magistracy, and general confusion is, to all appearances, sedulously cultivated rather than avoided.[5]

Testing the coherence of the law, and recognizing a chance to increase their market share, music halls began to introduce certain kinds of performances that the licensed theatres looked upon as their exclusive domain. In the larger West End music halls, the ones that catered for a more socially heterogeneous audience – and the ones most in competition with licensed theatres – the repertoire was dominated by ballet, pantomime, operatic selections and comic dialogue. In other words, precisely the kind of entertainment found on the stages of the smaller theatres near and along the Strand.[6] As Frederick Strange told the Committee, an evening's entertainment at the Alhambra, the music hall of which he was the proprietor, consisted of

> a grand chorus; after that a duet; after that a ballet, which we call the comic ballet; then a little more singing and tumbling, and after then the second

balled, 'the National ballet;' to follow that we have this selection [of opera] and a little tumbling; and perhaps another glee, and we finish with what we call a transformation scene.[7]

Just as the patentees and the managers of minor theatres had engaged in constant legal battles in the years before the Act of 1843, the managers of licensed theatres and music halls engaged in similar disputes in the 1850s and 1860s. Given the ambiguity of the licensing laws, conflict was unavoidable. But the legal results were inconclusive, and victories were won on both sides. In 1860, Benjamin Webster, then proprietor of the Adelphi, took Charles Morton to court for violating the 1843 Act by producing stage plays at the Canterbury without a theatrical licence. The offending performance was the pantomime duologue *The Enchanted Hash*, in which two actors played ten characters in a story that would not have been out of place in a holiday pantomime staged at the Adelphi or any other West End theatre. Morton was convicted, but his punishment was trivial: a small fine. The leniency of the sentence tells us that the courts understood just how unworkable the licensing laws had become.

Yet not every case resulted in a verdict against the music halls. In 1865, Horace Wigan, the young manager of the Olympic, brought a suit against Frederick Strange, proprietor of the Alhambra Music Hall, for an unlicensed performance of a ballet. In the case of *Wigan v. Strange*, the local magistrate found Strange guilty of violating his licence. But on appeal, the Middlesex bench overruled the decision and ordered that Strange's conviction be quashed. On that occasion, the judges maintained that because it was impossible to define the line between music and drama, it was impossible to prosecute someone for crossing it. There was no alternative but for the conviction to be overturned.[8]

But 'win some, lose some' was not the way to solve the problem, and as the music hall proprietors began to realize, the remedy would have to be legislative, not judicial. That is, Parliament would have to rewrite the law so that the Disorderly Houses Act of 1751 and the Theatres Act of 1843 no longer contradicted each other. Towards that end, Frederick Stanley, the lawyer for the London Music Halls Protection Society, contacted the Home Secretary, Sir George Cornwell Lewis, with proposed amendments to the 1843 Act. Lewis's successor, Sir George Grey, never put those amendments before Parliament.[9] Stanley remained vigilant, however, and in 1866 Parliament finally empowered a Select Committee to impose order on a rather chaotic state of affairs.

Over three months, the Committee received testimony from the Lord Chamberlain, magistrates, police officers, playwrights, theatre managers and music hall proprietors. Among the thirty-four expert witnesses were William Bodham Donne, the Examiner of Plays; the dramatists Dion Boucicault and Tom Taylor; theatre managers Benjamin Webster (Adelphi), J. B. Buckstone (Haymarket) and Horace Wigan (Olympic); and representatives of the London Music Halls Protection Society. On matters of professional rivalry, theatre managers and music hall proprietors presented arguments that were carefully rehearsed, completely predictable, and not always anchored in fact.

With pathos of nearly melodramatic proportion, theatre managers cried that they would suffer if music halls were allowed to present drama, opera or ballet. Music halls already enjoyed the advantage of allowing the audience to smoke, eat and drink from the comfort of their seats. If permitted to stage plays, so the argument went, they would draw yet more spectators. Before long, theatres would be empty, and Shakespeare would be forced to take up residence in the music hall, where he would play second fiddle to tobacco and whisky. The nobility of the drama was presumed to be incompatible with such pedestrian, and potentially immoral, activities as drinking and smoking. If music halls really wanted to perform drama, theatre managers declared, then they must become proper theatres and obtain licences from the Lord Chamberlain. Almost imperceptibly, the economic argument – that is, against rogue competitors – turned into an aesthetic and moral one – that is, in favour of high culture.

Yet such an argument, the music hall proprietors countered, was disingenuous. The theatres appointed themselves protectors of the national drama not because they cared about Shakespeare, but because they feared competition. Much like the managers of the minor theatres, when testifying before Edward Bulwer-Lytton's Select Committee in 1832, had argued for the abolition of the patent monopoly, music hall proprietors in 1866 advocated 'free trade': let theatres and music halls perform whatever they like and let the public decide for itself.

In the end, the Committee urged that music halls be allowed to offer 'theatrical entertainment' and that the Lord Chamberlain license them on the same terms as theatres. But this victory for music halls was purely symbolic. For just as Parliament in 1832 had ignored the recommendations of its own Committee, it did the same in 1866. The licensing laws were left unchanged: local magistrates continued to license music halls, while the Lord Chamberlain continued his policy of non-intervention. Meanwhile, music halls carried on presenting ballets, operatic selections and sketches that may or may not have been in violation of their licences, so bewildering had the enforcement of regulatory statutes become.[10]

For theatre scholars, the Committee's proceedings raise two problems: historiographical and cultural. The historiographical problem lies in the nature of the documentation. Running to over 300 pages, the published transcripts of the Committee's hearings certainly count as evidence. But evidence of what? With respect to Shakespeare and the music hall – a major theme of the Committee's hearings, although by no means the only one – the transcripts cannot be considered evidence of actual performances, for such performances never occurred. What we have is a body of *writing* about something that was imagined, but never enacted.

It is a critical commonplace to observe that loss is the constitutive feature of *all* performance, and thus the inevitable position from which performance scholarship is written. But in this instance we cannot speak of loss, since there never was anything to be lost. Here, the object of study is the *desire* for performance – and an unrequited desire at that. What we are grappling with is doubly absent, or at least doubly deferred: the unfulfilled promise of performance. In a way that recalls, uncannily, the spectral technology of Pepper's Ghost, we find ourselves gazing upon the reflection of a reflection.

But that does not mean we gaze upon nothing. Far from it. The 1866 documents are not evidence about the circumstances and conditions of performance, but an effort – however unheeded, however thwarted – to give performance *meaning*. Such a claim is not unique to this case; indeed, *all* evidence is always already a discursive formation; always already an investment in meaning. We can see that drive to ascribe meaning more clearly in the present example of Shakespeare and the music hall because there is no antecedent performance that the evidence might be presumed to document or otherwise recount. Indeed, it is the very lack of a stable referent for this piece of evidence that enables us to see how it puts into sharp relief a basic question of theatre historiography.

The cultural problem is a familiar one: in the mid-Victorian era, what was the state's interest in music hall audiences? Of course that audience was never monolithic, particularly in the West End; but generally, music halls were regarded as places of amusement for the urban working class. As Dagmar Kift has written, they catered for 'smalltradesmen, shopkeepers and their assistants, mechanics and labourers, as well as soldiers and sailors'.[11] Whether the Metropolitan in Edgware Road, the Canterbury in Lambeth, or Wilton's in the East End, the suburban audience was more socially cohesive, and represented an urban population found only infrequently in the larger West End theatres.

All music halls, but especially the suburban ones, were community-based establishments, drawing their audiences predominantly from among those who lived and worked in the area, or who grew up there and still maintained family or business connections. In a way that West End audiences did not, music hall patrons frequently arrived as groups, whether from work or home. The Chief Bow-Street Magistrate, Sir Thomas Henry, explained to the Committee that the 'advantage' of a music hall was that 'a man now takes his wife and part of his family with him ... whereas he used to go alone to the public-house'.[12] This communitarian ethos of the music hall, as we shall see, was seized upon by some members of the Select Committee as a means for enacting cultural reform.

By all accounts, however, the music hall audience was not on the verge of anarchy, not corrupting innocent women and children, and not debasing itself through depravity. None of the witnesses, not even those opposed to enfranchising the music halls, believed that the audiences were indecent, improper, or in any way threatening to public morals. After visiting the Canterbury, the magistrate George Norton declared the performance illegal but the audience exemplary: 'they were artizans, and I am happy to say very much with their wives and children sitting round those little tables and also enjoying the performances'.[13]

Especially when sitting round those little tables, the working class needed some attention, not the least because it was about to gain its political freedom. It is no coincidence that Parliament thought carefully about music halls and their audiences at the same time it thought about electoral reform. Indeed, the backdrop to the Committee's hearings was the campaign to enfranchise the urban working class – the very sort of people who spent their evenings in music halls. The means for that enfranchisement was the 1867 Reform Bill, which Benjamin Disraeli, giving voice to confusion and fear, famously called a 'leap into the dark'.

More boldly democratic than the Great Reform Bill of 1832, the second Reform Bill was introduced in Parliament by Disraeli, then the Tory Prime Minister, on 18 March 1867 and received royal assent five months later. Disraeli was right to call the bill a 'leap into the dark', for it doubled the size of the British electorate to about two and a half million. One-third of adult males became enfranchised, and for the first time the urban working class featured prominently in the roster of eligible voters. The expansion of the franchise was largely confined to cities and factory towns, the places where the industrial revolution had created both an upsurge in population and an underclass of the unskilled poor.

After 1867, the music hall audience (the adult male portion, that is) found itself politically empowered. All the more reason, then, that it should be prepared for its new role in an increasingly democratic society. This commitment to civic instruction explains why the people who advocated the extension of the franchise also advocated reforming the music halls. As I shall argue throughout this essay, the Committee (or at least its dominant faction) saw its task not to turn music halls into middle-class theatres, but into better versions of what they already were: the place where the soon-to-be enfranchised working class maintained a peaceful public sphere.

The Committee's self-assumed mission to give a stake in society to music hall audiences was itself the natural extension of the political sympathies of its forthright chairman, the thirty-five-year-old George Goschen. Like his fellow Liberals, Goschen championed free trade and markets unencumbered by government interference – hence, his push to lift the restrictions on music halls and to end the oligarchy of the licensed London theatres. As the newly elected politician remarked to his fellow parliamentarians in 1864, the purpose of government was neither to 'prevent' nor to 'stimulate enterprise' but rather 'to clear the field so that individuals might take their own course'.[14]

But there was a utopian vision underlying Goschen's classically liberal commitment to free trade and self-interest. The collective pursuit of self-interest must lead somewhere, and that somewhere was a broadly shared sense of a common national identity. Goschen supported the Reform Bill of 1867, confident that the urban working class was committed to upholding national unity, and would not descend into an anarchic mob. In that same year he published two articles on the subject for *St Paul's Magazine*, in which he declared his 'belief that all Englishmen are very much alike'.[15] That same commitment to national unity was the foundation of the utopian vision sketched out by the Committee under Goschen's forceful leadership.

And that is where the historiographical and the cultural problems *coalesce*. We have evidence about unrealized performances whose purpose was to find a cultural solution to a political problem. Shakespeare in the music hall symbolized the Committee's hope for a shared culture that would unite all segments of the population, but without bluntly imposing the values of the dominant upon the subordinate. Though it may be hard for us to understand today, the call for Shakespeare in the Victorian music hall was not an act of middle-class cultural oppression, not a tyranny of the majority, but a sincere attempt to find common ground beyond the entrenched boundaries of class, wealth and rank.

Not that everybody at the time saw it that way. Immediate denunciations came, predictably, from theatre managers, who engaged in a shameless defence of the national drama at the very moment of their greatest disloyalty to it. They opposed the enfranchisement of the music halls on the grounds that too much liberty would destroy legitimate drama. J. B. Buckstone, the Haymarket's manager from 1853 to 1878, believed that performing plays in music halls would be 'unfair to the theatre and degrading to the drama'.[16] But he also feared losing his gallery audience, who already visited the music halls. If gallery patrons could see plays at music halls, they would go nowhere else, because they could also eat, smoke and drink during the performance – and thus enjoy all their pleasures simultaneously.[17] Cutting to the chase, the Committee put to Buckstone a direct question: 'Is not your principal [objection] that you do not like competition?'[18] Buckstone, cornered, replied that no one 'can pay proper attention to the performance while he is eating'.[19] The Committee had the wittier (and stronger) case, for Buckstone's interlocutor retorted that no one 'eats with his ears'.[20]

Benjamin Webster, who had been running the Adelphi since 1844, also opposed the enfranchisement of the music halls on similar grounds. 'I think it is injurious to dramatic literature to allow theatrical performances in music halls, and also to the drama as an art.'[21] At least Webster admitted his hypocrisy: 'I took the chair to get free trade in drama [in 1843] and I have repented it ever since.'[22] But, still, he remained a hypocrite, for he was determined that no one else should benefit from 'free trade in drama'. Nelson Lee, manager of the City of London Theatre, similarly predicted that theatrical performances in music halls would

> degrade the drama, and do an injury in every way. I should be very sorry to see it ... Because there would be drinking, smoking, and eating, and the people could not pay attention to the context of the piece from the noise and buzz of gentlemen walking around at those places; the piece would be mutilated.[23]

It was an irony of the time that those who once had argued *against* restrictions on performances of Shakespeare (in 1832 and 1843) now argued *for* them. Having gained a commercial advantage for themselves, theatre managers were resolved that no one else should enjoy it. Free trade in the drama had its limits, and the boundary line of freedom was the line that separated theatres from music halls.

Appealing to Shakespeare's sanctity was but a ploy for theatre managers to protect their interests by preventing the music halls from becoming even more competitive. Even as they condemned (frequently without justification) music halls as sites of vulgarity and indecency, the licensed theatres showed little inclination towards Bardolatry. In 1866, productions of melodrama and burlesque far outnumbered those of Shakespeare. (Only two theatres out of twenty-five performed Shakespeare during the 1865–6 London theatrical season.) As the *Saturday Review* put it, theatre managers betrayed Shakespeare at every opportunity, but always in the 'high tone of morality'.[24] And that is exactly what Nelson Lee did when he declared that Shakespeare would suffer indignities in a music hall, because while Hamlet whispered one of his immortal soliloquies, a man in the audience might shout to the waiter for 'potatoes and a kidney'.[25]

A man in a music hall could indeed feast on 'potatoes and a kidney' while enjoying a performance. But that performance was never likely to be *Hamlet*, or any other Shakespearean drama, since music hall proprietors showed no interest in performing them – even if they could do so under law. By and large, what the music halls wanted to perform (but under the existing laws could not) were comic sketches, operatic selections, pantomime and ballet. No diffidence attached itself to this view, as if music hall proprietors doubted their own abilities, but might be coaxed by the Committee into performing Shakespeare. Nothing could be less true. Music hall proprietors had a strong sense of their own capacities and a healthily pragmatic understanding of what their audiences did – and did not – like.

For the music halls, Shakespeare was irrelevant: their audiences did not want it, their stages were not equipped to accommodate it, and their venues too noisy for anybody to listen to it. In the week that he appeared before the Committee, Frederick Strange, proprietor of the Alhambra, wrote an open letter to the *Era* on whether music halls should be allowed to perform scripted drama. Here is what he wrote:

> I assure Theatrical Managers, who have suddenly shown a great regard for Shakespeare off the stage, that I shall not desecrate him by performing him before an audience supplied with 'refreshments' by waiters at tables, instead of by orange-women and pot-boys . . . as at the Lord Chamberlain's Theatres. My turn will be served by the permission to represent operas and vaudevilles, in addition to the ballets, which now form the staple of my entertainment.[26]

Strange espoused the same line when he answered the Committee's questions, repeatedly declining to show the slightest interest in performing Shakespeare at the Alhambra. 'Although we want the thing thrown open', he granted, he '[did] not think that it would answer any music-hall proprietor's purpose to give any of Shakespere's plays at this moment in music-halls'.[27] If a new law so empowered him, still he would seek to produce only 'little operas dressed, and anything in the way of farce or pantomime'.[28] Repeatedly questioned on the point – are you *sure* that 'you would not have Shakespeare's plays performed at the Alhambra?' – Strange remained unyielding.[29] 'No, certainly not', he insisted; 'if it was thrown open to-morrow, I should not attempt one of Shakespeare's plays.'[30] Strange was willing to let the licensed theatres keep Shakespeare all to themselves, but it was not out of any desire to be accommodating. His mockery of the lip service paid to Shakespeare by theatre managers tells us that.[31]

Bewildered, the Committee tried to persuade its sceptical witnesses that getting Shakespeare into the music halls was a matter of national interest. Sometimes delicately, sometimes bluntly, and always with exasperation, the Committee insisted that Shakespeare should be performed in music halls because it would be 'an advantage to the public'.[32] This was not a view that the Committee arrived at sometime over the course of the hearings, as if it were gradually persuaded by the repeated Bardolatrous entreaties of music hall proprietors. No such entreaties were made. A close reading of the transcripts reveals the curious fact that the reformist majority on the Committee had made up its mind beforehand. Indeed, the *first* witness, Spencer Ponsonby of the Lord Chamberlain's Office, was asked whether it would be 'an advantage' for music halls to perform Shakespeare.[33] Tellingly, the question presumed that it *would* be.

The magistrate George Norton, asked if a music hall manager wishing to 'represent Shakespeare' should be 'denied that liberty', replied that the people who attend productions of Shakespeare would not enter a music hall because they 'would be very much annoyed by those little tables, and smoking, and so on'.[34] William Bodkin, a local judge, felt no discomfort in advising Parliament that the 'poorer classes' should *not* be allowed to 'enact Shakespearian plays whenever they liked', and certainly not in music halls, where their behaviour would insult the dignity of the drama. If the lower classes wanted Shakespeare so badly, then let them '[go] to the theatres'.[35]

It proved equally difficult for the Committee to convince music halls of the public 'benefit' of their performing Shakespeare. Because music hall managers did not rush to swear allegiance to the great national poet, the Committee had no option but to imagine that they did. And thus many of their questions were in fact completely severed from the reality of the situation. Something of a parallel universe was created in the hearings, for time and again the Committee referred to purely hypothetical cases: 'a person [i.e. a music hall proprietor] who desires to act Shakspere' or 'a person who wishes to represent Shakespeare'.[36] Such persons did not exist.

Frederick Strange faced particularly aggressive questioning. Although he had publicly declared that he would never stage Shakespeare at the Alhambra – it would not 'answer any music-hall proprietor's purpose' – the Committee, through ever more leading questions, urged him to change his mind.[37] Matters turned absurd when the Committee fabricated a scenario so preposterous that it was impossible for Strange to voice any dissent:

> If it was lawful to do so, and you found that the public taste was changed, and that there was a great wish for Shakespearian representations, if it paid you, you would put in on the stage, I suppose?[38]

The Committee succeeded in getting from Strange the answer it wanted – yes, he *would* put Shakespeare on the stage – but not for a moment was that his actual intent.[39]

Why did the Committee hammer away at the question? Indeed, it would be no exaggeration to say that the Committee *created* the question of Shakespeare in the music hall. And why did it frame the question not as a technicality about licensing laws, but as a broad issue of cultural politics? Because it thought about Shakespeare in a particular way – and in a way not shared by any of the expert witnesses whose testimony it received. Theatre managers and music hall proprietors thought about licensing laws in roughly the same terms: free trade, competition, and marketplace advantage. The magistrates and the police were concerned with public order and public morals. But the Committee had another item on its agenda: the promulgation of a shared national culture through the performance of Shakespeare in a popular place of recreation for the urban working class: the music hall. Shakespeare would not be the gift of the educated middle class to the uneducated working class – that was the patronizing agenda of philanthropists. Shakespeare was already the foundation of English culture and the source of its authority. And as such, he occupied a realm that transcended class, faction or self-interest.

The Committee refused to subscribe to the now familiar historiographical binary, as scholars such as Dagmar Kift have presumed, 'between a hedonistic and somewhat unbridled working-class culture and middle-class social reformers organised in temperance and purity movements'.[40] Certainly the music halls were right, as the Committee saw it, to resist the reformers. But they were wrong in how they went about it. For the true conflict was not between mindless but pleasurable amusement, on the one hand, and worthwhile but tedious rational recreation, on the other. Indeed, the Committee felt no desire to 'ad[d] another layer of tinsel' to the heavily-gilt stereotype of the working man who renounces gin and embraces prayer because a middle-class angel has revealed to him the path to salvation.[41]

Rejecting, as it were, both extremes, the Committee proposed a third way: fostering a shared culture in which the music hall had a legitimate place. Neither culturally bankrupt nor held hostage to the profoundly undemocratic (because mistrustful of the people) desires of middle-class reformers, the music hall could participate in a larger culture, but a larger *common* culture.

The Committee's vision of culture – idealist, utopian and egalitarian – was much like the one Matthew Arnold outlined in *Culture and Anarchy* (1869).[42] In that essay Arnold offered his classic (and now notorious) definition of culture as '[the] pursuit of our total perfection by means of getting to know ... the best which has been thought and said in the world'.[43] (Note the emphasis is not on 'the best', but on the perfection of the self.) Acting out, as it were, the values of *Culture and Anarchy*, the Committee took a stand against philistinism – and it was the *middle* class who were philistines, who believed that freedom and wealth were ends in themselves and not means to some greater end or goal.

Perhaps we find it hard to see this dynamic because our own work as scholars has taken us in a different direction. Many of us have been preoccupied, and with due reason, with histories of hierarchy, with threatened marginalized communities, ideological exercises, and hegemonic manoeuvres. Such has been the broad decentring trend not just of theatre history, but of humanities scholarship generally over the past two decades. But in consequence, many of us have not been looking at what Arnold looked at: culture as a galvanizing and unifying act; as the transcendent leap beyond a merely partisan self-interest. Many, perhaps most, scholars today do not subscribe to such liberal humanist beliefs. But the 1866 Committee *did* subscribe to them – and that explains why it made such a determined effort to get the music halls to perform Shakespeare.

The position I am proposing would lead us beyond the historiography of the music hall as exemplified in the work of Peter Bailey. Bailey notes, approvingly, that the so-called 'new cultural materialism' has 'redefined' culture 'beyond the elitist confines of "the best that has been thought and said" to embrace the ordinary and the popular'. That is a careless distortion of Arnold's view – tellingly, Arnold is quoted without citation – for the Victorian social critic would have opposed the 'elitist confines' that Bailey wrongly attributes to him.[44]

Current historiography, benefiting from the robust quantitative research undertaken by historians such as Tracy Davis, instructs us to read the history of theatrical licensing as a strand in the tangled history of free trade.[45] Unquestionably, there is much insight to be gained in such readings. Without disputing, then, the need to assess the economic dimensions of the Victorian theatre, let me suggest that the 1866 Select Committee points to something beyond economics, beyond free trade. What it points to is the *goal* of economic (or any other kind of) freedom. That goal, or greater end, is to seek our perfection through culture. What obstructs us, Arnold claimed, from attaining that greater end is the 'prevalent notion . . . that it is a most happy and important thing for a man merely to be able to do as he likes'.[46] But that is only one side of the coin. The other side of freedom is responsibility, and that responsibility is to use freedom for worthy purposes.

So how did the Committee translate Arnoldian values into its ambitions for the music hall? Just as the individual must be free to say what he likes – but then must say things that are 'worth saying', as Arnold insisted[47] – the music halls must be free to perform whatever they like – but then must perform things that are worth performing. Acrobatics, juggling and minstrel serenades were not worth performing. *Shakespeare* was. Just as culture, to perfect itself, must encourage, again in Arnold's words, the 'raw person' (meaning unfinished, not offensive) to like 'what is indeed beautiful, graceful, and becoming',[48] the music hall, in the Committee's vision, must not pander to its audience but encourage it to embrace something better.

Today, we probably regard such statements as patronizing, even oppressive. But for Arnold, and those who shared his beliefs, they were just the opposite: democratic and utopian. In the first pages of *Culture and Anarchy* he rejects the elitist view that culture is 'an engine of social and class distinction, separating its holder, like a badge or title, from other people who have not got it'.[49] Arnold distances himself from middle-class philanthropists who, however nobly intentioned, 'try to give the masses, as they call them, an intellectual food prepared and adapted in the way they think proper for the actual condition of the masses'.[50] He wants nothing to do with a false culture that seeks 'to indoctrinate the masses' with the creed of any 'profession or party'.[51] Striking again the note of inclusiveness, the note that struggles to reach our ears today, Arnold explains that

> If I have not shrunk from saying that we must work for sweetness and light, so neither have I shrunk from saying that we must have a broad basis, must have sweetness and light for as many as possible.[52]

Similarly, the controlling faction of the Committee understood culture as a project of transcendence, as an escape from a determinant, class-based view of society.

True, this is a middle-class idea in that middle-class people first espoused it. But ideas have to come from somewhere. And they have to *go* somewhere, too. And this idea was headed towards something beyond class interest.

In its drive to put Shakespeare on the music hall stage at the very moment when some in the music halls audiences were about to cross the threshold of modern democratic government, the Committee demonstrated its belief in culture as the solution to political problems. And a unifying culture was far more necessary for the 'new democracy', as Arnold put it, than the 'blessedness of the franchise'.[53] In a valiant, but failed, effort, the Committee tried to win support for a genuinely democratic culture – inclusive and participatory. And thus the Committee never wavered in its belief that music halls must remain music halls and continue with all the distinctive activities that made them so popular: the tables, the smoking, the eating, the drinking, and the wandering around.

But there would be something *added*, and that something was Shakespeare: a new figure, perhaps, for the music hall audience, but not – and this is the crucial point – an alien one. The music hall would produce Shakespeare on its own terms, not those of the West End: Shakespeare watched as you sat at your accustomed table, surrounded by your wife and children, as you smoked a cigar, drank brandy, and dined on potatoes and a kidney.

In an age fond of moralistic oratory, there is not a word of it in what the Committee said about music halls and their audiences. Unlike some of the theatre managers and police officers who gave testimony, the Committee did not patronize or condescend to music hall proprietors and audiences. Nor did they preach, but rather invited them to see for themselves the light of culture. (The light that is part of Arnold's 'sweetness and light'.) Ironically, the politicians were more progressive than those who testified before them. Immersed, as they were, in the narrow issues of market share and pecuniary advantage, theatre and music hall managers could not imagine a radically democratic culture. Most disappointingly of all, music hall proprietors did not know *how* to use the freedom they rightly demanded. They were, to invoke a philosophy of the day, utilitarians: they wanted to do as they liked. They wanted to ride the horse of freedom, but they did not know *where* to ride it, other than towards that cold and cheerless outpost called self-interest.

So instead of reading this moment in theatre history in the accustomed binary manner – as a hegemonic force (West End theatres, the middle-class) exercised over a marginalized community (music halls, the working class) – let us read it in a different way. One that is more aware of Victorian values, especially those we are unlikely to share – such as the belief that an idealist and utopian vision of culture cannot simply be reduced to the naturalized image of power, privilege and oppression. Let us read the desire for Shakespeare in the music hall as the articulation of a centre; a centre that would hold not by the magnet of ideology, but by the invitation of consensus. For the centre will hold only if people work to hold it, only if they cherish not, as Arnold put it, all that is 'unstable, and contentious, and ever-varying', but all that is 'one, and noble, and secure, and peaceful, and the same for all mankind'.[54]

Notes

1. *Report from the Select Committee on Theatrical Licences and Regulations; Together with the Proceedings of the Committee; Minutes of Evidence and Appendix*, in *Reports of Committees* (London: House of Commons Sessional Papers, 1866), 16:ii. The transcript of the Committee hearings is on pp. 1–333.
2. The first music hall, the Canterbury, near Waterloo Station, opened under the management of Charles Morton in 1851. During the 1860s the number of London music halls more than trebled. See 'Introduction' to Peter Bailey, ed., *Music Hall: the Business of Pleasure* (Milton Keynes: Open University Press, 1986), x.
3. *Report*, 1866, 42.
4. *Report from the Select Committee on Public Houses; Together with the Proceedings of the Committee* ... (London: House of Commons Sessional Papers, 1854), 14:xxv.
5. *Era*, 11 February 1866.
6. *Era*, 18 March 1866.
7. *Report*, 1866, 56.
8. See the testimony of William Henry Bodkin, one of the judges who quashed the conviction. *Report*, 1866, 67.
9. Peter Bailey, *Leisure and Class in Victorian England* (London: Routledge & Kegan Paul, 1978), 149.
10. Predictably, theatre managers continued to file lawsuits against the music halls. See *Era*, 4 November 1866; *Era*, 27 January 1867; *Era*, 11 December 1867; *The Times*, 30 October 1871; and *Era*, 15 February 1880. Not until 1912 were dramatic sketches finally legalized for performance in 'the halls', by which time the major West End music halls had become variety houses, and were thus virtually indistinguishable from theatres anyway.
11. Dagmar Kift, *The Victorian Music Hall: Culture, Class and Conflict*, trans. Roy Kift (Cambridge: Cambridge University Press, 1996), 62.
12. *Report*, 1866, 34.
13. *Report*, 1866, 51.
14. *Hansard* CLXXIV (3 May 1864), 2126; quoted in Thomas J. Spencer, Jr., *George Joachim Goschen: the Transformation of a Victorian Liberal* (London: Cambridge University Press, 1973), 17.
15. 'The Leap in the Dark', *St Paul's Magazine*, 1 (October 1867), quoted in Spencer, 25.
16. *Report*, 1866, 122.
17. *Report*, 1866, 126.
18. *Report*, 1866, 121.
19. *Report*, 1866, 121. The magistrate George Norton echoed Buckstone's position when he told the Committee that Shakespeare needed to be protected from the 'refreshment table' and the 'drinking and smoking' of music halls. *Report*, 1866, 53.
20. *Report*, 1866, 121.
21. *Report*, 1866, 106.
22. *Report*, 1866, 107.
23. *Report*, 1866, 180.
24. 'Theatres and Music-Halls', *Saturday Review*, 22 (18 August 1866): 203.
25. *Report*, 1866, 180.
26. *Era*, 15 April 1866.
27. *Report*, 1866, 57.
28. *Report*, 1866, 57.
29. *Report*, 1866, 58.
30. *Report*, 1866, 58.
31. At the outset of the proceedings, the London Music Hall Proprietors' Association declared that its members (about twenty establishments) were *not* demanding 'the right to produce stage plays'. J. Wilton, Secretary of the London Music Hall Proprietors' Association, letter to the *Era*, 13 May 1866.

32. *Report*, 1866, 45. Managers of the licensed theatres were given a rough ride, for the Committee mercilessly exposed their hypocritical preference for burlesque and sensation melodrama. See, for example, the hard-hitting questions put to Benjamin Webster, *Report*, 1866, 106–20.
33. *Report*, 1866, 5. There were a few conservative voices on the Committee who wished to limit the number of actors who could appear on music hall stages. But their dissenting views never prevailed, as Goschen steered matters decisively towards a recommendation for the lifting of all restrictions whatsoever.
34. *Report*, 1866, 54.
35. *Report*, 1866, 73.
36. *Report*, 1866, 54.
37. *Report*, 1866, 57.
38. *Report*, 1866, 66.
39. *Report*, 1866, 48.
40. Kift, 182.
41. *Cornhill Magazine*, 14 (July–December 1866): 285.
42. The essay was published in book form in 1869, but was written and published in serial form in *Cornhill Magazine* in 1867.
43. Matthew Arnold, *Culture and Anarchy*, ed. Samuel Lipman (New Haven and London: Yale University Press, 1994), 5.
44. Peter Bailey, *Popular Culture and Performance in the Victorian City* (Cambridge: Cambridge University Press, 1998), 2.
45. See, for example, Tracy C. Davis, *The Economics of the British Stage, 1800–1914* (Cambridge: Cambridge University Press, 2000), 17–41.
46. Arnold, 50.
47. Arnold, 34.
48. Arnold, 34.
49. Arnold, 29–30.
50. Arnold, 47.
51. Arnold, 48.
52. Arnold, 47.
53. Arnold, 44–5.
54. Arnold, 136.

13
What Is a Play? Drama and the Victorian Circus

Jacky Bratton

This chapter, like Richard Schoch's, focuses on cultural and historiographical boundary-crossing in the British performance world during the mid-century decades. But while he interrogates the preoccupation of the 1866 Select Committee with Shakespeare, my endeavour is to find a way to circumvent that middle-class Victorian obsession completely and discover the common experience of drama beyond the bard. To this end, I focus not on the music halls, but on that other nineteenth-century phenomenon noticed by the Committee: the circus. There, too, struggling theatrical managements found competition that they felt the need to suppress. I argue that in the plays presented in the circus ring and in the responses (both legal and critical) that they provoked, we may find traces of an alternative performance life very dissimilar from high Victorian realism, and an appreciation of the play that was free of the ever-tightening constrictions of the moral and literary conception of the drama.

There was nothing new in the ongoing attempt to prevent venues beyond the licensed theatres from presenting plays. In their protectionist manipulation of the laws, mid-century theatre managements defending their rights under the 1843 Act were simply continuing a battle previously waged by the Major theatres against the Minors; and in those earlier rounds of the fight, ideological issues had also loomed large, disguising, doubling or acting as a weapon in the commercial fight. In the early years, the mixture of entertainments that had been so acrimoniously discussed was not so much of Shakespeare with kidney and potatoes which concerned the 1866 Committee, as of the classic drama with the performing horse, which greatly enraged an earlier critical Establishment. The phenomenon of hippodrama and its popularity in the Revolutionary years is under examination. Jane Moody and Michael Gamer[1] foreground the paradox of the violent vilification and audience success of *Bluebeard* (1798) and *Timour the Tartar* (1811), performed with the aid of the stud from Astley's Amphitheatre, defiling the classic stage of Drury Lane. Critical fury was not, Gamer argues, because these shows brought a lower-class audience to the ancient theatre, but because the box and pit seats were crowded with fashionable enthusiasts for the culture of the horse.

In other words, Shakespeare's proper supporters, the management and audience of the Patent house, preferred a circus spectacle. Twentieth-century circus theoreticians have objected to the other side of this coin, the fact that Astley's was used for drama as well as physical display:[2] the riding and other physical feats in the circle were supplemented by a stage, and by drama that actually used ramps and fictions to link the two together. But some recent discussions are beginning to see the amphitheatre, the early nineteenth-century combination of circus ring and stage as a potent and perfect performance space. David Wiles, in his wide-ranging challenge to the historiography of performance space, spells out the modern discursive/theoretical conflict: 'from one point of view, early circus can be seen as an awkward hybrid' that 'sets up a binary opposition between circus as a space where things are done for real and the theatre as space of illusion' and, on the other hand, some see 'early circus as the perfect expression of its age, reproducing the Hellenic balance of stage and orchestra'. Excellent new historical work on Astley's by Marius Kwint takes this line, situating the amphitheatre as the best expression of late-Georgian sensibility.[3]

Less has been done so far to think through the role of the play within the success story of the circus in Victorian life. Brenda Assael, in the most recent publication on the subject, includes a chapter arguing that 'the equestrian military spectacle contributed to an important process of national mythmaking, one that did not originate with the state but arose within the unofficial, popular culture.'[4] But her taxonomy of circus performance confines this function to Astley's and its legacy in the first half of the century, and to the spectacular representations of the battles of Empire in the ring. However, circus managers throughout the century persisted in 'getting up' a wide range of pieces that took in farce, pantomime, domestic tales and romances as well as military spectacle, whenever they could get away with it, and sometimes when they could not, in the face of prosecution and repeated fines. Moreover, I would argue that allowed performances by clowns, riders and acrobats also often partook of the dramatic. The interesting speculation is how we might use these circus pieces to gain a fuller insight into the mid-Victorian experience and understanding of the nature of the dramatic. Two basic questions – why did the circuses persist in mounting plays, and what were their plays like? – give rise to a third, more interesting speculation: might a different and more complex understanding of Victorian plays arise from rereading the legal and conceptual arguments that surrounded the drama in the ring?

Battles in the courts: bumping into the scenery

Perhaps the major characteristic of the Victorian stage as we have understood it is the development of scenic illusion. The definitive modern work on this subject suggests that 'the nineteenth-century theater originates ... in Diderot's campaign for a more pictorial stage ... a more secure fiction – that is, a seamless dramatic illusion, a self-enclosed mimesis' leading to Irving's Lyceum as a fulfilment of that 'powerful aesthetic ideal'.[5] The Middlesex magistrate Henry Pownall, badgered by the 1866 Committee who did not want to hear his misgivings about the possibly inflammatory effects of allowing Shakespeare to be consumed alongside brandy-and-water, and indeed in places where sexual activity was rumoured to take place, maintained stubbornly that 'the principal point' that decided for his Bench whether a show was 'a theatrical entertainment' or not was 'whether there was scenery'. Eventually he admitted that scenery *without* acting is not exactly theatre, and even that acting itself is at least part of the theatrical event: 'if individuals come in in costume, and if they put themselves in certain attitudes, if they performed in dumb show certain things, all that would partake of a theatrical character.'[6] However, scenic illusion seemed to define, for the average armchair theorist of the theatre, what was a play.

In the court cases leading up to the 1866 Committee, scenery had been the *sine qua non* of the forbidden drama. In the course of the preceding decades, the magistrates to whom embattled managers appealed to stop encroachments upon their preserves tended to sympathize with those prosecuted, but found themselves obliged to find against showmen who went in for scenery. In 1861, encouraged by a successful prosecution in Margate, London managers pursued Morton's Canterbury Music Hall, Lambeth, for a piece called *The Enchanted Hash*. The defending barrister, in questioning William Smith, the acting manager of the Adelphi – a witness on the side, therefore, of the theatres, and one intent upon proving the piece was a pantomime – demanded to know whether he had ever seen a pantomime without scenery. He replied – judging by the response he got, it was a 'clever' answer designed to be beside the point – that he had: 'yes, a piece called *St George and the Dragon* at Hereford – at the Circus. (*laughter*)' Council replied severely, 'We are not talking of Circuses. Did you ever see a Pantomime, deserving the name of a pantomime, played in London without scenery as an adjunct?' to which Smith reposted that he had – at the Crystal Palace; and was admonished: 'This is trifling, Sir.'[7]

The magistrate's court did not want to talk about anything so low as the circus. But theatre managers nevertheless found circus a threat. Circus entertainment grew and grew, thriving mightily during the low mid-century years of the Victorian theatre. And as in the earlier case explored by Gamer, it was not only the poor and ignorant who chose the horse over Shakespeare. James Dawson, the Cornish circuit manager, lamented that 'There are many in this country who would gladly make a compromise with their conscience, and see a Play, if they could only lay the flattering unction to their souls that they had not been to a theatre' and so 'will rush to a Circus' to see ' "Billy Button the Tailor," or any other stupid vulgar piece performed, without any of the refinements of the regular drama'.[8] Consequently prosecutions for breaches of licensing laws were often brought against circuses in provincial centres, where theatre managers felt they could defend their turf. In Brighton on Boxing Day 1841, for example, Batty's circus opened *The Gnome King; or Harlequin and the Magic Eagle*, which was subsequently proven in court to contain fourteen lines of dialogue followed by 'tumbling, dancing, horsemanship, and tricks, but there was no scenery';[9] after an appeal at which they heard a great deal of lawyerly theatre history, the jury quashed his conviction. But circuses continued to be harassed into the 1870s, and just as pertinaciously continued to mount pantomimes and other pieces.

In the autumn of 1871, the Association of London Theatre Managers attacked Forester's-Hall off the Edgware Road, where Mr Charles Sinclair was alleged to be staging 'a regular Christmas pantomime' in a circus ring, relying on the absence of footlights and scenery to protect him from prosecution. Under the heading, once again, of 'What is a Play?' *The Era* reported the complainants' argument, which was that

> The piece was played in a Circus, but although there were no accessories, viz., a curtain and scenes, it was still a stage play. If it was not, any one might perform any act in Shakespeare in a public bar . . .

A professional witness told the court:

> It was a Circus, with seats round to accommodate about a thousand persons. When the horses came into the ring there was a side scene representing a house. There was a window in it, and steps from the ring lead up to the window. There was a trapeze fitted up, and the first part of the entertainment was feats of horsemanship. After the conclusion of the horsemanship the ring master thanked the audience, and said the entertainment would conclude with the comic Pantomime of *Ride a Cock Horse to Banbury Cross; or, Harlequin Old Mother Goose*. The acting of the piece took place in the ring. The first one to enter the ring was a man called Tom Tom Tivitt, who was riding, and was dressed in hunting costume, minus the boots. He wore a red coat and hunting cap with a peak, he is in love with the fair Rosabel, and says she shall not be engaged to the booby. He dismounts, walked up to the house, and knocks at the door. Rosabel appears at the window, and inquires who is at the door. He says it is your own Tom Tom Tivitt. She then leaves the house, and walks into the ring. She is dressed as a girl of the period. He seats her on the saddle, and is about to make off with her, when an equestrian party rides in, headed by Lord Foxbrush.

A great deal of riding about ensues, before Mother Goose appears and transforms the characters into the traditional harlequinade and, the witness continued:

> The usual chase takes place. The Clown says to the Pantaloon, 'Here is a doctor's shop' (pointing to the house). They knock at the door, the doctor comes out, and the Clown tries to buy the business. It was a regular Pantomime. He had been a great number of years in the Profession, and it was a Pantomime.

Cross-examined by Mr Leigh the witness said:

> The Pantomime was not played on a stage. The whole of the performance was played in a ring in presence of the audience. The side scene was not moved; it was used in the Harlequinade. The ring is covered with sawdust.[10]

When it suited the theatre managers, they asserted that Shakespeare performed in a bar room is the staging of a play and no elaborate set or accurate historical costume is really needed to constitute drama. Indeed, the fragment of the action quoted demonstrates that Shakespeare's method of indicating setting still made perfect sense to the audience at the circus: turning to the flat which had served previously, with no break in the performance, as his beloved's house, the clown says 'here is a doctor's shop'. The circus men try to argue that they have no stage, no footlights, their scenery stands exposed in the ring with the trapeze and the sawdust – what is thus done 'in presence of the audience' cannot really be an encroachment on dramatic art; but it clearly was, and they were fined – a shilling each.

The newspaper critics found the public taste for plays without modern scenery comically incomprehensible, or at least a fit subject for amused condescension. Take the *Era* report of Barrington's Circus, set up at Peckham for Christmas 1868–9. The reporter noted that the 'familiar evolutions' of horse and hoop were made much more attractive for a population otherwise starved of shows by the staging of a pantomime and a burlesque. He reflects that:

> in all purely equestrian establishments where dramas are supposed to be repres-ented without a stage or scenic effects, an immense amount of interest is left to the imagination of the audience, who, in taking the announcement that the scene now lies in Tartary, must picture before their eyes vast forests of gloomy pine, or boundless tracts of barren steppes. With this slight drawback, and if the spectator will be good enough to imagine the circle a lake, and sawdust the transparent water of Killarney, and also ignore the [non]existence of gorgeous scenery, he will find abundance at which to be pleased, and, indeed, highly amused, especially with the Pantomime, which, with the difficulties inseparable to a representation in an Arena, is a remarkably good one; and, if a Christmas piece is to be tested by the amount of laughter it provokes, then is the one at the Peckham Circus an admirable production. Certainly we have seldom seen more hearty mirth in a patent Theatre.[11]

He is concerned to make a point about the failures of the real theatres and, perhaps, the simplicity of the Peckham audiences; but his actual observation is that they had an imaginative ability which did not require the scenic aids that he, as a sophisticated reader of theatrical events, had come to regard as necessary. Moreover, the critic is either somewhat disingenuous or very blinkered by his presuppositions in lamenting the absence of scenic aids in evoking the plains of Tartary. In the staging of a fighting spectacular like the evergreen *Battle of Waterloo* or a processional play like *Timour the Tartar*, the verisimilitude of exotic costume, real horses, plenteous smoke and red fire, real men fighting close at hand, all seen in the round, surely more than made up for the simplicity or absence of painted representations of forest and steppe.

Battling for an audience: why act?

Despite prosecution, circuses continued to act, and audiences continued to find no difficulty in interpreting their dramas, without the scenic stage. A well-found circus management like that of the Henglers continued to 'get up pieces' despite staffing, logistical and sometimes licensing difficulties. Reasons are not hard to find. One of the on-going critical complaints about circus performance is that the display of skills for their own sake is inevitably lacking in variety. British circuses were a single-ring show: acts took place one at a time, and once you have seen a man turn fifty somersaults in a row or ride five horses standing, your second or fifteenth experience of the same feat will not have the same impact; there is only so far that the addition of yet more gyrations or the introduction of extra horses can go. On the other hand, if a man and horse gallop desperately over high leaps while impersonating Dick Turpin and his mare, or a semi-clad performer rides up a series of ramps lashed face upwards on the horse's back in *Mazeppa*, as part of a story, we have an ever-refreshed satisfaction in their success: the character's escape and survival (or, in the case of Turpin's mare Bess, her pathetic demise), while still inevitable, are made new and exciting for us by the thrill of the narrative. Hence the inexhaustible pleasures of the adventure movie. Circus proprietors who included drama in their repertoire of performance knew they were offering something that would draw audiences back in the successive weeks of their stay in town.

But one may go further in unearthing the Victorian playgoers' appreciation of the dramatic in the ring. Story-telling and dramatic illusion were deeply ingrained in much circus performance, and took many creative, rapidly moving forms. Dawson's remark about the 'stupid, vulgar' Billy Button the Tailor points to a performance by a singing clown, which was more like a music hall turn, in which one man presented a character dramatized by means of costume, action and a song. Tailors were the butt of circus as well as theatrical satire back into the previous century: 'The Taylor's Ride to Brentford' is the classic clown act of burlesque horsemanship, and clowns had many such comic impersonations in their solo slots. Two clowns have great play-making scope, enacting everything from 'settling an affair of honour' to 'the sentinel and the bear'; one clown, using only the ring-master, a table, a money-bag and a stuffed dog could produce a cod murder melodrama.[12]

Such practices extended perfectly legibly, for the circus audience, beyond the comic into exciting or moving performances on horseback. Andrew Ducrow, famous trick-rider and proprietor of Astley's, probably originated the practice of miming a whole story – such as the life of a sailor, from leaving home to fighting a battle to being wounded to returning to his beloved and meeting his child – while standing on the back of a running horse; more complex dramatically, requiring the reading of signs and symbols, was his transformation of the equestrian trick of driving many horses at once into a dramatic narrative. But the circus audience had no trouble in understanding that as he galloped along, standing on the back of first one horse, then picking up the reins of more horses as they entered the ring in succession, he was acting the part of a courier crossing Europe from St Petersburg to the North Sea. The horses he rode carried the flags of the nations he traversed; that was clear enough. Thus all kinds of acts might be framed, supported and given interest by an embedded fiction, signalled on the playbill and then carried out in the ring with minimal use of words. Four tumblers are billed as 'Trojan Youths Contending for the Laurels of Olympia', the fire-eater personates 'Langois Volcimane, the Fire King'.[13]

The bill might culminate in a more complete fiction: we have the testimony of James Frowde, clown and contortionist, for the nature of pieces like 'The Merry Coopers' or 'The Millers' Festival'. He recalls the latter as a

> scene, or rather equestrian ballet of action and words. The principal characters are the Miller, his Wife and Son, Dickie. All of the mill are at holiday, for 'tis the anniversary of the Miller's wedding day. At last a prize shall be given to the man who can imitate what they saw the Mountebank do on the green. Accordingly old Dobbin is brought in all caparisoned as though he was going to take the Master and Dame to market, and sent cantering round the ring, all the Millers vaulting and doing different tricks. The fun of the farce depends upon Dickie, who is always in the way, and imitating in a comic manner the tricks of the performer.[14]

The nineteenth-century dramatic stage also often included shows that embed acts, whether as a campfire entertainment scene introduced into *Henry V* or in the combination shows touring the American west which included a bar-room scene in which the actors did their personal turns. One might put films like John Baxter's *Say it With Flowers* (1934), which included a whole music hall bill, and shows with an exiguous narrative whose raison d'être is physical performance, like *Starlight Express* (Andrew Lloyd Webber, 1984) or *Riverdance* (Bill Whelan, 1995), in the same category. Arguably the circus 'fiction' is the more seamless and organic. Like the clown entrée of the comic rider peeling off ludicrous layers of clothes until he is eventually resplendent in spangles and expertise, the interplay between the fiction and reality – the miller and his family 'trying' to imitate the circus – is quite a complex comment on the spectrum of human skill on offer in this venue and audience responses to it.

Battles in the ring: getting up pieces

Farces, comic characterization, domestic transformations and pantomime deepen the mimetic layers of the circus. But I think we may also learn about their audiences' capacity to read the dramatic from a closer look at the most obvious of circus plays – the riderly spectacle and the military display. Circus and theatre proprietors, who knew what paid, stretched their resources to present mock battles, especially in times of national conflict. Such rituals of nation-formation, morale-boosting and the interpellation of the ordinary man as hero are part of the cultural function of theatre and, indeed, film, from *Henry V* (Laurence Olivier, 1944) to *Saving Private Ryan* (Steven Spielberg, 1998); only the on-going effort to define art as somehow outside the hegemonic power struggle – itself, of course, an ideological move – could prevent us recognizing how large a part they play. But the transaction was not necessarily as simple as the mocking witness contained in contemporary press reports might suggest. Many writers revelled in the affectionately-ironic description of Astley's epic *Battle of Waterloo*, an annual ritual involving hundreds of supers, horses, cannon and a thick pall of smoke. Novelists, memoir-writers and especially the self-congratulatory journalists of *Punch* elaborated upon their discovery that in the early Victorian imaginary, this re-enactment was scarcely surpassed by – indeed, was only hazily distinct from – the real thing.[15] But the possibility that the circus understood and even encouraged the irony with which its patriotism was greeted in some quarters should not be overlooked; and the sophistication of its stagecraft might be said to have gone over the heads of journalists intent upon sneering at what they took to be management failures in realism and audience simple-mindedness in overlooking them.

As in all melodrama, Amherst's text for *Waterloo* interlaces the spectacular with the comic, which qualifies the acceptance of heroic claptrap. But more than that, it makes a space for a character, Shaw the Lifeguardsman, whose simple and self-sacrificing heroism contrasts strongly with the patriotic loftiness of the generals, and whose story outlived the play as a whole in its ring popularity. Amherst's text as published in Duncombe's edition lists Shaw as played by the Astley's strong man Makeen, but it does not print the actual scene, which, presumably, did not need words. The point was that Shaw the prize-fighter, a simple man, fought in the battle against overwhelming odds and died still fighting. The Victorian clown Charlie Keith describes the management of the death within the play: 'At the finish of this act Shaw is killed by someone firing a pistol from the outside of the ring. He falls across the horse, and is so carried out. To give the act a more realistic appearance, when the pistol is fired the rider representing Shaw presses a sponge, soaked with red paint or dye, to his forehead, to make it appear like blood.'[16] In the course of time Shaw became detached from the main play and developed into a drama of his own, becoming one of the characters mimed on horseback, like Pickwick or Jack Tar. Henry Adams's version of him impressed a *Times* reviewer in 1831, who describes 'what is called a military act, on a horse at full gallop . . . his enlisting, drilling, arrival in London, his pugilistic exploits, his desperate fighting in battle, and his death, are described in very eloquent pantomime, which would be extremely good of its kind, independent of the great skill in horsemanship which he displays'.[17] By 1842, however, *Punch* is making fun of this 'equestrian biography':

The rider first appears in the dress of a countryman, with a bundle at his back and a larger bundle of carrot-coloured wig on his head. He jumps upon the broad saddle, and while standing upright upon it goes through a pantomime, from which he insists upon your supposing that he has first taken up the profession of a prize-fighter, and then enlists in the Life Guards. His dress changes as if by magic; for the clown to the ring deliberately hands him his helmet, sword, and other appurtenances to the jack-boots and red coat already displayed. All this time the horse trots round and round; two or three thumps are given on a big drum, which you are to mistake for the roar of cannon, and which are to cause you to fancy yourself a spectator of the Battle of Waterloo. Then the man in the middle of the ring, with the long whip and spangles, lashes the horse, and Mr Shaw goes to work in right good earnest, sword in hand. It is astonishing to see the execution he does with his weapon upon the air. You are to be quite horrified at the number of an imaginary French cuirassiers whom he indulges with a bed of glory. At length a terrible thump on the great drum announces that he is shot – he staggers about on the platform that forms the saddle at a rate which frightens you awfully, lest he should tumble off. Your fears are realised! And he rolls about in the sawdust in all the agonies of pantomime and death. Here your imagination is not further required, for the rest of the fight is real. A French soldier comes on from the place at which the charger goes off; and a combat ensues with the dying man, who, at the end of the tune played by the band, to which the combat is fought, kills his enemy. Another, another, another, and – yes – another Frenchmen sets upon the hero of prize-fighters; he fights them all; and, what is more, kills them! This is continued for some time, Mr Shaw slaughtering the Frenchmen in fours and sixes, till there is not room in the ring for any more dead bodies but his own, – he expiring at last from exhaustion. Four of the deceased warriors then get up and carry out the hero upon their shoulders, with his toes uppermost.[18]

The ironic, superior tone of the comic journalist is essentially self-congratulatory: he asserts that he is unmoved, indeed amused, by this unsophisticated spectacle and will make an amusing thing of it for the benefit of the *Punch* reader, who is flattered by the implication of shared cultural superiority. That ascendancy rests, importantly, upon the assertion of the superiority of the word to the act: the writer is unwilling to admit that any worthwhile theatrical illusion can be created or received in dumb-show without the aid of a written, verbal script. This understanding of much Victorian performance is unchallenged if we read only the literary record; but other witness is available, even in written forms. For example, a closer view of the act may be gained from the recently published autobiography of an ex-clown turned country gentleman, James Frowde; it reveals what might actually have been so impressive to the audience about the acting in this case. Frowde saw Shaw interpreted in the 1860s by the equestrian Alfred Cooke, for whose performance, he says, 'Musicians, horse and grooms were drilled, for every look and movement was to time and music, his death scene was very pathetic, soldiers in uniform at his death used to come in and in due form carry him out, his horse following him at slow time, to music of "Saul." The audience used to be awe bound, and then to applaud.' Frowde was working as a clown at the time, and was accustomed to create burlesque interaction with high moments of drama in the ring; but he adds here 'In this act, Cooke would not allow a clown and quite right.'[19] *The Battle of Waterloo* is a foundational text of British imperialist self-consciousness, and demands close attention as an emotionally complex performance as well as written text.

Hero combats and national identity: *George and the Dragon*

My final example of the contribution the circus ring made to the national drama is of one of its most loved and often-elaborated pantomimes – *George and the Dragon*. Deeply rooted in the folk tales of England, St George and the Dragon is a contender for most-played circus drama. A hero legend that combined George the soldier martyr, the defender of Christendom, with the Greek legend of the Virgin Andromeda whom Perseus rescued spread across Europe very early: it was said to have been brought to Iona by Bishop Arculf in the seventh century. The story appeared in Jacobus de Vortagine's collection of saints' lives around 1275 and was published in English by Caxton in *Golden Legends* in 1483. Its popular forms range from church wall paintings to chapbooks and ballads, and a saint or King George is a leading figure in the surviving texts of mumming plays. So here is a story with the deepest roots, and a drama that might have a life entirely transcendent of boundaries within the world of presentation. James Frowde, writing in the 1870s, provides a very clear example of the power of this myth to the Victorians, its place in the imaginary of the nineteenth-century child. Frowde was child of a leading circus family, the Henglers, through a daughter who married out of the circus. His mother obviously chose her family concern for the infant's first introduction to the play, which would have been in the early 1830s. He records:

> I remember being taken somewhere and there was a large rock with a door in it and a handsome lady was outside fastened with a chain to a stake, by the door or entrance to the cave. Her long black hair, refined and yet withal a pronounced Semitic face, showed to me Aunt Eliza, while spell-bound to see her under such extraordinary circumstances, a huge reptile, hideous in green scales and large fiery eyes, made its appearance over the brow of the rock, flapped its wings and swung its tail. My scream of terror, my shout for Aunt Eliza's assistance, my puny efforts to go to her assistance made, it seems, quite a sensation, and the hero spoiled the tragic effect, and caused much laughter. Thus early I made a melodramatic comedian's success.[20]

We have no text to tell us about the rest of the piece, but clearly little Jimmy vividly learned the fundamental lesson about performed fiction – and his particular familial relation to it – from the moment. No doubt this crisis was set in quite an elaborate frame, which he has forgotten.

The circus family embodied the St George story but it was widely and deeply known from the mumming plays. There is a long-standing debate around questions of continuity between these rural amateur entertainments and the hugely capitalized and commercial nineteenth-century forms. Peter Millington, for example, argues that much of the supposedly 'folk' drama of England since the eighteenth century is actually derived from the professional stage, with the black-face and patches costume of many sides doing hero-combat plays – the Saint/King/Sir George fights – derived from Harlequin himself.[21] Whatever the direction of traffic, there is certainly interplay right across the spectrum of entertainment. By the 1880s one could find St George the symbol of patriotism everywhere. In a late chapbook, *THE NEW MUMMING BOOK*, the traditional characters of the mumming play – George, the doctor, the King of Egypt, his daughter Sabrina – are a vestigial nugget of text hugely overshadowed by nationalistic sabre-rattling between representatives of England, Ireland, Wales and Scotland, on the one hand, and France, Russia, America and Turkey, on the other, which encloses the old action between two choreographed battles.[22] At Covent Garden, meanwhile, which in 1884 was converted into a circus ring, the ringmaster A. Henry licensed a very similar piece as a 'children's pantomime' in which dozens of girls rode about in fancy dress as champion saints, their equerries and flagbearers, still, in the midst of it all, speaking the mumming play lines of self-introduction, but also standing aside for other players to make meta-theatrical jokes about the old theatre's history as an opera house and to introduce music hall songs about mashers. The interleaving of theatre traditions could hardly go further than this highly commercialized example; but the drama is most strongly present through the middle decades of the century as a circus play.

The tale includes many disparate elements. The basic story has the champion George going to rescue the daughter of the King of Egypt who is about to be sacrificed to a dragon, which has already been fed cattle and then other children by the terrorized local people. In chapbooks from 1608 onwards stories were added to his triumphant moment of dragon-slaying. These had the saint first collecting a band of helpers, the seven champions of Christendom, a manifestation of the seven hero trope that finds its way into many later tales. His birth was transferred to England, and in particular to Coventry, where his father is called Lord Albert. Celebrations of the saint in his 'native' town included processions which merged with those celebrating Lady Godiva. The story so far was turned into pantomime by Charles Dibdin in 1822 and Amherst in 1829, but later that year found its real champion in the person of Andrew Ducrow; he and his stud transferred it, amidst the usual critical outcry, to Drury Lane under Alfred Bunn's management at Christmas 1833.

The equestrian company performed triumphantly at Drury Lane for sixty-two nights, into the next March, simultaneously staging the same play at Ducrow's own Amphitheatre in Whitechapel. He then took the piece back to Astley's itself when it reopened for the 1834/5 season. The script was supposedly by Barnard, but Ducrow recreated it to suit the stud and then licensed it under his own name for Astley's. It begins in a way that was becoming conventional in all kinds of panto, with a dark scene in an infernal region, in this case the lair of female demons who have captured a noble child and have him in thrall, laid out on a bed like Sleeping Beauty, while he grows up. Ducrow was a famously beautiful human specimen; presumably he had only to lie there to be admired. As the scene begins the hags are contending about who is to have him when he's old enough to be woken. He evades their designs, however, and a Coventry clown pops up, riding a disappearing mule, to be his servant and his spokesman – George never speaks throughout the play, since Ducrow's physical presence was much marred if he had to open his Cockney mouth. They set off home, rescuing on the way the seven heroes from paralysis by the dragon's breath – presumably a scene of the saintly knights being statuesque on horseback – as well as getting their horses shod – spectacle of a farrier's forge – and then adventure off again to Egypt, which is the other traditional setting of the piece, the place where the dragon is devouring the maidens. Ducrow calls it a pantomime on the title page; by the time he was back at the Amphitheatre with it, the high point was when the flying dragon lifted him bodily from his horse in the course of their terrific combat.[23] Despite press attacks, it was an equally huge success in the East End, West End and South of London, and it remained a dependable staple for circuses throughout the century. And at Christmas 2003, the eagerly awaited final episode of *The Lord of the Rings* on film included a stunning climactic moment when one of the champions of the West was lifted from his horse by the terrifying animation of a dragon – the Nazgul's flying steed. This is drama that requires no explanation or location in time to speak to our central cultural responses.

The last battle: how to read a play

What, then, does the circus play tell us about Victorian theatregoers and their understanding of the drama? Most importantly, I think, it suggests that they were not so very unlike playgoers before and after them as we have been led to suppose; that there is a strain, a tradition, one might say, of spectatorial experience which was neither debased by a brutalizing mass culture nor waiting to be rescued from it by the moral and educational inspiration of historicized Shakespeare and the illusionist stage. A large general audience continued to be moved and excited by narratives enacted in novel ways, and professional performers developed their story-telling skills through an increasingly rapid, referential, knowing, ironic and vivid representational code which is a precursor of the physical languages of modern entertainment. Despite, or aside from, the boundary-marking of theatre managers, the hegemonic moves of influential writers and the moral and legal support these enlisted for an ever-narrowing definition of the drama, audiences continued to enjoy and to read enacted fictions in ways no less sophisticated, nor less viscerally fuelled, than our own.

To attend to these spectators and what they saw, we need to read or read afresh the copious witness that exists to Victorian performance, without allowing ourselves to be directed and caged by the protectionist impulses of many of the Victorians who wrote it. We should attend to the copious critical reports to be found below the literary horizon – diaries, letters, amateur autobiographies, the reports of performance that appear in the provincial entertainments columns of *The Era* – not just to the waspish commentaries of disappointed or aspiring dramatists writing as London theatre critics in *Punch* and *The Times*. We can read the proceedings of the Select Committee of 1866 with a similarly acute consciousness of their particular impulse – their educationalist agenda. And we need to ask presentist questions about the performances they describe: what was the emotion, the lived cultural experience that this clown burlesqued, that this standing rider sought to mimic and make strange, that this mock-battle captured in its clouds of gunpowder and trumpet-calls? Our answers are inevitably partially presentist too; but our imaginative effort and that wider view we allow ourselves will perhaps begin to free us of the constricting assumption that 'the Victorians' had no understanding of the nature of (the) play.

Notes

1. Jane Moody, *Illegitimate Theatre in London, 1770–1840* (Cambridge: Cambridge University Press, 2000), 69–72; and Michael Gamer, 'A Matter of Turf: Romanticism, Hippodrama, and Legitimate Satire', *Nineteenth-Century Contexts*, 28.4 (2006), 305–34. He made the point that 80 per cent of the box office for hippodrama at Drury Lane came from box and pit receipts – hence, from the upper classes.
2. See, for example, Antony Hippesley-Coxe, *A Seat at the Circus* (Hamden, CT: Archon Books, rev. ed. 1980), 24–5.
3. David Wiles, *A Short History of Western Performance Space* (Cambridge: Cambridge University Press, 2003), 199; and Marius Kwint, 'The Legitimization of the Circus in Late Georgian England', *Past and Present*, 174 (2002): 72–115.
4. Brenda Assael, *The Circus and Victorian Society* (Charlottesville and London: University of Virginia Press, 2005), 61.
5. Martin Meisel, *Realizations: Narrative, Pictorial, and Theatrical Arts in Nineteenth-Century England* (Princeton: Princeton University Press 1983), 432.
6. *Minutes of Evidence Taken Before the Select Committee on Theatrical Licences and Regulations 19 March to 8 June 1866*, #432, p. 17, and #725, p. 28
7. Report of the Lambeth Police Court hearing, *The Era*, 3 March 1861: 10.
8. *The Autobiography of Mr James Dawson* (Truro: J. R. Netherton, 1865), 126–8.
9. Report of the East Sussex Quarter Sessions, *The Times*, 11 January 1842.
10. 'What is a Stage Play?' *The Era*, 29 January 1871.
11. Barrington's Circus, Peckham, *The Era*, 5 January 1868.
12. See George Speaight, 'Some Comic Circus Entrées', *Theatre Notebook*, 32 (1978): 24–27; John H. Towsen, *Clowns* (New York: Hawthorn Books, 1976); and Jacky Bratton and Ann Featherstone, *The Victorian Clown* (Cambridge: Cambridge University Press, 2006).
13. Bill for Hengler's Grand Cirque Variété, Curzon Exhibition Hall Birmingham, 30 May 1866; copy held by Birmingham Central Library.
14. Bratton and Featherstone, 99–100.
15. See J. S. Bratton, 'Theatres of War: the Crimea on the London Stage 1854–5', in D. Bradby et al., *Performance and Politics in Popular Drama* (Cambridge: Cambridge University Press, 1980), 119–38
16. Charles Keith, *Circus Life and Amusements* (Derby: Bewley and Roe, 1879), 47.
17. *The Times*, 27 May 1831.
18. *Punch*, vol. 2, 1842: 22.
19. Bratton and Featherstone, 107.
20. Ibid., 41.
21. Peter Millington, 'Mystery History: the Origins of British Mummers' Plays', *American Morris Newsletter*, 13.3 (Nov./Dec 1989), 9–16; also available at http://freespace.virgin.net/peter.millington!/Mystery_History.htm
22. *The New Mumming Book: the Four Champions Of Great Britain: Showing how St. George of England; St. Patrick of Ireland; St. Andrew, of Scotland, and St. David, of Wales conquered the Representatives of all Nations* (Leeds: C. H. Johnson, n.d. [c.1879–1884]).
23. See A. H. Saxon, *The Life and Art of Andrew Ducrow and the Romantic Age of the English Circus* (Hamden, CT: Archon Books, 1978), 270–7.

Index

(Theatres and other performances spaces are listed together)